IMAGINING CONSUMERS

STUDIES IN INDUSTRY AND SOCIETY

Philip B. Scranton, *Series Editor*

Published with the assistance of the Hagley Museum and Library

RELATED TITLES IN THE SERIES

David A. Hounshell, *From the American System to Mass Production, 1800–1932: The Development of Manufacturing Technology in the United States*

James P. Kraft, *Stage to Studio: Musicians and the Sound Revolution, 1890–1950*

Lindy Biggs, *The Rational Factory: Architecture, Technology, and Work in America's Age of Mass Production*

Pamela Walker Laird, *Advertising Progress: American Business and the Rise of Consumer Marketing*

IMAGINING CONSUMERS

DESIGN AND INNOVATION FROM
WEDGWOOD TO CORNING

REGINA LEE BLASZCZYK

The Johns Hopkins University Press • Baltimore and London

32174

© 2000 The Johns Hopkins University Press
All rights reserved. Published 2000
Printed in the United States of America on acid-free paper

9 8 7 6 5 4 3 2 1

The Johns Hopkins University Press
2715 North Charles Street
Baltimore, Maryland 21218-4363
www.press.jhu.edu

Library of Congress Cataloging-in-Publication Data will be found at
the end of this book.
A catalog record for this book is available from the British Library.

ISBN 0-8018-6193-4

Photograph of Union Square interior, china floor, 1870–1905, copyright
Tiffany & Co. Archives, 1999. Not to be published or reproduced without
prior permission. No permission for commercial use will be granted except
by written license agreement. Pyrex and Corning Ware images courtesy of
Corning Consumer Products Company. PYREX is a registered trademark of
Corning Incorporated.

For Nellie, a Woolworth shopper
with Tiffany tastes

CONTENTS

Color plates follow page 160

ACKNOWLEDGMENTS

Imagining Consumers had its genesis in the 1980s, when I worked on the research staff at the Smithsonian Institution's National Museum of American History. During this decade, the NMAH director Roger Kennedy encouraged his staff to undertake serious scholarly research and wrestle with tough historical questions. Washington's rich resources attracted dozens of university scholars to NMAH, many of whom were pioneering the study of consumerism. Through exhibition projects, the Tuesday Colloquium, and conversations with visiting academics, I became stimulated by the debates about consumer society, which offered promising paradigms for putting the material world in historical context. More important, I discerned a missing component in the emerging body of literature. With some notable exceptions, including Neil McKendrick's seminal work on Josiah Wedgwood and Thomas Bentley, historians were examining consumer society from every vantage point except that of the companies that made the goods. Few considered the strategic intersection of design practice, consumer taste, and changing demand.

To explore how manufacturers and retailers figured into the creation of consumer society, I undertook several projects that laid the foundation for this book. At George Washington University, I completed a master's thesis on product design and development, working under the tutelage of the cultural historian Bernard Mergen, in the Department of American Civilization, and of the business historian William C. Becker, in the Department of History. For NMAH, I curated exhibits and assembled collections of artifacts and documents relating to the pottery and glass industries, concentrating on the everyday objects used by consumers in a range of social classes. In 1988, I received a Smithsonian Institution Research Opportunities Grant from the Office of the Secretary and traveled to the Midwest, where I recorded oral histories with aging designers, salesmen, and managers. These experiences fueled my determination to examine how home furnishings companies—firms that made and distributed the most commonplace and meaningful artifacts of the American consumer revolution—created effective links to their audiences.

When I left the Smithsonian in 1989 to pursue a doctorate and an academic career, I chose a graduate program that promised to foster my growth as a historian of American business, technology, and culture. Fortunately, I found strong mentors and excellent funding in the Hagley Program, Department of History, University of Delaware. Four scholars—David A. Hounshell, Anne M. Boylan, Glenn Porter, and Philip B. Scranton—listened, advised, and commented on my research, writing, and thinking for much of my graduate career. Concurrently, I continued to draw sustenance from the Smithsonian, revisiting NMAH as a predoctoral fellow under the sponsorship of Steven Lubar, Robert C. Post, Susan H. Myers, and Charles McGovern. During my two-year fellowship, Steve Lubar and Bob Post, my sponsors in the Department of Science and Technology, provided much of the encouragement that furthered my scholarly growth. As always, Susan Myers guided me through thick and thin, granting me access to the documents, artifacts, photographs, and staff under her care in the Department of Social History. Bonnie Lilienfeld, Sheila Machlis Alexander, Shelley Foote, Anne Golovin, David E. Haberstich, Eric Long, Lori Minor, Dane Penland, James Roan, Rodris Roth, Lonn Taylor, Roger White, Helena Wright, and others aided my research in countless ways.

This book would not have been possible without the generosity of executives and professional staff at four firms: Homer Laughlin China Company, Salem China Company, Kohler Company, and Corning Incorporated. In West Virginia, Homer Laughlin's owner-managers granted me unrestricted access to historical records in the art, engineering, executive, research, and sales departments. Trained in history and law, company president Marcus Aaron II, nicknamed "Pete," took a genuine interest in my project. As I visited his office with weekly reports of my discoveries from the company's dusty dungeon, Pete Aaron acted as a sounding board for ideas, and, on my behalf, he compiled valuable data from the confidential financial records. Joseph M. Wells Jr. listened quietly and carefully to my questions and, drawing on his lifetime of experience in the pottery business, pushed me in the right directions. Joseph M. Wells III, the company's executive president, imparted his enthusiasm for Homer Laughlin's future. But my extended visits to the East Liverpool district would have been less productive and enjoyable without the support of the art department. With an interest in design history, art director Jonathan O. Parry first welcomed me to his division in 1986, when I began studying Frederick Hurten Rhead. During my trips to Newell, Jonathan and his staff warmly opened their design annex to me, so that Homer Laughlin became my home away from home.

At the Salem China Company, J. Harrison Keller and his son Gary Keller made their archives accessible to me during the late 1980s, eventually donating these materials to NMAH's Archives Center and Department of Social History. Harrison Keller, part of the pottery trade since the late 1930s, had preserved Salem's enormous sample collection, which includes the products of his firm and competitors. Similarly, the longtime salesman Rudy Linder had squirreled away departmental memoranda in a deserted area of the factory. Although relatively modest, Salem's collection provided an important complement to Homer Laughlin's exhaustive records.

At the Kohler Company, the Communications Department hosted my stay in 1993, and Peter Fetterer, Cheryl Prepster, and Leah Weiss guided me through the archives. Once the firm opened the executive files of Walter J. Kohler and Herbert V. Kohler, Cheryl demonstrated her patience and skill in facilitating long-distance research. In the summer of 1997, we exchanged countless phone calls, as she diligently sifted through recently released files to locate documents. Cheryl's efforts immeasurably strengthened my interpretation of Walter J. Kohler's efforts to imagine the consumer.

Among the firms in this study, Corning Incorporated alone has a records management program staffed by professional archivists, who extended a warm welcome to me as the first business historian using the firm's papers. From 1990 through 1997, Michelle L. Cotton, working under the division chief Stuart Sammis, used her knowledge of American history to provide direction. The former designer Jerry E. Wright shared his knowledge and files, while Tony Miday enthusiastically retrieved records boxes. During his tenure as chief executive officer, James R. Houghton granted me permission to use the Houghton Family Papers, and Nina R. Houghton, widow of Arthur A. Houghton Jr., gave me access to her husband's papers, all housed in the Department of Archives and Records Management.

From Boston, Massachusetts, to Madison, Wisconsin, professional staff at the following institutions made my visits stimulating and fruitful: Corning Museum of Glass, Hagley Museum and Library, Winterthur Library, Baker Library at Harvard Business School, Perkins Library at Duke University, Olin Library at Cornell University, Arents Library at Syracuse University, Kent State University,

Massachusetts Historical Society, Maytag Archives, Good Housekeeping Institute, East Liverpool Museum of Ceramics and the Ohio History Center at the Ohio Historical Society, New Jersey State Museum, Society for the Preservation of New England Antiquities, Trenton Public Library, Tiffany & Company, Museum of American Glass at Wheaton Village, and State Historical Society of Wisconsin. In addition, I thank several funding sources: Corning Museum of Glass for a Rakow Grant; Early American Industries Association for a grant-in-aid; Business History Conference for the John E. Rovensky Fellowship; State Historical Society of Wisconsin for the John C. Geilfuss Fellowship; and Duke University's Hartmann Center for the History of Advertising, Marketing, and Sales for the J. Walter Thompson Fellowship. At Boston University, Dennis Berkey, the dean of the College of Arts and Sciences, provided a summer travel stipend; the Material Culture Fund, resources for illustrations and manuscript preparation.

As I revised my dissertation into a book, I benefited from the feedback of scholars at Boston University and the broader academic community. In BU's American Studies Program, colleagues Bruce J. Schulman, Claire Dempsey, Richard Candee, Karen Bishop, Elysa Engelman, Paul V. Schmitz, and Ruth Gallagher put in their two cents. In the History Department, Professor Emeritus Saul Engelbourg gave sage advice on the penultimate draft. In the Office of Presentation Graphics, Ron Mistretta lived up to his reputation as "media man" with last-minute aid on photos and charts. An alumna of the Art History Department, Patricia Johnston, evaluated portions of the manuscript with the eye of a gifted scholar of visual culture. From Bentley College, Marc Jeffrey Stern contributed his knowledge of the pottery trade. Beyond Boston, Robert J. Brugger, Catherine E. Hutchins, Glenn Porter, and Philip Scranton offered incisive readings at a critical moment.

Over the years, countless scholars provided helpful comments at conferences, workshops, and brainstorming sessions. I am indebted to Sally Clarke, Robert Friedel, James Gilbert, Carolyn M. Goldstein, Mary Ann Heilrigel, Gary Kulik, Kenneth L. Lipartito, Jacqueline McGlade, Roland Marchand, Jeffrey L. Meikle, Mark Rose, Marguerite Shafer, Kathryn Steen, Nina de Angeli Walls, and William W. Walls. Shelley Nickles deserves special thanks for reading chapters and for sharing her unpublished manuscripts. Without question, Shelley's input confirmed and deepened my understanding of the industrial arts and industrial design traditions.

Laboring over my revisions in New England, I missed the Washington-Delaware corridor, where institutions such as the Smithsonian and the Hagley

Museum and Library encourage vigorous scholarship on the modern material world and the cultural dimensions of American business and technology. That supportive intellectual environment midwived and nurtured this study of producers and their strategic ties to consumers. In a fitting tribute to those origins, I am pleased to see this book published in Hagley's Industry and Society Series by the Johns Hopkins University Press.

IMAGINING CONSUMERS

Introduction

BETWEEN THE CIVIL WAR and World War II, the United States emerged as an industrial giant and a consumer society. Economic growth provided more Americans with ready-made clothing, brand-name foods, and imitation cut crystal. During Great Britain's eighteenth-century consumer revolution, only middling and wealthy sorts could enjoy luxuries like Chippendale chairs, Boulton belt buckles, and Wedgwood vases. A century later, a significant percentage of the American population, including workers, experienced rising living standards that made earlier developments pale by comparison. Consumption for ordinary people was made in America, and the companies this book explores—firms providing commonplace items like Sears mail-order glassware and Woolworth pottery dishes—figured prominently in the process that marketing impresario Paul T. Cherington described in the 1930s as the "democratization of things."[1]

A complex dialogue between American tastes and business tactics undergirded the transformation to consumer society. Successful companies recognized that satisfying shoppers' practical and stylistic needs offered these firms a competitive advantage that could generate sizable profits. Manufacturers collected information about consumers piecemeal, using all their wits to decipher demand—to determine what shoppers wanted, how much, and at what price. A company's survival rested on its ability to envision its target audiences and to design products for them; it depended on the process of imagining consumers. The objective of customer satisfaction lay at the heart of this strategy.

Much in this argument is at odds with our understanding of a corporation's role in the evolution of consumerism. For decades, scholars have portrayed manufacturers and retailers as malignant manipulators, employing the tools of persuasion to mold women into passive shoppers and assembly line workers into depoliticized automatons. Americans who have come of age since the 1950s—recalling repetitive TV commercials, sanitized shopping malls, and monotonous product designs—may believe that advertising shapes desire and creates demand. But the coercion thesis misconstrues the American consumer revolution, which instead aimed to satisfy diversity. Historians have overlooked these facts primarily because they have been searching in the wrong places, accepting high-profile big businesses such as Procter & Gamble, Coca-Cola, and General Motors as the norm.

During the late nineteenth and early twentieth centuries, more Americans than ever could buy the new products pouring out of the nation's industrial heartland. Although consumers purchased such disposable goods as Heinz catsup, Camel cigarettes, and Lux soap, they hardly designated such heavily advertised products as prized possessions. Those brand names alerted shoppers to quality and signified corporate rather than consumer identity. Instead, rich and poor invested a good deal of meaning in the durable goods that made houses into homes. Ubiquitous china closets, whatnot shelves, and buffet cabinets suggested that pottery and glassware mattered more than many other things. Courtly associations made these objects attractive to the socially ambitious; brilliant colors and interesting textures appealed to the artistic. These durable, yet fragile, artifacts symbolized blood ties, anchored memories, and expressed private longings. Between social climbing and visual delight, Americans found a wide spectrum of reasons for treasuring pottery and glassware—all as individual as the consumers themselves.

As Americans endowed these objects with great personal significance, potteries and glassworks fixed their eyes on the consumers. For the most part, those firms ignored the "managerial revolution" taking hold of the companies that made soap, cigarettes, sheeting, cereals, and canned goods, the large corporations often described as the harbingers of modern marketing. Although professionally managed big businesses in the core economy sought to enlarge sales of standardized goods through direct consumer advertising, firms in the periphery concentrated on studying consumers and responding to their desires rather than trying to build markets by creating new needs.

The firms making household durables were entangled in a complex market-

At home with prized possessions, Wilmington, Delaware, 1888. Hagley Museum and Library

ing web that encompassed enormously powerful retailers and incredibly demanding shoppers. Getting caught in a tug of war between supply and demand
threatened their very well-being. To stay in the game, producers had to remain
flexible, which meant knowing how to switch from one style to another as fashions changed. The emerging systems of mass and bulk production, two manufacturing modes favored by big businesses, signaled a retreat away from flexibility. More fashion-conscious firms, looking for production prototypes, had to
rely on their roots in the Old World.

The American consumer revolution in the late nineteenth and twentieth century, arising in response to the demands of a highly variable market, owed much
to its smaller eighteenth-century British predecessor, especially in design, production, and marketing. As Great Britain industrialized and its population expanded in the mid-1700s, workshops and factories drew sustenance from the
growing demand for fashionable goods among the upper and middle classes, who
were enjoying a rise in per capita incomes. Citizens of the world's most prosperous empire, Britons eagerly showed off their wealth. The upper crust led the

way, indulging material passions on fanciful gardens, private zoos, extravagant clothing, magnificent mansions, and lavish furnishings to create the "treasure houses of Britain." The middling sorts followed suit, using their newfound wealth to emulate the lifestyles of the rich and famous by purchasing copycat products. Manufacturers fed on the consuming frenzy, producing a bewildering array of fashion goods to adorn people and their palaces, townhouses, and cottages.[2]

Among the most coveted objects of the British consumer revolution were porcelain and pottery. For decades, wealthy Europeans had indulged in china collecting. After the Dutch East India Company began importing significant amounts of Chinese porcelain in the 1640s, a rage for decorating interiors with china baubles swept across the Continental courts. One prince, Augustus the Strong, King of Poland and Elector of Saxony, engaged a chemist to uncover the secrets of porcelain manufacturing. In 1710, Augustus established the first royal china works, at Meissen; by midcentury, nobles across Europe were investing in private factories that made the fragile aristocratic bibelots. Other royals opened porcelain works at Berlin, Frankenthal, Fürstenberg, Höchst, and Nymphenburg in the German principalities; Vienna in Austria; Capo di Monte and Doccia in Italy; and Buen Retiro in Spain. The French king, Louis XV, added cachet to his Sèvres line by personally supervising the yearly sale. When the porcelain rage crossed the English Channel, British capitalists, recognizing a timely investment opportunity, gave china mania a new twist. As the customs of drinking tea, coffee, and hot chocolate became hallmarks of English civility, the market for costly teatime accessories expanded. In response, entrepreneurs founded factories for making bone china (an imitation porcelain that contained calcined animal bones) at Bow, Chelsea, Derby, Longton Hall, and Lowestoft. When the technical and financial challenges of chinaware production proved overwhelming, many English bone china companies failed. However, the porcelain craze inspired English earthenware potters, who possessed the technical skills essential to success, to join the ranks of manufacturers catering to Britain's emerging consumer society.[3]

The most renowned earthenware potter of the British consumer revolution was Josiah Wedgwood, founder of the dish-making dynasty that bears his name today. Born to a family of peasant potters in Staffordshire in 1730, Wedgwood belonged to a generation of artisans who changed the pottery trade. Whether in London, the countryside, or the colonies, consumers clamored for stylish table accessories; and Staffordshire potters rose to the occasion. Between the 1750s and 1780s, the towns around Stoke in north Staffordshire emerged as a hotbed of innovation. By adopting refined materials, the division of labor, and, ultimately, steam power, Staffordshire artisans transformed the potter's craft into a cutting-edge trade. The most astute entrepreneurs kept their eyes on the market, where fashion dictated novelty. Responding to baroque tastes, the region's most celebrated midcentury potter, Thomas Whieldon of Fenton Low, made teapots, plates, and table ornaments in glazes that mimicked the appearance of costly tortoiseshell. Whieldon and other potters, who experimented with flint and white clays, also produced two types of poor man's porcelain, that is, modestly priced white stoneware and cream-colored earthenware. In this cauldron of creativity, Wedgwood came of age, drawing inspiration and comradery from like-minded artisans.[4]

A technical virtuoso who by 1783 enjoyed membership in the Royal Society for his work on the pyrometer, Wedgwood also clearly understood the benefits of keeping the customer in focus. Following a five-year partnership with Thomas Whieldon, Wedgwood established his own pottery at Burslem in 1759. During the Seven Years' War between France and England (1754–63), the colonial market, a mainstay for Staffordshire potters, declined. Undaunted, Wedgwood forged ahead to expand his domestic trade. Aided by contract modelers (skilled artisans who designed product prototypes for flat fees), he tapped into the desires of middle-class Britons for beautiful tableware. By the early 1760s, slumping sales suggested that shoppers had tired of white stoneware and tortoiseshell; they wanted something different. With modeler Daniel Greatbatch, Wedgwood developed a stunning baroque line covered with green and yellow glazes, including tea items each shaped like the cauliflower, a favorite English vegetable.[5]

Like most potters, Wedgwood sold his goods by shipping packages of goods to merchants for resale; but in the 1760s, he opened a London warehouse, which took advance orders. Persnickety shoppers browsing through the self-service store and selecting services from samples or pattern books expected the finished goods to be uniform in quality. Although striking, Wedgwood's popular green glaze behaved unpredictably in the kilns, and picky customers complained about the inconsistencies. To resolve this problem, the potter buckled down in his laboratory, applying his talent for chemistry to perfecting a reliable cream-colored earthenware. He knew that the end of the French war would reopen important markets, especially on the Continent. In 1765, Wedgwood's tedious experiments paid off, as dependable cream-colored trials started emerging from his kilns. Shoppers so liked creamware that Wedgwood soon discontinued the green glaze; and, with his cousin Thomas, he set up an larger factory for making this so-called useful ware. The new line especially appealed to Britain's middling classes, who aimed to distinguish themselves from the small fry in part through consumption. In fact, creamware epitomized middlebrow taste; it cost less than English or Continental porcelain and looked more attractive on tables than common redware dishes, pewter plates, or wooden trenchers.[6]

Wedgwood did more than perfect a formula; he aggressively promoted creamware by seeking patronage from the right customers. During the 1760s, Wedgwood cultivated the interest of Sir William Meredith, the member of Parliament for Liverpool, who sent the potter china patterns to copy and recommended other highbrow clients. After his lines gained popularity among the local aristocracy, Wedgwood welcomed factory visits from the duke of Marlborough, Lord Gower, and Lord Spencer. Recognizing the market value of snobbery among the targeted middlebrow audience, Wedgwood looked higher up the social ladder for customers. When Charlotte, wife of King George III, ordered a green and gold tea service in 1765, Wedgwood jumped at the chance to earn the title, Potter to Her Majesty. The queen's imprimatur lent prestige to creamware, making it de rigueur. The potter made the most of this celebrity endorsement, broadcasting the queen's patronage on his bill head, in the London papers, and on the signboard of his showroom. Wedgwood amassed a fortune by selling spin-off products, which he called Queensware, to social climbers. In 1767, the potter marveled over this accomplishment: "The demand for this said *Creamcolour*, Alias *Queens Ware*, alias *Ivory* still increases. It is really amazing how rapidly the use of it has spread almost over the whole Globe, and how universally it is liked. How much of this general use and estimation is owing to the mode of its introduction—and how much to its real utility and beauty?" Within a few decades, Wedgwood's Queensware—and imitations made by dozens of Staffordshire factories—came to symbolize the aspirations of status-conscious shoppers throughout the Western world.[7]

Indeed, Wedgwood thrived by learning how the emulation engine worked and harnessing its energy, a task that he tackled most effectively with the aid of his principle partner, the Liverpool merchant Thomas Bentley (1730–80). After their fortuitous meeting in Liverpool in 1762, Wedgwood and Bentley developed a friendship that solidified as a formal business partnership in 1769. By the time he met Wedgwood, Bentley had more than two decades of commercial experience under his belt; he had trained in business with a wholesale wool and cotton merchant in Manchester, operated a successful Liverpool wool warehouse, and was about to enter the partnership of Bentley & Boardman, general merchants serving the colonies in North America and the West Indies. Just as important, Bentley boasted a classical education, which endowed him with a fluency in languages; he had also traveled to France and Italy, where he cultivated a passion for antiquities. Wedgwood and Bentley perfectly complemented each other; the peasant potter's technical knowhow and the urbane merchant's wide-ranging interests fused into a redoubtable combination. Indeed, Bentley was more than Wedgwood's confidant, co-investor, and fellow advocate for the Trent & Mersey Canal; he provided the Staffordshire man with an aesthetic link to the marketplace, a lifeline to the cosmopolitan world of fashion. Put simply, the cultured Bentley was Wedgwood's secret weapon in the war to conquer the pottery trade.[8]

When Wedgwood told Bentley, "You have taste," the potter did more than flatter the merchant; he ventured his opinion about what really mattered to a manufacturer anxious to capitalize on consumer society. Although Wedgwood counted among Staffordshire's success stories by the mid-1760s, this enterprising craftsman understood that his country schooling and craft skills could only take him so far. Wedgwood had visited London and Liverpool enough to know that triumph in the wider world depended on connections and comportment that lay beyond the purview of a backwoods artisan. It depended on links to the beau monde, to the people who mingled in tight-knit circles, inflected their voices in distinctive ways, and wore the latest London fashions. In England's ranked social order, this community of tastemakers remained off limits to Wedgwood's small artisanal clique. To leap across social barriers, the potter turned to Bentley, whose routine duties as a merchant and whose amateur pursuits in art, literature, and science provided entree into cultured circles. With a dignified appearance and personable manner, the knowledgeable Bentley easily impressed the fashionable members of society. Using his social contacts, Bentley helped to put Wedgwood ware on the map.[9]

By the late 1760s, Wedgwood and Bentley recognized that a niche market awaited the pottery that was ready, willing, and able to feed the vogue for neoclassicism. In the era of the grand tour, wealthy Britons returned from their pilgrimages to Rome and Athens longing to recreate the monuments of classical civilization. The elite architects Robert Adam and James Wyatt designed interiors that reflected the fashionable "Augustan" taste (named after the Roman Emperor Augustus, a great connoisseur and art patron), and the London cabinetmakers Thomas Chippendale and John Cobb made matching furniture decorated with urns, garlands, and swags. When the shortage of genuine antiques forced architects to embellish rooms with mock classical vases made from wood or silver, Wedgwood and Bentley seized the moment. By 1767, Bentley agreed to join a partnership for the production of so-called ornamental wares; two years later, Wedgwood & Bentley commenced operations at the new Etruria factory (named after the site of a popular Italian archeological dig). Between 1769 and 1780, the partners acknowledged consumer sovereignty and crafted a strategy aimed at meeting demand, rather than shaping it. Their partnership demonstrated how close ties between a manufacturer and his consumer liaison augmented design practice.[10]

Wedgwood & Bentley perfected techniques that registered the nuances of consumer taste and channeled this information into the factory's design shops. While Wedgwood supervised operations in Etruria, Bentley moved to London, where he ran an enlarged showroom on the corner of Newport Street and St. Martin's Lane. (In 1773, Bentley relocated the facility to more fashionable quarters on Greek Street in Soho, a chic shopping district; he also opened showrooms in other stylish locations, including Bath, the great spa town.) In the London shop, Bentley coddled the upper crust, small and large. Here, the Russian counsel submitted Catherine the Great's commission for the "Frog Service," some nine hundred pieces to be used at the Chesmenski Palace at La Grenouil-lière (the Frog Marsh). Just as important, the firm planned new products based on Bentley's observations in the store, contacts with the cognoscenti, and evaluations of avant-garde trends. It was probably at Bentley's urging that Wedgwood added famous artists to the payroll, including John Flaxman of London, who designed celebrity medallions for gentlemen's curio cabinets. When Bentley noted why shoppers preferred certain products, Wedgwood gratefully acknowledged the feedback. Such was the case when the potter learned that English women liked the stark contrast between the whiteness of their skin and the blackness of basalt. "Thanks for your discovery in favor of the black Teapots," Wedgwood told Bentley. "I hope *white hands* will continue in fashion, and then we may continue to make *black Teapots* 'till you can find us better employment." So the story went, Bentley sizing up the fashion scene and Wedgwood heeding his recommendations.[11]

The manufacturer-retailer team never hesitated to make what the market demanded; early on, the partners learned to set aside personal preferences in favor of consumer taste. "I have a very small vase which was dug out of Herculaneum," Wedgwood told Bentley. "I do not see any beauty in it but will make something of it." The partners' achievements rested on their prescient acceptance of the market, which was propelled by the engine of emulation. When a

Wedgwood & Byerley showroom, York Street, St. James's Square, London. Showrooms played a major role in Wedgwood's marketing strategy. From Rudolph Ackermann, *Repository of Arts, Literature, Commerce, Manufactures, Fashions, and Politics* (London, 1809), Smithsonian Institution Libraries, Smithsonian Institution

"violent *Vase madness*" swept across England one shopping season, Wedgwood recounted how the trickle-down process worked. "The Great People have had these Vases in their Palaces long enough for them to be seen and admired by the *Middling Class* of People. . . . Their character is established, . . . and the middling People would probably buy quantitys of them at a reduced price." Those unable to afford ornamental jasper or basalt found that Wedgwood's useful goods—the tea, table, and toilet lines made at Burslem—filled the bill. Although Wedgwood priced his Queensware higher than competitors' copies, consumers still coveted the line. The high price was part of the snob appeal. For a humble cottage dweller, nothing seemed more elegant, refined, and beautiful than a precious piece of cream-colored ware, which was fit for the Queen.[12]

Marketing practices only partially accounted for Wedgwood's rise as Staffordshire's leading light; a good deal also rested on his manufacturing innovations. Along with other eighteenth-century English and Continental entrepreneurs, Wedgwood pioneered a production model that minimized proprietary risk, reduced fixed costs, and maximized skilled labor's input. Using a manufacturing system that historians call *flexible specialization*, or *flexible batch production*, these firms deliberately made short runs of highly varied goods, quickly changing from one color, fashion, style, or price as the market dictated. This practice was ideal for creating the novel, high-quality products that eighteenth-century shoppers craved. Whether the line was Zurich watches, Sheffield cutlery, Paris cabinetry, or Staffordshire pottery, manufacturing flexibility ensured profits.[13]

Changes in production practice appeared in tandem with the redefinition and relocation of skill among the Staffordshire potteries. Europe's porcelain manufactories had divided work into a number of tasks, employing workers who specialized in particular jobs, such as modeling, firing, and enameling. By the 1760s, the Staffordshire potteries also relied on the division of labor; Wedgwood followed the mark, introducing disciplinary improvements such as the factory bell, the punch clock, and the list of rules dictating appropriate behavior. Among workers, two new types of labor aristocrat—the modeler and the china decorator—had an enormous influence over design practice and the appearance of Wedgwood's lines. During the 1770s, the challenge of creating attractive, uniform, and consistent products had become a problem of monumental dimensions. To resolve the issue, Wedgwood asked contract modelers to simplify his cream-colored line. By eliminating fanciful rococo handles, finials, and feet, the modelers revamped the look of Queensware, introducing plain shapes and smooth surfaces. The straightforward styling not only appealed to consumers versed in neoclassicism; but as Wedgwood told Bentley, it also allowed the factory to lower "the price of workmanship."[14]

To achieve economies in Queensware manufacturing, Wedgwood reduced production runs by limiting the number of shapes in his factory's oeuvre; but at the same time, he dramatically expanded his decorating options. On the shop floor, workers made the plain shapes by using expedients such as molds and lathes. In turn, china decorators gave each piece a distinctive look by adding delicate embellishments, such as enameled pictures copied from design books. There was no limit to the variety of patterns that decorators could use on simple plates, bowls, cups, pitchers, dishes, and tureens. (Wedgwood also subcontracted with the Liverpool printers Sadler & Green, which employed decorators to apply specially made engraved transfers on to items.) With this system, Wedgwood avoided inventory buildups, asking his china decorators to embellish blanks only after the orders arrived. Aiming to "make such *Machines* of the *Men* as cannot Err," Wedgwood retrained his workers for the new precision-oriented jobs, such as casting with molds, using lathes to trim items, and painting pictures with enamels, which enhanced the neoclassical style of Queensware. To sharpen the artistic skills of apprentices, he placed them in drawing and modeling classes. Geared up for state-of-the-art production, Wedgwood's practical men (as apprentice-trained artisans were called in the parlance of the day) made hundreds of different novel products.[15]

By the time of Bentley's death in 1780, Wedgwood & Bentley had perfected a design and development system that linked factories to distant fashion centers, providing the producer with mechanisms for reading consumer preferences. Customers flipping through Wedgwood's catalogue or browsing through his showrooms in London, Bath, or elsewhere saw useful and ornamental wares in a spectrum of patterns. Dozens of manufacturers copied these lines. For decades to come, the story remained the same: the name Wedgwood symbolized high-quality ceramics, and status-conscious shoppers throughout the West coveted this china. Just as enduring, Wedgwood's labor-intensive, batch-production manufacturing techniques and his informal market research methods, including his acknowledgment that merchants could play a major role in deciphering consumer taste, influenced manufacturers on this side of the Atlantic Ocean.

In the nineteenth-century United States, potters and glassmakers emulated the example of Wedgwood & Bentley as they went about the tasks of designing, manufacturing, and marketing desirable products. The names of the master craftsman and his merchant colleague were revered by generations of practical men, who understood how much the partners contributed to the potter's art. More important, these artisans embraced the Wedgwood-Bentley model of organization, design, production, and marketing, which had become standard practice in the Staffordshire potteries. When British practical men immigrated to the United States, they carried the tradition of imagining consumers to the North American shores.

If European tastes had varied, those in the United States ranged even farther, given the population mix and the land's sheer size. Flexible specialization, which emphasized the reading of consumer desires and the creation of an endless flow of novel lines, perfectly suited the enormous and highly diversified market. The Wedgwood-Bentley batch production system that dominated many American potteries was emblematic of the modus operandi in dozens of other industries that produced household furnishings. Whether they made furniture, silver, rugs, textiles, or glassware, such manufacturers embraced flexible specialization, which emphasized responding to what the market wanted. As these producers discovered, few Americans blindly aped the consuming behavior of their economic betters. More often, consumers noted elite styles, smiled sweetly, and proceeded to shop for items that better suited their distinctive subcultures. Producers responded by adjusting the Wedgwood-Bentley system of fashion feedback, fine-tuning it to work in a heterogenous market. Focusing on the cultural dimensions of this "other side of industrialization"—on product design and development in the home furnishings factories that once dotted the landscape from Boston to Chicago—has consequential implications for understanding the clockwork that made the American consumer revolution tick.[16]

Like their European predecessors, many potteries and glassworks remained tightly controlled family firms, passing managerial responsibility from generation to generation. With family tradition dictating commitment to communities and industries, owner-managers evinced little interest in horizontal consolidation or vertical integration, two growth tactics pursued by large national corporations. Instead, these owner-managers played active roles in daily operations, often hiring practical men to help oversee particular aspects of batch production. Such concentration on factory matters left owner-managers with little time, energy, or interest for looking beyond the established way of doing things in an attempt to manipulate demand.

Indeed, owner-managers concentrated on the most important task at hand: getting their audiences in focus. Although few took merchant partners like Bentley, most manufacturers relied heavily on feedback from *fashion intermediaries*, astute consumer liaisons whose jobs entailed studying markets, evaluating tastes, and making product recommendations. Identifying these fashion brokers as the primary agents of innovation turns the canon of design history inside out and upside down. Generations of connoisseurs have studied high-style craftsmen, self-appointed reformers, and high-profile "name" designers. Little attention has been paid to the evolution of household products between the decline of the craftsman and the ascendancy of the consultant industrial designer. Between 1865 and 1945, fashion intermediaries of various stripes—practical men, shopkeepers, salesmen, retail buyers, materials suppliers, art directors, showroom managers, color experts, home economists, advertising experts, and market researchers—assumed the major responsibility for the way things looked. Rather than impose their tastes, the most accomplished read the marketplace and cooperated with factory managers to design products for a spectrum of audiences. By contrast, the leading lights of reform, from the Aesthetic and Arts and Crafts movements on down to the "good design" campaigns of the Museum of Modern Art, attempted to foist consensus on a heterogenous portfolio of consumer products. Such efforts ignored the variability of tastes, the flexible production practices of the nation's home furnishing factories, and the egalitarian nature of the American consumer revolution.

Batch manufacturers helped to democratize consumption primarily by way of the mass merchandisers they served. Before the department store's rise as the bourgeois consumption palace, other retailers extended the possibility of consumerism to an enormous proportion of the population. Chain stores like the Great Atlantic & Pacific Tea Company and the F. W. Woolworth Company targeted urban immigrants, with their lofty dreams of abundance and little cash to spare. The chain stores needed enormous quantities of inexpensive china and glass to give away as premiums or to sell for modest sums. Making carload after carload of this tableware for such retailers, factories and workshops advanced the American sense of shared "wealth."

Gender also figured into corporate strategy. By the twentieth century, mass-market manufacturers understood their audiences as primarily female. Fashion intermediaries, who were often men, faced one of their greatest challenges in crossing gender boundaries in order to understand, interpret, and satisfy women's material expectations. The most successful of them achieved this end, taking tips from shoppers on which designs would sell. To be sure, the batch production format did not penetrate all segments of the home furnishings trade; newcomers to consumer products, unaware of these feedback loops, experimented with corporate elixirs like industrial design, credit sales, mass advertising, and market research. Consistently, however, these firms learned an important lesson: whether for reasons of price, utility, or style, women refused to buy items that they did not really want—no matter how much money producers had spent on enticement.

By no accident did clusters of batch producers dominate the industrial landscape at the moment when consumerism came to revolve around women and domesticity. These specialized manufacturers, much more than big businesses, ushered the transmogrification of a fragmented group of provision seekers into a nation of highly differentiated consumers. Make no mistake: supply did not create demand in home furnishings, but demand determined supply. Whether china decorators or art directors, the most successful design innovators created practical goods that delighted the senses, rather than exotic items that seduced, tantalized, and disoriented. Artistic protagonists concerned with imposing "good taste" found few supporters in the home furnishings trades, in which many different tastes were the order of the day. Firms catering to the enormous mass market admitted that design and development was an interactive process that took place at the intersection of supply and demand, a process best facilitated by seasoned fashion intermediaries experienced in the task of imagining consumers.

CHAPTER 1

Cinderella Stories

Few American women experience girlhood without learning the tale of Cinderella, the servant who finds happiness as a princess with the aid of magic and, more important, a portfolio of fashionable consumer goods. Forbidden to attend a ball by wicked relatives, the impoverished maiden labors in the kitchen while her ugly stepsisters bedeck themselves for the fete. Following their departure, Cinderella enjoys a visit from her fairy godmother, who outfits the beauty with costume, coach, and livery designed to capture royal attentions. After blissfully dancing with the enchanted prince, Cinderella dashes from the ballroom to meet her gift-giving godmother's midnight curfew, losing a crystal slipper in her flight. Ultimately, this artifact reunites the lovers, for Cinderella's precisely calibrated glass shoes fit only her. The infatuated prince scours his kingdom for his true love, finally locating his bride-to-be, Cinderella, the girl whose foot slides into the glittery slipper. United, the two live happily ever after, so the story goes.[1]

For centuries, the Cinderella story has offered girls and women a paradigm for reaching emotional fulfillment and financial security through marriage and domesticity. Yet this tale about culturally sanctioned gender roles also reveals much about the centrality of material goods in building individual identity and negotiating interpersonal relationships. Without question, Cinderella's transformation from a kitchen wench to a dazzling belle depends on a fairy's gifts, and emancipation from her evil keepers requires the goodwill of a male protagonist, who symbolizes a future of marital bliss. Still, Cinderella captures the prince's attentions and secures his devotion by using an ensemble of fanciful consumer products. This constellation of things amplifies her natural beauty into the courtly good looks that catch the prince's fancy, turn his head, and hold his gaze. The material message in this romance resonates loud and clear: women can use objects to set agendas and achieve ends within the realms of courtship, marriage, and family.

The Cinderella tale operates on many metaphorical levels, and its object lessons bear upon the study of cultural production in nineteenth- and early twentieth-century America. As in this make-believe romance, domesticity figured boldly in the culture and economy of Victorian America, infusing interactions among manufacturers, retailers, and consumers of household artifacts with creative dynamism. Through the activities of selecting, receiving, purchasing, and using artifacts, consumers forcefully challenged producers' capabilities and expectations. Much like fairy godmothers, managers in manufacturing, retailing, and advertising constantly reassessed the marketplace, designing and redesigning products to meet purchasers' needs and fancies. In companies producing household accessories, the goal of satisfying consumer tastes contoured decision making from the board room to the shop floor. Just how glass manufacturers imagined the tastes and met the expectations of real-life Cinderellas, giving form to the market basket of household glassware, is the subject of this chapter.

During the nineteenth century, people's yearnings for objects that helped define their individuality and social position shaped managerial strategy in factories and workshops making two kinds of glassware: mass-market and high-end lines. Put simply, the pressed and cut glass trades drew sustenance from three sequential, sometimes overlapping, cultural systems: gentility, domesticity, and distinction. Early in the century, the rise of genteel culture, with its emphasis on ritual, midwifed the glass pressing trade, an industry segment that faced almost no competition from rival materials or imported wares. From the Civil War through the Great War, glass factories responded to the emerging cult of domesticity by adopting new formulas, equipment, and furnaces to achieve significant productivity gains and to create inexpensive, mass-market products. By the 1880s, pressing factories watched the emergence of cutting workshops devoted to making distinctive lines, that is, objects with snob appeal. By century's end, the consumer glass industry had bifurcated into the pressing and cutting trades, each with its own share of design, production, and marketing challenges.

In each branch, decision makers relied not on designers per se but on fash-

glass, made in the United States or abroad, required a substantial financial expenditure, and well-off men remained its primary purchasers. In 1817, President James Monroe visited the glassworks of Bakewell, Page & Bakewell in Pittsburgh, ordering decanters, wine glasses, tumblers, and dishes for the executive mansion. While Monroe may have selected Pittsburgh glass to demonstrate presidential confidence in American industries, other men bought table accessories for different reasons. Some appreciated costly table glass as man-to-man gifts; during the 1820s, the former treasury secretary Albert Gallatin presented the Delaware gunpowder manufacturer E. I. du Pont de Nemours with a pair of decanters. In men's eyes, glassware could function on several levels; crystal showed knowledge of gentility, demonstrated wealth, signified fraternal bonds, solidified friendships, built political alliances, and sealed business deals.[4]

Regardless of how and why each gender embraced refinement, the unfolding of genteel culture provided entrepreneurs in the home furnishings trades with avenues for enlarged sales. Beginning in the 1820s, glassmen like Deming Jarves, proprietor of Boston & Sandwich Glass Company in Massachusetts, developed new technologies, including mechanical presses outfitted with metal molds and dies, that increased productivity and elaborated design possibilities. Among early pressed products, the cup plate—a coaster for the tea-drinking ritual—best speaks to the glass industry's relationship to gentility. A late afternoon pastime, the tea ceremony provided refined Americans with the opportunity to gossip, flirt, network, discuss politics, and celebrate accomplishments; in Philadelphia, Otis found himself invited to two or three "gentlemen's dinners and tea parties" each day. English and Chinese potters, who dominated the United States ceramics market, had long made teapots, caddies, cups, saucers, and other equipage for this ceremony, which also had a set of prescribed behaviors. The advice author Eliza Leslie reminded readers of the *Lady's House Book* about the advantages of "little cup-plates or cup-mats" for teatime. To imbibe properly, a tea drinker first poured the hot liquid into a saucer to cool, resting the cup on the coaster—a 3½-inch shallow dish—to avoid soiling the table. Genteel consumers so coveted cup plates that between 1827 and 1860 American pressing factories produced more than eight hundred different designs.[5]

Following the introduction of pressing, the consumer glass industry entered a period of unprecedented growth. In 1825, Jarves employed seventy workers at Sandwich; by 1852, five hundred. Sandwich's good fortunes, built on vernacular gentility, coincided with expanded glassware production in the mid-Atlantic states and, more notably, in the Pittsburgh-Wheeling area of the upper Ohio

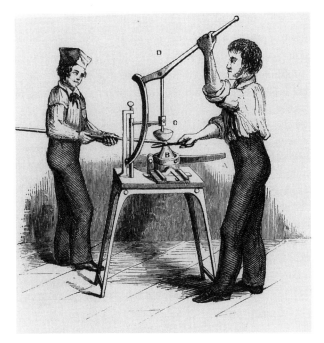

Pressing a piece of glass tableware. A worker drops a gob of hot glass (B) into a metal mold. Another lowers the plunger (D), shaping the molten glass (C). From Apsley Pellatt, *Curiosities of Glass Making* (London, 1849), Smithsonian Institution Libraries, Smithsonian Institution

River valley. For glassmakers, the so-called Pittsburgh district possessed tremendous geographic advantages; it had good supplies of bituminous coal, high-silica sand, and potash, all essential raw materials in glass production. For table glass manufacturers, the area had another lure: ready access to western markets via the railroads and the Ohio and Mississippi Rivers. By 1857, Pittsburgh's thirty-four glass factories turned out $2.6 million worth of glass products per year; more than a third of these plants fashioned pressed items. Located on the National Road and Baltimore & Ohio Railroad, Wheeling sported a smaller glassworking center, with three substantial glass factories within the city limits.[6]

In *Reminiscences of Glassmaking*, Deming Jarves boasted that pressing had so reduced manufacturing costs that tableware consumption had multiplied tenfold in thirty years. When Jarves published his memoirs at the end of the Civil War, more than three-fourths of the glass tableware made in the United States originated in pressing factories. Few would deny his claim that the new technology democratized glassware consumption. Once a precious commodity "prized and displayed as the treasure and inheritance of the wealthy," wrote Jarves, glass tableware by the 1850s could be found in "the humblest dwellings." The pressing revolution enabled even the "poorest and humblest" person to discard pewter plates and wooden bowls and "decorate his table" with glassware "at a cost barely more than that of one of his ordinary day's labor." Yet what stands out most about Jarves's comments is the gender of his imagined consumer.[7]

At a time when metropolitan merchants like A. T. Stewart of New York City, proprietor of the country's leading dry goods emporium, encouraged women to embrace shopping as entertainment, Jarves described the pressed glass consumer as male. However strong the temptation to dismiss his language as literary convention or gender legerdemain, Jarves's pronoun choice may reflect a reality wherein men purchased glassware or, like Otis decades earlier, assisted their spouses. Reports of men's consuming escapades abounded. In 1838, the Philadelphia correspondent for the *Boston Atlas* described one of the city's leading crockery stores, Joseph Kerr's China Hall, as filled with "classically beautiful" marble vases from Italy, "superb" porcelain sets, "elegant and showy glass wares," and male shoppers, including the famed Massachusetts orator, Daniel Webster. The aging Jarves could not foresee the future. At midcentury, shopping was turning into a feminine leisure-time activity. Some observers had discerned faint outlines of this shift in the 1830s; editors at *Godey's Lady's Book* and *Graham's Magazine,* who perceived luxury in stark opposition to the valued

Women browsing in china shop. From Horace Greeley, *The Great Industries of the United States* (Hartford, 1872), Hagley Museum and Library

quality of sentiment, had condemned women and girls who frequented stores for pleasure rather than out of necessity. By the 1850s, this critique of luxury waned as editors of magazines and authors of etiquette manuals accepted material indulgence. To shop for fabrics, dishes, and other objects of personal and domestic adornment signified mature womanhood; and to teach a girl to consume joined tutoring in sewing, embroidering, and cooking as a serious maternal duty. When Caroline Dunstin of New York City shopped for Christmas gifts in 1856, she purchased toy "cups & saucers" for her little girl, a consumer-in-training. The cultural system of gentility began to yield to domesticity, with its need for highly ornamented goods that spoke to familial taste. None other than the lady of the house, with her presumed natural affinities for beauty and home life, would select the goods indicative of her family's middle-class position. At the close of the Civil War, the glass trade stood at a crossroads; perhaps Jarves, a founding father of pressing technology, had retired at an opportune moment.[8]

The Mold Maker's Sphere

> The metal molds for the manufacture of pressed glass are made upon the premises of each manufacturer; and as the production of a novelty is a point aimed at by each, as an important element of success, the getting up of new designs demands a considerable amount of care and attention.
> —George Wallis, "New York Industrial Exhibition," 1854

As gentility and domesticity reshaped the tableware market, pressing techniques transformed work in the glass industry in ways that affected design and innovation. Most notably, the pressing trade witnessed the birth of a new breed of labor aristocrat: the mold maker, who with his journeymen determined the appearance or look of pressed glassware. When George Wallis, head of the School of Art & Design in Birmingham, studied American industry on Parliament's behalf in 1853, he observed the seminal role of mold makers in "getting up . . . new designs."[9] Trade journalists agreed that the boss mold maker's "taste and fancy" plus his "ceaseless and watchful attention" to the marketplace made him indispensable to a glassworks seeking consumer dollars.[10]

Mid-nineteenth-century pressed glass manufacturers realized advantage through a tricky balancing act, seeking equilibrium among quality, quantity, price, and novelty. They continued to press dishes, bowls, compotes, egg cups, vases, toothpick holders, sugar bowls, pitchers, candlesticks, and lamps in hundreds of designs. They also competed for market shares with a new line: the four-piece set consisting of a creamer, spoon holder, sugar bowl, and butter dish. Glass sets visually complemented the heavy white ceramic ware known as ironstone that merchants had imported from England in substantial quantities since the 1840s. Pressing factories differentiated these sets by decorating them in a variety of molded motifs: leaf, flute, crystal, honeycomb, diamond, and so forth. Created for the formal evening meal, glass sets bridged the cultural systems of gentility and domesticity that vied for Americans' attentions as the nation recovered from the Civil War.[11]

A factory's chief mold maker aided this design initiative by harnessing his unusual combination of skills: mastery of metalworking technologies, an understanding of glassworking processes, and a sensitivity to the fashion system. Often, a mold maker had apprenticed in another glass plant or in a contract mold shop, experience that provided him with a knowledge of competitors and their likely design strategies. Routinely, he collaborated with the factory's general manager and chief salesmen to evaluate the potential reception of new forms and styles. Factory salesmen returned from the field with reports of changing tastes that could fire a mold maker's imagination. Mechanics supplemented travelers' feedback with their own knowledge of art and design. Some searched broadly through American culture, looking to fine art, architecture, and other industrial arts for suitable motifs. By copying flowers from wallpaper samples, geometric borders from architectural books, and nut-shaped finials from silver products, some mold makers created eclectic lines that presented new interpretations of old themes. Others found inspiration in their personal lives: John Ernest Miller, chief mold maker at the Pittsburgh glassworks of George Duncan & Sons from 1874 to 1892, saw in his wife's beautiful countenance the model for his famous Three-Face pattern. Always, attentive mold makers acknowledged the agency of consumers, who voted for their favorite products with their purses.[12]

While most mold makers remained employees, some used their craft skills to segue into management; often, mechanics' firms enjoyed wide reputations as artistic and technical innovators. After working for the New England Glass Company (NEGC) in Cambridge, Massachusetts, the mold maker John H. Hobbs moved to Wheeling in the 1850s to found Hobbs, Barnes & Company (renamed Hobbs, Brockunier & Company in 1863). Once established as a maker of high-quality novelties, the firm undertook chemical experiments that would alter the pressing trade and propel the Pittsburgh district to the forefront of consumer glassmaking. Superintendent William Leighton Sr., also from NEGC, developed viable formulas for lime glass in 1863 or 1864. This glass contained bicarbonate of soda as a melting agent, making it cheaper than the lead glass, fluxed by lead oxide, common in pressing factories. The low density of lime glass meant that it cooled and became rigid sooner than lead glass, so that managers could demand that workers press items faster. By reducing the costs of both materials and labor, Leighton's formula soon became the favorite at Hobbs and at other pressing factories in the Pittsburgh district.[13]

At Central Glass Company in Wheeling, German-born mold maker John Oesterling manipulated the visual and tactile components of lime glass, rearranging ordinary shapes, forms, and motifs into mosaics that delighted potential purchasers. In Oesterling's day, a good design combined considerable familiarity with a pinch of newness, such as his Cabbage Rose pattern, patented in 1870. To create this line, Oesterling applied a stylized low-relief rendition of the prickly garden shrub *Rosa centifolia* to standard forms, such as goblets, spoon holders, covered bowls, footed bowls, and celery vases. He crowned covered bowls with high-relief acorn finials that showed off his understanding of naturalistic forms and his mastery of metalworking techniques. Oesterling also looked to other pressed glass patterns, perhaps drawing inspiration from Alonzo C. Young's 1869 design patent for acorn-topped dishes produced by the Boston Silver Glass Company. No sooner had Oesterling emulated Young's novel finial than mold makers working for McKee & Brothers and Adams & Company, both in Pittsburgh, copied other components of the New Englander's design. Like Oesterling's work, these patterns trumpeted the brilliance and clarity of lime glass, while touting the sculptural potential of pressing technology. Equally important, all these designs, including Cabbage Rose, testified to the rapid transmission and mutation of patterns in the pressed tableware business.[14]

As prices fell and purchasing power rose during the 1880s, industry commentators for the *American Pottery and Glassware Reporter* acknowledged that, more than ever, a firm's survival depended on its responsiveness to consumer taste. Prominent glassworks managers confirmed journalistic observations that fashion had transformed the marketplace. Writing to Boston from Wheeling in 1886, William Leighton Jr., who had succeeded his father as superintendent, confided to colleague Thomas Gaffield: "The progress of glassmaking during the last half dozen years has been decidedly toward the artistic." Whereas the American glassmaker of the past had been "simply an artisan," the successful manufacturer of the prosperous mid-1880s had to be "be something of an artist" so that he could "be constantly producing new and beautiful things." The impetus for this change, he argued, came directly from consumers. Products that were "simply useful without beauty" found "a poor market." Manufacturers could no longer second-guess what people wanted; they had to monitor major cultural shifts, regional tastes, competitors' lines, and more. Leighton "kept exceedingly busy now, more so than ever," supervising the development of lines that would meet "the demands of the people for novelty and beauty."[15]

Similarly, managers in pressing factories grasped for ways to improve pattern offerings to enlarge their sales to mass merchandisers. More and more, these factories bypassed wholesalers, which for generations had bought glassware on credit and distributed it to small retailers. By the 1880s, pressing factories preferred to do business with department stores, chain stores, and mail-order houses, which placed large orders, paid cash on delivery, and kept down transaction costs by distributing goods directly to consumers. Department stores sold pressed glass on tight margins; when making room for new stock, they cleared out items at cost. Chain stores like the Great Atlantic & Pacific Tea Company built up customer loyalty by offering shoppers free gifts of pressed glass after so many purchases of tea, coffee, and sugar. In 1887, Montgomery Ward & Company surprised rural crockery merchants by adding modestly priced glass sets to its mail-order catalogue. As mass retailers undercut prices, urban china and glass stores carped about the erosion of the traditional crockery trade. Much to these shopkeepers' dismay, the symbiotic relationship between pressing factories and mass merchandisers led to ever lower prices, which threatened to push small retailers out of the distribution chain.[16]

To accommodate high-volume customers, glassworks managers reevaluated their approaches to product design, innovation, and promotion. Factories introduced new patterns at the beginning of each year to capture the trade of mass retailers, who planned ahead for seasonal sales, including the frenzy leading up to Christmas. Large urban department stores like R. H. Macy & Company in New York and John Wanamaker's in Philadelphia helped to convert the religious holiday of Christmas into a secular shopping event with tantalizing window displays and thematic interiors that celebrated consumerism and gift giving. While planting the seeds of desire, mass retailers implored manufacturers to create items with greater gift appeal. As retailers threatened to desert stodgy factories for those in the aesthetic vanguard, glassworks managers pressured mold makers to design ever more unusual forms, enlarging the potpourri of objects known today as Victorian bric-a-brac. In Pittsburgh, Henry Franz patented a mold for

Pressed glass goblets. By the 1880s, mold makers had created novel patterns that transformed mundane tableware into desirable consumer products. National Museum of American History, Smithsonian Institution

a sleigh-shaped dish, while Miller created salt cellars shaped like glass slippers for wishful Cinderellas. The drive for novelty also affected factories' merchandising practices, encouraging glassworks to refurbish showrooms in ways that appealed to retail buyers. The sample rooms of Adams & Company in Pittsburgh, noted *Pottery and Glassware Reporter* in a typical passage in 1885, "have been newly papered, painted, and decorated, and their appearances now may be suitably designated as gorgeous." Ultimately, glass factories joined forces with nearby Ohio River valley potteries to sponsor the semiannual, later the annual, shows of the Associated Glass & Pottery Manufacturers in Pittsburgh.[17]

Comparable to the furniture industry's trade exhibits, each china and glass show ran for several weeks in early January at the Monongahela House, a hotel close to Pittsburgh's industrial area. Over several decades, the "Pittsburgh show" became the pottery and glass industry's largest advertisement. As was customary in trade shows, factory salesmen rented commercial suites, where they laid out their company's new lines for visiting buyers to scrutinize. With a store's recent Christmas statistics in mind, a buyer could plan next fall's sales as he circulated through room after room of factory exhibits. Generally, he studied competing displays, made notes on patterns and prices, and returned home to

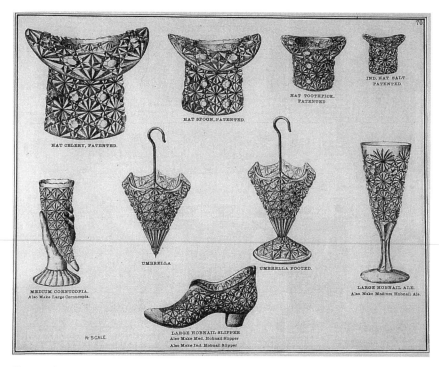

Glass novelties by imaginative mold makers. From *George Duncan & Sons, Manufacturers of Fine Flint Glassware* (Pittsburgh, ca. 1890), George A. Fogg

contemplate orders. Once buyers grew accustomed to making pilgrimages to Pittsburgh, the annual model change became an institutionalized aspect of design practice in potteries and glassworks. Indeed, the "mania for turning out new styles" that gripped mass-market manufacturers would have an enormous effect on the design process during the early twentieth century. By that time, the responsibility for design would shift away from skilled factory artisans—such as mold makers and their equivalents in the pottery business, china decorators—to the retail buyers who had urged producers to speed up innovation.[18]

No matter where consumers looked for household necessities, they bumped into glass tableware, made ever cheaper and more ubiquitous by advances in glass chemistry and the mold maker's craft. According to the *New York Mercantile Gazette,* pressing factories made "goods of real beauty in form and style" at prices that placed them "within the means of every class of the public." Even the poorest Americans, including factory workers in the nation's industrial cities, could own pressed glass. In New York City, itinerant peddlers, like "one old Italian," filled small handcarts with western glassware acquired at auction and pushed them along the side streets and alleys of the most impoverished neighborhoods, calling out their wares. These vendors furnished the city's poor with Pittsburgh's "beautiful glass in all its varied colors." Everywhere, budget-conscious Cinderellas envisioned how pressed glass might transport them to a higher level of material achievement. The price was right, the risk low, the promise great: Why *not* buy into this more gracious world?[19]

While suburbanites, immigrants, and farmers admired the look of pressed glassware, detractors castigated it as mock crystal, criticizing mechanics for designs that embarrassed industrial art. Molds, remarked one observer in *Pottery and Glassware Reporter,* could never produce "outlines and angles sharp enough" to "attain the beauty and perfection of cut glass." Pressed glass, charged elitists, paled in comparison with the real thing: costly crystal. "Imitation cut glass," wrote a journalist in *Harpers New Monthly Magazine,* "can always be distinguished from the genuine expensive article by the inferior luster and the unavoidable rounded edges." In the pressing trade, managers, salesmen, and mold makers paid little attention to these critics, knowing that they had interpreted the material desires of their target audience, people with modest incomes. Out of this collaboration emerged an aesthetic that flaunted the pressing industry's chemical and technical achievements, including the mold maker's talents. Owners of pressed glass appreciated its clarity, its excellent design and finish, its widespread availability, and its reasonable, if not outright cheap, price. Pressed glass represented the quintessential democratic consumer product; cut glass, its antithesis.[20]

Crystal City, Cutting Edges

> The appointments of modern tables indicate with no less certainty the progress of nations and individuals in refinement, luxury and wealth.
>
> —*New York Mercantile Gazette,* 1871

As the nation's class structure congealed after the Civil War, newly wealthy consumers flaunted their riches in the accumulation, display, and use of sumptuous objects, from Italian Renaissance furniture and Old Master paintings to Newport "cottages." Encouraged by gallery owners like Samuel P. Avery, who ran the Fine Arts Room on Fifth Avenue at Fourteenth Street in New York, successful businessmen developed a taste for art collecting. European painting, sculpture, engravings, and antiques counted among the most desirable treasures, but most things exceptional, elaborate, and expensive filled the bill. Delicate, breakable glassware spoke of the owner's disposable wealth, and as did precious gems and shiny porcelains. Millionaire coal baron Henry Clay Frick accumulated extensive holdings of European paintings, sculpture, furnishings, and ceramics, as well as American crystal, which he displayed in the intimate dining quarters at Clayton, his house in Pittsburgh. To Frick, the ability to indulge his whims for such costly—and easily cracked, chipped, or shattered—goods signified financial and social security, his place at the apex of the wealth pyramid. The foppish Caldwell Colt, heir to his father Samuel's gun-making fortune, appointed the cabin of his yacht, the *Dauntless,* with fine crystal. Once a luxury for kings, cut glass now belonged to America's industrial princes and other self-made aristocrats, who in the United States sat upon pedestals that the Old Country reserved only for inherited wealth. Rich crystal epitomized "good taste"—and entrepreneurs like Frick and leisured gentlemen like Colt, who lived on industrial fortunes, coveted good taste.[21]

Like Frick and other self-made men of the new business class, an invigorated cut glass industry emerged from the economic, cultural, social, and political shifts that followed the Civil War and Reconstruction. The stupendous showing of American factories at the United States Centennial International Exhibition of 1876, in Philadelphia, ushered in the birth of the crystal glass industry. Among the 130 glass companies present at this world's fair, Americans contributed one-third of the exhibits. The Centennial Exhibition's great attractions included the model plant of Philadelphia's Gillinder & Sons, in which demonstrations of the glassmaking process mesmerized visitors. Leaving the miniature factory, spellbound spectators became glassware consumers as they purchased souvenirs decorated to their specifications by cutters and engravers. In the Gillinder store, the twenty-nine-year-old Frances Mower Scott, who traveled from Schuylkill Falls to Fairmont Park by horsecar, purchased two pitchers and a pressed glass slipper, which later found a permanent place among other heirlooms in her granddaughter's china cabinet. Few left the Gillinder exhibit without newfound enthusiasm for the glassmaker's craft and for the enticing products that glass factories could make.[22]

The cultural excitement generated by the world's fair combined with geographic, demographic, and political factors to lay the foundation for a glass-cutting renaissance. The 1870s discovery of deposits of high-silica sand in the Berkshire hills of western Massachusetts meant that glassmakers no longer had to import this key ingredient. The immigration of European cutters and engravers to the United States during the Franco-Prussian War solved the long-standing problem of scarce skilled labor. Finally, protectionist tariffs supported by Republican administrations gradually increased ad valorem duties on cut and engraved glassware from 30 percent in 1861 to 45 percent in 1883. If American glassmakers had their way, the 1883 tariff would have reached 60 percent, but manufacturers' entreaties fell on deaf ears in Congress. Still, by the early 1880s, protectionism barred all but the most expensive cut glass from entering the American market.[23]

By that time, an infant cutting industry appeared in a handful of cities in the Northeast and Midwest, including Toledo, Ohio; White Mills, in central Pennsylvania; and Corning, in upstate New York. The cutting trade featured two branches. On the one hand, manufacturers such as Christian Dorflinger & Sons in White Mills hired factory artisans to ornament pieces of blown or molded lead crystal made in their own furnaces. On the other hand, independent cutters like Thomas Gibbons Hawkes of Corning procured blanks from glass factories and importers, employed workers to devise and cut the designs, and assumed responsibility for selling the final product. By 1900, the Irish-born Hawkes, who had learned the cutting trade in America, operated the most successful workshop in the Crystal City, as Corning citizens designated the nation's cut glass center. There, the cutting business thrived in the shadow of the town's largest employer, Corning Glass Works, which made specialty glass products for railroads and electrical manufacturers as well as high-quality blanks for cutters. By the 1920s, when the sun had set on the cut glass vogue, the Crystal City had seen more than three dozen cutting and engraving shops rise and fall within its boundaries.[24]

Like other cutting entrepreneurs, Hawkes realized that the division of labor could expedite the crystal-making process, so his facility resembled a small factory with some sixty artisans laboring on stationary assembly lines. In long window-lined rooms, under the supervision of a foreman, employees worked at frames, that is, steam-powered apparatuses consisting of rapidly revolving disks, which were sprinkled from overhead funnels with wet abrasives. As production coordinator, the foreman reviewed incoming orders, marked blanks with pattern outlines, and assigned tasks, in turn, to roughers, smoothers, polishers, and engravers. A rougher crudely incised a design's outline on the blank in preparation for the highly skilled smoother, who applied the labyrinthine decorations—networks of stars, fans, and diamonds—that endowed crystal with much of its beauty. Next, a polisher restored shine to a piece by buffing it with different

Cutting workshop, Corning, N.Y., 1890s. Juliette K. and Leonard S. Rakow Research Library, Corning Museum of Glass

grades of wheel-mounted abrasives. Finally, an engraver added embellishments such as family crests, initials, dates, mottos, and flowers, as specified by the customer. Although artisans reproduced standard decorations again and again, the endless mixing of motifs enabled cutting shops to produce novel items.[25]

In the home furnishings trade at large, cutting workshops enjoyed a reputation as design leaders that fused technical ingenuity with craftsmanship to create a distinctively American style of glassware. By the 1880s, cutters introduced their "brilliant" mode, which excited even the harshest critics of American pottery and glassware, including Eurocentric importers in Boston and New York City. By combining high-silica sand and lead oxide in batch formulas, Corning Glass Works produced extremely thick, highly refractive blanks; Hawkes's employees, in turn, engaged their craft skills and artistic wherewithal to decorate these pieces with detailed, bold designs. When the cutter Philip MacDonald embellished some tableware with a dazzling nova that "shone with the brilliancy of ten thousand closely set jewels," Hawkes patented the design, called Imperial Russian Star. The combination of exceptional lead glass, energetic incising, and showy patterns endowed American crystal with a clarity, luminescence, and intricacy that differentiated it from Anglo-Irish and Continental products. Moreover, brilliant crystal embodied the material aspirations of upper- and middle-class Americans, who wanted distinctive objects that reflected their ambitions if not their social positions.[26]

Introduced during the art craze of the 1880s, brilliant cut glass differed from other art products—from whatnot shelves, Japanese fans, and the like—in its popularity among male shoppers. As costly purchases, crystal inevitably fell into men's domain, but cut glass owed its masculine appeal to something other than price. Prismatic cut glass sparkled, diamondlike, in dimly lit dining rooms, flattering the owners' wealth, status, and taste. Why a Gilded Age entrepreneur like Frick valued such ostentation is apparent; but why men from the old and new middle class treasured cut glass requires more probing. Like their female counterparts who celebrated the past by dressing in colonial garb, men of the established middle class may have purchased glassware in old English designs to establish a link with an imaginary eighteenth-century golden age. In great-grandfather's day, educated men such as physicians, attorneys, teachers, and proprietors knew where the middling lot stood: between the gentry and the lesser sorts. By the 1880s, such men felt uneasy about their status as they battled upstarts for the middle rungs of the social ladder. Ironically, the objects of their distrust, salaried men from the new middle class, also experienced uncertainty about their role in industrializing society. Among the first to work in nonproprietary and nonclerical jobs at telegraph agencies, railroads, insurance companies, government offices, and other bureaucracies, these men often lacked mentors who might have shown them the proper way to do business. While women of the new middle class learned about manners, dress, and ritual from etiquette books, their men emulated behavior prescribed in popular, business, and trade magazines. The *Decorator and Furnisher* carried an illustration of a bachelor's cabinet designed by the Broadway interior decorator Edward Dewson; this elaborately carved pièce de résistance was outfitted with cubbyholes for glass decanters, goblets, and smoking accessories. When firms like Christian Dorflinger of White Mills advertised cut and engraved decanters in the *Commercial and Financial Chronicle,* the salaried managers who read this major business weekly surmised that gifts of glass might figure into their corporate exchanges. Indeed, owning objects with artisanal origins perhaps quelled managerial anxieties, imaginary and otherwise, over the loss of a bucolic craft world supposedly diminished by the rise of national corporations.[27]

In this context, the greatest admirers of Hawkes's crystal included midlevel managers connected to the nation's first big business: the railroads. When visiting upstate New York to buy signaling equipment from Corning Glass Works, railroad men learned about the Crystal City's cut glass trade by strolling down Market Street, which had show windows filled with the latest brilliant patterns. By the 1880s, railroaders saw trips to Corning less as dull purchasing sojourns and more as a chance to mix business with pleasure. On their trips home, railroad men mulled over the expensive crystal they had seen. Some, like Osborne Sampson, an agent for the Adams & Westlake Company, one of Chicago's leading railroad suppliers, and J. T. Crocker, purchasing agent for the Chicago, Milwaukee & St. Paul Railway, later wrote to Hawkes to secure cut glass gifts for their relatives, friends, and colleagues. In 1885, John S. Brewer, a Chicago agent for a Bridgeport railway supply company, ordered glass plates for one of his "RR friends." Brewer's gift functioned to bolster, to impress, and to flatter. Regardless of what meanings the recipient assigned to Brewer's glass gift, the keepsake facilitated the continuation of a collegial exchange and helped to augment sales.[28]

As men demonstrated their appreciation of brilliant cut glass, manufacturers and retailers honed in on the male consumer by offering accessories specially designed for masculine settings, such as libraries, smoking rooms, and offices. The trade journal *China, Glass and Lamps* described tobacco jars, whiskey and brandy flasks, decanters, and punch bowls encased in silver, ornamented with horn, and engraved with figures of yachts, dogs, or horses as "fashionable presents for men." Focusing on the male audience worked splendidly. Men not only selected rich cut glass as gifts but they also pampered themselves with personal purchases of these fancy things. One Philadelphia businessman of modest means, Moses LaRue, a retired coal yard proprietor, stocked the dining room in his three-story house in Spring Garden with porcelain dinnerware, a silver-plated tea service, finger bowls, and other assorted glassware. In Ohio, the engineer Edward Orton Jr. received a cut glass cologne bottle as a party prize. Whether atop the social ladder or somewhere in the middle, men prized rich cut glass for multiple reasons: as instruments of corporate solidarity, as objects of personal desire, as symbols of social status, and as reminders of earlier accomplishments.[29]

In this marketplace, glass cutters strove to remain attuned to the social, economic, and cultural changes that fostered consumers' infatuation with novelty, quality, and beauty. Innovation and profits depended on both craft skill and on proprietary alliances with retail merchants. As Wedgwood and Bentley had demonstrated a century earlier, a merchant in touch with his customers harvested meaningful data about tastes and purchasing habits. For decades, china and glass importers on this side of the Atlantic had emulated the Wedgwood-Bentley formula, informing British suppliers about the types of goods suited to American tastes and pocketbooks. In 1826, the Baltimore jobber Matthew Smith had implored his Liverpool shipper to "avoid drab and cane" colors, "except in low-priced articles" for the urban trade and to send "dinner sets of light patterns," as demanded by "retail buyers" in the country. More than fifty years later, Hawkes turned to the retailing world for help in imagining cut glass consumers.[30]

Hobnobbing with Highbrows

Parties buying rich cut glass from me are very exacting and will only receive that which is perfect in every way.
—Richard Briggs, 1884

When Hawkes opened his cutting workshop in 1880, he realized that the marketplace had been transformed since his arrival in the United States. As urbanization accelerated, the marvels of the nation's great metropolises lured curious visitors and ambitious residents from far and wide. Attractions included the capacious dry goods emporiums that had sprung up in New York, Chicago, Philadelphia, and Boston since midcentury and that were evolving into full-fledged department stores. In them, shoppers could buy every imaginable consumer product, from hoopskirts to gas lamps, made by the nation's workshops and factories or imported from abroad. By 1881, the ground floor alone at Wanamaker's Grand Depot on Market Street in Philadelphia featured crockery, glass, millinery, linens, toys, stationery, books, shawls, shoes, and more. In the shadows of these consumption palaces stood shops specializing in particular lines: furniture, clothing, jewelry, fancy goods, china, and glassware. Shoppers meandering around northeastern seaports also browsed through importers' warehouses, where the newest goods lay awaiting the wholesale and retail trade. Whether rich or poor, consumers who visited the great downtowns of the 1880s found stores catering to every pocketbook, stores filled with items that promised to help Americans define their changing social roles.[31]

By the 1880s, Boston and New York enjoyed a healthy rivalry as distribution centers for pottery and glassware; in these ports, Hawkes sold his crystal through high-end importers who doubled as jobbers and specialty retailers. Among Boston's tightly knit community of china and glass dealers, Hawkes found his Bentley, his liaison to the world of consumers: Richard Briggs. Born into a dish-selling dynasty established in 1798, Briggs assumed responsibility for his family's business in 1861, riding on the splendid economic opportunities ushered in by the Civil War. At that time, Otis Norcross, Boston's leading crockery merchant, had created the Earthenware Association, which united jobbers in price, credit, packaging, and freight agreements until its dissolution following the Panic of 1872. In 1883, several factors—the onus of national tariff policy, the threat of discrimination by western shippers, and tough competition from mass retailers and their suppliers, the pressing factories—encouraged Boston's crockery men to regroup as the Earthenware & Glassware Association. Both organizations in large measure united dealers as "a mercantile class," whose interests could be advanced by cooperation rather than cutthroat practices. Members adhered to formal price-fixing plans and to gentlemen's agreements that divided markets according to product types. Perhaps because of his firm's eighteenth-century legacy, Briggs reigned as Boston's highbrow china dealer, as the man of eloquence and "good taste," who served the city's political, intellectual, literary, and business elite.[32]

New Englanders of the 1880s who traveled to Boston, the self-described Hub of the Universe, could shop for china and glass in more than three dozen factory showrooms, retail shops, and wholesale storehouses. In part unscathed by the Great Fire of 1872, the crockery district lined both sides of Franklin Street, where the city's major dealer, Jones, McDuffee & Stratton, successor to Otis Norcross & Company, operated its main six-level store, which housed a stock of English, French, German, and American pottery and glass reflecting the diversity of Victorian taste. However, the firm specialized in the Asian blue-and-white ceramics or "India and Japan china," which had found favor among fashionable young Bostonians who followed the Japan craze. Nearby, at the corner of Devonshire, sat the airy new store of Abram French & Company, purveyors of "everything from costly Sèvres to cheaper everyday goods." If this variety boggled the senses, shoppers had only to walk down Franklin Street to the more modest retail store of Mitchell, Woodbury & Company, which sold plain goods like brown Rockingham and white ironstone. So the story went in New England's crockery town, with each merchant picking a specialty and sticking to it.[33]

While the *Crockery and Glass Journal* in 1884 called Franklin Street the "flocking place" for Boston's crockery men, the trade weekly admitted that Richard Briggs enjoyed a thriving business—"he flocks all alone by himself"—

Jones, McDuffee & Stratton's warehouse, one of the largest stores in Boston's crockery district during the 1880s. Society for the Preservation of New England Antiquities

on Washington, the equivalent of Philadelphia's Chestnut Street and New York's Broadway. Briggs's store rested smack in the middle of Newspaper Row, dubbed the "most crowded thoroughfare in Christendom" by the travel writer Karl Baedeker in 1883. Home to eleven papers, this news haven extended from the Old State House on State Street to the corner of Milk, the birthplace of Benjamin Franklin. Boston's main shopping strip, government buildings, and financial district lay within walking distance, as did the posh residences of Beacon Hill and the Back Bay. Like other Washington Street merchants, Briggs drew customers from the seats of power and money.[34]

By the last quarter of the century, people with class and people who aspired to class flocked to Briggs China & Glass Warehouse. By tradition, members of "old Boston families" knew that Briggs respected the status quo, with its hierarchies of rank and aesthetics. The distinguished statesman Charles Sumner had so appreciated Briggs's store that he never walked by "without dropping in to admire and select from the new importations." Members of New England's intelligentsia, from Oliver Wendell Holmes to Ralph Waldo Emerson, crossed the street from the famous Old Corner Bookstore to browse among the costly porcelains fresh from Limoges, Sèvres, Carlsbad, Berlin, Leipzig, and Dresden. If one needed a gift for a member of these families, shopping at Briggs's promised to yield results. When one of Longfellow's daughters received a present from her Uncle Tom, the package bore the markings: "With Great Care. Miss Annie Longfellow. From Richard Briggs." Briggs's celebrity clientele, along with his expensive stock, probably impressed curiosity seekers. To the empowered, Briggs offered a place for indulgence. To social climbers, his shop played a different role, providing an education in "good taste"—what it was and who had it.[35]

Inheriting a concern with a conservative reputation, Briggs did everything to sustain that legacy. In cultural matters, nothing appealed to elite Bostonians more than heritage; items had to originate in Europe or to boast high prices to hold Brahmin attentions. Like other crockery dealers, Briggs annually traveled abroad to select goods from the stocks of Venetian glassworks and French porcelain factories. He also visited Staffordshire, enlisting potters in his pet projects. In 1871, Briggs worked with Josiah Wedgwood & Sons to create his Elder Brewster teapot. Modeled after a piece of Chinese export porcelain in a wealthy Bostonian's collection, this American Colonial Revival novelty catered to the passions of upper-class New Englanders for a mythic Pilgrim heritage. In 1880, Briggs asked Wedgwood to make his Longfellow jug, a pitcher ornamented with a portrait of the Cambridge poet and passages from his 1878 verse, "Keramos." When Briggs advertised the Longfellow jug in *Frank Leslie's Illustrated Newspaper,* he did so with the confidence, grace, and dignity characteristic of "good taste." With such products, Briggs gave expression to his clients' yearnings for a heroic past and for exotic lands peopled by contented craftsmen. Not by accident had Briggs chosen Wedgwood, Potters to Her Majesty the Queen, as his collaborator. Ever since Wedgwood and Bentley courted the gentry with Queensware in the late eighteenth century, the firm had epitomized high-quality ceramics among status-conscious consumers, who looked up the taste ladder for models worthy of emulation.[36]

During his European buying trips, Briggs assembled a large sample collection, later cajoling factories and workshops to devise lines after these prototypes. In this respect, he played the role of a manufacturer's agent who interpreted tastes and suggested new designs to employers. In 1883, Briggs sent Hawkes a valuable "antique metal tray" as a pattern for bowls, sugars, creamers, salts, and other pieces. "I may be mistaken," the confident merchant boasted, "but it seems to me" that the new shape "will be the most attractive . . . ever gotten up." Similarly, George M. Howard, Reed & Barton's agent in Philadelphia, shipped an old English tea set to his firm in Taunton, Massachusetts: "In my opinion, this would make a desirable tea set now, in fact feel quite sure it would sell, provided the price was right." Again and again, Briggs forwarded drawings to the Crystal City, sketches that delineated precisely what, in his opinion, consumers would buy, be it a salt cellar, a candlestick, a decanter, or a liquor bottle. Always, Briggs engaged British or Continental reference points. To his customers, nothing expressed better taste than copies of fine European craftsmanship, untainted by uncouth American experience.[37]

As crockery dealer to Boston's upper crust, Briggs paid careful attention to the appearance of his store, the composition of his stock, and the look of his products. Given that his job entailed acting as a consumer watchdog, he welcomed those with "good taste" to his doors, while selectively beckoning the most discerning newcomers to join the luxury-goods game. In this conservative way, he shaped taste, especially among novices with dollars to spare. Throughout, Briggs recognized the value of determining what kinds of products pleased those who really mattered. By the time he was doing business with Hawkes in the 1880s, Briggs had seasoned his interpretations of consumer desires with well-oiled mechanisms for imagining the highbrow marketplace.

Briggs's taste thermometers included his china-decorating service, in operation since the 1860s. To furnish hotels with customized products, crockery merchants had long employed china decorators to embellish wares in their stores. At Briggs, shoppers could visit the decorating room, open to the public from Monday through Thursday of each week, where they saw artisans transform plain china into customized products. In turn, individuals might submit their own sketches for execution on imported porcelain blanks. In a series of household chats for James T. Field's *Atlantic Monthly* (later published as *The House and Home Papers*), Harriet Beecher Stowe praised Briggs for his attentiveness to consumer desires. Stowe appreciated the possibility that, at his china-decorating room, a woman could obtain household accessories "exquisitely painted with the wild-flowers of America, from designs of her own." More important, his china-decorating service facilitated communication with customers and magnified his ability to stock the right goods. As consumers sought self-expression through the purchase of individualized ceramics covered with copies of their own artwork, Briggs watched their ideas unfold. Once this information supplemented his aesthetic capital, Briggs used it to his benefit, sharing data about colors, shapes, and motifs with potters and glassmakers to design new generations of consumer products.[38]

Another of Briggs's taste-measuring devices was constant observation on the selling floor. As customers contemplated prices, quality, and shapes and demanded bits of this and that, Briggs made mental notes about what less-discerning witnesses might regard as insufferable nitpicking. Some shoppers valued engraved glass "lighter than paper," while others fancied dramatic deep cuts or overall etching. Occasionally, consumers carried goods home, unwrapped their parcels, and discovered scratched ice-cream dishes or off-color glasses. An "often-critical" woman complained to Briggs about some "far from brilliant" tumblers; she found the glass "clear enough" but with "no life." The Boston merchant tried to avoid the disastrous publicity such incidents could trigger by immediately returning unsatisfactory items and demanding "first class" replacements. What constituted perfection to Briggs's customers was as diverse as they were. The merchant's job entailed sorting through the eclectic tastes of his customers—their insistence on better metal, deeper cutting, and more graceful shapes—until he understood exactly what they wanted.[39]

To ease the burden of product development, Briggs invited customers to submit glassware designs for execution by manufacturers. Some customers saw this opportunity as the chance to acquire accessories that matched family heirlooms; a Russian bottle, carried to American shores by one man's father, provided a template for new drinking utensils. Others asked for novel forms, including glass platters "somewhat like the usual china meat dishes." The most confident clients devised new shapes and patterns. One woman believed that the inverted cover of a cheese dish, paired with a punch bowl stand, would make a gorgeous flower holder. A Washingtonian helped Briggs design a thistle pattern, modeled after English prototypes. In a critical letter, this articulate shopper posited that the line's tumblers would "be more effective, and decidedly more brilliant, if there was occasionally a line of deeper or broader cut." If Briggs ignored her advice, this well-traveled consumer argued, then his New York rival, Gilman Collamore & Company, would surely capture the market with similar items already on display in its Fifth Avenue store.[40]

Like other crockery men catering to the carriage trade, Briggs mediated the terrain of aesthetic risk that linked cut glass manufacturers and highbrow markets. He exercised a degree of autonomy, for he could encourage customers to buy certain products, including those that yielded greater profits. He printed booklets, trade cards, and advertisements that recommended certain household accessories; to some extent, he thus shaped desire. Still, Briggs knew that audiences wielded a powerful tool over producers: personal choice. When celebrities like the Swedish soprano Jenny Lind and the Brazilian emperor Dom Pedro paused in Boston, they bought expensive items at Briggs's store. But not every client wanted or could afford such sumptuousness; one out-of-town clergyman

Customer's sketch for a glass decanter, given to Richard Briggs and forwarded to Thomas Hawkes, 1888. Juliette K. and Leonard S. Rakow Research Library, Corning Museum of Glass

found the china shop so tempting that he begged the desk clerk at the Parker House, a quality hotel at School and Tremont Streets, "to give him a room as far removed as possible from Briggs's gallery of treasures." In the luxury-glass trade, businesses could not long make or stock items that consumers refused to buy; neither could they force people to participate in conspicuous consumption. Yet for those who wished to partake, rules of etiquette, style, and demeanor governed both selection and use. Ultimately, consumers laboring under cultural constraints dictated the survival or the extinction of goods in the glass market basket. Few appreciated these fashion facts better than Boston's broker of fine crystal in "good taste," Richard Briggs.[41]

Westward Ho!

> Pressed glass is so cheap, so plenty, and so pretty, there is no excuse
> for even the humblest household's lacking a full supply.
> —Emily Holt, *Encyclopedia of Household Economy,* 1903

As Hawkes and merchant collaborators like Briggs designed cut glass tableware that graced upper- and middle-class dining rooms, managers of pressing factories coped with the metamorphosis of their trade. Building on Leighton's formula for lime glass, Pittsburgh-area glassmakers had developed faster presses, water-cooled plungers, mold-heating furnaces, and the fire-polishing process. This technological ensemble, in turn, heightened expectations for productivity among managers, who sped up the shop floor and the pace of design innovation. As the fashion game soured into bitter rivalry, losers fell by the wayside.[42]

Eager to keep their firms afloat, Pittsburgh glassmen pursued several options. Ongoing price wars had led glassworks managers to believe that horizontal consolidation would eliminate fierce competition, stabilize declining prices, and boost earnings, as developments in the railroad, oil, iron, steel, and meatpacking industries promised. In 1891, thirteen pressing factories in Pennsylvania, Ohio, and West Virginia fused their financial and technical wherewithal, merging into a new corporation, the United States Glass Company. Others saw natural gas as their savior, as a means of reducing manufacturing costs and improving product quality; by the late 1880s, hardly a glassworks in the Pittsburgh district used coal, except as a backup fuel. Still others sought new beginnings in greener pastures farther west, in Ohio and Indiana, where local boosters beckoned with free fuel, cheap land, and cash bonuses. New production centers, from Tiffin and Fostoria in Ohio to Gas City and Muncie in Indiana, dotted the midwestern landscape wherever gas proved to be plentiful. By 1890, half of the pressed glass made in the United States came from factories in these boom towns.[43]

These new factories secured their future by hitching their wagons to the rising star of mass merchandisers, including mail-order houses. To meet these clients' volume needs, managers reduced production costs by adopting tank furnaces, which increased throughput by permitting round-the-clock operations. Initially developed for German steelmakers by the Siemens brothers, these furnaces, which produced an ample supply of hot glass on a continuous basis, enabled factories to experiment with semiautomatic presses, to run hand presses faster, and to dispense with the fire-polishing process, which endowed pressed tableware with considerable gleam and glitter. As a result of this technological cyclone, Indiana tableware became the cheapest in the trade. By 1900, the national average wholesale price for a hundred pieces of glass was $4.00. However, in terms that sketched the shape of competition, it stood at $5.48 in West Virginia, $4.43 in Ohio, $4.35 in Pennsylvania, and only $2.31 in Indiana. Once the semiautomatic rotary press appeared after 1900, factories enjoyed enormous productivity gains, as an average worker's output increased from thirty-one to sixty-five pieces per hour.[44]

By the turn of the century, mold makers, the pressing industry's labor elites, realized that their craft had reached stasis. Indeed, these mechanics had enjoyed a golden age between the 1850s and the 1890s. They had stretched the boundaries of metalworking practice to patent multipart molds for pressing complex forms, expanding the glass set to include a sugar bowl, creamer, celery holder, spoon holder, butter dish, nappies, and compotes. Few antebellum glassmen could have imagined the range of products shown in the mail-order catalogue that Sears, Roebuck & Company distributed in 1895. Sears's large footed compotes, pressed in a single step, seemed worlds apart from the humble cup plate. Yet by the 1890s, mold makers could do little more to enlarge the options for novelty. Increasingly, pressing factories defended their market positions by concentrating production on a limited number of forms, which they varied with surface alterations. Having exhausted the lexicon of patterns, mold makers looked up the social ladder for inspiration. More and more, they copied brilliant cut glass.[45]

In 1903, Sears offered customers with modest budgets five sets of "beautiful imitation cut glass": Pride, Victoria, Desplaines, Westmoreland, and Jubilee. The timing dovetailed perfectly with the rise of domesticity and its hallmark custom, formal dining. Over the course of several decades, urban and suburban women, aided by hired immigrant servants, embraced the highly orchestrated evening meal, a practice once reserved for elite households. In *House-Plans for Everybody* (1879), architect S. B. Reed illustrated the ideal "comfortable and genteel" home: a single-family dwelling with a first-floor kitchen, parlor, and dining room. Etiquette books devoted pages to tips on furnishing dining areas and conducting mealtime parties. To make the correct impression on guests, a homemaker had to select a matching table, chairs, and sideboard proportionally suited to her dining room. "Set the table as beautifully as possible," *Hill's Manual* urged in 1881. "Use only the snowiest of linen, the brightest of cutlery, and the cleanest of china." More than ever, prescriptive writers deemed dining accessories as fitting tools for inculcating children with middle-class manners. As Marion Harland argued in *House and Home,* a boy was "more apt to sip noiselessly from a cut-glass goblet or a china cup" than from a heavy mug. Overall, writers of advice books encouraged readers to think of evening meals as occasions that celebrated the home and family. By stocking its catalogue with glass sets and matching pottery services, managers at Sears extended the promise of middle-class domesticity to rural and small-town women.[46]

"It is difficult to decide," noted journalist Harriet Edwards in *Harper's Bazaar* in 1900, "whether glass or silver play the more important role in the decoration of the table." Undoubtedly, some women shared Edwards's uncertainty about the household goods that flooded the market at the turn of the century. More often, they used these goods in ways as distinctive as each woman was herself. While some consumers saw glassware as instruments for impression management, they frequently imbued these objects with intensely personal meanings. When David and Sarah Walmsley celebrated their fiftieth wedding anniversary in 1887, these former slaves, who owned a Delaware farmstead, received a glass vase molded with diamond-shaped facets from their six children. Sarah Walmsley stored her pressed treasure atop a cupboard, until special family dinners warranted her using it along with her best linen napkins, gilded chinaware, and silver forks. A humble mass-market object, this "strawberry diamond" vase nonetheless registered the Walmsleys' remarkable accomplishment: the long journey from agricultural servitude to participation in consumer society. Just as Cinderella's costume and coach signaled her yearnings for a better life, pressed glassware could symbolize a woman's hopes, aspirations, and ideals while connoting her faith in the sanctity of the traditional life-sustaining institution, marriage.[47]

American Beauties

> Cut glass in this country has become so popular that it now rivals the precious metals in its sale in various forms for gifts.
> —*Scientific American Supplement*, 1902

In 1890, a commentator for the *Jewelers' Circular* noted how shifts in demographics and aesthetics—the growth of a "large middle-class population possessed of sufficient means and taste to appreciate the best efforts of the glass cutter"—had propelled luxury glassware to the forefront of American consumer culture. To be sure, wealthy sorts still bought the most expensive crystal. In 1902, the *New York Tribune* reported that "one of the Vanderbilts," who owed their riches to railroads and finance, had purchased some cut glass champagnes that cost of $500 per dozen. However, top-echelon households bought but a minuscule proportion of American crystal. Members of the northern professional and managerial classes—physicians, attorneys, small businessmen, engineers, educators, government workers, and corporate bureaucrats—enjoyed disposable incomes that allowed them to buy refined table accessories. To cultivate rising middlebrow demands, cutting workshops lowered prices by reducing the amount of skilled labor involved in production. Most notably, they started polishing pieces by dipping them in acid, rather than employing a felt wheel and putty powder, and introduced specially molded blanks impressed with the facets of a design. These cost-reducing measures encouraged New York merchants to open cutting workshops, where semiskilled workers simply sharpened the angles on imported pressed blanks. Even experienced retail buyers working for department stores like B. Altman & Company in New York had difficulty distinguishing between items made from "figured blanks" and genuine handmade crystal.[48]

As the retail price of brilliant cut glass fell, manufacturers competed for consumers' dollars by embracing mass advertising, promotional gimmicks, and brand names. "To tell cut from pressed glass is no difficult task," Christian Dorflinger of White Mills told readers of *Century Magazine* in 1889, "but to distinguish between the different grades of cut glass is not so easy." To those uncertain about their social standing, the solution lay in buying branded products, which carried the assurance of quality and the status associated with accessories like Wedgwood ware. "It is useful to know," continued the *Century* advertisement, that the best glass "in the world is Dorflinger's American Cut Glass." For middlebrows, the hobbies of giving, receiving, and collecting nationally advertised brand-name glassware symbolized their affiliation with the new economic order, embodied their wishes for material abundance, and spoke to their aspirations to distinction.[49]

Few men better understood how perceptions of rank, notions of propriety, and conceptions of integrity affected consumers' choices than one of the principal architects of the cut glass boom and the creator of a branded crystal that bore his name: Edward Drummond Libbey (1854–1925), president of the Libbey Glass Company in Toledo. Libbey spent his early career in East Cambridge, Massachusetts, where he learned the business of glassmaking from his father, a former Jarves employee. In 1874, Libbey joined his father, William L., in NEGC's management, taking charge of the blowing and pressing works at the older man's death in 1883. Libbey inherited a firm that had been shaky since the Civil War, when Pittsburgh lime glass factories had eroded NEGC's share of the consumer market. His attempts to put the company on solid footing by hiring Englishman John Locke to design fancy glass lines like Amberina, Pomona, and Peachblow failed in the light of waning tastes for aesthetic goods, heated patent battles, and tough competition. Following bitter strikes by the American Flint Glass Workers' Union, Libbey closed NEGC and abandoned Massachusetts for Ohio in 1888, moving west to take advantage of fuel supplies, expanding markets, and open shops. In Toledo, he established W. L. Libbey & Son Company, producing cut glass tableware, art glass, railroad signal ware, and lighting glass. In 1890, the company diversified into electrical goods during a strike that paralyzed Corning Glass Works, the major supplier of glass components—bulbs, tubing, and filament—to incandescent lamp makers. While reaping most of its profits from these quantity-production lines, the firm (renamed the Libbey Glass Company in 1892) owed much of its prestige to cut glass.[50]

Shortly after his arrival in Toledo, Libbey's fortunes became entwined with those of Michael J. Owens, a glassworker-turned-inventor who was determined to mechanize glassblowing. Libbey's managerial acumen and Owens's mechanical capability merged into a redoubtable combination. Together, these men developed technologies that transformed bottle making from a craft to a continuous-process industry. As Owens's ideas matured into workable, patentable, and profitable machines, Libbey secured capital for the Owens Bottle Machine Company, which built and licensed them to American bottle factories. Ultimately, the Libbey-Owens collaboration had its greatest impact on branches of the glass industry making standardized goods, in which managers embraced mechanization to facilitate the throughput of lighting components, containers, and windows. Libbey's growing fortune, made by advancing mechanized production, enabled him to nurture his favorite project: Libbey crystal.[51]

Ironically, Owens contemplated his mechanical revolution in 1893 at the World's Columbian Exposition, where he supervised Libbey's stupendous celebration of craftsmanship. Inspired by Gillinder & Son's highly successful Glass Exhibition Building of 1876, Libbey secured the exclusive American concession for making and selling glassware at the Chicago world's fair. Ignoring bankers' advice to tighten his belt, Libbey poured money into a huge display. A picturesque Italianate structure that accommodated some five thousand people, the Libbey Glass Works stood centrally on the Midway Plaisance, a short distance from the sensational Ferris wheel. Inside the Libbey building, visitors watched artisans blowing and pressing intricate items and saw cutters transforming blanks into beautiful novelties. In a mirror-lined chamber known as the "crystal art room," they found cut glass products glittering under the bright light provided by the new illuminant—electricity. One spellbound journalist from the *Jewelers' Circular* termed it "a room lined with diamonds."[52]

If Libbey envied the grand prize awarded to Hawkes's glassware exhibited by New York's Davis Collamore & Company at the 1889 Paris Universal Exposition, he soon had his satisfaction. His pavilion served as a magnet to visitors, who swarmed through the building in astonishing numbers; according to the guest register, about forty thousand tourists passed through the glassworks during the early weeks of the fair. Bathed in electric light, the Libbey pavilion exuded a phantasmagoric glow, a spellbinding magic. "The prettiest sight of all," noted one anonymous woman in her special fair diary, "is the Libbey Glass Works." One European princess admired the cut glass so much that she ordered some for herself, conferring on Libbey the title, Glass Cutters to Her Royal Highness Infanta Dona Eulalia of Spain. The Libbey exhibit also excited retailers and culture critics, including the fair's judges, who honored the glassworks with six blue ribbons and a gold medal. Men and women of all ages took souvenirs home; each received a little spun-glass bow on the end of a stickpin. Twenty-one-year-old Elizabeth Esther Mower of Philadelphia, niece of Frances Mower Scott, purchased a yellow glass slipper, which she treasured throughout her life and which she passed on to younger female relatives, along with a set of six world's fair demitasse spoons.[53]

Libbey's decision to show off at the fair put his company in the spotlight just as national economic policy gave advantage to the cut glass industry. In 1890, the McKinley tariff raised the duty on all pressed and blown glass from 45 to 60 percent. Although the short-lived Democratic tariff of 1894 slashed the rate to 40 percent, the Republicans reinstated protectionist tariffs in 1897 and 1909, restoring the duty on ornamented glassware to 60 percent. The Underwood tariff reduced the rate to 45 percent in 1913, but the Great War halted the law's implementation. Essentially, the 60 percent rate remained in effect for the thirty years between 1890 and 1920—and the cut glass age took off. Anticipating ever greater demand, in 1903 Hawkes built his own factory in Corning—the Steuben Glass Works—to ensure his workshop of a steady supply of blanks. Retailers bought less and less European cut glass every year; one importer cut his foreign purchases from $100,000 in 1893 to $15,000 in 1903.[54]

Although he channeled much energy into his alliance with Owens, Libbey still devoted considerable time to the Libbey Glass Company, which served as a proving ground for his theories about public relations, advertising, and consumer markets. Inspired by fair goers' enthusiasm, he hired Kate Field, a popular advice columnist from Washington, D.C., to write *The Drama of Glass,* a booklet that documented the Libbey pavilion. As Field's book piqued consumer interest in his products, Libbey determined to solidify his company's position as glass cutter to the middle class. Gearing up his public relations engine, Libbey scrutinized the glass trade, lest he repeat his mistakes of the 1880s. More aware of what middlebrow audiences expected of household goods, he masterfully combined three elements—status, quality, and reasonable pricing—to craft "Libbey" into the leading brand of American cut glass.[55]

As he conceived his brand strategy, Libbey capitalized on men's ongoing fascination with certain types of objects, including crystal. In college, young men often savored their first taste of consumerism by decorating dormitory rooms to suit personal fancies. At Yale University in 1899, one group of seniors decorated their suite with pictures, books, photos, tobacco jars, and beer steins. After graduation, men continued to purchase smoking, grooming, and drinking accessories, including cigar jars, toilet bottles, whiskey jugs, wine decanters, claret jugs, knife rests, cordial sets, and punch bowls. To build brand loyalty among male shoppers, Libbey wooed them with fabulous stories about rich and powerful men who owned pieces of masculine glassware. With much fanfare in 1898, Libbey presented Ohio's favorite son, President William McKinley, with a stupendous fifty-pound cut glass punch bowl, patriotically ornamented with stars, stripes, and shields. Using the White House as a springboard, Libbey's press releases, picked up by the trade and popular press, touted the punch bowl as a great achievement of American industry.[56]

To develop a reputation for fine crystal, Libbey went even farther. Playing off the notion of separate spheres, he manipulated prescribed gender roles to construct a new market for cut glassware: crystal as a wedding present. During the 1870s, Henry Ward Beecher had condemned the custom of giving wedding presents and the habit of displaying them for all to see on the marriage day. Beecher's ascetic diatribe fell to wayside when the formal public wedding joined the panoply of consumer celebrations in the next decade. Attendance at a festive wedding ceremony helped community members express their support of a marriage; giving luxury gifts like silver or glassware demonstrated a stake in the domestic ideal. Swayed by mass advertising and public relations gimmicks, male consumers started to think of crystal as appropriate presents for women, especially young brides. By the 1890s, wedding invitations regularly specified the bride's favorite gift, and "crystal weddings" became the vogue.[57]

During the fin-de-siècle decade, retailers encouraged manufacturers to reconceptualize standard lines as wedding-related gifts as a way of enlarging markets for household accessories. Porcelain factories pioneered this theme, and cut glass makers hurried to catch up. In 1891 Walter Scott Lenox, proprietor of Ceramic Art Company in Trenton, New Jersey, received a perplexing order for some porcelain "engagement cups." "But what is an engagement cup?" queried Lenox. "Oh, after-dinner, coffee, or anything of that kind," replied the scheming merchant, "as pretty and delicate as you can" make them. After receiving his porcelain delicacies, the dealer launched a ballyhoo promotion, telling fashionable shoppers that a betrothal warranted giving the bride an "engagement cup and saucer." Others joined Lenox's china works in seeking wedding dollars. Frank Haviland, a New York importer with porcelain factories in France, used *Century Magazine* to promote his dinner, oyster, soup, fish, game, salad, and ice-cream sets as "elegant wedding or holiday gifts." Both Dorflinger and Higgins & Seiter, a china and glass retailer with stores in New York City and Newport, Rhode Island, invested in advertisements that suggested that women desired cut glassware. Such campaigns targeted readers with discretionary incomes, including men with money to spend on expensive presents. Soon, Libbey embraced national advertising to outdo his rivals, publicizing crystal in *Century, Cosmopolitan, Harper's, McClure's*, and *Saturday Evening Post*. In a series of promotional booklets distributed by retailers—*Things Beautiful, American Beauty,* and *The*

Gentle Art of Giving—Libbey advised on the fine art of table setting and on the
selection of feminine gifts. Fittingly, the beauties in *American Beauty* included
the famous red rose, Libbey glassware, and the object of the gift giver's admiration—the lovely bride.[58]

Still, the rise of Libbey's firm as glass cutter to the middle class depended on
variables largely out of his control. Unexpectedly, his world's fair exhibit served
as a focusing device for the cut glass era by capturing the attention of retail jew-

elers. Having traveled to Chicago for a convention, jewelers in droves toured the World's Columbian Exposition, enthralled by the electrified displays. Up until then, only the most sophisticated urban stores had dared to stock cut glass; however, jewelers realized that Libbey-style showmanship might entice shoppers to buy crystal. In Elmira, New York, a young clerk, J. R. Sprague, watched his employer install a miniature crystal art room modeled after the one in the Libbey pavilion. No matter where Sprague went at the turn of the century, he found a jewelry store "similarly equipped" with a "cut-glass room lined with mirrors and lighted with electricity." Consumers relished the fanfare as well as the objects that sparkled in the bright light. Across the country, hundreds of crystal rooms, in jewelry stores and dry goods establishments, helped shoppers to solidify memories of the fair. When Sprague opened his own shop in the early 1910s, he found that customers often asked for "Libbey," which they remembered from "the cutting exhibit at Chicago."[59]

As jewelers became the major vendors of brilliant crystal, they pursued the male glass connoisseur. When men shopped at jewelry stores to buy the intensely intimate accessories—rings, pins, brooches—for their sweethearts, wives, sisters, aunts, and mothers, they encountered elegant displays of rich cut glass set up by retailers who understood crystal's subliminal allure as a mock jewel. The visual association of crystal with precious gems allowed middle-class men, some of whom studied geology and collected rare stones, to buy cut glass without compromising their masculinity. By the 1890s, few men frequented department stores, which managers had consciously feminized for the enjoyment of women shoppers. Although B. Altman, Stern Brothers, and Siegel-Cooper in New York, Wanamaker in Philadelphia, and Marshall Field in Chicago carried crystal, men tended to turn to the more sparingly decorated jewelry stores, with their club-like atmosphere. There, male clerks put male shoppers at ease as they contemplated purchases of gems, watches, silverware, and crystal. In such surroundings, men like Orville Taylor, Henry Gardner, and Oliver Drack, who in June 1908 attended the Chicago wedding of Louise Schoenberg and Barrett Conway, purchased the crystal goblets, the cruets, and the compote that appeared next to their names on the couple's wedding present list. With jewelers in their pockets, Libbey and other cutters deepened the national market for gifts of glass.[60]

Between 1890 and World War I, the fancy for cut glass reached its zenith, as manufacturers and retailers promoted cut glass as the "solution to the wedding-gift problem." Producers capitalized on gender relations, encouraging men and women to live out their Cinderella fantasies. To streamline gift selection and wrapping, retailers sold wedding present china, glass, and silver in custom-made, satin-lined boxes. While the guest's chores lessened, the recipient's task grew more complicated. Etiquette dictated that a bride devote months to writing thank-you cards "for all sorts of cut-glass presents—punch bowls, finger-bowls, dinner-glasses, wine-glasses, ice-cream dishes, bonbon dishes, decanters, and vases." When Pauline Cashman married Freeman J. Condon, the *Newburyport Daily News* covered the couple's "brilliant wedding" on the front page. "Liberally remembered by their multitude of friends," the newlyweds received 194 presents, 58 of them crystal. From May through August, this Massachusetts bride extended her gratitude, in person or in writing, to each acquaintance, friend, and relative. Such thanks necessitated her knowing something about different crystal forms and their uses, so that she could make appropriate remarks. Once the excitement had passed, real-life Cinderellas like Pauline Condon assumed responsibility for setting dinner tables with their new glassware, with or without the help of servants. Crystal weddings like this one became so popular that furniture factories created a new type of dining room display case, the glass-fronted china cabinet or china closet, just for storing glass gifts. If left on open shelving, crystal attracted dust and risked breakage; safe behind the transparent doors of a china cabinet, glassware glistened for all to see and admire.[61]

Sizing up the money, time, and energy devoted to the dining ritual, some observers lashed out against the cultures of domesticity and distinction, condemning the formal dinner party as a flagrant example of conspicuous consumption. In 1895, the journalist Robert Grant used the pages of *Scribner's Magazine* to satirize "the modern American woman of refined sensibilities" who instructed her servants to serve multicourse meals using every "article of virtu" in the house. "Modern dinner tables," he complained, had "too much fuss and feathers." The fashion for putting out every piece of crystal, silver, and fine china had reached such extremes that guests could no longer see the table linen. Etiquette mandated that every inch of the table top must be covered with paraphernalia: baskets of ferns, dishes of confections, and even candlesticks with pink lamp shades. Brides "worried" that their wedding presents might not include enough crystal to set every plate with "an array of cut glass or Venetian glass." Grant lobbied for simpler days, simpler meals, and simpler table decorations. No sooner had Edward Drummond Libbey perfected his marketing strategy than spectators denounced crystal.[62]

One of the most vindictive judgments came in 1919, when *Scribner's* published F. Scott Fitzgerald's "The Cut-Glass Bowl," a short story about the domestic life of Evylyn Piper and her prized possession, a huge crystal punch bowl. In 1892, just as the fad for cut glass took off, middle-class Evylyn breaks the news of her impending marriage to another suitor, Carleton Canby. The spurned admirer spitefully promises a wedding present as hard, beautiful, empty, and transparent as the object of his thwarted desire: a crystal bowl too gorgeous and expensive for the fashion-conscious bride to throw out, give away, or hide in the attic. As Canby anticipates, the vain Evylyn places the object of virtu in her dining room, where it, along with her "marvelous china," impresses status-conscious visitors like Mrs. Roger Fairboalt, who realizes that such a *"huge* cut-glass bowl" had cost a pretty penny. Like the spirit of a jilted lover, the bowl comes to haunt Evylyn as it eerily presides over a series of tragic events during her troubled marriage. Ultimately, when a maid misplaces an ominous telegram from the War Department, Evylyn instinctively knows that she will find the death notice for her son in the punch bowl. As the story winds to a close, the anguished Evylyn, grief stricken by her son's death, grabs her bowl, runs out the front door, trips on the stone steps, and falls to her death—with the prismatic object shattering to smithereens in the darkness. Fittingly, Evelyn dies just when the fashion for cut glass ended, given fatal blows by wartime shortages of labor and raw materials as well as by the criticism of formal dining.[63]

By no accident did the author Fitzgerald select a cut glass punch bowl to symbolize Evylyn's beauty, entrapment, and demise. In his literary mind, this objet d'art perfectly embodied the constraining aspects of the materialistic consumerism that he both envied and loathed. As a historical document, the story evinces the rise and fall of the cut glass age; as a diatribe against consumer society, it reflects the emerging modernist aesthetic that valued simplicity, efficiency, and scientism over the accumulation and display at the heart of the cultures of gentility, domesticity, and distinction. Since the 1890s, this alternative had appeared piecemeal in magazines and advice books: "Do not fill your homes with a profusion of bric-a-brac," warned Frank A. DePuy in *The New Century Home Book* in 1900: "Two or three pieces of fine ware will do." When Fitzgerald wrote his cut glass tale, the penchant for austerity had begun to influence the habits of gift givers. Among her wedding presents in 1919, Pauline Condon found several pieces of Pyrex baking ware, a new heat-resistant oven ware designed with efficiency in mind. A simpler aesthetic had budded.[64]

CHAPTER 2

China Mania

DURING THE EARLY 1880s, the air of prosperity at the three-story brick work-shop of Jesse Dean impressed visitors to Trenton. An immigrant from Stafford-shire, England, who had opened his New Jersey china-decorating business in 1867, Dean supervised a "little army of fifty operatives" at the "finest decorating establishment in this country." His employees—men, women, and children—expertly used a range of embellishing technologies, from gilding and painting to transfer printing and photoceramics, to make products for a variety of consumer groups. They filled orders for both stock patterns and one-of-a-kind pieces, cre-ating products for working girls and First Ladies, and even offered lessons and other services to amateur china painters. Fittingly, contemporaries dubbed the master of this busy, versatile workshop the "champion decorator."[1]

Jesse Dean (1845–1926) became the most celebrated among the dozens of artisan-entrepreneurs who operated china-decorating workshops in the major American centers of pottery production and distribution. For a brief period dur-ing the mid to late nineteenth century, these men thrived by interpreting the vagaries of consumer taste, either as independent manufacturers or as contrac-tors to potteries. During the 1870s, pottery managers had recognized that em-bellishment provided a means for satisfying diverse groups of consumers, sell-ing more goods, and improving profits. Increasingly, they relied on the services of china decorators, skilled artisans who knew how to add value to factory blanks, making them attractive and marketable. In this period, the industrial design profession as we know it today did not exist. Instead, apprentice-trained practical men like Dean functioned as surrogate designers, helping potters to imagine consumers and to create products accordingly.

The china decorator's heyday as product designer paralleled the rise and fall of an art craze that permeated American culture during the last three decades of the nineteenth century. All socioeconomic classes benefited from a long decline in prices that expanded the number who could participate in the emerging consumer society. As people could buy more for their dollars, middle- and working-class shoppers strove to fill their homes with "artistic" mass-market goods—machine-carved bedsteads, stamped silver plate, decorated chinaware— that simultaneously expressed individuality, betokened a social class's aesthetic preferences, and testified to participation in mainstream culture or industrial capitalism. As the nation recovered from the depression of 1873–79, factories from Providence, Rhode Island, to Chicago, Illinois, turned out ever more furnishings and accessories geared to satisfying the material and psychological needs of a diversified population. At the moment when critics like Charles Lock Eastlake promoted reformist designs, the nation's batch producers recognized the folly of bowing to any monolithic concept of good taste. Just as Americans stratified by class, ethnicity, geography, and other factors, their preferences also divided into countless variations. To accommodate those differences, mass-market manufacturers created artistic items in a hierarchy of price categories, each distinguished by its own grammar of ornament, standards of workmanship, and criteria for beauty.

This egalitarian art craze midwived a fad for collecting and painting ceramics, which in turn figured prominently in a major cultural development: women's transformation from housekeepers into consumers (for the differences between the prescriptive approach and the actual practice, see the two figures showing dining rooms). Among artistic household objects, mass-market pottery—ubiquitous and sometimes free or inexpensive—enabled ordinary women to own a piece of material perfection and, through that experience, to partake in their own cultures of beauty. As the art craze took off after the 1876 world's fair, shoppers found store windows filled with colorfully decorated ceramics, made ever cheaper by price wars. Retailers, schools, and ateliers offered lessons in china painting, which sharpened women's artistic skills but more often whetted their appetites as consumers. Although some wealthy Americans bought goods embellished with sunflowers, lilies, storks, frogs, and other motifs of the Aesthetic movement, most people satisfied their cravings with less expensive items, such

Dining room, with table laid for dinner. From *Miss Corson's Practical American Cookery and Household Management* (1885), Printed Book and Periodical Collection, Winterthur Library

Dining room with unmatched tableware and mock china cabinet, 1888, Wilmington, Delaware. Hagley Museum and Library

as moss rose tea sets, photoceramic pictures of loved ones, and colorful decal-decorated dinnerware, all made by U.S. factories and workshops. The job of deciphering the wants, needs, and desires of this new art-conscious client—the woman consumer—fell into the hands of practical men like the china decorator Jesse Dean.[2]

The Roaring Lion: Staffordshire in America

Dean had learned his trade at Samuel Alcock's Hill Pottery in Staffordshire, the pottery-making region of England that had been supplying the United States with most of its refined tablewares since the 1760s. Linked to the North American market by a network of loyal importers in large Eastern cities, Staffordshire potteries continued to dominate this trade for much of the nineteenth century. During the 1820s and 1830s, the Philadelphia jobber George M. Coates redistributed English goods acquired from commission agents, auctioneers, and manufacturers to general storekeepers in Pennsylvania, Delaware, and New Jersey. Similarly, Boston importers supplied imported ceramics to retailers in Massachusetts, Vermont, and New Hampshire. Some British potteries operated agencies in New York, where representatives gathered firsthand data about customers. During the 1840s, agents from three Staffordshire firms—Ridgway, Mayer, and Davenport—watched the retailing scene from their downtown showrooms, writing home about fashions and fads. As long as these channels linking Staffordshire potteries to American consumers operated smoothly, the United States ceramics industry remained a fledgling.[3]

During the 1840s and 1850s, several factors chipped away at the dominance of English imports and encouraged the nascent American pottery tableware industry. While the United States market stimulated growth in Staffordshire, trade hegemony enslaved nearly one-third of English potteries to the United States economy. Intense competition for shares of the vast American market resulted in price wars and speedups (the acceleration of production without wage increases). The better-capitalized firms built well-lighted, spacious factories; those on the economic edge cut corners. At midcentury, the towns that composed the Staffordshire ceramics district—Hanley, Burslem, Tunstall, Longton, Fenton, and Stoke—experienced a major recession, resulting in reduced wages, widespread unemployment, and the migration of the industry's highly skilled, apprentice-trained artisans to the United States.[4]

Equipped with specialized skills, many English practical men found ready employment in upstart American potteries, where they commanded top dollar. Charles Coxon secured a modeling job at Edwin Bennett's Queensware factory in Baltimore. Isaac Davis ran a crockery store in Trenton and, after the Civil War, worked as a modeler and mold maker for the city's new whiteware potteries. Eventually, ambitious practical men joined forces with investors or capitalists to establish potteries in budding ceramics centers on the East Coast and in the Ohio River valley. Arriving in 1842, William Bloor operated a porcelain works in Greenpoint, New York, before moving to Trenton, where he joined Joseph Ott and his nephew, John Hart Brewer, in opening the city's first china works. Jabez Vodrey worked for an ill-fated Indiana pottery before setting up his own factory in East Liverpool, Ohio. Frequently, practical men oversaw daily operations at the new potteries, and capitalists remained distant or silent partners. From across the ocean, the owners of British potteries eyed their industry's progeny with a mixture of pride and suspicion, as Staffordshire expatriates imparted craft secrets in exchange for potential fortunes promised by the conquest of the enormous American market.[5]

Recasting the American ceramics industry in an English mold, practical men knew that flexibility on the shop floor and attentiveness to consumer desire went hand in hand. Anglo-American potteries were loosely connected workshops supervised by seasoned journeymen rather than integrated, centrally run factories. An inside contracting system preserved craft secrets while providing managers with a well-disciplined workforce. Under this system, managers contracted work to senior journeymen, who assumed responsibility for hiring, monitoring, paying, and disciplining members of their crews, which included skilled, semi-skilled, and unskilled workers often selected from among their relatives. Eventually, the family-wage system collapsed, but the practice of subcontracting remained well into the twentieth century.

The advantage of the Anglo-American batch production system rested in its ability to respond quickly to changes in taste. Each unit—whether dedicated to mixing clay, grinding glazes, forming ware, tending kilns, or decorating goods—could readily switch from one product to another. Such shifts in production remained especially cheap and easy in decorating rooms, where workers applied patterns to blank shapes. The ability to mix an extensive repertoire of patterns with a limited number of shapes yielded considerable visual diversity while minimizing a factory's fixed costs. This flexibility helped small, poorly capitalized companies to compete in a fashion-conscious environment. As long as consumer

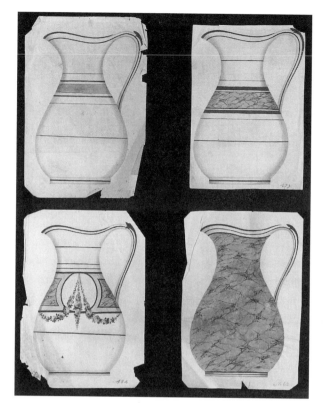

Watercolor sketches for patterns on pottery pitchers, 1870s. Ott & Brewer Company Papers, Joseph Downs Collection of Manuscripts and Printed Ephemera, Winterthur Library

desires drove the marketplace, embellishment remained the best way for potteries to achieve visual novelty.

In design and development, Staffordshire traditions dictated who made decisions about new shapes and patterns. During the nineteenth century, potteries employed modelers, mold makers, copperplate engravers, and china decorators. Although the largest potteries might employ several of these artisans, many could afford to pay only one person as an all-around design expert—typically, the china decorator. This person served as an artistic jack-of-all-trades under one of several titles: chief decorator, head decorator, or art director. Wearing his workingman's breeches, the chief decorator oversaw operations in the factory's decorating department, where he employed helpers to do menial tasks for day wages and supervised individuals learning the trade on piecework. Wearing his artist's beret, the chief decorator stretched his creative abilities by dreaming up patterns, collaborating with engravers on printed decorations, and supervising modelers and mold makers as they worked on shapes. A fiercely independent breed, china decorators had long shied away from the routinized factory environment, preferring instead to work in their homes or in small workshops as contractors to potteries, as they had for generations. When English potteries cut costs in the 1840s by introducing white granite—a heavy, durable ironstone that depended on novel shapes for its eye appeal—these decorators witnessed a diminishing demand for their services. Looking across the Atlantic Ocean, they envisioned bright futures for themselves in the budding American ceramics industry.[6]

In the United States, English china decorators often acclimated themselves to the china and glass business by working for urban merchants serving luxury markets. In Eastern seaports, they secured jobs in the ateliers of crockery men like Boston's Richard Briggs, for whom they customized ceramics with gilded inscriptions, repaired broken porcelains, and created matched additions to painted dinner services. With its rapidly growing bourgeois population, New York City, even more than Boston, attracted china decorators seeking to expand their fortunes. By the 1850s, the nation's leading style center boasted dozens of stores, warehouses, and workshops specializing in china and glassware. On Broadway, the monumental emporiums of Haughwout & Dailey, Davis Collamore & Company, and John Vogt & Company stocked fine tableware, parlor bric-a-brac, and library busts from European factories. West of Broadway, importers like Haviland, Blanchard & Company and Thomas A. Rees filled substantial warehouses with fancy French porcelain. When real estate development pushed northward after the Civil War, the city's upscale retailers, including its growing dry goods establishments, followed in pursuit of the carriage trade. The exodus allowed china and glass importers to expand their operations and create a virtual "crockery quarter," covering several blocks of lower Manhattan. At midcentury, however, china and glass merchants still jostled for space with other wholesalers and retailers in the city's busy commercial district.[7]

In this cauldron of commerce and consumption, china decorators—and their glass industry equivalents, cutters and engravers—found ready employment. William Leigh and Thomas Maddock, formerly of Staffordshire, opened a china-decorating workshop in Haughwout & Dailey's prosperous Broadway store. By the early 1850s, their subcontracting shop employed a hundred workers, and their products received accolades from the American Institute of New York, a mechanics' organization, and the New York Crystal Palace, an 1853 exhibition of manufactures modeled after the sensational world's fair in London two years before. Working in Manhattan exposed practical men like Jesse Dean, then decorating wares in James Shaw's atelier, to the ebbs and flows of the great port, where they forged friendships with potential employers, employees, and business partners. Stints in the crockery trade also familiarized immigrant artisans with the full range of metropolitan tastes: "I amused myself by drawing patterns I had seen," wrote Bohemian engraver Louis Vaupel in his memoir. Dreaming of an era when highly embellished tableware would grace every American home, some practical men used their New York experience to land factory jobs. Vaupel accepted a position at the New England Glass Company in East Cambridge, Massachusetts, while Dean looked to nearby Trenton, which held great promise as a pottery center.[8]

When Dean arrived in the United States during the early 1860s, Trenton housed a handful of potteries that manufactured several grades of white ceramics (whiteware), including CC (cream, or common, colored), WG (white granite, a type of ironstone), and china (porcelain). Wartime inflation and tariffs, which resulted in higher prices for English, Continental, and Asian ceramics, spurred the growth of the city's pottery industry. As Congress hiked import duties in 1861, 1862, and 1864 to raise revenues for the war, potters in New Jersey's capital wrested the CC and WG trade away from the Staffordshire factories and the urban importers. In 1860, American ceramics accounted for only 38 percent of the pottery and porcelain used in the United States. A decade later, pottery made in the United States, including plain white "Trenton goods," constituted 58 percent of those wares.[9]

Following the Civil War, ambitious china decorators saw bright careers for themselves in Trenton's pottery industry. In 1866, the twenty-one-year-old Dean left New York City for New Jersey, establishing a workshop with the aid of his mother and sisters, all Staffordshire decorators who "knew just what to do and how to do it." If Dean hoped for ready success, he soon met disappointment. Although wealthy New Yorkers bought decorated porcelains, many Americans believed that such luxuries encouraged corruption. One morality tale spoke to this concern. Visited by a peddler hawking "beautiful glass dishes and china ornaments," Mrs. Smith mistakenly traded her husband's best overcoat, worth about twenty dollars, for some bibelots worth about two dollars. Discovering her error, Mrs. Smith, ashamed that she had given precedence to market transactions over family matters and had been duped to boot, "went quietly down into the parlor," removed the vases, and "hid them away in a dark closet" for perpetuity. In 1869, Catherine E. Beecher and Harriet Beecher Stowe reiterated the themes of the china ornament story when they urged readers of the *American Woman's Home* to subordinate aesthetics "to the requirements of physical existence" and "to means of higher moral growth." The ownership of fancy chinaware could not be taken lightly, lest ruinous evil invade the virtuous household. Distrust of luxury and the consumer penchant for "white crockery" portended ill for china decorators. Looking back on the 1860s, one practical man later recalled, "There was no money, no work, plenty of debt, and no encouragement." In spite of these obstacles, Dean and a handful of other Trenton decorators remained firmly committed to their craft, maintaining that American purchasing habits would change in their favor.[10]

After the Fair

So many things date from the Centennial Exposition of '76. Among them the taste for decorated china.
—Mary Gay Humphries, *The House and Home,* 1896

In 1886, a trade reporter for *Crockery and Glass Journal* noted that "all classes and conditions of people" bought decorated pottery and porcelain more than ever before. The financial and social elite still patronized cosmopolitan china stores, antiques dealers, and jewelers. A pair of monumental blue-and-white vases so obsessed the well-to-do artist Edward Darley Boit that he carried these Japanese porcelains back and forth between his Boston home and his Paris apartment; when John Singer Sargent painted Boit's four daughters in 1882, the girls stood in the shadows of their family's prized possessions, which, all told, crossed the Atlantic Ocean sixteen times. On a more modest level, middle-class women purchased embellished pottery for their homes, while their husbands, brothers, and fathers—lawyers, bankers, restaurateurs, clerks—bought those goods as clubhouse accessories, public dining room accouterments, or gifts to colleagues. Men purchased shaving mugs emblazoned with mottos, initials, and pictures, which they displayed in their local barber shops; in Massachusetts, C. G. Ellis, who operated a West Sandwich lumberyard, owned a mug decorated with his name and a picture of a lumberman driving a wagon. Even the poorest Americans, who once had only the plainest dishes, discovered that, for a few extra coins, they could own decorated tableware on sale at the new variety chain stores, buy painted cups and saucers from urban street vendors, or obtain dinnerware as premiums with purchases of food staples at tea stores. During the 1870s and 1880s, the passion to possess decorated ceramics engulfed many Americans: men and women, managers and workers, rich and poor, city dwellers and rural folk. China mania was an inclusive phenomenon—and a relatively new one.[11]

The broader significance of this collecting craze lies in its relationship to a major shift in gender and consumption. Throughout the nineteenth century, both men and women had shopped for domestic necessities; however, by the 1870s and 1880s, several factors fused to reshape women's desires and revamp cultural perceptions of their role in the marketplace. The popularity of trade exhibitions, the retailing revolution, the rise of industrial arts education, and the feminization of particular handicrafts, including china painting, figured into this equation. Simply put, American women exited the Civil War as housewives, and they entered the 1890s as consumers. China mania loomed large in this consequential transformation.

The United States Centennial International Exhibition of 1876, in Philadelphia, encouraged the penchant for accumulation, display, and embellishment by exposing ten million visitors to an astonishing array of new goods. More than previous world's fairs, the throngs who visited the Philadelphia exhibition included large numbers of people from the middle and lower classes. Familiar with the annual shows sponsored by local and regional artisans' institutes, such as Philadelphia's Franklin Institute and Boston's Massachusetts Charitable Mechanic Institute, working people traveled to the Quaker City to see the shoppers' extravaganza par excellence. The mechanically minded found much to admire, including the highly publicized Corliss steam engine and Alexander Graham Bell's telephone. Those with interests in household products also enjoyed a visual feast. The sprawling Main Building, Agricultural Hall, Machinery Hall, Women's Pavilion, and smaller structures erected by industries, states, and guest nations all contained displays of the newest furniture, textiles, silverware, musical instruments, paper goods, clocks, glass, and ceramics.[12]

In the gigantic Main Building, visitors saw pottery and porcelain made by the forty or so companies that belonged to the new United States Potters' Association (USPA), a trade association established to promote the interests of the nation's whiteware manufacturers. Seizing the fair as an opportunity to publicize their industry's growth since the war, USPA firms created a series of exhibits designed to upstage their foreign competitors. Companies from Trenton and East Liverpool contributed displays, with New Jersey's Etruria Pottery presented a raft of prize-winning products. Etruria's owner-manager, John Hart Brewer, had engaged the services of the Canadian sculptor Isaac Broome, who dabbled in terra cotta, tile making, and china painting, to create pieces that evinced the firm's commitment to the production of high-quality porcelain. Broome captured visitors' attentions with his enormous baseball vase, which celebrated the sport on the eve of the National League's birth. East Liverpool potters contributed more utilitarian lines, as did the Laughlin Brothers, who won a medal and a "highest diploma." Shakespeare Laughlin tended the USPA exhibits, and ever the charmer, he delighted in "answering the many questions put by the ladies." He also encouraged them to visit nearby Trenton and "spend hours in the potteries." Lest tourists forget the potters after the fair, USPA firms prepared inexpensive patriotic souvenirs that consumers could take home.[13]

Despite the USPA's valiant efforts, critics reserved their praise for the products of foreign factories. Guidebook authors ignored American ceramists—except to dish out vicious attacks. Writing for the *Boston Herald,* one journalist termed the American porcelain "so poor as not to be noticeable artistically." The anonymous author of *Gems of the Centennial Exhibition* decried the "thorough lack of artistic pottery of American make," condemning the products as "tawdry and commonplace" compared to imported specimens. These exhortations signaled the beginnings of the protracted crockery wars, with United States factories struggling to assert themselves in the shadows of high-profile rivals.[14]

Indeed, even ordinary fair goers must have thought American pottery and porcelain looked unsophisticated next to European and Asian goods, as foreign factories simply had better designers, factories, products, and display techniques. Berlin's Royal Porcelain Manufactory mounted a striking chinaware exhibit in the long Main Building. Nearby stood the great pyramid of Spanish water jars, which seemed about to topple over—but never did. French and English factories presented splendid showpieces. One English firm, Minton, stunned viewers with its Prometheus vase, a breathtaking work some four feet high, covered in a bright turquoise glaze, and crowned by a figure of the Greek god of fire. The Japanese pavilion whet visitors' appetites for Asian ceramics. There, Stephen Terry of Hartford, Connecticut, took notes on his favorite items; other fair goers purchased porcelain trinkets from concessionaires.[15]

At the auction held at the fair's close, affluent men and women bid on impressive exhibition pieces. In many cases, men dominated the bidding. During the auction, the gentlemen-scholars James Jackson Jarves (son of glassmaker Deming Jarves), Edward S. Morse, and Ernest F. Fenollosa, New Englanders who pioneered the study of Asian art, bought objects for their impressive Far Eastern collections, which they eventually donated to the Museum of Fine Arts in Boston. Business elites also flocked to the sale. These men not only possessed

Auction room, Fairmont Park, at closing of the United States Centennial International Exhibition, Philadelphia, 1876. From Frank Henry Norton, editor, *Frank Leslie's Illustrated Historical Register of the Centennial Exposition, 1876* (New York, 1877), Hagley Museum and Library

the requisite discretionary income but they also knew that objets d'art, such as china, glassware, jade, jewelry, precious metalwork, textiles, painting, and sculpture, advertised their wealth. A fan of Asian porcelains who had shopped at world's fairs in London, Paris, and Vienna, the Baltimore merchant and railroad magnate William T. Walters added significant pieces of Japanese pottery to his collection. The publisher of the Philadelphia *Public Ledger,* George Washington Childs, splurged on some English fireplace tiles, assorted Russian bric-a-brac, and Minton's Prometheus vase, which he put on display in his newspaper office. Such artistic decorations impressed Child's business associates, educating his colleagues and employees in the nuances of cutting-edge taste. The auction lengthened the life of the world's fair, stretching its influence into the ensuing decades.[16]

The tremendous popularity of the Philadelphia fair led some observers, like the advice-giving journalist Mary Gay Humphries, to credit the exhibition with revamping American taste. Reminiscing in 1893, Alfred T. Goshorn, the Cincinnati businessman who oversaw its operations, claimed that the exhibition had done nothing less than give birth to "esthetic culture." In conceptualizing the show, Goshorn and fellow planners had aimed to educate manufacturers on the sales potential of good design and to instill consumers with a love of "culture and taste." Two decades later, Goshorn savored the results. To him, the show had transformed Americans "from a people absorbed in the pursuit of material prosperity" into a people who appreciated the "higher refinement" that art brought to their lives. However strong the temptation to accept boosters' claims about the exhibition as an aesthetic watershed, evidence suggests a far more complex story of the fair's impact. More accurately, the fair infused Americans with confidence in the nation's future as an industrial power just as the country emerged from the ordeal of Reconstruction and struggled with the economic depression ushered in by the Panic of 1873.[17]

After the exhibition, however, several factors shaped Americans' aesthetic awakening and stimulated desires for household products, including decorated ceramics and glassware. In a backlash against ironstone, critics decried plain white dishes as old-fashioned and ugly, advocating a new look partially inspired by Asian design. John Trowbridge, a journalist for *Atlantic Monthly*, remarked in 1878 on the allure of ceramics painted with butterflies and bugs, motifs drawn from Far Eastern art. The same year, design ideologue Clarence Cook condemned "cold, unthinking" white china in favor of blue-and-white porcelain, claiming white ceramics "took the yellow out of the butter, made the milk look blue, cast suspicion on the tea, took all the sparkle out of the sugar," and accounted for wholly unappetizing table settings. Most readers of this invective could not afford the antique Asian porcelains that met Cook's standards for beauty. Still, many middle-class people accepted his implied link between physical well-being, wholesome eating, and embellished ceramics.[18]

While prescriptive literature was bringing the gospel of aestheticism into the middle-class parlor, other mechanisms were familiarizing Americans with the pursuit of beauty by putting gorgeous things on display in public spaces. Everywhere men and women went, they saw fashionable domestic accouterments made in the industrial belt, which stretched from Boston to Chicago. Fairs sponsored by local, regional, and national institutions continued to exhibit household products. In cities from New York to Cincinnati, cultural philanthropists founded museums to house permanent collections of fine and applied arts. "Our Industrial Expositions, our Art Museums, and our Schools of Design," noted USPA secretary George W. Oliver, "have done and are doing much to educate all to a higher appreciation in Art." Most important, the great commercial transformation now known as the retailing revolution placed the new manufactured furnishings, especially ceramics, before more and more people. Chain stores like the Great Atlantic & Pacific Tea Company stocked inexpensive porcelains decorated with the moss rose motif, which they gave away to consumers who purchased the requisite amounts of coffee, tea, and sugar. At the opposite end of the taste spectrum, the elite art-goods merchandiser Tiffany & Company filled entire floors of its Union Square store with imported ceramics, from brilliantly colored majolica flowerpots to heavily decorated demitasse sets. Among retailers catering to middle-class shoppers, china and glass warehouses and a small group of cutting-edge department stores embraced china mania with particular fervor. Their managers saw the pottery craze as a window of opportunity to advance the quest for middlebrow dollars.[19]

Through carefully planned merchandising strategies, crockery shops and elite department stores attempted to engender in middle-class women a passion for decorated pottery and porcelain. Together, these retailers strove to transform crockery purchasers into chinaware consumers, encouraging housekeepers to replace whiteware with decorated goods that showed off individual taste and familial social status. Since historians have pointed to department stores as the primary architects of the consumer ethos, a qualifier is warranted. During the 1870s and 1880s, very few dry goods emporiums had transformed themselves into full-fledged department stores with sections dedicated to furniture, silverware, housewares, china, and glassware. Only exceptional stores—for example, New York's R. H. Macy & Company and Chicago's Marshall Field—carried household goods by the 1880s. Significantly, those stores tested the waters by establishing china and glass departments managed under contract by experienced crockery men, who excelled in interior design and street-front display. By no coincidence, L. Frank Baum, founder of the National Association of Window Trimmers and editor of *The Show Window*, spent several years as a traveling salesmen for Pitkin & Brook, one of Chicago's leading crockery and glass wholesalers. His on-the-job experience taught Baum much about the art of seduction, which he later applied in his children's book, *The Wizard of Oz*. Similarly, dry

China floor at Union Square store, Tiffany & Company, 1870–1905, copyright Tiffany & Co. Archives, 1999

goods emporiums recognized that they could profit from seasoned crockery men's experience in ordering, stocking, and, most important, displaying household products.[20]

Macy braved the home furnishings frontier in 1874 by adding china and glassware to its stock at the urging of Nathan Straus, a partner in L. Straus & Sons, one of Manhattan's leading crockery importers. As trade journals recount the legendary encounter, Straus, eager to capitalize on the northward movement of the city's high-class retail trade, strutted into Rowland Macy's Sixth Avenue dry goods store with two beautifully decorated porcelain plates tucked under his elbows. Artifacts in hand and years of crockery experience under his belt, Straus persuaded Macy to grant him and his brother Isidor a contract to set up a china department. Within a few years, the china and glass section became the store's most profitable department. Shoppers flocked from "Ladies Mile," the strip of Broadway that housed Manhattan's fashionable retail stores, over to Sixth Avenue to browse through the Strauses' novelties. As veterans of the crockery quarter, the Strauses adapted what they knew about pleasing chinaware buyers to the creation of displays that enticed women away from Broadway. "The profitable part of the china business arises not from the sale of the goods which people must buy," Isidor Straus confided to a business associate, "as much as from the sale of goods that are bought through the tempting manner in which they are exposed to the masses passing to and fro in a popular establishment." Macy's seductive china and glass displays aimed to stir feelings of envy, inadequacy, and discomfort. More important, they encouraged impulse buying. By artfully show-casing fragile china and glassware, the Strauses, like Wedgwood's Bentley a cen-tury earlier, endowed these goods with a cachet that appealed to consumers versed in the art craze. Riding on their success with the chinaware department, the Straus brothers gained control of Macy's store by the late 1880s. As they often reminded others, the Strauses triumphed by drawing on merchandising skills developed in the crockery business.[21]

While embryonic department stores like Macy's fostered china mania under the auspices of crockery showmen, old-guard crockery establishments also did much to reorient feminine attitudes toward ceramics. The *New York Press* noted that American women loved to visit china and glass shops, where they inspected everything "new and pleasing to home adornment and use." Just as other shops created a clothes-conscious female consumer, china stores large and small helped to persuade women that decorated dishes represented essential and fashionable household products. Leaders in the business drew their inspiration from promi-nent events: "The great World's Fair of '76 at Philadelphia was epoch making in our history," pronounced Jerome Jones, president of Boston's leading china warehouse, for its displays had "stimulated the taste of Americans to have some-thing better than white ware in their homes." By 1882, Jones, McDuffee & Strat-ton (JMS) employed young female clerks to wait on customers at its main store on Franklin Street. Jones decided to hire saleswomen after seeing them in Lon-don showrooms, later explaining that female staff provided the "the woman's point of view." These counter girls not only sold dishes but also sized up cus-tomers and reported their observations to superiors. Feminine "taste" under-wrote JMS's success; the partners called on these surrogate consumers for brief-ings before departing on buying excursions to Europe and Asia, where they selected items, including "India and Japan china," likely to be "generally accept-able" among Boston shoppers.[22]

Getting the right goods was only one of the crockery men's tasks; as depart-ment stores accustomed shoppers to material delights, other retailers had to fol-low suit or suffer the consequences of looking like poor relatives. "Storekeepers who are lacking in . . . correct arrangement should call to their assistance their wives or other female relatives," advised the *American Pottery and Glassware Reporter*, "as good taste in such matters is inherent in the tenderer sex, and they would soon bring order out of chaos." At JMS, the partners may have depended on their highly valued saleswomen to arrange goods in ways that would encourage female shoppers to walk through the door, browse, and spend. Everything about the decor in the 31,000-square-foot space encouraged indulgence. The large windows, filled to capacity with sparkling French crystal chandeliers and Asian vases wrapped in serpents and dragons, drew customers inside, where they found a spellbinding ceiling covered "with a legion of pitchers of various colors and designs." If department stores qualified as the consumption palaces of the high Victorian era, speciality warehouses like JMS operated as only slightly less elaborate rivals. Filled with artistic wares, these consumption mansions beguiled women with beautiful things artfully displayed to touch, admire, and buy.[23]

Crockery houses had a distinct advantage over budding department stores in the pursuit of feminine ceramics dollars. Since at least the Civil War, women had watched in admiration as china decorators working for merchants transferred their designs on to pottery and porcelain. Importers like JMS, already outfitted with decorating workshops, could readily respond to the burgeoning interest among middle-class women in china painting, the handicraft inspired by post-centennial art fever. To nurture, promote, and benefit from the fad, these merchants threw open the doors of their ateliers to amateurs.[24]

It had taken nearly a quarter century for this to occur because of the resistance of British immigrant china decorators. At midcentury, a group of New York women had asked china merchants Haughwout & Dailey to offer classes. The merchants initially denied the request and squelched the women's ambitions because the china decorators, feeling the crunch of the Panic of 1857, had threatened a citywide strike if Eder Haughwout "sent out a teacher to train up ladies to the profession." If genteel women entered the trade, the practical men had argued, the paintresses (as female painters were called) would "take bread" from the mouths of male artisans. Twenty years later, a new generation of china decorators and crockery merchants sang a different tune when the ladies knocked.[25]

As cultural notions about gender roles shifted, women began to realize their creative impulses in work outside the home. Earlier in the century, employment opportunities for middle-class women had been limited to teaching, shopkeeping, dressmaking, and a handful of other occupations. Since the early 1870s, manufacturers, artisans, and retailers had been listening to British educator Walter

Smith, who as director of the Massachusetts School of Design in Boston championed jobs in art industries as fitting for women. In his estimation, women's "quickness and aptitude" balanced men's "muscular superiority," so that a "sensitive touch and quick perception and delicate hand" made them perfectly suited to activities like wood carving, engraving, drawing, and painting. Based on the ideas of Arthur Cole and other British industrial arts advocates, Smith's 1873 book, *Art Education, Scholastic and Industrial,* captured the attention of American educators, manufacturers, and retailers concerned about the large numbers of women left widowed or single by the Civil War, the shortage of skilled workers, the threat of unrest among immigrant labor, and the growing hunger for fancy goods. In 1877, the pottery industry's premier trade weekly, *Crockery and Glass Journal,* pronounced: "Decoration is an employment both adapted to the feminine mind and congenial to it." By the early 1880s, the Philadelphia School of Design for Women, the Maryland Institute School of Art & Design, the Art Students League in New York, and other schools broadened their curricula to include china painting.[26]

If industrial arts education exposed women to the possibilities of china painting, the celebrity of accomplished female ceramists in Cincinnati encouraged countless aspirants. In 1873, several Queen City socialites, including Mary Louise McLaughlin and Maria Longworth Nichols, studied china painting at the Cincinnati School of Design under the watchful eye of Benn Pitman, a zealous British advocate of women's place in the art industries. Twenty-two years later, Pitman summarized the philosophy that drove his work in Cincinnati: "Let men construct and women decorate." Pitman's students showed samples of their china painting in the Women's Pavilion at the Centennial Exhibition but felt humbled by the displays of Limoges faience and Japanese porcelain, returning to the Midwest determined to expand their ceramics horizons. Between 1877 and 1880, McLaughlin published two widely distributed books for amateurs: *China Painting* and *Pottery Decoration under the Glaze.* In 1879, McLaughlin, Nichols, and other women founded the exclusive Cincinnati Pottery Club, which operated off and on until 1894. The energy emanating from the Queen City inspired editors at national periodicals. By the early 1880s, magazines as diverse as *Art Amateur* and *Harper's Weekly* touted the accomplishments of Cincinnati's china painters before the public eye with lavishly illustrated, feature articles.[27]

In contrast to fancy work, a feminine parlor activity, china painting was a ladies' pastime inexorably linked to the marketplace. To learn this technically sophisticated craft, women had to take lessons, buy specialized supplies, and pay

China paintresses plying their art in the 1880s. Jean King Collection, National Museum of American History Archives Center, Smithsonian Institution

technicians to fire their work. They could study china painting at art schools like the Maryland Institute. They could also visit public libraries, reading periodicals like *Art Interchange, Art Worker, Art Amateur,* and *Art Student* and searching natural history books for images worthy of copying. Yet for the most part, paintresses had to rely on the crockery establishment for instruction, materials, and firings. No one understood the symbiotic relationship between amateurs and practical men better than George Ward Nichols (Maria Nichols's spouse), who had watched Cincinnati's ladies struggle to learn the potter's art. In 1878, he directed would-be china painters who read his book, *Pottery: How It Is Made, Its Shape and Decoration,* to avoid bottlenecks by seeking expert advice from the men who made "a business of decorating and baking pottery."[28]

During the late 1870s and 1880s, paintresses in search of perfect blanks, mineral paints, and technical services knocked on the doors of urban crockery stores, china decorating workshops, and artists' supply shops. In response, crockery stores began offering lessons, firings, and supplies. China men like Jerome Jones and Richard Briggs, who had long used their ateliers as apparatus for the advancement of product design, quickly realized that a modest investment in amateurs' services promised considerable return. Lessons and firings both attracted potential customers and provided new vehicles for monitoring tastes. For china decorators, the pottery painting fervor offered means to earn better livelihoods. Theodore Walter worked days as a decorator for Boston's crockery dealers and moonlighted as a china painting instructor at his shop on nearby Beach Street. Chicago's Phillips & Company routinely fired amateurs' work; in Trenton, so did Jesse Dean. The English-born John Bennett instructed pupils in his studio and at the Society of Decorative Art, a charitable organization formed by New Yorkers in 1878 to promote woman's industries. At his store under the Cooper Institute, Charles L. Hadley sold French blanks and fired decorated goods. Through city directories, newspapers, trade journals, and art periodicals, crockery merchants and china decorators beckoned amateurs to their ateliers.[29]

Lessons in china painting prepared some women for positions as factory designers, but on the whole such opportunities remained limited. Among USPA potters, only D. F. Haynes, president of the Chesapeake Pottery, hired middle-class women trained at the Maryland Institute to work as professional designer-decorators in his Baltimore factory. For the most part, women versed in china painting and other feminine handicrafts used their knowledge to earn their living as teachers and to act judiciously as homemakers and shoppers. By the 1880s, keeping house had become a complex art. The enlargement of middle-class culture through exhibitions, etiquette books, popular magazines, and other vehicles of refinement created an uncertainty as to proper manners, dress, and interior decoration. Advice books like *Good Form Dinners* prescribed practices that made the selection of the right linens, silver, china, and glass seem as complicated as building a bridge. Which size fork for fish, olives, shrimp, and sweets; which flowers signified joy, sorrow, or contemplation; which color best flattered a certain guest's complexion; the list of rules and regulations boggled the mind. Implicitly, art educators like Emily Sartain, principal at the Philadelphia School of Design for Women, held that women needed special training to decipher such prescriptions and to perform their domestic duties. Sartain admitted that the bulk of art school graduates would never secure jobs in industry; instead, they would make up "an informed and appreciative public" equipped with the visual tools to recognize, buy, and use well-designed household products. "We educate not only the producer," she explained in 1890, "but the consumer."[30]

In this context, the experience of Alice Simons, a professional china painter and self-styled participant in the Aesthetic movement, bears scrutiny. A single woman, Simons taught school in South Carolina and New York City before studying art in Paris. By 1881, she had established a studio on Chestnut Street near John Wanamaker's Grand Depot in Philadelphia, offering classes in drawing, china painting, and French. Mingling in artistic circles, Simons skirted the edge of bohemia while remaining genteel and respectable. Through her drawing teacher, Charles Leland, Simons even met Oscar Wilde during his 1882 American tour: "I immediately entered into a conversation with him," Simons excitedly wrote to her sister, Elise du Pont, who lived nearby in Delaware, "and we sat down, sans façon, on a table together." At one point, she hoped to become an "editress to an art journal which is in contemplation." The journal remained a pipe dream; the challenge of finding students and customers, arduous. "Miss Lewis came to see me on Sunday afternoon," Simons wrote about one china painting colleague in January 1882. "She says she has been speaking, on every possible occasion, to get me pupils, and I believe her. If only I could get orders enough, I would not care about the pupils." Hard at work on a portrait plaque of a family friend in Manhattan, Simons hoped the successful completion of this china painting commission would bring "some more orders from New York." Simons became so frustrated by her meager earnings as a china painter, drawing instructor, and French teacher that she contemplated joining a nunnery.[31]

Yet Simons's training had stirred her desires for beautiful surroundings, and she channeled much of her creative energy and artistic knowledge into decorating her studio and her home on a tight budget. "I *must* have a music stand for my portfolio and some things to hold the . . . plates on the wall," she told her sister while setting up her Chestnut Street atelier. Sometimes, well-to-do pupils, like Mrs. Charles Whelen, bestowed their generosity. On one occasion, Simons returned to her work space to discover a Wanamaker gift box filled with "a bundle of Japanese decorations for the studio." Most of the time, though, Simons had to settle for a combination of family hand-me-downs, inexpensive furniture, and her own creations. After moving to Germantown to share a rented house with her brother Tom, Simons let her imagination run wild as she turned her new quarters into an artistic wonderland. She saw the potential for expression everywhere. Even the "little wooden mantle" in her bedroom looked as if it had been "made expressly for a lambrequin." "Tom and I are going to make an aesthetic table to put in the bay window," Simons wrote to her sister, when she was setting up her front parlor in May 1882, "and I am going to cover the top with cotton flannel, then make a fancy cloth out of my hideous (spoiled) green dress and put the fringe you gave me around it." Preparing for her aging mother to join the household, Simons outfitted the older woman's sleeping quarters with a carved walnut bed, a matching mirror, and a white bedspread from Wanamaker, all for less than twenty dollars. Short of cash, she planned to "manufacture a toilette table out of a barrel." During the art craze, countless women must have shared Simons's passion for beauty, her commitment to china painting, and her chagrin with the unpredictable marketplace. Using her knowledge of form, line, and color to set artistic standards for her home, Simons exemplified the china painter who applied her training to making do as a consumer.[32]

Although gender conventions, industry prejudices, and economic constraints relegated many aspiring paintresses to the realms of the amateur or the impoverished professional, women's work in china painting affected pottery fashions in two major ways. As Simons's experience shows, china painting often endowed women with a love of beauty that governed their choices as housekeepers. By contrast, another Philadelphian, Miriam Louise Scott, gave up china painting after a few lessons, deciding the pastime poorly suited to her pocketbook and temperament. Women like Scott bought ceramics to satisfy their desires for beautiful possessions. As friends, neighbors, and employees, including servants, followed suit, china mania permeated American culture. In every village, town, and city, noted Mrs. Oliver Bell Bunce in the *Decorator and Furnisher,* china painters made pottery and porcelain into fashionable household accessories. By sharing their knowledge of artistic principles, china painters became pottery proselytizers. In daily interactions, these ceramics evangelists disseminated what one industry commentator in 1889 termed the "correct appreciation of what constitutes excellence in the beautiful art of the potter."[33]

Furthermore, the china painting fad fundamentally reoriented producers' perceptions of who their customers were and what they wanted. In dealing with paintresses on a daily basis, producers—china decorators, crockery merchants, and pottery managers—came to see that women made most of the ceramics purchases. In potters' eyes, men who occasionally bought Shakespeare busts, showy Japanese vases, and barbershop mugs fell into the category of the connoisseur or collector. Women, who purchased items for everyday dining and decorating, constituted an enormous market, which producers needed to understand better. To pry open the door to feminine taste, producers used china painting as a lever. By the mid-1880s, annual exhibitions mounted by the Massachusetts Charitable Mechanic Association and the American Institute of New York featured special fine art sections that spotlighted china painters' work. Manufacturers and retailers encouraged the feminization of these exhibitions, which had once functioned as trade shows, by offering prizes to outstanding women designers. At the 1883 Cincinnati Industrial Exposition, male judges drawn from the city's business class smiled favorably on Annie Collins, a china painter from Newport, Kentucky, awarding her products a "gold medal for artistic design, brightness of color, and general finish," and on hometown artist W. H. Bristol, whose "tasty grouping and natural modeling" received a silver medal. Annual exhibitions, sponsored by museums, art schools, governments, and trade associations such as the USPA, became showcases for amateurs' work and vehicles by which producers gained further insight into women's tastes. The designs that china painters put on plates, vases, and teacups gave manufacturers and retailers some indication of what they expected from factory-made ceramics. Hence potters introduced highly figural designs in the 1890s because china painters like Alice Simons loved to cover porcelain blanks with cupids and other sentimental figures. By the time the china mania peaked, producers had a clear idea of who their primary customer was: she was a woman and a consumer.[34]

During the mania's heyday, people of modest incomes also opened their eyes to the possibilities of decorated pottery and porcelain as appropriate demarcators of social class, personal identity, and aesthetic sensibility. Moreover, as prices fell, shoppers realized that they could buy attractive embellished china for little more than the cost of plain whiteware. As they demanded better products, distributors learned that the vogue, if handled properly, offered a means for increasing sales. Thus the nation's crockery shops took on a new look. Store windows no longer brimmed with English ironstone or plain Trenton goods but featured printed, painted, splattered, sponged, gilded, and otherwise embellished wares. With the eclipse of white goods, china mania generated a bitter struggle between importers and American manufacturers over who would get the juiciest pieces of the pottery pie.

Design Frontiers

> It is all decorated goods . . . decoration without end, either as to price or variety.
> —*Crockery and Glass Journal*, 1882

Into the 1880s, New Jersey led the nation in pottery production, and Trenton was the state's jewel in the ceramic crown. There, fourteen potteries and a handful of decorating workshops, modeled after English prototypes, busily manufactured a wide variety of whiteware. Enjoying the protectionist tariffs initiated during the Civil War, Trenton's pottery factories had long since captured the market for undecorated table, tea, and toilet ware previously dominated by English potters. Unable to loosen importers' hold on eastern markets, firms like Mercer Pottery Company had bypassed established distribution channels to fill the demand for inexpensive plain goods in the Far West. At last, as the nation emerged from the six-year depression that began in 1873, the American eagle, the mascot of some potters in the United States, seemed destined to soar high over a humbled British lion. The impending triumph proved chimerical. Stunned by Trenton's rise as a ceramics center, New York importers regained their toehold in the American market with the introduction of richly decorated wares.[35]

Jockeying with importers for control of the United States market, Trenton's potters retaliated on the decorative front by escalating the production of embellished goods that responded to what John Hart Brewer termed "the sentiment of the masses." At first, the decorative skirmish boded well for practical men like Jesse Dean, as potters demanded more and more services from china decorators. Observers for the R.G. Dun credit agency noted that Dean enjoyed a "good business," while his competitors struggled. Trenton's champion decorator opened a showroom in New York's crockery district and his salesmen drummed up trade in the West. Jobbers like H. Leonard & Sons in cities as far away as Grand Rapids, Michigan, stipulated that Trenton's potteries send Dean blanks for customization. But as the demand for decorated goods grew, the city's pottery managers became frustrated by delays associated with the outside contract system. To protect themselves against design piracy, to cut costs, and to expedite output, potteries established on-site facilities for china decorating: the American Crockery Company had decorating rooms by the early 1870s, the Mercer Pottery Company by 1873, Ott & Brewer by 1875, the Glasgow Pottery by 1878, and the Willets Manufacturing Company by 1881.[36]

In these factory departments, potteries created highly detailed, colorful designs by using the English method of overglaze called printing and filling in, which was introduced to Trenton by the ex-Staffordshire decorator Thomas G. Edge. This technique reduced costs, increased productivity, and extended the range of ornamental possibilities. Under the watchful eye of a chief decorator, working-class women and girls applied printed patterns and accented them with enamels. A shape could be covered with a pattern in any style, from classical to Japanese; the motif could be complex or simple; and the price high or low. As the Progressive Manufacturing Company, a distributor of Trenton ceramics, boasted in its advertising leaflet that consumers of "any taste" could now find decorated New Jersey pottery to match the carpets and furniture in their homes.[37]

1. THE FURNACES OR KILNS. 2. INTERIOR OF THE GLAZING-FURNACE. 3. DECORATING VASES. 4. CHARGING A KILN. 5. GILT-BANDING TABLE-WARE. 6. PRESSING OUT OR STAMPING THE WARE. 7. CARRYING TO THE DIPPING-ROOM. 8. PUTTING THE WARE TOGETHER.

NEW JERSEY.—THE POTTERY INDUSTRY OF TRENTON—THE PROCESSES OF FINE-WARE MANUFACTURE ILLUSTRATED.
FROM SKETCHES BY A STAFF ARTIST.—SEE PAGE 294.

The pottery industry of Trenton, New Jersey. Trenton led the nation in pottery production, and china decorators were its guiding lights. From *Frank Leslie's Illustrated Newspaper*, June 23, 1888, Trenton Public Library

The new technology gave New Jersey potters a weapon against importers, but foreign competition soon compelled Trentonians to seek other methods that would reduce costs while enhancing product appearance. Although less time consuming than hand techniques, printing and filling in remained a labor-intensive proposition. Trenton potters complained about the lack of female workers: "I would put fifty fillers-in at work this morning," lamented one manager, "if I could find them without taking them away from other potters who want them as badly as we do." Given the restricted labor supply, Trenton ceramists searched for ways to eliminate the process of accenting transfer prints with enamel colors. The trick entailed figuring out how to create detailed, refined embellishments in a single step.[38]

Racing to develop one-step decorations, Trenton's ceramists pursued two innovations: decalcomania and photoceramics. The first method, decalcomania, was a technique for creating special chromolithographic pictures that could be fired onto pottery, porcelain, and glass. Since the mid-nineteenth century, American and European chromolithographers had been printing colorful decals on specially prepared paper, which manufacturers like the Singer Sewing Machine Company applied to their products. By the late nineteenth century, American art stores sold decals to women for their fancywork creations. When advising budget-conscious readers how to "make do" with little money, the *Decorator and Furnisher* suggested that women construct bric-a-brac from chipped, cracked, or broken crockery by using metallic paints and colorful decals, which could be stuck on like postage stamps. To journalists writing for this interior decorating magazine, decals offered women an easy, inexpensive way for turning ugly white pottery into attractive, colorful parlor ornaments. Taking cues from the popularity of decals, Trentonians surmised that chromolithography held the key to the future of pottery embellishment.[39]

During the mid to late 1870s, Trenton's leading factories tried to adapt decals to ceramics production, only to find the task technically daunting. Ceramic decals required the interweaving of three strands of knowledge: chromolithography, speciality papermaking, and ceramics chemistry. At Ott & Brewer's Etruria Works, the art director Isaac Broome grew frustrated with the firm's expensive experiments and soon abandoned them. In 1879, Haviland & Company, importers that manufactured porcelain in Limoges, made President Rutherford B. Hayes's tableware, which the French factory covered with decals of American flora and fauna. Amid much fanfare, Haviland patented the Hayes designs and, from its Manhattan store, marketed spin-off dinner services for general consumption. The triumph ruffled Trentonians' feathers. In retaliation, the East Trenton Pottery Company put its decals or "chromo-lithographic enamels" on exhibit at the American Institute in 1879. Walter Scott Lenox and Charles Frederick Ulrich, though, saw this as an opportunity to get rich quick.[40]

The Lenox and Ulrich partnership to perfect ceramic decals was as colorful and short-lived as it was experimental. Their eccentricities may explain why their liaison attracted so much attention from the trade journal columnist who documented the experiments in great detail. Neither partner was a practical Staffordshire man. Trained as an artist, Lenox had learned the decorating trade at Trenton's Dale & Davis Pottery under the tutelage of Elijah Tatler, whom he succeeded as art director. In 1879, Lenox entered into a series of partnerships that established his reputation as one of Trenton's technical and artistic leaders. Ulrich, his first partner, had studied drawing, genre painting, and lithography in New York and Munich and, after returning to the United States, had been indicted for currency counterfeiting. After he had served as a witness for the prosecution in several criminal cases, the court released him on his own recognizance. Having promised to "never be found in the business of engraving counterfeit plates again," Ulrich decided to apply his skills as an engraver to Trenton's decorating trade. In a small shop, he and Lenox experimented with ceramic decals, which they called "chromo-enamels." The partners created at least five decal patterns, including a morning glory decoration that reportedly rivaled the colors achieved by Boston's Louis Prang, the nation's most celebrated chromolithographic printer. After the dissolution of their partnership in late 1879, Lenox and Ulrich continued to explore decal technology at the New Jersey Pottery Company before returning to conventional decorating techniques during the early 1880s.[41]

Although Trenton ceramists failed to perfect decals, they succeeded in creating another one-step decorating technology: photoceramics. By the 1880s, Dean picked up the gauntlet for the new photographic technique. When he hired François Schmalz, a European chemist who claimed knowledge of applying photographic images onto ceramics, competitors raised their eyebrows in skepticism. Schmalz embodied the essence of what was absent from the American ceramics industry but present in Europe: expertise in chemistry and physics, which could enhance manufacturers' knowledge of materials and processes. Confidence in his own judgment and an affinity for risk induced Dean to collaborate with Schmalz, who claimed that he could adopt heliotype, a photomechanical printing technique, to ceramics production.[42]

For decades, technologists—anxious to overcome the limitations of photographs, which could tear or fade—had experimented with photoceramics. In 1865, the Rockwood Photo-Engraving Company won a silver medal at the American Institute fair for its images on porcelain. Dean probably had seen Rockwood's so-called heliographs when working in New York; therefore, he could recognize the credibility of Schmalz's claim. He also realized that mastering a technology to create inexpensive high-quality images would give him immeasurable advantage as the demand for decorated goods grew. Moreover, consumers viewed the new technology favorably. While living in New York in 1875, would-be china painter Alice Simons had a photograph of her nephew Frances transferred onto porcelain. Dean hoped to tap into the photoceramics interests of art-minded consumers like Simons. By early 1882, the combination of Schmalz's theory and Dean's practical knowledge resulted in the perfection of the patented helioceramic process.[43]

Like any entrepreneur developing a new product, Dean sought to capture and express the cultural ideals of his target audience. The capacity of helioceramics to preserve all types of images for eternity made these ceramics appropriate for the Victorian parlor, or "memory palace." In advertisements, Dean boasted that the "beautiful process" allowed his firm to "produce the most exquisitely toned pictures, of any person, place, or thing." In taking this approach, he capitalized on the perception that photography, a medium capable of capturing and saving images, suited middle-class ideals of refinement. Photographs of all sorts, from stereocards to *cartes de visite,* allowed men and women to live vicariously, remembering departed loved ones, imagining inaccessible experiences, like a trip to Yosemite Valley, or replicating past events, such as a night at the theater. Whereas ordinary photographs, printed on paper, could fade, Dean's images, fired onto porcelain or refined white earthenware, were virtually imperishable.[44]

As they experimented with new technologies, Dean and other china decorators faced a dilemma. They had to innovate to survive, but their experiments with new designs and new technologies, successful or not, threatened Trenton's potters. Witnessing the adventurous spirit emerging in the city's workshops, pottery managers knew that the lucky decorator who discovered the Eldorado of embellishment would possess a mighty advantage in the struggle to gain control of the American market. Rather than invest in design frontiers, Trenton's conservative pottery establishment turned its back on china decorators, instead speeding up the shop floor and seeking additional protectionist legislation to save the day. The design trials of decorators combined with the fears of potters undercut Trenton's whiteware trade.

The Crockery Wars

Turning away from technological frontiers, American potters took the British lion to task in the political arena. In 1882, the USPA and its powerful Republican allies in Congress slammed importers with the crockery clauses of the Morrison tariff, which significantly raised duties on earthenware. The Trenton potters John Hart Brewer and John Moses blamed the inferior performance of potteries in the United States on exorbitant wages and materials costs. Dissidents like Isaac Broome, formerly Ott & Brewer's art director and most recently in charge of Trenton's newly established design school, castigated American potters for their poor taste, lack of foresight, and other crimes against common sense and industrial art, but his cries went unheeded. When the USPA achieved increased protection, effective in mid-1883, importers shuddered—and then went about business as usual.[45]

Following the passage of the Morrison tariff bill, New York crockery dealers promoted a new favorite—European porcelain—with the fervor, flashiness, and fanfare characteristic of their bustling metropolis. At the time, New York's china and glass trade encompassed entire city blocks in lower Manhattan. Adjacent to

Photoceramic technology, which allowed consumers to memorialize loved ones like Aunt Regine Valentine. National Museum of American History, Smithsonian Institution

the city's older retailing section, the crockery quarter stretched west and south from Broadway and Chambers Street, covering the area between City Hall Park and today's World Trade Center. Out-of-town buyers staying at the Astor House, a luxury hotel known as "headquarters of the crockery merchants," had only to venture off Broadway to revel in china and glass heaven. What importers could no longer get from Staffordshire to sell at competitive prices they ordered from France and Germany, where many of them operated their own china factories. The low-wage economy throughout much of Continental Europe kept exported porcelain so inexpensive that American duties mattered little. Indeed, the putting-out system enabled foreign factories to embellish ware for pennies. On Barclay Street, the quarter's main thoroughfare, O. A. Gager carried C.F.H. chinaware made by E. Gerard, Dufraisseix & Morel in Limoges, while A. Klingenberg stocked amusement park novelties like alphabet plates covered with Coney Island scenes from his own French decorating shop. At the modest store of John C. Vogt, paintresses chose from "a very complete assortment of fine white china for decorating purposes," all made by the importer's two Limoges factories. No matter where visitors looked in Gotham's dish district, they encountered the message that Europe's porcelain factories made the world's finest ceramics.[46]

By promoting foreign chinaware, New York's importers continued to feed the longings of consumers at the upper end of the social pyramid, those with old riches or new money who looked to Europe for models of deportment, demeanor, and display. The design reformers, interior decorators, and art-conscious consumers who read *Decorator and Furnisher* and *Art Interchange* valued highbrow aesthetics and all things Continental. Wealthy Manhattan men learned through business, social, and philanthropic networks to toe the party line regarding the superiority of French, German, and English porcelain. Rich crockery dealers like Nathan and Isidor Straus touted the virtues of expensive European china while drinking, discussing investments, or attending charity events with fellow business elites. In other cities, ideas disseminated through similar channels. The Philadelphia publisher George Washington Childs bought porcelains from Sèvres, Berlin, Worcester, and Derby to complement the Prometheus vase he had purchased at the Centennial Exhibition auction. The Boston banker Rogers L. Barstow learned about the desirability of French china from collegial business exchanges and, in 1881, went so far as to bypass local crockery men to acquire a set of gilded, personally monogrammed, and richly painted dishes directly from Haviland & Company in Limoges at a cost of $700. Few Americans could afford or even wanted such expensive dining and dessert accessories, which spoke of lavish entertaining and a large staff of servants in Barstow's Dorchester home. Yet to this ambitious Bostonian, owning European porcelain evinced his social, financial, and material accomplishments. The china's associations with France, the Continental locus of good taste, signified Barstow's accomplishments in ways that undoubtedly impressed guests, who admired the glittering porcelain at his dinner table.[47]

The crockery merchants who flooded the United States with European porcelain fundamentally changed the market basket of imported ceramics for decades to come. In 1880, English earthenwares made up 70 percent of ceramics imports; by 1890, they accounted for only 56 percent. Encouraged by lower duties on china, importers substituted Continental porcelain for British pottery. In doing so, they altered Americans' perceptions of what constituted desirable dishes. Through lavish advertising in newspapers, city directories, trade journals, and magazines and through aggressive posturing on the sales floor, crockery men preached the gospel of precious porcelain. They bombarded consumers with the idea that Continental European china signified quality, status, and good taste. Fashionable dinnerware had to be made of fine white porcelain; inexpensive earthenware should be relegated to the pantry, summerhouse, and workers' cottages. "It must be English, you know," or "French, you know," became the motto of consumers satirized by the figure of Miss Majolica Dare, a china maniac whose pottery pleasures depended on the ownership of foreign porcelain.[48]

This marketing ploy was so successful that even consumers on society's fringes learned to equate Continental china with the good life. When an investigative journalist for the *New York Evening Sun* toured tenements on the East Side in 1887, one working-class woman served him a modest meal, a "little piece of uninviting cold salt beef," bread, potatoes, and tea, on a set of imported porcelain in the moss rose pattern. Astounded by the "pretty dishes" that "contrasted strangely with the plain wooden chairs, uncovered deal table, and bare walls," the *Sun*'s inquisitive writer complimented his hostess on her table appointments. Proud of her free tea-store dinner service, this impoverished New Yorker confidently boasted to the middle-class newspaper snoop that her porcelain dishes were "just as good as any you'll see in the grand houses on Fifth Avenue!" To her and other such consumers, spin-offs of luxury products expressed an affiliation with the good life of the rich and powerful, who showed off their finery in the Easter Parade.[49]

Back in Trenton, the crockery wars fractured the profitable interdependence

Miss Majolica Dare, a fictional resident of Farragut Square in Washington, D.C., satirized as the typical china maniac swooning over her bric-a-brac. From *Clay-Worker*, July 1896, Hagley Museum and Library

of potteries and workshops. As factories turned their backs on independent artisans, Jesse Dean scrambled for orders—and for reliable sources of supplies. During the recession of 1885, Dean incorporated his business with capital from New York and Philadelphia china dealers, who appreciated his national reputation, photoceramic hubris, and decorative pluck. Dean's urban experience had engendered him with an appreciation of merchants' ability to measure taste. He recognized that dealers' frequent face-to-face contact with shoppers could provide him with intelligence indispensable to his understanding of fashion, and he routinely called on his business partners in New York and Philadelphia to advance his knowledge of markets. Crockery men provided Dean with a steady stream of imported blanks, ceramic colors, and other necessities—and with re-

Breakfast Set, Consisting of 37 Pieces
Given for one book of Eastern Estate
Premium Trade Marks

BREAKFAST SET OF 37 PIECES

8 Cups and Saucers . .	16	Pieces
8 Plates	8	"
8 Oatmeal Dishes . . .	8	"
1 Sugar Bowl	2	"
1 Platter	1	"
1 Cream Pitcher . . .	1	"
1 Round Deep Dish . .	1	"
	37 Pieces	

DINNER SET OF 82 PIECES

12 Small Plates . . .	12	Pieces
12 Large Plates . . .	12	"
12 Fruit Dishes . . .	12	"
12 Cups and Saucers .	24	"
12 Individual Butter . .	12	"
1 Pickle Dish . . .	1	"
1 Sauce Boat . . .	1	"
1 Covered Dish . . .	2	"
1 Platter, medium size . .	1	"
1 " large size . .	1	"
1 Cream Pitcher . . .	1	"
1 Vegetable Dish, round . .	1	"
1 Sugar Bowl	2	"
	82 Pieces	

Dinner Set, Consisting of 82 Pieces
Given for two books of Eastern Estate
Premium Trade Marks

Dinner Set, Consisting of 110 Pieces
Given for three books of Eastern Estate
Premium Trade Marks

DINNER SET OF 110 PIECES

12 Small Plates . . .	12	Pieces
12 Medium Plates . .	12	"
12 Large Plates . . .	12	"
12 Fruit Dishes . .	12	"
12 Individual Butter . .	12	"
12 Soup Plates . . .	12	"
12 Cups and Saucers . .	24	"
1 Covered butter with drainer	3	"
1 Platter, medium size .	1	"
1 " large size . .	1	"
1 Covered Dish . . .	2	"
1 Vegetable Dish, oval .	1	"
1 Sauce Boat	1	"
1 Pickle Dish	1	"
1 Sugar Bowl	2	"
1 Cream Pitcher . . .	1	"
1 Vegetable Dish, round .	1	"
	110 Pieces	

TEA SET OF 52 PIECES

12 Tea Plates . . .	12	Pieces
12 Cups and Saucers , .	24	"
12 Fruit Dishes . .	12	"
1 Sugar Bowl . . .	2	"
1 Cream Pitcher . .	1	"
1 Cake Plate . . .	1	"
	52 Pieces	

Tea Set, Consisting of 52 Pieces
Given for one book of Eastern Estate
Premium Trade Marks

Moss rose china to be given to tea customers as premiums. From Eastern State Tea Company, *Catalogue of Products and Premium Prizes* (New York, 1900), Morris Library, University of Delaware

ports on changing styles and consumer preferences. Two decades after leaving James Shaw's atelier, the feisty Dean had come full circle, again dependent on merchants for his survival.[50]

Trenton's Eclipse

During the 1890s, the heightened demand for ornamented chinaware accelerated the fierce rivalry among the nation's potters, china decorators, and crockery importers. Potteries making inexpensive wares began to imitate costly designs, and prices fell. Factory managers increased output at the expense of product quality and workers' earnings. As prices for printed and filled-in goods plummeted, managers pressured factory decorating rooms to hasten the pace of production. In this cutthroat environment, independent china decorators complained mightily about unprofitable business, and many closed their shops. In Trenton, Jesse Dean's attempt to protect his business through incorporation temporarily provided him with capital, a steady source of supplies, and information about the market, but the move failed to serve him in the long run. As the nation moved toward financial panic and depression in 1892, Dean, heavily indebted to crockery men, filed for bankruptcy.[51]

Dean's insolvency not only coincided with the country's economic crisis but also corresponded with major transformations in the United States ceramics industry. Accolades bestowed on ceramists at the World's Columbian Exposition in 1893 testify to those changes: among American potteries, only the Homer Laughlin China Company, a major manufacturer in East Liverpool, Ohio, received medals. As the nineteenth century drew to a close, firms in the expanding East Liverpool district, which consisted of the central "Crockery City" and nearby towns in Ohio, Pennsylvania, and the upper panhandle of West Virginia, became the major suppliers of pottery to mass merchandisers—department stores, mail-order houses, premium vendors, and, most important, chain stores. A range of interrelated factors, from geography to technology to managerial savvy, facilitated East Liverpool's ascent. In terms of design, western potteries created a high degree of visual diversity at reduced costs during the 1890s, when they started decorating products with decals purchased from English ceramics printers. With decals, these firms met mass distributors' demands for huge quantities of inexpensive, highly decorated tableware.[52]

Trenton decorators had failed in their attempt to broach the mass market by experimenting with decals. Making decals compatible with ceramics presented a complex challenge. European ceramists had toyed with decals since the late 1830s, and their technology did not achieve perfection until the 1890s, when potters, color manufacturers, and ceramics printers pooled their expertise to create a special paper that suited both pottery shapes and enamels. By 1898, firms like the Potters' Decorative Supply Company and the Chromo Transfer Company, both in Staffordshire, used duplex paper to make decals for English and American potters. In the twentieth century, English printers such as the Universal Transfer Company in Hanley continued to refine decals through the use of rotary offset printing and photolithography. These firms employed staff artists, who created entirely new designs and who adapted drawings supplied by potteries for chromolithographic printing. Ceramics printers made decals to manufacturers' specifications and guaranteed not to sell those designs to competing potteries. In time, decal manufacturers would eclipse china decorators as the pottery industry's embellishing experts.[53]

The ascent of decals, the ideal one-step decorating method, solved the decorating dilemma that had plagued American potters for decades. Potteries were no longer content to ornament their products with simple motifs, which importers loved to mock. Only the imagination of the factory's art director, who collaborated with the decal manufacturer to create new designs, limited the decorative possibilities. After the introduction of decals, low-paid working-class women known as decal girls applied decorations onto blanks under the watchful eye of a male superintendent. This labor strategy allowed potteries to cut production costs significantly. The widespread use of decals thereby furthered the de-skilling process that had begun with the adoption of printed embellishments in the 1870s.[54]

The expansion of low-cost tableware manufacturing in the East Liverpool district, combined with heated clashes against New York importers, brought enormous changes to Trenton's whiteware potteries. Generally, USPA firms faced tough challenges in the 1890s, one of the most volatile decades in the history of the American pottery trade. A contraction in sales coincided with the general depression in 1892 and 1893, a strike by the National Brotherhood of Operative Potters in 1894, and a trade recession spawned by the Wilson tariff from 1894 to 1897, which favored importers. The Trenton potteries suffered more than their rivals in Ohio. When New York crockery men flooded the market with imported porcelain, they forced Trentonians out of the middlebrow tableware trade on the East Coast. At the same time, East Liverpool potteries, which sped up production to a dizzying pace, eroded New Jersey's hold on markets for low-end goods in the West and the South. The shrewdest Trentonians dealt with this shifting balance of power by altering their product mix, honing in on the growing market for sanitary plumbing fixtures, such as sinks and toilets. By the turn of the century, New Jersey's ceramics city led the nation in the production of sanitary fixtures.[55]

China decorating all but vanished in Trenton. Arthur Mountford, for one, fled to East Liverpool; as Homer Laughlin's first art director, he managed the decorating rooms, painted elaborate showpieces for special exhibitions, and facilitated the company's acceptance of decals. In these, he achieved a certain degree of financial security, found an avenue for artistic expression, and tackled new technical challenges. By about 1900, like-minded, shrewd china decorators found it more inviting to sell their knowledge to a corporation rather than to run their own workshops. For those intrigued by the technical dimensions of the potter's art, a position with a well-capitalized East Liverpool pottery provided the chance to investigate decorating technology at the cutting edge and to design products for the exciting new mass market.[56]

Jesse Dean demonstrated greater resiliency and tenacity than most china decorators. A few years after his bankruptcy, his shop again thrived; a staff of sixty-five employees decorated blanks, using a range of techniques, including photoceramics. Ever the opportunist, Dean capitalized on his technical expertise by selling decorating supplies to the East Liverpool potteries. Still, Dean spent his remaining career primarily serving the limited market for high-style pottery and porcelain. As the operator of one of Trenton's few surviving decorating workshops, Dean built on his reputation for "the higher class" of embellishments, including the ornamenting of "odd pieces in white china." In 1899, George Washington Clarke, Homer Laughlin's chief salesman, inquired if Dean could decorate a tea set in the heavily encrusted gold style made famous by the Royal Worcester Porcelain Company in England. Indeed, Dean's skill in reproducing so-called Worcester-style decorations was probably unparalleled, since the most discerning men in the ceramics industry ordered his wares for their personal consumption. Ironically, Trentonians remembered Dean not for his photoceramics but for his copies of elaborate English-style ornamentations that the importers had introduced into the American market.[57]

Dean's nineteenth-century career provides a metaphor for the rise and fall of china mania and Trenton's golden age of pottery production. A practical man, Dean clearly had little if any time for the muses, struggling to make a living along with other Staffordshire immigrants in New Jersey's crockery city. Many failed while Dean succeeded. Admirers exalted Dean for his supposedly extra-ordinary creativity and his outstanding technical abilities, but the business survival of Trenton's leading decorator depended on how well his products met the expectations of consumers of myriad tastes, which in turn hinged on his understanding of a subtle contradiction. Those who comprehended the underpinnings of china mania recognized that the economic growth providing consumers with the means for enjoying artistically furnished homes primarily stemmed from accelerated industrial production. Trenton's potters and decorators fathomed this equation—but not as well as their rivals in East Liverpool, who readily and rapidly expanded their potteries to accommodate growing tableware markets in the 1890s. If Dean passed judgment on decals, he did so in silence. More likely, Trenton's aging champion decorator watched the marketplace with resignation, as factories in the East Liverpool district, in the twentieth-century Staffordshire of America, placed novel and beautiful household goods within the grasp of more and more consumers.

CHAPTER 3

Beauty for a Dime

IN DECEMBER 1899, W. Edwin Wells, general manager of the Homer Laughlin China Company in East Liverpool, mused over a letter from Clinton Pierce Case, domestic crockery buyer for F. W. Woolworth in New York City. Anxious to lessen his store's dependence on foreign manufacturers, Case wanted to build a relationship with a "good American house," a reliable pottery providing "good goods and plenty of them at fair prices." Wells (1863–1931) recognized the tremendous potential of dime stores, and he responded by urging Case to visit his factory after the midwinter show of the Associated Glass & Pottery Manufacturers in Pittsburgh. What transpired that January may never be known, as neither potter nor buyer discussed the meeting in subsequent correspondence. One thing is definite: the two men possessed complementary agendas. Wells understood that Case had enormous cash resources at his disposal and knew that few American potteries could meet his demands for quality, quantity, and price. By early 1900, the pottery manager and the dime store buyer were on the way to establishing an alliance that would profit both of their firms into the middle of the twentieth century.[1]

Wells's tenure as Homer Laughlin's general manager (1899–1930) and his pursuit of the Woolworth account coincided with major transformations in American retailing that affected the pottery industry. By coordinating the flow of household goods through the economy, chain stores enabled shoppers of modest incomes to participate in consumer society. Urban tea stores like the Great

Atlantic & Pacific Tea Company (A&P) gave away pottery and glassware, and dime stores or five-and-tens sold inexpensive tableware, catering to the tastes of a wide range of consumers, from farmwives to mill girls. Together, these distributors made pottery acquisition into an unintimidating process, figuring prominently in the "democratization of things."[2]

As the retailing revolution unfolded, East Liverpool potteries elbowed each other for business with mass merchandisers, which promised to liberate them from an unpromising future of contention with crockery importers over slim wedges of the jobbing trade. Firms unable to fill large orders at the right prices fell to the wayside, but volume-oriented potteries achieved prominence in the premium and dime store trade. Wells's courtship of Case fit into this highly successful corporate strategy. Proud to serve budget-conscious consumers, he gave a populist twist to a queenly phrase, emblazoning the motto, "Makers of American Pottery for the American People," on the company's promotional literature. If Old World factories looked up the social ladder and back in time for authentication, let it be. Wells found much to admire in the American present. He enjoyed hustling for a share of the vast profits to be made by doing business with mass merchandisers. At his retirement in 1930, Homer Laughlin China Company was the world's largest pottery; its most important customer was Woolworth, the world's leading five-and-ten.[3]

As Wells pushed Homer Laughlin to the forefront of the mass market, the imperative of determining what shoppers wanted forced him to revamp long-standing practices for imagining consumers. In this transition, the efforts of Wells to evaluate those practices and to institute new ones proved crucial. Making goods for tea stores like the A&P and five-and-tens like Woolworth tested the mettle of the pottery industry's established style referees, china decorators who had been trained in Staffordshire to read middlebrow and highbrow tastes. Unwillingly, these men handed the mantle of artistic authority over to consumer liaisons better attuned to popular culture. The new fashion intermediaries included well-traveled factory salesmen and decalcomania importers. At Homer Laughlin, the jobber-turned-salesman George Washington Clarke fully saw his responsibility as involving the study of consumer tastes in faraway places. By the early twentieth century, decalcomania manufacturers acted as surrogate art directors for the East Liverpool potteries. Decal man Rudolph Gaertner, an energetic German ceramist who operated an all-around design office in New York City, provided stylistic recommendations. However, the most important change in design and development came with the ascendancy of the chain store crockery buyer as primary fashion intermediary. As Wells collaborated on new products with Case and his successor, William F. Newberry, he helped to create inexpensive ceramics that pleased millions of American consumers, providing Woolworth's shoppers with "beauty for a dime."[4]

Makers of American Pottery for the American People

When the United States Potters' Association held its 1889 convention, prescient managers were alive to the fact that their industry's fate rested in the mass market. Although foreign factories made 95 percent of the ceramics purchased by "the rich," association president Thomas Maddock happily reported that American firms produced most of the pottery used by "the poor and middle classes." Since the centennial, USPA potters in Trenton, New Jersey, had waged a persistent but fruitless war against New York importers for control of the large middlebrow market on the East Coast. More successfully, USPA firms in the new "crockery city" of East Liverpool, Ohio, penetrated two major markets with their cheap, decorated goods: the vast Far West, which completion of the transcontinental railroad had opened, and the low-end East Coast market, which had expanded incrementally with urbanization. By 1889, Trenton's moment as a whiteware center had passed; East Liverpool moved to take its place. "Poor indeed" was the American home that did not own some tableware from the Crockery City.[5]

When Wells joined Homer Laughlin as bookkeeper that year, the company had struggled for more than a decade to make "the greatest amount of the best ware at the lowest cost" in a tiny, technologically unsophisticated factory. Founded in 1871 as Laughlin Brothers, the pottery became a sole proprietorship in 1877, when Homer purchased Shakespeare's interest. Among the sixteen East Liverpool firms in the USPA, Homer Laughlin ranked sixth in size, as classified by kiln capacity (a long-standing measure of a pottery's productive potential). Encouraged by awards at the 1876 fair, founder Laughlin picked up the gauntlet for aesthetic reform, both within the USPA and in his pottery. Taking inspiration from the Ohio River valley's sublime beauty, his china decorators embellished products with "purely American subjects" in an effort to turn copycat potters on their heads and to overturn the design traditions that encouraged the worship of European styles. At a time when most American factories still labeled their wares with the British seal (a royal lion, a unicorn, and a coat of arms), Laughlin expressed his patriotism with a unique eagle-and-lion trademark.[6]

HOMER LAUGHLIN
Mfr of PREMIUM STONE CHINA. EAST LIVERPOOL, OHIO.

SHAKESPEARE.

FINE DECORATED WARE

Buyers before placing their orders should see the New Shape ''Shakespeare,'' as it is without doubt the finest design ever offered to the American trade. It is having a large sale. I am now prepared to supply to the trade, car-load lots in bulk, which saves the usual cost of packages, and reduces breakage to a minimum. I have special facilities for safely packing in bulk, being the only White Ware Manufacturer in East Liverpool owning a railroad siding at my own works. Price lists, discounts, etc., furnished applicants.
                    Very respectfully yours,

                                                    HOMER LAUGHLIN

Homer Laughlin's lion and eagle logo. Designed in the 1870s, the image of the American eagle devouring the British lion (upper left) reflected Laughlin's dreams for a prosperous United States pottery industry. Advertisement in *Pottery and Glassware Reporter*, April 22, 1886, Smithsonian Institution Libraries, Smithsonian Institution

If Laughlin's facilities were small, so were his markets. In terms of merchandising, most East Liverpool potteries, including Homer Laughlin, depended on middlemen or jobbers to buy, store, sell, and deliver products to retailers, often on credit. The potteries worked especially hard to build good relations with jobbers in expanding midwestern and western markets. During the late 1870s, T. Rigby & Company, the owner-operator of the Broadway Pottery Works, shipped his goods to jobbers in Ohio, Indiana, Michigan, Illinois, and Wisconsin, which paid traveling salesmen to "drum up" business among storekeepers. These drummers toured the countryside by wagon and rail, armed with photographs and chromolithographs of dishes. After china mania midwived the craze for decorated pottery, many sold goods "by sample," circulating from town to town with enormous sample trunks in tow.[7]

A pottery heavily tied to wholesalers could encounter problems on the design front. Put simply, the jobbing system eliminated the direct link to shopkeepers, who had direct links to consumers. To bridge this gap, factories hired their own salesmen to evaluate local trade conditions, push the lines to retailers, and keep the managers informed of changes in fashion and taste. The field letters of factory salesmen read like primitive market research reports. In 1888, the Homer Laughlin salesman James C. Shaw circulated through the Southwest, leaving Chicago in early March: "I am paving the way for a good fall trade all over Texas," he enthusiastically wrote, "and I think we will have our share of it." In Corsicana, Shaw "struck it lucky" when he found jobber W. M. Tatum unpacking crates from Wallace & Chetwynd. "I had the satisfaction of comparing wares," Shaw reported on the moss rose decorations. "I always like to do so," he stroked Laughlin's ego, "as it does me good as I know we will always come to the top." In San Antonio, the jobbers snubbed him: "I have tried hard to sell your goods in this place but could not succeed." Wagner & Chaboh "would not buy at any price"; Newton & Weller were "pleased with the goods" from Wheeling Pottery; and the clerk at Riedel & Legler disdained all American ware. "I don't like him," Shaw reported, as "he has a bad look." After having no success in Forth Worth ("The crockery men of this city seem to have a dislike for your ware"), Shaw looked forward to the trek into New Mexico and Colorado. Puffing up their company's products, spying on competitors, reporting on truculent jobbers, negotiating orders, interpreting local tastes, and venturing opinions on designs: these tasks kept the salesman-cum-intermediary busy.[8]

Meanwhile, George Washington Clarke, the proprietor of a wholesale crockery house in Denver that imported English and German china, had joined the

Homer Laughlin roster of jobbers, becoming the "man of the hour" for his genius in consumer mediation. From his first order in 1889, Clarke displayed talents peculiarly suited to the pottery's aspirations as ceramics conquistador of the West. He was flashy, abrupt, resourceful, artistic, and in the right place at the right time. Once sales confirmed his suspicions that Homer Laughlin goods were just the thing, Clarke successfully lobbied to become the firm's exclusive western representative. In many respects, his jobber's experience enabled him to extract market data more effectively than could china decorators or factory salesmen. In his Denver warehouse, Clarke watched country storekeepers handle goods, listened to their praise, and tolerated their "kicks." When these small-town retailers resisted his sales pitches, the crackerjack salesman heeded the fine points of their condemnations—Homer Laughlin toilet sets had glazes that crazed, its tea sets lacked the handsome motifs like those of Knowles, Taylor & Knowles—and passed them on. More than Shaw, Clarke—by virtue of talent, savvy, and experience—knew how to translate kicks into proposals for technically viable, artistically appealing, and commercially successful products. In the mid-1890s, Clarke pondered the notion of introducing a new shape geared to the western trade, including the burgeoning California market. He designed just such a line, named Golden Gate after the strait connecting the Pacific Ocean to San Francisco Bay. Although details of the design transaction remain unknown, Clarke's design appeared in the 1896 Homer Laughlin catalogue. Within a year, he received an appointment as the pottery's sales director.[9]

Even when he supervised factory salesmen, Clarke continued to value hands-on experience and spent much of his own time drumming up business in boomtowns and port cities, from Chicago to San Francisco. These stints on the road kept his sales skills in top form. On a typical stopover, Clarke traversed a business district to notify retailers of his arrival, laid out samples in a commercial suite at a hotel, and showered visitors with orations on Homer Laughlin's wonderful chinaware. Sometimes his rooms adjoined those of other pottery salesman, so that customers drifted among them while mulling over selections. Clarke enjoyed friendly shouting matches with rival crockery men, boasting about his products while sneaking glimpses at their goods. If a customer ultimately favored the man next door, Clarke wasted little time on self-pity and instead calculated the dollars lost and the reasons why.[10]

Just as important as drumming up sales, Clarke scrutinized towns and their inhabitants, studying private and public spaces to advance his understanding of consumption habits. He was a polished taste detective. As a known quantity in some circuits, Clarke enjoyed private spaces and personal pleasures that were off limits to ordinary salesmen. Dining at clients' homes, he took note of the interior decorating styles, including any distinctive choices in pressed glass, table linens, floor coverings, and furniture that expressed local tastes. Even the smallest details—violets in window boxes, green ribbons on bodices, patterns on silverware—clued Clarke into fads that could be harnessed to puff up goods and design new lines. If women liked purple blossoms in their front gardens, they might look favorably on pottery covered with similar flowers. If men wore scarlet neckties, they might buy fancy shaving mugs decorated with bright red decals. To Clarke, the consummate salesman, no feature of the material world lacked significance: every piece of minutiae evinced some aspect of taste; every habit could be interpreted and translated into a motif with commercial value.[11]

As he canvassed the marketplace, Clarke set down his observations in daily letters to Laughlin and Wells. This correspondence reveals much about the information corridors in the retail crockery business, for documents like these were the primary conduits through which data about consumers' desires reached manufacturers. In these shorthand messages, Clarke referred cryptically to stippled gold bands or to lily of the valley motifs, and the managers knew how these patterns looked, how they were priced, and who in East Liverpool made them. When he reported that consumers in Salt Lake City found Homer Laughlin's teacup in the St. Denis shape too large and that Montanans considered the firm's Catalina toilet set inferior to competitors' designs, his bosses in Ohio got the message. Clarke's letters demonstrate how the consumer feedback loop, essential to design and innovation, operated in the pottery business.[12]

Just how much Clarke's letters influenced the appearance of Homer Laughlin lines depended on several factors, including the probable size of a customer's orders. More and more, Laughlin and Wells exercised managerial prerogative to limit their pottery's output, exerting restraint in dealing with small-time retailers and jobbers. When one jobber in San Francisco asked Clarke for plates with a "scroll rather than a sprig design . . . not unlike no. 412, but much smaller," managers refused. Even with a batch production setup, it would be sheer folly "to get up new designs every month or so, or to get up every design that customers may happen to think they fancy!" Orders for relatively unique embellishments increasingly fell under the purview of china decorators like Trenton's Jesse Dean, a specialist in niche markets. Yet none of this implies managerial insensitivity to the marketplace. If "every customer on the books" in Montana demanded simple patterns or if the most important jobber in California repeatedly asked for toilet sets in "good strong colors," Laughlin and Wells did their best to respond. The trick to surviving in the competitive 1890s entailed learning when to say yes and when to say no to requests for design variation.[13]

Yet by the fin de siècle decade, the Homer Laughlin product portfolio and its design and development strategies started to assume their modern contours. Like manufacturers of pressed glass, western potters discovered that a "mine of wealth" awaited "prospectors" with the right "dynamite." Blasting middlemen out, potteries could dig deep into the mass market and realize significant profits. When Clarke secured orders from Marshall Field & Company, his bosses bent over backward to accommodate Chicago's leading department store. As American glass factories had discovered, prestige came with the Field's account. The store's china department was so stupendous that Philadelphia's John Wanamaker sent spies to take notes. The Field account also signaled a major triumph against New York crockery men, who had so long dominated the department store trade. This victory was peculiar to the West however; on the East Coast, the powerful propaganda machines of importers like L. Straus & Sons had prejudiced retail buyers against American wares. Homer Laughlin and other East Liverpool firms searched for a different entry point into the mass market; some chose to expand their client base in the premium, or scheme, goods trade, with its enormous orders from gift-giving businesses.[14]

The gift scheme dated to the 1870s, when tea stores like the Great Atlantic & Pacific Tea Company pioneered the practice of giving away premiums with their products. These stores sold pantry goods at elevated prices and, to encourage shoppers to return, issued coupons or tickets, which consumers collected and then redeemed for household goods. Aware that women comprised nine-tenths of their customers, managers looked for giveaways with feminine appeal. By the early 1880s, "every red front tea store in the country" brimmed with cheap cutlery, pictures, and kitchen gadgets, as well as glassware and crockery, which women most favored.[15]

Tea stores publicized their gift system with chromolithographic advertising cards, which women collected, talked about in their parlors, and pasted in enormous keepsake scrapbooks. Trade cards targeted local audiences through racial, ethnic, and class references and biases. In the textile city of Lowell, J. Buckley's Acme Tea Company appealed to the racial prejudices of working-class consumers with pictures of an African American farmer in embarrassing situations. In New York City, the A&P targeted middle-class women by using American Colonial Revival motifs depicting elegant living. The backs of the cards featured

Grand Union Tea Company, possibly Waterville, Maine, 1898–1903. Society for the Preservation of New England Antiquities

descriptions of the tea store's products, prices, and gifts. Through trade card advertising, tea stores trained consumers to expect more from retailers than staple items. Premiums became a much-anticipated element of the shopping experience.[16]

The scheme-ware business took off during the 1890s, when consumers suffering from the economic depression welcomed the prospect of getting small household goods for "nothing." The success of tea stores with ceramic giveaways led other businesses to opt for cheap, showy, and durable pottery as enticements. By 1901, consumers who bought soap, baking powder, cigars, cereal, newspapers, theater and music hall tickets, shoes, books, and beer could anticipate receiving dishes with their purchases. Even that bastion of middle-class respectability, the *Ladies' Home Journal*, offered dinnerware premiums to subscribers. As they learned to take gifts for granted, shoppers grew impatient with stores that reneged on reliability, quality, and quantity. One coffee and tea dealer, Hartford's Lincoln, Seyms & Company, explained how the gift system

THE FORTUNE-TELLER.

WHAT DOES THIS LOVELY MAIDEN SEE ? ✻ AND HERS GOOD FORTUNE E'ER MUST BE.—
HER FORTUNE IN A CUP OF TEA!. ✻ SHE BUYS FROM THE GREAT "A & P."
COPYRIGHT 1886 BY THE GREAT ATLANTIC & PACIFIC TEA CO. N.Y.

Colonial Revival trade card, Great Atlantic & Pacific Tea Company, New York City, 1886. Society for the Preservation of New England Antiquities

could backfire: "A woman comes into a retail store and buys a pound of our coffee, and she gets with it a cup and saucer. She comes in again and buys another and so on, until she has three cups and saucers. The next time she comes in the place, the dealer has ordered a different kind, and she can get no more of the first. You can see very readily how the woman would be annoyed, as she originally started in with the idea of getting a set to match." To avoid confrontations and ensure repeat purchases, tea stores had to secure dependable shipments of these premiums. Some large distributors integrated backward into pottery production. In 1901, the Larkin Soap Manufacturing Company, which used giveaways in the mail-order soap business, opened a pottery close to its Buffalo suds factory. With Larkin, women like Sarah M. Peters of Schuylkill Falls, Pennsylvania, sponsored soap-selling parties and earned a chest and a sewing cabinet, which she picked up at the Philadelphia redemption center. However, most premium vendors had little time, interest, and capital to invest in manufacturing. They needed established potteries to make the small items—cups, saucers, bowls, shakers—that fit in food packages or on crowded store shelves. The pottery that secured the business of a large scheme customer like Chicago's American Cereal Company, which packaged Quaker Oats, received substantial orders. Still, only the largest, most up-to-date factories could rise to the challenge of the fast and ruthless scheme-goods trade.[17]

The acknowledged leader in the scheme-goods business was the Sebring family, which personified the rags-to-riches myth of Horatio Alger's novels. Inspired by consumers' enthusiasm over giveaways in their small East Liverpool grocery store, the seven Sebring brothers—described by the Dun credit agency as "pushing sort of men"—switched to pottery manufacturing in 1887. To readers versed in crockery lingo, their trade journal advertisements for "bulk car lots" signaled a pledge to high volume, low prices, simple decorations, and quick deliveries—every scheme user's dream. Premium vendors responded so enthusiastically that, by the Great War, the Sebrings controlled an empire of more than a dozen scheme factories. In part, the family's unrivaled success stemmed from clan leader Frank A. Sebring's refusal "to be anything but modern." In his eyes, being a modern potter simply meant stretching the limits of the batch production system to meet the needs of the most up-to-date mass merchandisers.[18]

From the depressed 1890s through the early 1900s, premium orders sustained many East Liverpool potteries. Scheme-ware distributors, caring little if their giveaways compared favorably to dishes actually purchased by the housewife, pressured scheme-ware factories to compromise quality in favor of high volume and low prices. Running at a frenzied pace, potteries expected flaws on some 25 to 40 percent of their output; decorating shops covered the ugliest of these defects with printed and filled motifs, gilding, airbrushing, and decalcomania. Horrified, some members of the USPA's Art & Design Committee condemned scheme decorations as the epitome of "crudity, flashiness, and cheapness."[19]

Judgments about quality and taste aside, the real problem with the scheme-ware business lay in the unpredictable shifts in demand. When importers captured the "great cereal schemes" for 1903, the USPA estimated a loss of a million dollars, or 7 percent of members' annual sales. A year earlier, the Union Pacific Tea Company had deserted Homer Laughlin for a foreign supplier after finding Laughlin's salad bowl prices a "trifle too high." Refusing to tolerate such erratic conditions, resourceful East Liverpool potters diversified their customer portfolios. Survival depended on strengthening ties to large regional jobbers and on building new accounts with scheme-ware users, department stores, mail-order houses, and five-and-tens. This strategy worked beautifully for Homer Laughlin. The fast-moving scheme-ware business covered manufacturing costs; sales to other mass merchandisers provided profits.[20]

Mass retailers placed unprecedented demands on East Liverpool's quantity-production factories. Every day, the mail delivered messages from buyers demanding that managers give priority to *their* orders, and buyers for scheme ware were the most demanding. The representative of the American Cereal Company pressured managers at Homer Laughlin to ship him four thousand dozen decorated bowls a week for use in Quaker Oats promotions. The buyer for Union Pacific Tea Company commanded Wells to "fill . . . orders immediately" so the company could meet the demand for premiums, which it had created through "extensive advertising." Mail-order houses joined the chorus. P. A. Murkland, crockery and glass buyer for Sears, Roebuck & Company, begged Wells for a freight car of Pink Rose dinner sets to fill orders that poured in following a mail advertising campaign. Dime store men also chimed in. The assistant buyer at S. H. Kress & Company needed some showy loss leaders for the gala opening of his new store in Knoxville, Tennessee. Daily correspondence always brought new challenges as big crockery customers chanted, more, more, cheaper, cheaper.[21]

Pottery executives tackled changing market conditions in several ways, all characteristic of nineteenth-century batch manufacturers. Collectively, they continued to embrace associationism as a control mechanism. Through the USPA, proprietors attempted to regulate markets and prices by negotiating for favorable shipping rates, bargaining with organized labor over wages, creating standard sizes and prices, and lobbying for higher tariffs. At the level of the firm, some coped by speeding up production, others by expanding old factories or building new ones—sometimes deserting East Liverpool for greener pastures. Between 1898 and 1903, more than a dozen companies constructed large, modern facilities in nearby Ohio towns: Carrollton, East Palestine, Lisbon, Minerva, Salem, Salineville, Sebring, and Wellsville. The expanded pottery district included towns in western Pennsylvania and the panhandle of West Virginia. Between 1901 and 1914, more than two-thirds of American tableware would come from these factories.[22]

Starting in the late 1890s, managers at Homer Laughlin aggressively pursued many of these firm-level tactics. Laughlin and Wells incorporated the Homer Laughlin China Company in 1896; a year later, the Pittsburgh investor Louis I. Aaron (1840–1919) and his sons, Marcus (1869–1954) and Charles I. (1872–1947), bought a large block of stock. Wells became general manager in 1899, Laughlin gradually withdrew his capital to invest in Los Angeles real estate, and the Aarons assumed top slots. The new executives began refurbishing old facilities and erecting new plants in Crockery City's growth area, the East End, so that Homer Laughlin became America's largest pottery manufacturer in 1901. Next, Wells and the Aarons pooled their capital, incorporating a Homer Laughlin subsidiary, North American Manufacturing Company (NAMC), whose wholly owned companies built the town of Newell, West Virginia, across the Ohio River from East Liverpool. At Newell, NAMC constructed a village for workers and factories for Homer Laughlin and the Edwin M. Knowles China Company, another firm partially owned by the Aarons. A suspension bridge across the Ohio River and streetcar lines operated by NAMC firms connected Newell to East Liverpool. Completed in 1906, Homer Laughlin's Newell facility, Plant No. 4, was reputed to be the most up-to-date pottery in the world.[23]

In 1899, the general manager, Wells, made his first important executive decision about design, hiring Arthur Mountford (1850–1917) as the firm's full-time art director. Mountford's impressive credentials included a Staffordshire apprenticeship, training at the Hanley School of Art, and experience in English and American factories. After arriving in Trenton in 1888, Mountford had worked as chief decorator for Burroughs & Mountford's Eagle Pottery, operated by his brother. New Jersey ceramists revered Mountford as an Old World craftsman who knew all the secrets of the china-decorating trade. Mountford expected a high degree of autonomy at Homer Laughlin, as befit his ability and experience, but he soon discovered that the reality was otherwise. Wells solicited the art director's opinions on products, authorized him to supervise modelers and decorators, and charged him with procuring decals from Staffordshire. However, when Wells established a new design committee to oversee the creation of shapes and decorations, the members included managers like Clarke but not Mountford. Times had changed, and pottery executives expected practical men to listen and obey.[24]

Soon after Mountford's arrival, conflict broke out between the new art director and salesman extraordinaire Clarke. Clarke's achievements in building up the western trade had earned him a seat of honor at the firm. With a flair for design,

Clarke loved nothing better than to plan new shapes and patterns and to share those ideas. The salesman's aesthetic excursions infuriated Mountford, who saw them as threats to his artisanal authority and to the entire Staffordshire system. He refused to cooperate with Wells and the design committee, adopting an especially obdurate posture toward Clarke. The sales chief retaliated; he characterized Mountford as a ne'er-do-well, subjecting the art director to ridicule in letters to Wells. If the Englishman lacked inspiration, contended Clarke, he should "spend some afternoon in Pittsburgh," browsing through the shopping district. There, he would find stores filled with "a number of most excellent treatments by Tatler," one of Trenton's leading china decorators, "including a sort of yellow pansy, which he should be able to reproduce." Wells came to share Clarke's irritation with the art director: "I have been after him constantly for three weeks" to create a new rose wreath motif, and he "finally started to work on it!" Cognizant of the rarity of practical men like Mountford, Wells tolerated him for his technical expertise. Hostilities continued to rage for years. Clarke eventually rose to a vice presidency at Homer Laughlin, but Mountford left in 1909, accepting a position with the small Edwin Bennett Pottery in Baltimore. Clarke's rise, Mountford's fall: representing flip sides of a coin, these men's fortunes underscored larger transformations in an industry in flux.[25]

Welcome to the Five-and-Ten

As mass retailers bought more and more Homer Laughlin products, men who spent their days in offices far from East Liverpool extended their reach into design practice. Unlike Mountford, these men knew little about the inner workings of dust-filled potteries. In many respects, they shared Clarke's experience and outlook. Their apprenticeships had been served in the stockrooms of country stores, at the counters of urban emporiums, and on the road with sample trunks. These men were the specialized agents of the nation's new shopkeepers, and the subject of their expertise was the American consumer.

By 1900, a plethora of home furnishings, accessories, and equipment poured out of the nation's batch production factories and workshops: furniture, carpets, draperies, lamps, stoves, bric-a-brac, glassware, pottery, and more. Wherever shoppers looked, they found retail stores overflowing with enticing goods: specialty shops, general stores, home furnishings emporiums, hardware stores, department stores, gift tea stores, and dime stores. Among these retailers, five-and-tens like Woolworth most effectively extended consumer society to within the reach of the lower classes. Adapting many of the cost-cutting principles perfected by the railroads and the steel industry, the dime store pioneer Frank W. Woolworth so reduced retail prices for ordinary nonperishable housewares that even factory workers with modest earnings could indulge in a few luxuries. With a mass audience in mind, he eliminated the wholesaler, eschewed the extension of credit, carried nothing that sold for more than a dime, tagged all his goods with fixed, nonnegotiable prices, and embraced a location-is-everything strategy. Refusing to do business in small communities, Woolworth opened stores on the "Main Streets" of good-sized cities, choosing sites with the densest sidewalk traffic. By the turn of the century, Woolworth's five-and-tens counted among urban America's landmark retailing institutions.[26]

With good reason, early twentieth-century observers noted that five-and-tens owed their livelihoods to "the woman with a shawl"—the recent immigrant who had not yet been Americanized. When crockery buyer Clinton Pierce Case contacted Wells in 1899, Woolworth already operated more than fifty "strictly 5 & 10 cent stores" in carefully selected urban locations in the industrial belt that spread across the New England and Mid-Atlantic states. In Pennsylvania alone, one of the nation's leading industrial states, the chain owned stores in all the major cities and market towns: Allentown, Bethlehem, Harrisburg, Lancaster, Philadelphia, Pittsburgh, and Reading. New York City's first Woolworth's opened in 1896 at 259 Sixth Avenue, close to elite department stores like B. Altman, Stern Brothers, and Bonwit Teller, but rarely attracted "upper crusters" searching for bargains. Primarily, it drew shoppers from the swarms of working people who labored nearby or who walked across town to run errands. "Foreigners as a class go to the cheaper class department store and to the 5 and 10 cent stores for everything," sniffed a trade journalist in *Hardware Age*. "These stores demand cash and if it were not for their foreign trade, they could not exist in most communities."[27]

Woolworth's investment in the rising tide of urbanization augured well for a volume-oriented pottery. The urban character of five-and-tens appealed to Wells, who, like Frank Woolworth, fixed his eyes on the pocketbooks of pennywise working people. The European immigrants and rural Americans who populated the nation's growing cities were a ready market for inexpensive household goods. After witnessing tea stores introducing china and glass to "thousands of families who might not otherwise have discovered these luxuries," Wells suspected that dime stores might extend pottery consumption to even greater numbers of people. Indeed, the five-and-ten's facade seemed to call out to the "shawl

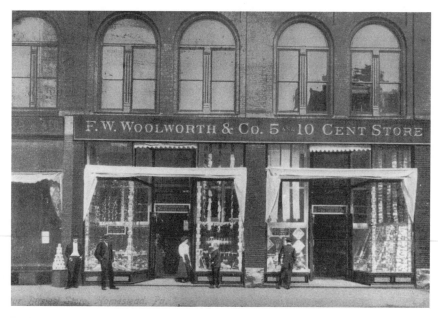

The busiest Woolworth store in the country, 1911. This five-and-ten operated in the shadow of the U.S. Steel works in Homestead, Pennsylvania, and stocked Homer Laughlin's inexpensive pottery. Homer Laughlin China Company

trade." Bearing the founder's name, bright red-and-gold signs—once used exclusively by teas stores—hung across display windows filled with judiciously arranged merchandise. Unlike department store display artists, who mounted theatrical, thematic, and surreal exhibits aimed to stimulate shoppers' fantasies, Woolworth window dressers created tidy, repetitive arrangements that emphasized their store's affinity with quantity production and the real accessibility of abundance. While department stores tempted and intimated, dime stores beckoned and delivered. Created for eye-level viewing, a Woolworth window encouraged pedestrians to stop, look, study the goods, think about the clearly marked prices, and go inside, where beautiful and affordable goods abounded. Among all the products in the dime store, crockery had the visual and symbolic properties that made it ideal for window displays. To the shawl trade, no objects better epitomized American respectability than pretty dishes, the things that ladies kept in their china cabinets.[28]

At the time that Case contacted Wells, retailing operated both as an institution for coordinating the flow of goods through the economy and as a vehicle for imagining consumers. Charged with interpreting demand, retail buyers had to distinguish the solid components of taste, such as quality intolerance and decorative preference, from its ephemeral elements, including whims for odd colors. Before the advent of formal market research, buyers used their wits to develop an understanding of consumers' material desires. If they were to stock goods that would sell quickly on tight margins, Woolworth buyers had to understand Woolworth shoppers. They took this responsibility seriously, for the five-and-ten's survival and their own fortunes hinged on their success in distinguishing fast-selling goods from potential duds.

The store's first crockery buyer, Case, enlarged his knowledge of dime store shoppers in several ways. First and foremost, he assimilated a good deal from his urban environment, much as Clarke had studied his western circuit. At 280 Broadway, Woolworth's executive offices stood in the heart of New York's major commercial district, where fashion was the name of the game. On Frank Woolworth's orders, people-watching became mandatory among buyers. Like other New Yorkers, Case loved to window-shop, and he often spent hours roaming Manhattan's retailing districts. Pretending to be an ordinary consumer, he studied the sumptuous windows on Ladies' Mile, where large department stores like Lord & Taylor vied for women's dollars. Out of the corner of his eye, Case sized up passersby as they looked. When crowds gathered around an especially "live" window, he joined the hordes, scrutinizing the dress, manners, and accents of people as they ogled the goods. Inside the Woolworth stores on Third Avenue in New York and on Fulton Street in Brooklyn, he studied shoppers as they browsed, handled the merchandise, mulled over choices, and finally bought the goods. He listened to shoppers' remarks about a store's layout, appearance, and stock. No detail seemed insignificant. Based on his observations, Case formulated a partial vision of Woolworth shoppers' preferences in his mind's eye. He drew on these fragmentary images when collaborating with manufacturers to design new products.[29]

To further his knowledge of consumers, Case also relied on feedback from Woolworth store managers, who understood the tastes of their communities. Woolworth often selected store managers from among local Anglo-American residents, who, in turn, hired salesgirls fluent in the appropriate foreign language as well as English. While ethnicity may have been a stumbling block in some instances, French Canadians in Lowell and Slavs in Pittsburgh learned to feel at ease with their Woolworth managers. Local shoppers trusted him to provide reliable merchandise, from wooden spoons to woolen kerchiefs, that would not break, wear out, or go out of style too soon. In his daily routine, a Woolworth manager scanned the selling floor, watching consumers handle, talk about, and buy goods. He listened to shoppers' concerns about prettiness, pricing, and performance, even if it meant working through a translator or using pantomime. Keeping communications channels open helped a manager to select products for Case's seasonal circulars and to conduct market research for the New York office. When planning new pottery lines, Case sent factory samples to store managers, who solicited customers' opinions on these patterns-in-progress. Involving consumers in the development process furthered goodwill, although such consultations occurred only a few times a year. More typically, managers shared market data with Case in routine letters to New York. When a particular line of Homer Laughlin china tickled shoppers' fancies, the manager in Fitchburg, Massachusetts, reported that the pattern was "going some" or "selling great." If consumers complained about a shape, form, or decoration, managers also passed this on, by letter or in person.[30]

Case encouraged managers to visit Woolworth headquarters, finding time in his busy schedule to meet with them. Throughout the year, Case kept abreast of regional and local variations in taste by studying stores' monthly sales reports and manufacturers' shipping statistics so that, when a local manager appeared at the door, Case already knew much about that store's crockery department. Case pressed the manager to elaborate on letters and statistical summaries and encouraged him to handle samples and to speculate on how his customers might receive the new lines. Over the course of an hour's chat, Case artfully extracted a wealth of information about shoppers' preferences for colors, shapes, and decorations. Although the mechanisms had not changed since Clarke's heyday, the responsibility for imagining consumers had passed to the crockery buyer and, in part, to his assistants, the store managers.[31]

Committed to giving consumers the "most at least cost," dime store buyers like Woolworth's Case looked for products that met strict criteria. Whether dishes, dolls, or dust mops, a store's stock had to be of good quality, to sell at a price lower than the competition's, and to make a profit. By no means did buyers purchase shoddy products to foist on unwitting customers, for indignant shoppers, disappointed with "bargains," would take their cash to competing five-and-tens, hardware stores, or speciality shops. "Customers will not bring goods back when they are not just right," explained one dime store crockery man in 1914, and "we simply lose trade when we put these goods out." Neither could buyers impose highbrow tastes on the purchasing public. None lasted in Woolworth's organization by trying to remake shoppers in the images of socialites from Park Avenue or suburbanites from New Jersey. Without question, crockery buyers brought their own aesthetic values to bear on their product choices, but decades of experience in mulling over the tastes of different groups and distant places modulated those preferences. In the dime store trade, the permeable boundaries between manufacturers, retailers, and consumers allowed the voices of potential pottery purchasers to resound in Homer Laughlin offices and factories. Consumers, in essence, spoke through the mouths of Woolworth's crockery buyers, the pottery industry's latest fashion intermediaries.[32]

Decal Aesthetics

> Rudy is here. Now we can get some new patterns!
> —Pottery managers' chant, East Liverpool

Like other big-time crockery buyers, Case realized that pottery covered with inexpensive decal decorations offered the best avenue to satisfying the tastes of "the poorer classes," who frequented five-and-tens during the early twentieth century. If china mania had stimulated technical change and the rise of one-step pottery decorations in the 1880s, the end result was the adoption of decalcomania as an alternative to the more labor-intensive process of printing and filling in. Perfected by English ceramists during the 1890s, decals soon appeared on most East Liverpool products. Bold, colorful, and eye-catching, decal pottery looked beautiful in the Woolworth window displays, designed to lure pedestrians, bicyclists, and trolley riders into the store.[33]

The heightened demand for decals had major ramifications for design practice and the definition of aesthetic skill within the American pottery industry. During the 1900s, some potteries tried to produce decalcomania only to discover, like Trenton decorators before them, that decal manufacturing required knowledge beyond their purview. They turned to decal importers like Palm, Fechteler & Company, Palm Brothers, and Rudolph Gaertner to obtain sheets of decals from specialty printers overseas. Little by little, decal men like "Rudy" Gaertner assumed the technical and artistic responsibilities once shouldered by practical Staffordshire men like Jesse Dean and Arthur Mountford. "Our decal manufacturers," reported the USPA's Art & Design Committee, "have taken the position of art directors to our potteries." Crockery buyers, in particular, appreciated the decal man's enthusiasm as a welcome respite from the sometimes sluggish East Liverpool potteries. When J. J. Parkhurst of Kress asked Gaertner to create some "conventional border patterns," the decal man quickly responded. When Case pressed Wells for a "new bright pattern" of small flowers to replace the fading "extreme fashion of large flowers," Gaertner speedily provided decals with miniature blossoms in brilliant colors. To pottery managers and crockery buyers, Gaertner was an embellishing wizard whose time had arrived.[34]

Between 1901 and his death in 1932, Gaertner—affectionately nicknamed by East Liverpool potters as the "decorative father confessor"—played a pivotal role in design and innovation at Homer Laughlin. An engineer by training, Gaertner, who became America's leading supplier of decals for ceramics, also fancied himself a gentleman, so he felt at ease straddling the gap between technology and art. Born in Prague to a potting family, Gaertner received his degree from the Institute of Technology at Carlsbad in 1893. He apprenticed in German and French china works, managed his family's porcelain factory, and in 1896 joined Frank Schroeder & Company, a German manufacturer of ceramic decorating supplies and a pioneer in decal printing. Five years later, Gaertner traveled to the United States as Schroeder's New York sales agent. Within a year, the ambitious immigrant had established his own importing firm, incorporated in 1905 as R. Gaertner & Company. His personal tastes extended to impeccably tailored suits, a handsome office on West Broadway, lunches at the Manhattan Club, and evenings at the Metropolitan Opera. A complicated and colorful personality, Gaertner specialized in supplying decals to the five-and-tens and scheme-goods users, which absorbed 50 to 80 percent of the pottery made in the East Liverpool district. In 1908 alone, Gaertner and his small staff of artists designed a hundred or so new mass-market decals.[35]

For any one Woolworth decoration, Wells, Case, and Gaertner often engaged in a months' long exchange of letters, telegrams, watercolor sketches, decal samples, and artifacts. The process went something like this. Once Wells and Case decided that Woolworth needed a new pattern, they contacted Gaertner, who mobilized his firm. In his office, staff artists first painted watercolor sketches, drawing inspiration from such design sources as wallpaper fragments, printed textiles, and English china. If Wells and Case liked these sketches, Gaertner began the time-consuming process of procuring sample decals from abroad. Choosing a printer was determined by the look that the design required: English firms such the Universal Transfer Company in Hanley used "dust printing" methods, which were appropriate for brilliant colors and detailed designs; German firms like George Nitzke & Company excelled in wet printing, which suited simpler patterns and quantity print runs. When the decal proofs arrived, Wells consulted his decorating department chief, a technical expert who suggested production-enhancing alterations. Next, Case evaluated the decal's likely market appeal. Finally, Gaertner telegraphed his printer with instructions on modifying the pattern. So the decorative turnstile revolved, stopping only when Wells and Case deemed the new Woolworth pattern just right.[36]

Without question, dime store dishes differed recognizably from both the more costly department store lines and the cheaper scheme goods. In many respects, the patterns were the twentieth-century ceramic equivalents of the ornamentation on nineteenth-century machine-made furniture. Stylistically related to costly handcrafted cabinetry, these inexpensive furnishings were distinguished as a group by their simplified decoration. Similarly, the Woolworth pottery patterns—colorful bouquets, neoclassical festoons, and chromatic bands—harked back to motifs painted on highbrow porcelain; but here, too, taste and technology fused to endow these inexpensive dishes with an identifiable aesthetic. Decal printing suited highly refined pictorial representation impossible to achieve at comparable cost with painting, giving dime store pottery a distinctive look of its own.[37]

Neither the new way of designing products, which privileged decal suppliers and retail buyers over china decorators, nor the decalcomania aesthetic lacked critics. The managing director of Baltimore's Bennett Pottery, Henry Brunt, condemned dime store and premium wares: "Made in the most slipshod manner," these vulgar goods constituted a "menace to art." Like Mountford (whom he would hire in 1909), the opinionated Brunt belonged to a dying breed of practical Staffordshire men. He lamented the demise of the apprenticeship system and longed for a revival of decorations like Jesse Dean's fancy gold work. During the early 1890s, Brunt's elegant porcelains had won judges' hearts at the World's Columbian Exposition, earning awards for Bennett. Boasting of his accomplishments at the Chicago fair, Brunt hoped that others might follow in his footsteps and focus on highbrow lines.[38]

By the time Brunt penned his 1907 diatribe, the high-end market lay beyond the reach of most American potters and china decorators, whose rising labor and materials costs prohibited fancy goods production. For supervisory jobs in decorating departments, managers routinely passed over practical potters in favor of American-born men like E. Samuel Hilton. More of a superintendent than a craftsman, Hilton, who worked for the Anchor Pottery Company in Trenton, even spoke the language of management. His identity and pride stemmed from his "capital stock," that is, from executive ability, industry, economy, honesty, and push, rather than from artisanal knowledge and craft skills. At Homer Laughlin, Edward L. Carson, a graduate of the Spring Garden Institute, one of Philadelphia's trade schools, directed Wells's decorating rooms. Carson's education provided him with a minimum of technological know-how and a maximum of obedience to authority. Hilton, Carson, and factory men like them perfectly complemented decal importers like Gaertner. They adjusted his designs to accommodate particular technical conditions—nothing more, nothing less. While Brunt grumbled, perspicacious managers and crockery buyers, who foresaw bright futures in quantity production, pressed ahead with decal pottery, laboring to gratify rather than to judge mass-market tastes.[39]

Back to the Five-and-Ten

Following the Pittsburgh show every January, crockery men traveled to East Liverpool, where they visited the potteries and finalized the details of their annual contracts. At Homer Laughlin, year after year Wells rolled out the red carpet for dime store men, treating Case and other Woolworth executives, including treasurer Charles C. Griswold, to meals in the city's best hotels and to tours of his factories. Wining and dining aside, the agenda included plenty of wheeling and dealing. The men spent countless hours in the pottery's sample room, studying hundreds of samples laid out on tables. Shapes embellished with competing decals sat side by side for comparison. Here, the Woolworth buyer had a library of objects at his disposal, and he readily communicated the subtleties of his preferences to Wells. To those versed in material goods, an object was worth a thousand words; with artifact in hand, Case could elaborate on details impossible to deal with in letters. This leaf had too much yellow; that rose, too little pink. This gold band looked too thick; that gold filigree, too fussy. The conversations first revolved around decoration—and then volume and price. In their deliberations, the men considered sales statistics for the previous year's patterns, allowing consumer choice to dictate the fate of shapes and decorations. In absentia, dime store shoppers exerted a powerful influence over both merchant and manufacturer during these big midwinter meetings.[40]

Case wanted distinctive motifs that consumers would recognize as Woolworth designs, motifs that might resemble, but that could not be identical to, those sold by other five-and-tens. If consumers wanted matching dishes, they could complete their set only by returning to a Woolworth store. In this way, the five-and-ten encouraged shawl ladies to emulate Anglo-American habits by purchasing

Homer Laughlin factory sample room, ca. 1910. Homer Laughlin China Company

dishes that matched. Whether or not dime store consumers followed these pre-scriptions may never be known. Those who wanted to be "American" probably did, while others remained happy with a mix of designs. Unlike middlebrow shoppers, who might use elaborate European services to impress dinner guests, married working-class and farm women bought five-and-ten dishes to serve food in pantries and kitchens. These people ate, rather than dined. Single wage-earning women who lived in boarding houses, hotel rooms, or small tenements cheered up their tiny abodes with inexpensive dime store ceramics. Unfettered by a middlebrow taste culture that mandated the acquisition and display of exten-sive tableware sets, Woolworth shoppers may have stocked their cupboards with goods in a variety of decorations, shapes, and forms. Stylistic variety was integral to working women's tastes—and to the homey dime store aesthetic.

While the imperative of divining and satisfying Woolworth shoppers shaped their decisions and actions, Wells and Case's task of obliging the purchasing public remained a difficult one. Consumers accustomed to quantity-production goods, such as packaged cereal and soap, anticipated the same level of depend-ability from their household accessories. Even rural women, who ordered pot-tery from mail-order houses, would not tolerate irregularities like off-color flow-

Dime store dishes displayed on top of makeshift china cabinet in home workers' New York tenement, ca. 1900. Pottery bric-a-brac and pressed glass punch bowl with hanging cups can be seen in adjoining room. Lewis Hine Collection, Eastman House, Rochester, N.Y.

ers, poorly applied gold trim, or crooked sprigs. "I know that you make due allowance for the fact that your customers must buy their crockery blind," Wells wrote to buyer P. A. Murkland at Sears, Roebuck & Company in 1911. "Women are inclined to be a little exacting about their tableware," he continued, and they "may sometimes return goods to you which . . . do not happen to be just as they expected." The refinement of the senses, a process whose origins sociologist Norbert Elias traces to early modern Europe, unfolded to embrace mass-market consumers. A host of factors, including the rise of mass merchandising itself, contributed to this "civilizing process." Like Sears customers, Woolworth shoppers refused to lower their standards, rejecting pottery that deviated from certain norms.[41]

A discerning lot, Woolworth's customers possessed notions about "good goods" that had jelled long before they entered the five-and-ten. Indeed, a large part of a local managers' job entailed selecting the right stock from the range of decal options—sprays of "small roses and lily of [the] valley," borders with "small, neat gold lace," sprigs of pink hawthorn, clusters of "rambler roses, leaves, and small flowers," lustrous bands in green and gold, and classical festoons in gold—listed on the annual circulars provided by the New York buyer. A Woolworth store serving a predominately Slavic community offered different items than did five-and-tens with Italian, German, or Irish customers. Regardless of ethnicity, consumers—who might have endured irregularities from printed and filled-in decorations during the 1880s—expected symmetry and consistency in decal patterns by the 1900s. After women in Lancaster, Pennsylvania, scoffed at a Homer Laughlin line decorated with a particular pink floral decal, Woolworth's manager J. U. Troy explained to the home office why this ten-cent pattern did "not sell": the "shade of the rose" was often very brown or "very, very pale." Troy, like other Woolworth managers, abhorred being obliged to discount imperfect items because his profits accrued on such close margins. Case laid the problem on the pottery's doorstep, and Wells begged for mercy on technical grounds. Declaring pink the "most treacherous color" in the potter's palette, he argued that "things . . . unexplainable and almost unbelievable" could happen to "large pink patterns in the kilns." An unsympathetic Case responded that few of the women who shopped at Woolworth's 189 stores appreciated "brick-colored pinks" and fewer still enjoyed seeing "three different" shades of a single color "on one plate." Woolworth shoppers wanted tried-and-true colors, and Case insisted that Wells fix his pink problem. In the same year, the crockery buyer refused some pickle, baking, and bone dishes in old-fashioned shapes, even at a special discount, on the grounds that "the ladies" would not buy these items "simply because they are cheap." Case would have been foolish to act otherwise, for success in the five-and-ten business depending on satisfying ladies' desires.[42]

In the first decade of the twentieth century, Case had established a model for dime store pottery purchasing that extended beyond procurement. He and Wells spoke the same language and thought about business in much the same way. Low prices, high volume, rapid delivery, and novel decoration; both men understood these concepts. As the two allies collaborated on patterns, they took their signals from culture and competition. This method of imagining consumers worked splendidly, contributing to the rapid growth of Homer Laughlin. In 1892, the pottery had operated one factory employing 124 workers; by 1910, the company ran four factories in Ohio and West Virginia with 1,800 workers. Gross sales increased more than twelvefold during the century's first decade: in 1898, sales totaled less than $200,000; in 1910, $2.5 million. The fate of

BIRDSEYE VIEW of East Liverpool, Ohio, plant of The Homer Laughlin China Co.

FRONT VIEW of Newell, W. Va., plant of The Homer Laughlin China Co.

Homer Laughlin's gigantic potteries, geared up for quantity production. From *The China Book* (Newell, W. Va.: Homer Laughlin China Company, 1912), National Museum of American History, Smithsonian Institution

Homer Laughlin seemed to be inexorably linked with that of Woolworth; but the next decade tested the tie between the pottery and dime store, as both firms coped with major shakeups.[43]

Tempest in the Teapot

> Much as a thunderbolt out of the clear sky, comes the Kress store, opened but little more than thirty days ago. Their manager, Mr. Champion, tells me they have already sold practically a car of crockery, that he has an order for a second car, and that every indication points to their selling five or six cars a year!
>
> —George Washington Clarke to W. Edwin Wells, 1911

In December 1911, Clarke displayed more than his usual flamboyance in writing to Wells from Arizona. S. H. Kress & Company, the southern-based dime store, had just opened a new store in Tucson, creating a quite a stir. At a moment when most five-and-tens converted existing buildings into stores, president Samuel H. Kress had established a corporate architectural department expressly for the purpose of giving his 5-10-25-cent stores a dignified look. When a Kress building appeared on Main Street, its shiny yellow brick facade did indeed glisten like a thunderbolt. When Tucson's Kress opened, consumers showed their confidence in mass retailing by shopping in their Sunday best. Not all Tucsonians welcomed "the advent of the Kress stores"; at least one china-shop owner wallowed in deep depression. "Clothed in sackcloth and ashes," Clarke reported, "no more pathetic a figure than Mr. W. J. Corbett, who may be said to fairly exude dejection at every pore, can possibly be imagined." To this shopkeeper, Kress's opening portended the "passing of any possible profit in the crockery business." All told, the consumer exodus to Kress so dejected retailers that Clarke described Tucson, potterywise, as "the city of the unburied dead."[44]

Clarke's account of the Tucson incident anchored Wells and Homer Laughlin ever more firmly to the five-and-ten trade, in which mass retailers like Woolworth and Kress promised endless orders. Such tales also propelled scheme-ware potteries—threatened by a new mass-market entrant, cheap Japanese porcelain—into action. They decided to take advantage of the plight of retailers like the Tucsonians to create new markets for giveaway pottery. Scheme-ware potters transformed the gift idea into a cure-all for china stores, hardware stores, furniture stores, flour mills, and bakeries suffering from slumping sales (plate 1).[45]

As firms like the West End Pottery Company, which ran a six-kiln factory in

East Liverpool, orchestrated the premium trade's face-lift, they suddenly discovered consumers' needs and desires. What women wanted became a major talking point in the West End's marketing strategies. Behind closed doors, potters had long acknowledged their market's feminine character. At the apex of the china-collecting craze of the 1880s, the USPA's Art & Design Committee had encouraged paintresses to submit designs to its exhibitions in the hope of tapping into women's aesthetic sensibilities. In 1890, the Baltimore potter D. F. Haynes acknowledged the "very great improvements in the taste of the public, particularly the female portion of the community, who buy the crockery." More recently, Wells in 1908 testified at congressional tariff hearings that "women buy the pottery." The difference with premium potters of the 1910s lay in their deliberate use of gender to lure new customers into the scheme-ware business. "Show me a woman who takes pride in her home and who doesn't love to have nice dishes," the West End's chief salesmen wrote in its 1910 catalogue. A woman "will go out of her way in order to deal with a merchant who is giving away dishes as a premium for quantity or cash purchases." Harry A. Epstein, a retailer in Berlin, Wisconsin, became a believer. Every May, he used a fail-safe formula to lure farmwives to his anniversary sale. He ordered some inexpensive "pretty plates," advertised these giveaways, and watched the "women folks" march his way. "Offer a dish to a lady free," Epstein explained, and "she will walk to town to get it." Women's tastes became a weapon wielded by scheme potters against cheap imports and, in turn, by small retailers against mass merchandisers.[46]

Meanwhile, Wells channeled most of his energy into resolving a different kind of problem. Homer Laughlin experienced its first major upheaval of the decade following the gigantic Woolworth merger of 1911, in which the firm absorbed six major East Coast competitors. By January 1912, the new F. W. Woolworth & Company controlled more than six hundred five-and-tens in the United States, Canada, and England. In 1910, Woolworth, F. F. Kirby, and S. H. Knox & Company accounted for less than 30 percent of Homer Laughlin's total sales. Two years later, sales to the enlarged Woolworth expanded to 36 percent; by 1916, to 40 percent. In 1916, Woolworth sold $87 million worth of goods; that year, the chain bought $1 million in crockery from Wells alone. Homer Laughlin, with seventy-eight kilns, made most of the nation's dime store pottery; its biggest competitor was the W. S. George Pottery Company, a thirty-two-kiln firm established in 1911 by china decorator William Shaw George, in East Palestine, Ohio.[47]

These five years had wrought considerable changes at the dime store's main offices. With considerable fanfare in 1913, Frank Woolworth moved his company into the newly constructed Woolworth Building, a thirty-five-story Gothic Revival tower at the corner of Broadway and Park Place. Fittingly nicknamed the Cathedral of Commerce, the world's largest skyscraper was built with $13 million in nickels and dimes. The firm's structure soon became more hierarchical and bureaucratic. The number of buyers expanded from ten to nineteen, many of them midlevel managers from the ranks of the consolidation firms. Responsible for selecting specific lines of merchandise in each of the six hundred five-and-tens, these men now relied on inspectors to study stores, redefining their own jobs more narrowly around specific product categories. When Case accepted a promotion to top management in 1915, William F. Newberry, formerly with F. F. Kirby & Company of Wilkes-Barre, Pennsylvania, succeeded him as the American crockery buyer.[48]

In Newell, Wells took pleasure from Newberry's appointment; the two men already knew each other, as the buyer had stocked Kirby's crockery departments with Homer Laughlin's products. (The son of a train master for the Pennsylvania Railroad, Newberry grew up in Scranton, one of three brothers who pursued retailing careers. His handsome sibling, Charles, joined Woolworth as its sheet music buyer; later, this dashing ladies' man joined a third brother to form the J. J. Newberry Company, a small competitor.) William Newberry suited the specialized position of pottery and glassware buyer very well. Passionate about dishes, he knew that women endowed pottery with special meaning. His enthusiasm, expertise, and stylish vision dovetailed perfectly with Frank Woolworth's postmerger strategy for refurbishing his stores and reaching out to middle-class shoppers. If the dime store were to expand upmarket, buyers must select items that had middlebrow appeal and looked attractive in windows. To Newberry, there was no better choice for head-turning displays than crockery, stacked tall in geometric formations that suggested order, utility, and abundance. Under his auspices, Woolworth's crockery departments would gain a reputation among middle-class consumers as *the* place to go for good-looking everyday dishes.[49]

In a two-decade business collaboration that matured into a warm friendship, Newberry and Wells slowly reenvisioned Homer Laughlin's dime store pottery to reflect the new emphasis on middle-class taste. Like Case before him, Newberry ordered goods from several East Liverpool factories, buying his best items from Homer Laughlin. When he searched for pottery with "prestige," Wells shouldered much of the burden for decorative development. Soon, the buyer showed his fussy side: "Now as you well know, deterioration in the decorations will hurt the business very quickly." The aesthetic high priest, Gaertner, often served as mediator between the dime store's crockery buyer and the pottery's general manager. "I explained," Gaertner wrote to Wells in 1913, the impossibility of putting "borders with gold" on festooned plates without accommodating "the demands of the decal girls for higher wages" and pushing the retail price beyond the ten-cent limit. Wells and Gaertner saw Woolworth's quality campaign as a double-edged sword. Both men's firms enjoyed the increased business, but both recognized that Woolworth had them in an economic squeeze. "If it is necessary to give Woolworth's better and more costly patterns every year," Gaertner complained, "it will not be possible for us to stand the difference!"[50]

Yet times were good. At the start of the twentieth century, American potters controlled a lion's share of the United States market, and the Great War dropped more business in their laps as production at European factories slowed. Between 1910 and 1920, ceramic imports from Germany declined from $3.5 million to $995,000 a year; imports from war-torn France, from $1.5 million to $666,000. Customers who had once scoffed at American ceramics hammered on the doors of East Liverpool's factories. Homer Laughlin sales skyrocketed, as department stores like New York's Bloomingdale Brothers and Gimbel Brothers searched for new supplies of high-quality dinnerware. To replace supplies of low-end European china, Sears also expanded its orders to Homer Laughlin. By 1919, rural consumers flipping through the Sears catalogue found more than two dozen dinner sets, in Violet Spray, Pink Rose, and other Homer Laughlin patterns. Sales to department stores and mail-order houses, Wells later revealed, accounted for all of the pottery's profits between 1916 and 1920.[51]

High-volume mass merchandisers also reevaluated their crockery policies. During the war, Brooklyn soap maker Kirkman & Sons, which promoted Borax with pottery premiums, terminated gift giving. At Woolworth, Newberry patiently watched potters cope with circumstances beyond their control: the virtual collapse of the railroads, the union's insistence on wage increases in response to soaring inflation, and scarcities of raw materials, fuel, and decalcomania. In 1915, Gaertner responded to wartime difficulties in getting decals by opening his own print shop in Mount Vernon, New York, and showing Newberry several lines, including a blue bird pattern, featuring American-made decals. Thinking these novelties would "be an attraction" among fashion-conscious customers at his "larger stores," Newberry approved the new lines, but soon afterward Gaertner encountered wartime shortages of paper, colors, and lithographers, which delayed the print shop's startup. The next year, Wells turned down Woolworth's orders for seasonal items, including Passover plates sold during the "Jewish

Easter" on the Lower East Side, because Homer Laughlin found it impossible to obtain the necessary decals. Unable to get his crockery orders filled, Newberry more and more turned to stocking his departments with pressed glass, whose manufacturers suffered fewer bottlenecks. The Great War cut a deep wound in the Homer Laughlin–Woolworth relationship. In 1916, Woolworth accounted for 40 percent of the pottery's gross sales, measured in dollars. By 1917, the percentage dropped to 35 percent; by 1920, to 20 percent.[52]

Although the war redefined Homer Laughlin's relationship to five-and-tens, it more generally gave a big boost to the sales, profits, and egos of American pottery manufacturers, setting a confident tone for the Jazz Age. By one estimate, American factories made 90 percent of the pottery distributed in the United States between 1918 and 1920. Looking forward to a bright future, USPA managers channeled their earnings into new technologies and capital improvements. A new generation of Sebrings, bearing the family's torch for modernity, established a model of technical innovation that other potters, including Homer Laughlin, would follow in the 1920s. To retain their share of the diminishing scheme-ware trade, Frank A. Sebring and his son, Charles Leigh Sebring, took dramatic measures to cut production costs, installing labor-saving equipment and hiring a ceramics chemist to test inexpensive American raw materials. Most notably, the chemist successfully experimented with ball clays, cheap clays not often used because of impurities that gave products an off-white color. At Homer Laughlin, managers fiddled with technical matters as well; but in the immediate postwar years, Wells's greatest concern lay, not with production, but with marketing.[53]

During the Great War, buyers visiting the Homer Laughlin factories boldly vented their opinions about the potters' facilities in East Liverpool and Newell. They lambasted Wells: nowhere else had they seen such shoddy hotels, factories, and sample rooms; Old World managers knew how to court visiting customers in style. Warming to their topic, buyers became increasingly vocal. One veteran dealer, Pittsburgh's Louis Reizenstein, boasted to the USPA about his sixty business trips across the Atlantic Ocean. Crockery men loved nothing more than to travel abroad and revel in luxury, and Wells knew that after reconstruction, buyers from Bloomingdale, Gimbel Brothers, Butler Brothers, and Sears would flock to the Continent for café au lait, chocolates, and crockery—unless he took drastic measures to prevent such a mass exodus.[54]

Although weary of the jeering, Wells nevertheless took buyers' descriptions of foreign showrooms to heart. Determined to retain wartime market shares,

Wells, who had accumulated a fortune during the boom, reinvested his profits in a fabulous Renaissance Revival display room that he opened to the trade in early 1922. Located above the factory's executive offices, the 50-foot-by-150-foot showroom, appointed with plaster moldings, oak display counters, stained-glass windows, leather chairs, wall tapestries, Oriental carpets, and mulberry-colored velvet draperies, exuded the posh atmosphere of an exclusive men's club. A gilt-framed portrait of Wells hung in a place of honor. Even when visiting buyers in New York City or enjoying some golf on the nearby links, the general manager presided over his fiefdom like a Medici prince, making sure that order presided. In effect, Wells had sized up the desires of Eurocentric crockery men, creating an environment that fulfilled their expectations. Impressed, the *Pottery, Glass, and Brass Salesman* devoted a feature to the display room, comparing it to a smaller version at Lenox China in Trenton. The Renaissance-style showroom testified to Wells's marketing abilities, which would meet new challenges during the final decade of his career.[55]

Any Color, as Long as It's Yellow

During the 1920s, the tremendous growth of chain stores dealing in groceries, drugs, clothing, and 5-and-10-cent merchandise encouraged observers to nickname the decade the chain store age. The unbridled expansion of grocers such as A&P and First National, which together operated more than 18,000 stores by 1930, most often drew criticism from the champions of rugged individualism, community spirit, and entrepreneurial capitalism. More pertinent to this story were five-and-tens, which expanded in number and continued to sell the goods that consumers needed to construct personal identity and convert empty living spaces into homes. The number of Woolworth stores alone increased by more than 50 percent, from 1,111 to 1,881; sales more than doubled, from $141 million to $289 million. At this gargantuan chain, shoppers found costume jewelry, cosmetics, and perfume for bodily adornment; little trinkets to give friends and loved ones on special occasions; and bric-a-brac like pottery, glass, doilies, and plastic ornaments that enlivened china cabinets, dresser tops, and kitchen tables. Among the many affordable products for home and family, Woolworth dishes with pretty floral decals mattered immeasurably to consumers making statements about self, ethnicity, and class.[56]

By 1923, sales from Homer Laughlin to Woolworth had rebounded from their wartime slump and accounted for 33 percent of the pottery's business.

Newberry's position in this revived relationship allowed him to wield more power than ever before, and he used it without hesitation. "The only thing that will help us out," he apprised Wells in May 1923, "is more merchandise." To be sure, Newberry's chant for "more" echoed the words of Case, who had begged Wells for "good goods and plenty of them" many years before; yet the context of accelerated competition among five-and-tens set Newberry's command apart from his predecessor's appeal. Although Woolworth dwarfed other limited-price variety stores like the Detroit-based S. S. Kresge & Company, these other chains gained market shares in particular regions of the country. For example, west of the Mississippi River, Woolworth stores lost crockery sales to Kresge, which had purchased Michigan's Mount Clemens Pottery Company in 1920. Mount Clemens's unbelievably cheap dishes came out of tunnel kilns, continuous-flow ovens that enhanced volume to levels previously unimaginable. As Newberry implored Wells to "find a way to give us an increased output which will put our stores in shape to meet the full demand," he suspected that Kresge's managers had discovered something good. He wanted Homer Laughlin to jump on this technological bandwagon, no matter what feats it entailed. Unknown to Newberry, the pottery's board of directors had already authorized the construction of a new facility, Plant No. 6, equipped with tunnel kilns. For Wells, second-guessing powerful buyers had long been part and parcel of doing business in the mass market.[57]

Next, Newberry broached design matters and addressed again the prewar subject of the "prestige" factor. Hoping to make his department into the five-and-ten's greatest attraction, the crockery man envisioned up-to-date dish sections filled with stylish lines that window dressers would choose for enticing, electrically illuminated displays. Planning for spring 1926 sales, Newberry in late 1925 asked Wells to replace two older patterns, dating from 1917 and 1922, with an entirely new decoration "appropriate for our business." This coincided with Wells's designs for giving the Homer Laughlin repertoire a face-lift. Anticipating a line with wallop, Wells authorized laboratory experiments on colored clays and glazes, which laid the groundwork for Woolworth's best-selling crockery line of the 1920s: Yellowstone dinnerware.[58]

The impetus for the venture into colored ceramics came from two sources: consumers and competition. Before the Great War, the quintessential Woolworth shopper had been a "woman with a shawl," who browsed through five-and-tens for inexpensive chinaware for her room or tenement kitchen. During the 1920s, the dime store's crockery departments bustled with middle-class

A Woolworth show window at night. From *Chain Store Age*, September 1926, Baker Library, Harvard University

consumers looking for dining accessories. Several factors accounted for the infiltration of middlebrow taste. The expansion of factory and office jobs for working-class women and nativist intolerance of Southern and Eastern Europeans contributed to perceptions of a servant shortage. Concurrently, Prohibition affected cooking, dining, and drinking practices. In many upper- and middle-class households, the unavailability of both alcohol and suitable servants circumscribed menus and made impossible the preparation of French dishes requiring wine, sherry, or other liquor. Urbanization and the growth in apartment living confronted women with limited cabinet space for hundred-piece dinner services, including precious heirlooms. Without good domestic help, the right ingredients, and enough storage space, homemakers reevaluated consumption habits inherited from their grandmothers, reconfiguring their visions of the ideal meal and the perfect dining ensemble. Informal dining and easy eating came into vogue; and middle-class women learned to appreciate Woolworth's open-stock crockery department, which provided fashionable, carefree table settings with little investment of time and money. Like previous generations of Woolworth shoppers, middlebrows could buy dishes one by one, picking and choosing the number of plates, bowls, and serving items they needed at a fraction of department store prices.[59]

Wells also scrutinized his competitors, paying special attention to his longtime rival, the Sebring Pottery Company. Modifying their scheme-ware expertise to suit the consumer boom, the Sebrings honed in on credit sales during the early 1920s. The "chronically dead broke" family in need of new dishes suddenly had a slightly larger array of options: buy Homer Laughlin ware piece by piece at Woolworth or get a Sebring dinner set as a premium, a trade-in, or an installment purchase. Furthermore, in 1923, Charles Leigh Sebring took advantage of his firm's wartime ball-clay experiments, introducing creamy clay bodies and glazes that softened the appearance of bright decal patterns. Consumers relished this warm look, especially on the Barbara Jean shape, introduced in 1923 and copied by rivals "almost line for line." Sebring's yellow palette resonated with scheme-ware customers, who appreciated the way golden dishes harmonized with different woods, fabrics, and paints. The Golden Maize line reached a wide audience through grocery stores, which used it as a premium to stimulate sales of Chef Coffee. The Royal Ivory porcelain line found ready customers among retailers like Atlanta's Myers-Miller Furniture Company, which devised trade-in deals similar to General Motors' strategy that encouraged car owners to move up. Shoppers at Myers-Miller turned in their "old, cracked, faded, out-of-date dinnerware" and received a $5 discount on a Royal Ivory set costing $39.95. Aware of Sebring's success with yellow dishes, Wells pressed his laboratory to speed up its experiments on colored clays and glazes. Other East Liverpool potters also scrambled to design yellows that would "knock your eyes out." Giving a ceramics twist to Henry Ford's famous phrase, East Liverpool potters joked that any color, "as long as it is yellow," would sell.[60]

As Homer Laughlin's chemist experimented in the fall of 1925, Wells and Newberry jointly conceptualized the aesthetic details of Woolworth's Yellowstone line. At a moment when market researchers started to quantify purchasing patterns for other home furnishings manufacturers, these men still drew on personal experience to profile the potential consumer for the new line. Again and again, Wells and Newberry debated the intricacies of color, shape, decoration, quality, utility, and price. In daily letters, they speculated about possible audience reactions to tiny changes, from the angles of the octagonal edge to the positioning of decal decorations. These two collaborators fully understood, expected, and appreciated the uncertainties inherent in product design and development for the mass market.[61]

Wells and Newberry took their initial hints on household taste from store managers and pottery competitors, but they needed better data to fuel the product's takeoff, turning to experts inside and outside the developmental firms. During Yellowstone's genesis, data never flowed smoothly and steadily along a well-maintained path between Woolworth's headquarters and Homer Laughlin's front office. Instead, it trickled, gurgled, sputtered, and bubbled through the two companies in all directions. Both Wells and Newberry had nurtured private coteries of taste trustees, and each routinely solicited these fashion intermediaries' opinions on shapes, decorations, colors, and other variables. Newberry's decorative darlings still included local managers, who enthusiastically responded to Yellowstone prototypes, invariably hazarding that the new product would "stimulate . . . business." Crockery buyers from other stores who saw samples in Newberry's office also sang Yellowstone's praises, predicting a "strong drift" toward the line among Woolworth's consumers in 1926.[62]

By the mid-1920s, Gaertner functioned as Homer Laughlin's proxy art director, and Wells tapped the information banks of his favorite fashion intermediary for the Yellowstone project. The decal man collaborated on the decorations, and he provided samples of English pottery as models for the octagonal shape. Most important, Gaertner networked in New York's home furnishings trade on behalf of Wells and Newberry, seeking counsel on domestic decorating trends from big-city merchants like Ovington Brothers, a large china and glass importer. At the Ovington warehouse, he solicited the opinions of one MacIntosh, perhaps "the best-posted buyer of high-grade china and earthenware in the world." MacIntosh confirmed Wells's suspicions that few American consumers cared for bright, bold, modernist designs—for "jazz in color."[63]

Yellowstone emerged as a conservative product well suited to the tastes of Woolworth's customers. The line was modernistic, rather than modern. Its color was offbeat, not startling. Its shape was different, not shocking. In short, Yellowstone took possession of the stylistic middle ground acceptable to the dime store's broadening spectrum of shoppers. The new product added a tad of distinction to Woolworth's crockery department yet provided Homer Laughlin with real reductions in manufacturing costs. The color disguised the slight imperfections that could earmark white goods as off-quality; a large percentage of Yellowstone production, hence, was best-of-kiln and sold at first-quality prices.[64]

In early 1926, Newberry held a preliminary sale of decorated Yellowstone ware at Store No. 1000, Woolworth's flagship, which sat in the heart of Manhattan's fashionable shopping district at Fifth Avenue and Fortieth Street, across from the New York Public Library. The store attracted consumers from all backgrounds, who made it into one of the most prosperous five-and-tens in the coun-

try. One Miss Williams from the J. Walter Thompson advertising agency summarized it all: "Woolworth's is Coney Island on Fifth Avenue." Noisy, crowded, and "smaller than any other stores in town," the midtown Woolworth attracted bargain-hunting women from Park Avenue and Tenth Avenue who "consider a trip to the 10 cent store good fun." Upper-class owners of Pierce Arrows and Cadillacs who visited this "Woolies" bought low-priced dishes for "country places and everyday use." From the perspective of Newberry, there was no better venue than Store No. 1000 for market testing a new product. He reported to Wells that the first decal design was a "big hit," the next "was better," and the third proved to be *"the pattern."* "People bought everything," Newberry exclaimed. "Every customer who came in wanted . . . to make up a dinner set." Like other successful dime store lines, Yellowstone stimulated shoppers' senses and encouraged impulse buying; in short, this ware sold itself. Anticipating immense orders, Wells converted his new tunnel kiln facility, Plant No. 6, to Yellowstone production. If reading consumers as they shopped was good enough for Newberry at Woolworth, it certainly was good enough for Wells and Homer Laughlin.[65]

Wells spent most of his career encouraging shawl women to participate in American consumer culture, and he did this by producing household accessories that retailers gave away or sold cheaply. Rather than packaging respectability with the idea of uplifting tastes, Wells and like-minded managers such as Frank A. Sebring modified middle-class aesthetics to suit working people's needs. However, they soon discovered that premium and dime store dishes had enormous appeal among other groups. Victorian dining customs trickled downward; informal eating habits, upward. The same was true for styles. By the interwar years, the shopper who carried a "Woolworth's pocketbook" was recognized for her "Tiffany tastes," and vice versa. Potteries in the East Liverpool district, and their cohorts in mass retailing, facilitated the exchange between middlebrow and lowbrow culture.[66]

Creating tableware that attracted, delighted, and satisfied mass-market shoppers entailed the refinement of the design and development practices inherited from Staffordshire potteries. By the twentieth century, many English practical men seemed out of touch with American tastes, which ranged across a broad spectrum. As producers searched for ways to communicate with shoppers, they brought new fashion intermediaries into the fold. This transformation is indicative of the growing complexity of the production and distribution system, wherein cutting-edge batch producers vied for profitable orders from expanding retailers. In this competition, volume mattered, but the right looks mattered too. To get tastes in focus, pottery managers came to depend on crockery men, whose success in "buying right" hinged on knowing the customers.[67]

By the late 1920s, the pottery and glass industries entered a new phase in design and development. Crockery buyers continued to loom large in aesthetic interpretation, but smart pottery managers recognized they needed an edge. Yellowstone's reception demonstrated that Woolworth stores could attract customers from all walks of life and that doing so was profitable. Indeed, as the five-and-ten reached up the social ladder, it redefined "the masses" to include the middle class. Back at the factory, Wells came to believe that it would be ever more difficult to find design solutions within the existing decalcomania framework. Ultimately, pressures from mass merchandisers forced Homer Laughlin to make dramatic changes to its design practice.

CHAPTER 4

Fiesta!

THE FOUR HUNDRED CROCKERY BUYERS attending the 1936 midwinter show of the Associated Glass & Pottery Manufacturers in Pittsburgh swarmed around the exhibits of the Homer Laughlin China Company, attracted by colorful pottery shown against a backdrop of a Spanish flamenco dancer. Among the hundred factory displays, the talk of the show was Fiesta tableware, a department store line that came in bright monochromatic colors: orange-red, deep blue, cucumber green, egg yolk yellow, and rich vellum. Buyers from all retailing sectors—five-and-tens, mail-order houses, department stores, and premium vendors—commented to factory salesmen J. Donald Thompson and George B. Fowler on how well Fiesta captured the mood of Depression Era America. The line's round shapes exuded a wholesome feeling; its signature molding—concentric circles—seemed futuristic yet quaint; its imaginative mix-and-match colors suggested sunshine, merriment, and brighter days to come. Crockery men agreed that Fiesta's tempered modernism would strike a chord with shoppers yearning for inexpensive foils to austerity. The hoopla surrounding Fiesta's debut attested to consequential changes in design practice at the world's largest pottery.[1]

Traditionally, when pottery managers created new lines, they looked to an amalgam of experts—to salesmen, chief decorators, modelers, crockery buyers, and decal suppliers—for help in imagining consumers. Homer Laughlin's Yellowstone tableware epitomized this design method. The tremendous success of

Fiesta! A Depression Era sensation. Window display unit, 1936, Homer Laughlin China Company

Yellowstone convinced general manager W. Edwin Wells to look beyond tried-and-true design methods, leading him to establish an in-house art department. Since his 1927 arrival, art director Frederick Hurten Rhead, the man responsible for Fiesta's development, had worked diligently with crockery buyers to update Homer Laughlin's mass-market offerings. At the 1936 show, Rhead chatted with inquisitive buyers, waxing eloquently about Fiesta and his other designs, including Oven Serve, a versatile refrigerator-to-oven line, and experimental silk screen decorations of plaids, wreaths, and polka dots. Fiesta's reception was the crowning achievement of his career and symbolized Homer Laughlin's commitment to stylistic innovation in a time of social and economic crisis.[2]

Rhead's hiring and the creation of Fiesta tableware coincided with major shakeups at Homer Laughlin, in the pottery industry, and in the economy. During the interwar years, Wells and Joseph M. Wells, his son and successor as general manager, initiated an expansion and renovation program designed to strengthen Homer Laughlin's alliances with mass merchandisers and to safeguard its reputation as potters to "Her Majesty—The American Housewife." The boom-and-bust economy of the 1920s and 1930s rattled the United States Potters' Association (USPA), destroying many less-efficient potteries. The "giant among dishes" survived by virtue of its size—and a product-diversification strategy that aimed to produce tableware for every pocketbook. In tough times, Homer Laughlin looked upmarket for customers, creating Fiesta in an effort to penetrate the department store trade when F. W. Woolworth and Company, Quaker Oats Company (the successor to the American Cereal Company), and other volume distributors reduced their low-end crockery purchases.[3]

As the 1920s came to a close, Homer Laughlin hovered on the fringes of the whirlwind stylistic revolution known as modernism, an outgrowth of and response to industrialization and urbanization. Modernists grappled with rapid technological advances, including Fordist mass production, by simultaneously celebrating and critiquing the past, present, and future. Rhead designed products that aimed to put consumers at ease with a world full of uncertainties. Fiesta incarnated this approach. Rhead's tactics put him at odds with consultant industrial designers like Walter Dorwin Teague, who aimed to uplift taste and to precipitate social change with the tool of styling. Rhead saw himself not as a tastemaker but as an expert in technical processes and an experienced fashion intermediary. While consultants tried to impose their tastes on clients and consumers, Rhead, as in-house art director, studied women's preferences, listened to crockery buyers, and designed products accordingly. This fundamental difference helps explain the commercial success of Fiesta and the poor reception of streamlining, the consultants' cure-all for Depression Era woes.

Adjusting to the New Tempo

As the "new American tempo" rapidly transformed consumer society during the late 1920s, factories making everything from automobiles to clothing and furnishings scurried to increase output, lower prices, and hasten the pace of design and innovation. The best-known instance of this phenomenon occurred at General Motors, which wrested leadership in the automobile industry away from the Ford Motor Company by engaging the cogs of flexible mass production and consumer-conscious design to make a range of colorful, stylish cars for "every purse and purpose." In the dry goods trade, hosiery mills hired stylists to upgrade the look of women's silk stockings; in home furnishings, glass factories devised new methods for intercepting the moth of style before it metamorphosed into a new, fashionable butterfly. William A. B. Dalzell, manager at the Fostoria Glass Company in Moundsville, West Virginia, led the way by establishing an art department, which promptly broke away from the tired look of imitation cut glass and introduced a new line of pastel tableware that gave Fostoria high visibility in the department store business. With characteristic deliberation, W. Edwin Wells slowly but surely joined the ranks of managers who acknowledged that design fever might be harnessed for corporate gain. In his eyes, design might fit into Homer Laughlin's strategy given the right art director and the right complement of manufacturing facilities.[4]

During the 1920s, several factors—rising energy costs, high union wages, railroad shipping boycotts, a flood of cheap Japanese imports, and shifting demand—eroded the prosperity that the Great War had brought to many United States potteries. Declining demand forced many companies to shut their doors. Between 1922 and 1929, the average household spent 6.8 percent of its annual budget on china and glassware, expenditures that paled next to those for the previous era, 1898–1916, when consumers spent 13 percent of their incomes on tableware. "Nearly every dollar of the average family income is spent before it is earned," Wells told USPA members, nervous about their future. "It is mortgaged against installment purchases." With the exception of chain stores, installment houses, and scheme-ware users, retailers ordered less and less pottery every year. By the end of the decade, Homer Laughlin was a juggernaut in an otherwise declining industry, controlling one-third of the output among the USPA's forty firms. In 1927, the pottery's daily output of Yellowstone dinnerware, made for Woolworth, could form a ten-mile line, "stretching from the Battery in New York to the Harlem River and three miles beyond." Never before had the firm experienced such a volume of orders. Yet these developments did not free Homer Laughlin from a long-standing commitment to flexible production, fashion, and style. To ignore these matters at a moment when women shoppers clamored for smart goods would have been foolhardy.[5]

When Paul Nystrom published *Retail Selling and Store Management* in 1925, he lent his authority as a retailing guru to an idea that had been folk wisdom among American potters for decades; women made the vast majority of household purchases, some 80 percent. The prosperity decade saw the culmination of the long trend in the feminization of shopping. Although couples shared decisions about credit purchases of pricey durable goods such as living room suites, bathroom fixtures, and kitchen appliances, women carried out most cash-and-carry transactions. In the 1920s, they shopped more—and they did so with heightened expectations in terms of style, novelty, and quality. "The housewife," wrote Wells in 1923, "is insisting on more and better dishes than she thought she needed or could afford in the old days." Women voted for their favorite styles by buying certain goods and letting others sit on store shelves. For retailers, the message was clear: Women wanted up-to-date pottery to match other smart household accessories.[6]

Never before had the twins of fashion and style mattered so much to Homer Laughlin's profits. As Wells coddled important buyers in his plush Renaissance Revival showroom, he grew weary of the badgering of crockery men, for even those who procured the most ordinary pottery bid him to give more for their dollars. In 1926, when Quaker Oats reinstated the practice of providing cereal eaters with pottery premiums, buyer William A. O'Grady knocked on Wells's door with big orders—and requests for customized patterns. Similarly, when R. H. Richards at Kirkman & Son in Brooklyn coordinated the soap manufacturer's reentry into giveaways after a seven-year hiatus, he demanded "excellent" patented designs that "must not be furnished to anybody but to his firm." The fastidious Charles Newberry and a Mr. Evans, respectively the president and china buyer at J. J. Newberry Company, a five-and-ten, wanted "gaudy, elaborate decorative tableware." Powerful, persnickety, and opinionated, some twenty big-time buyers consumed about 80 percent of Homer Laughlin's output, flaunting their bulging billfolds to intimidate Wells into jumping on the stylistic treadmill.[7]

Initially, Wells called on his faithful colleague in decorative affairs, the decal man Rudolph Gaertner, to help actualize buyers' wishes with chromolithographic embellishments. However, by the mid-to-late 1920s, the decalcomania business buckled under potters' demands, lithographers' wages, government duties, and foreign printers' delays. After his foremost competitor, Meyercord Company, withdrew from the ceramics business in 1920, Gaertner had borrowed money from Homer Laughlin to expand his Mount Vernon print works, envisioning a bright future for American decal manufacturers. Although his factory made a "cheaper grade of patterns," Gaertner still imported high-grade decals, relying on English and German factories for his best designs. In ill health, Gaertner became impatient with buyers, whether Newberry or O'Grady, who pressed for evermore fashionable decorations for less and less money. Yet probably better than anyone in American pottery trade, Gaertner, the surrogate art director to the East Liverpool potteries, comprehended the commercial value of art. When Wells sizzled over buyers' entreaties, the decal man calmly proposed a simple solution: hire a designer.[8]

If memories of Arthur Mountford prejudiced him against art directors, Wells only needed to look at his firm's great rival, Sebring Pottery Company, to see how a factory design division might augment sales in modern times. Sebring retained its advantage in the scheme-ware business during the 1920s by investing in a ceramics laboratory, tunnel kiln technology, and an art department, whose staff created the warm Royal Ivory porcelain and Golden Maize line that took the pottery trade by storm in 1923 and 1925. The Sebring family never let moss grow underfoot. Learning through trade gossip about Kirkman's plans to reorder pottery premiums in 1925, managers at the Sebrings' Limoges China Company rushed two sweet-talking salesmen to Brooklyn, where they barraged Richards with seductive samples and promising prices. Without Gaertner's intercession, Limoges might have expropriated Kirkman's orders from Homer Laughlin. By 1927, the Sebrings assumed a defensive posture when other East Liverpool firms, including Homer Laughlin, started to imitate the successful Golden Glow, Golden Maize, and Antique Ivory wares they had created for installment-purchase houses. The artistic Charles Leigh Sebring fixed his gaze on the growing department store trade and, in the summer of 1927, inaugurated a developmental project on Umbertone, a tinted clay body the color of café au lait. News of this venture quickly spread among pottery managers, who chatted daily on the links of the East Liverpool Country Club or over lunch at Flemington's tavern adjacent to the Travelers' Hotel.[9]

Ever watchful, Wells made one of his last major decisions before his retirement. If flashy "Charlie" Sebring could capitalize on the design craze to create lines that would turn shoppers' heads, so too might Wells engage the mechanisms of fashion to please exasperating buyers and to offer more variety to Woolworth and other five-and-tens. Gaertner, determined that his favorite and his largest customer not be outdone by Charlie Sebring, arranged for Wells to meet Frederick Hurten Rhead, research director at American Encaustic Tiling Company (AETCO) in Zanesville, Ohio. Gaertner, who had collaborated with Rhead on decals since 1924, realized that this practical Staffordshire man, who loved consumer products, felt isolated and otherwise dissatisfied in the tile business. He also knew that Rhead had admired Wells since 1902, when, as art director for a Wheeling firm, he heard managers identify Homer Laughlin's executive as "the coming man in the pottery field." While the details of their meeting are unknown, Wells found Rhead had the right qualifications to direct his new art department. (Besides Sebring's activity, precedents existed for in-house design facilities. For decades, the USPA's Art & Design Committee encouraged close cooperation between pottery managers, designers, modelers, and decorators; by 1924, every East Liverpool pottery had its own modeling shop, the first step toward internalizing the design process.) In August 1927, Wells rolled out the red carpet from Newell to Zanesville, luring Rhead to the East Liverpool district with promises of a juicy salary, a dedicated staff, and spacious workrooms. The gigantic Homer Laughlin appeared to be the ideal proving ground for his theories about product design and consumer markets. When news of Rhead's hiring reached the Woolworth Building, crockery man William F. Newberry, pleased as punch, immediately congratulated Wells on his "splendid move."[10]

Ceramic Art Engineering

> There is more than one personal taste.
> —Frederick Hurten Rhead, 1931

Rhead's fifteen-year career at Homer Laughlin (1927–42) coincided with the formative years of the industrial design profession in New York, but as a factory art director working in the manufacturing heartland, Rhead saw himself in opposition to slick "art evangelists," such as Teague, Raymond Loewy, and the younger Russel Wright. These consultants attempted to create a public image of the designer as tastemaker, and they hoped to stimulate demand for their services primarily among appliance manufacturers, from General Electric to General Motors, that is, among companies that could afford their high fees. Rhead also appreciated the importance of styling, but he comprehended it in a different way. Whereas consultants sought to create a distinctive American style that would improve public taste and alleviate the country's economic ills, Rhead believed that no catholic fashion would succeed in a pluralistic society like the United States. In his eyes, streamlining, the favorite style mode of design consultants, was far too monolithic, technocratic, and utopian for American consumers. Women who shopped at Woolworth in Fall River, Massachusetts, or who bought dishes on the installment plan from the Columbus Furniture Stores in Montana would never fall for it. Overall, Rhead was more attuned to the heterogeneity of American popular culture and more constrained by it, in his factory job, than his heralded rivals.[11]

Rhead so opposed New York consultants that he renounced their label, *industrial designer*. Instead, he described himself most often as "an experienced practical potter and executive." As such, Rhead claimed allegiance with the interwar era's conservative applied arts establishment, whose outspoken proponent was John Cotton Dana, director of New Jersey's Newark Museum from its founding in 1908 until his death in 1929. In contrast to the high-profile industrial design movement, whose practitioners aimed to build clients primarily among quantity production firms, the applied or industrial arts tradition consisted of an atomized network of older, flexible batch production industries, manufacturers' associations, trade journals, museums, and design schools. As the "apostle of the applied arts," Dana tried to make sense of this fragmentation, using the curator's medium, the museum exhibition, to endow industrial arts with cultural legitimacy. Through shows like Beauty Has No Relation to Price, which featured Yellowstone tableware and other dime store merchandise, Dana hoped to teach museum visitors to discern and appreciate beauty in everyday things. From these object lessons, workers and consumers, respectively, might learn to make and to select home furnishings that were up to date and well designed.[12]

Gaining celebrity for his epigram, "An industrialist is an artist," Dana defined himself in opposition to Richard F. Bach, founding director of the industrial arts division of the Metropolitan Museum of Art, whom he berated as an elitist, a historicist, and a romantic proponent of handicraft. Beginning in 1917, Bach mounted a series of industrial arts exhibitions of contemporary objects with antecedents in the Met's historical collections. Without question, Bach had aesthetic uplift in mind when he encouraged the nation's textile, wallpaper, furniture, pottery, and glass industries to take inspiration from objects in the Met's holdings. Since consumers revered period styles like English Colonial, Dutch Colonial, Spanish Mission, Chippendale, and Sheraton, Bach contended, why should contemporary manufacturers not look to the best examples of these styles? To practical men who designed products for industry, ideological differences between Dana and Bach mattered less than their shared advocacy of the industrial arts tradition. As befitted their needs, practical men picked up either man's gauntlet to carve out lucrative careers as guiding lights to batch manufacturers. In ceramics, Rhead was an aesthetic superstar who provided Wells with understandable, attainable solutions to the pressing problem of styling for a buyer's market.[13]

Indeed, the industrial arts tradition ran through Rhead's veins, and he continually emphasized this when dealing with those conservative pottery managers who viewed artists and designers as irresponsible, temperamental idealists. Rhead heralded from a prominent family of Staffordshire artisans, whose members served as chief decorators and art directors in major English potteries. While still an art and design student at Stoke-on-Trent, the youthful Rhead accompanied his father to Brownfield's Guild Pottery, where he learned to design new shapes and decorations in his parent's office. He met the region's most experienced art directors and accepted invitations to observe design and development practices at their factories. By age nineteen, Rhead taught his own courses in an industrial arts school and directed the art department at Wardle Art Pottery, a small firm specializing in colorful art wares. Believing he had reached "the top of the tree" in the English potteries, at age twenty-two Rhead immigrated in 1902 to the United States, where he readily secured a series of positions in firms seeking knowledgeable practical men. Of Rhead's subsequent ten jobs, two positions—his art directorship at Roseville Pottery Company and his research directorship at AETCO—most influenced his Homer Laughlin career. Working at these Zanesville firms, Rhead discerned how American potteries might tap the tremendous potential of the burgeoning mass market.[14]

From 1904 to 1908, Rhead collaborated with the Roseville plant superintendent John J. Herold, who streamlined the production of art pottery based on his understanding of the emerging ideas of the efficiency engineer Frederick Winslow Taylor. At a moment when most pottery managers still guessed at shop floor expenditures, Herold, a German-born decorator-turned-manager, scrutinized workers' actions, closely calculated costs, and replaced rule-of-thumb methods with techniques that promised to augment output, reduce waste, and improve product quality. Just as the stopwatch signified Taylorist practice, a powerful pocket magnifying glass symbolized Herold's predilection for detection, surveillance, and analysis. Nicknamed the "quarrelsome Dutchman" by irritated workers, Herold extended his rationalization project to Roseville's design department, enlisting the newly hired art director in his drive for efficiency. After methodically studying consumers' tastes, Rhead and Herold revamped Roseville's lines, junking obsolete jardinieres covered with runny red and green glazes reminiscent of "gangrene" in favor of up-to-date art ware with mellifluous names such as Della Robbia and Olympic. Rhead considered Herold to be a model practical man; and he carefully watched the energetic entrepreneur use whatever means were available (product design, brand name marketing, and national advertising) to elevate Roseville's products in consumers' eyes. Leaving Ohio to lecture, teach, and work in small art ware factories in New York, Missouri, and California, Rhead found that potteries could operate as modern industrial enterprises rather than as haphazard craft shops. A slew of unsuccessful ventures, including the failure of his own Santa Barbara pottery, dampened Rhead's spirit, but a job offer from the world's largest tile works—a promising position as a designer of sanitary fixtures, terra cotta, and decorative tiles at AETCO—rekindled his enthusiasm.[15]

In 1917, the fashion for colorful building materials known as architectural faience burgeoned, and AETCO's managers hoped to exploit this market by hiring an expert designer and colorist to direct their research department. At AETCO for ten years, Rhead sharpened his chromatic skills under the tutelage of Léon Victor Solon, a Staffordshire man who ran the company's New York showroom and worked with architects on tiled interiors. (As the nation's foremost architectural colorist, Solon eventually designed the color scheme for the Rockefeller Center.) At the tile works, Rhead devoted much of his time to developing new clay bodies, colored glazes, and product lines but soon became disillusioned because AETCO managers clung to "archaic" business methods and manufacturing technologies. By 1923, Rhead felt "too much alone" and longed for a job in a progressive clay-working plant with managers sympathetic to "the many commercial possibilities open to this . . . undeveloped industry."[16]

During the 1920s, Rhead assumed a series of leadership positions in the newly formed art and design division of the American Ceramic Society (ACERS), and he used this professional organization, dedicated to the technical advancement of the ceramics and glass industries, as a platform for promoting his theories—and his career. Rhead mocked the dusty developmental practices that dominated the American ceramics industry, painting an unflattering portrait of factory personnel and plant managers. He condemned "czarist" factory engineers; castigated chief decorators with a "talent for art" but little market awareness beyond the best-sellers they copied; and mocked sales managers, covered with "patina," who could not fathom the unpopularity of "standard lines of ten or fifteen years ago" and blamed sluggish sales on the poor judgment of crockery buyers. As a curative for stylistic inertia and poor sales, Rhead urged manufacturers to establish in-house departments for "decorative ceramics research." In these factory divisions, art directors versed in production methods, design techniques, housewares trends, and consumer taste might collaborate with scientists and technologists, respectively skilled in "materials, mixtures, and process control" and "plant design and equipment," to create goods in fulfillment of "any market requirement." In 1927, Rhead described the art director's responsibilities under the rubric "ceramic art engineering"; in doing so, he equated design expression, bridled by formal rules of perspective and theories of color coordination, with the contingent process of invention, the engineer's domain. During the golden age of engineering, this choice of words marked Rhead as a cutting-edge theorist, who sought to apply an engineering viewpoint to the problem of designing consumer products. A few years later, New York advertising impresario Earnest Elmo Calkins coined the phrase "consumer engineering" to describe his agency's approach to stimulating demand during the Great Depression. Calkins saw consumer engineering as a "new business tool" for "shaping a product to fit more exactly consumers' needs or tastes" in order to "keep pace with rapidly changing habits and ways of living." Its major objective: "to learn what people want and adapt the goods to these wants." By similarly proposing to rationalize the slippery job of design and development, Rhead sought to galvanize managers of leading firms in the hope of achieving his ambition for an art directorship in a pottery devoted to "large-scale production."[17]

At first glance, Rhead's proposition for bridging the realms of "ceramic art" and "engineering" seemed like the musings of a transplanted English dreamer versed in the antimodernist ideology of the Arts and Crafts movement. This sentimental veneer hid the makings of a corporate expert cognizant of new quantity-production methods and modern management practices that had gained footholds in big businesses like steel and autos. Without hesitation, Rhead exploited his English charm and erudition, for these assets softened his invective among conservative American pottery managers, who still esteemed Staffordshire traditions as the apex of the potter's art. In reality, Rhead idolized British potteries less than many American managers, for his youth in the Five Towns left him with indelible memories of secret glaze recipes, impenetrable craft hierarchies, a repressive family wage system, and devastating trade depressions. Exposure to both sides of the Anglo-American potting trade, combined with his observations of United States industry in general, led Rhead to theorize that the future of potteries reliant on changing tastes and on volume distribution rested in a fusion of American and British manufacturing methods. Rhead's theories dovetailed with the massive modernization at Homer Laughlin, wherein Wells grafted quantity-production practices in the form of tunnel kilns onto a time-honored batch production setup.[18]

As an expert in ornament, shape, and color, Rhead filled his office at Homer Laughlin with the tools of his trade, including art books, historical artifacts, and extensive files on American, English, and European factories. From Herold, Rhead learned to keep meticulous records, recording daily accomplishments in a desk dairy. Yet the business of determining what Homer Laughlin's customers wanted depended on more than competent draftsmanship, potting know-how, good librarianship, and curatorial skills. It required studying women as they selected, purchased, and used objects, making sense out of the evidence drawn from these observations, and, ultimately, applying that information to new generations of products. Whether buying a wedding gift for a bride, dining at a friend's home, or browsing through the china and glass displays of department stores in Pittsburgh, Cleveland, and New York City, Rhead perpetually contemplated consumers in action. At a moment when most pottery manufacturers still viewed the consumer as "an uncertain quantity," Rhead attempted, through these observations, to discern in his "slow and rambling manner" precisely what "various groups really like—and why."[19]

Rhead ventured to develop an understanding of consumer tastes just as social scientists started to categorize people according to income, education, and expenditures for the benefit of industrial capitalism. Building on the tradition of Progressive Era budget experts, sociologists Robert Lynd and Alice C. Hanson classified population segments by purchases of goods such as food, clothing, and appliances for their contribution to *Recent Social Trends in the United States*. In Rhead's eyes, such researchers' generic descriptions of furniture, curtains, toasters, and stoves were of little use; managers in style-conscious companies needed to know the type of furniture, the color of the draperies, the brand of the toasters, the age of the stoves, and so forth. "I would like to see a chart showing some approximate classification of the public taste," he wrote, with "some estimated proportion for each distinctive style, with price ranges and potential volume for each group." In essence, Rhead longed for tabulated results from consumer surveys. But only a few large publishers, including the Curtis Publishing Company, and major advertising agencies, such as J. Walter Thompson, had scientific methods for collecting and analyzing survey data. This kind of fact gathering was time-consuming, costly, and available only to large accounts. Lacking access to such capabilities, Rhead saw it as his job to explicate the subtleties of consumers' ceramics choices—delineating preferences for white or ivory clay bodies, for floral or geometrical motifs, and for gilding or lack of gilding—and to make sense of such details on behalf of Homer Laughlin and its retail customers.[20]

Without question, Rhead's foray into market research drew heavily on well-established developmental practices in American potteries and glassworks, for his approach to imagining consumers depended on firsthand observation. Wells, Newberry, and Gaertner comprehended the value of scrutinizing the marketplace, but these men admitted befuddlement when they tried to discern motivation. Rhead avoided the pitfalls of trying to define desire, a task better suited to philosophers than to product designers. Instead, he focused his energies on reading the material world and evaluating what he saw in ways that he believed would be useful to his firm. Trained during his boyhood to look, Rhead believed that he could decipher preference patterns often incomprehensible to contemporaries other than seasoned crockery buyers.[21]

Rhead's youthful experiences shaped his worldview in other ways, for he employed an English model—the template of a hierarchical society with inviolable class boundaries—to interpret what he encountered on the American landscape. In Rhead's mind, consumers used all many objects—houses, automobiles, clothing, pets, and furnishings—as powerful communicators, and they did so to demarcate social class. Tastes varied among America's six major socioeconomic groups—immigrant, working, lower-middle, upper-middle, upper, and elite classes—but preferences within each had the endurance of "religious beliefs." For the most part, the greatest influences on taste included daily social interactions, fashion trends, and "advertising propaganda." Just as ecclesiastical rituals changed slowly from generation to generation, class-based taste preferences evolved sluggishly, and dramatic shifts occurred only occasionally as revolutionary jolts. In this context, beauty often seemed an immutable and monolithic ideal, particularly to tastemakers wearing blinders that obscured their views of all but the pinnacle of the social pyramid. In categorizing consumers, Rhead displayed remarkable tolerance for their tastes. Any loathing, he reserved for the rich. With derision, he described "good old DARs" and "society-page experts" like "Mrs. Van Demon" and "Mrs. Push Rusher II" as status mongers who surrounded themselves with "pedigrees of parents, pups, pots, and pictures," rode around in Pierce Arrows and Cadillacs, and shopped at exclusive china shops for dishes by Wedgwood, Spode, or Minton—all for the sake of flaunting their so-called good taste. In Rhead's eyes, what constituted beauty to one social class often held no appeal to other groups, and the manufacturer that realized this fashion fundamental would come out on top.[22]

Just as important, Rhead's roots in the British class system supplied him with a perspective on American society that prompted a reevaluation of Thorstein Veblen's and Georg Simmel's trickle-down theories. These original deterministic theories held that the eager masses, consciously or not, emulated the lifestyles and consumption habits of elites. Rhead believed that sometimes consumers saw their economic betters as material paragons, but more often, they did not. Those indoctrinated by the educational system to appreciate "boiled-down" art, such as high school graduate "Ethyl Smith" and college graduate "Sarah Hunt," shopped at five-and-tens and department stores searching for dinnerware patterns in "styles and types which they have been told are in good taste." Status emulation figured into these women's lower-middle and middle-class tastes. The more typical dime-store shopper bought Woolworth's dinnerware not because she wanted to copy the mayor's wife but because she found it affordable, practical, and beautiful. "Mrs. Jim Brown," an elevator operator's spouse, selected decal dishes because these inexpensive objects matched the wallpaper and curtains in her three-room apartment. Mrs. Brown took as much pride in her dime-store dinnerware as did "Mrs. Vassar-Yale" in "her best porcelain." Price and prettiness shaped the product expectations of working-class women, for whom making do on small budgets mattered more than making appearances. Each social class possessed a distinctive material vocabulary for self-expression, but women in the upper echelons coveted the lifestyles of the rich and famous to a greater extent than did those who struggled simply to pay their bills.[23]

Rhead was on target vis-à-vis motivation. Wealthy consumers such as Arthur A. Houghton Jr., heir to a glassmaking fortune made in Corning, N.Y., patronized Tiffany & Company's Fifth Avenue store, where he bought costly Minton china. Looking up the ladder, social climbers satisfied their longings with Wedgwood spinoffs; working women, with American pottery. In 1937, Katherine Wicks Perry, a New Jersey bride of a congressional aide living in Washington, D.C., bought on a "pleasure trip" to England a Wedgwood dinner set in the Grosvener pattern, embellished with a hand-tinted Florentine border of griffins, leafy scrolls, and cattle skulls (plate 2). Around the same time, Elizabeth Petrowski, a mill operative working for the American Woolen Company in Lawrence, Massachusetts, purchased from a house-to-house canvasser a yellow dinner set for her twenty-two-year-old daughter's hope chest, selecting a floral decal pattern that suited Nellie's traditional tastes (plate 3). For decades, Perry and Petrowski each cherished their sets—for different reasons. Perry loved her bone china for what it said about her "good taste." During the 1980s, the aged invalid suspiciously eyed a researcher visiting her rest home bedside; by careful voice inflection and word choice, Perry emphasized the elite European origins of her service, using the phrase "my Wedgwood" to impress the inquisitor with her knowledge of beautiful, expensive things. In contrast, Nellie Petrowski never thought twice about who made her East Liverpool dishes. Nonetheless, she for decades displayed the service in a glass-fronted china cabinet built into the kitchen of her four-room flat. Used only for holiday dinners—Thanksgiving, Christmas, New Year, and Easter—the fragile earthenware remained impeccable when Petrowski gave it to her daughter as an heirloom in the mid-1980s. To Petrowski, the dishes were more than eye-catching decorations and special occasion utensils. A divorced mother of three, Elizabeth Petrowski had acquired Nellie's set by pinching pennies, by saving a bit every week from her meager and unpredictable paycheck earned at American Woolen. Bought with "blood money" during the Great Depression, "Babci's dishes," as the yellow dinner service was always called, symbolized a working-class woman's determination to help her daughter participate in American consumer society, against unbelievable odds.[24]

More inclusive in many respects than earlier theories on consumption, Rhead's ideas were influenced by cultural values that marked certain groups as insiders and others as outsiders. While he coined clever Anglo-American names to describe major economic groups, Rhead lumped some people into generic categories, arguing that "colored" folks and "immigrants" shared preferences for "primitive" colors and decorations. These conjectures about the hoi-polloi are unsurprising given Rhead's British roots and the context of the interwar years, when nativism reshaped immigration policy, fed resurgent racism, and more. During these decades, native-born white workers perceived African Americans and immigrants as extreme examples of primitive cultures; Rhead understood this perspective. As he began the slow, complicated process of deciphering taste, Rhead identified Homer Laughlin's customers as members of the larger Anglo-American culture that he and his superiors understood, respected, and targeted as their main clientele.[25]

Rhead survived at the helm of Homer Laughlin's art department by embracing two cardinal principles: first, the consumer was sovereign; second, design was a collaborative process. Above all, he believed that only consumers, rather than self-appointed art reformers, could "tell the manufacturer what to make." Like all historic actors, Rhead lived in the real world, which inevitably constrained him. Since few consumers articulated ideal china preferences—only "exceptional" people asked clerks for products "not seen in the stores"—Rhead had to figure out women's desires in the tried-and-true manner, relying on retail buyers as fashion intermediaries. At the same time, he had to satisfy his bosses, steering clear of decorations that raised the hackles of cost-conscious managers and engineers. Again and again, Rhead explained successful creative development as an "organizational activity" involving a "pooling of ideas," likening his job to that of a movie director, to provide artistic atmosphere, orchestrate decorative action, and smooth ruffled feathers.[26]

The Wave of Modernism

> When we speak of "styling," we have the crux of the whole problem
> of development, a problem which concerns an understanding of
> what we are making now, and why; of what the other fellow is mak-
> ing now, and why; of what we will make next, and why.
> —Frederick Hurten Rhead, 1941

From Wells's perspective, Rhead arrived in the nick of time; the "wave of modernism" sweeping across the home furnishings trade brought economic opportunities. The expensive handcrafted objects displayed at Paris's Exposition Internationale des Arts Décoratifs et Industriels Modernes in 1925 cast a long shadow. One after the other, large urban department stores across America mounted pseudo-Parisian exhibits featuring products with a modern twist, including china and glassware. The American manufacturer fortunate enough to secure orders from one of these high-profile retailers received considerable newspaper and magazine publicity. Through Marshall Field and similar stores, glassware by Fostoria and its major competitor, A. H. Heisey & Company, often appeared in articles and food advertisements in the *Delineator, Good Housekeeping,* and *Better Homes and Gardens.* For a batch production pottery like Homer Laughlin, whose budget, variable output, and modus operandi prohibited investment in national advertising, such gratis exposure, combined with the cachet associated with being displayed in a department store china section, had immeasurable appeal. Wells and Rhead ventured to capitalize on this prestigious and profitable trade.[27]

None of this is to suggest that Wells contemplated letting go of his lucrative business with Woolworth, the great consumer bazaar (figure 1). More than anyone, Homer Laughlin's general manager realized that his bread and butter depended on high-volume, mass-market accounts. In 1927 Wells added a second tunnel kiln facility, Plant No. 7, to his Newell site to sate the appetites of hungry chain stores, scheme users, and mail-order houses, but recent failures in the East Liverpool district alarmed him. To safeguard his firm's future, he sought to broaden and deepen its client base. Confident of Homer Laughlin's standing

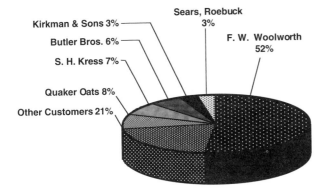

Kirkman & Sons 3%
Butler Bros. 6%
S. H. Kress 7%
Quaker Oats 8%
Other Customers 21%
Sears, Roebuck 3%
F. W. Woolworth 52%

Figure 1. Homer Laughlin China Company, sales to six largest customers as percentage of net sales, 1927. *Source:* Homer Laughlin China Company, Executive Files

with volume distributors like Woolworth, Quaker Oats, and S. H. Kress & Company, Wells looked for greater visibility in upscale markets, to department stores like Cleveland's May Company, St. Louis's Famous-Barr, and New York's R. H. Macy & Company, all of which promised access to consumers willing to pay a little bit more for "something different."[28]

To a veteran potter like Wells, the notion that artifacts played important psychological roles in consumers' lives came as second nature. Furthermore, this cool-headed student of the material world realized that object symbolism was undergoing a fundamental transformation that accounted for underconsumption in the pottery industry. Rightfully, Wells surmised that the success of firms like General Motors, which encouraged Americans to climb the "ladder of consumption" with automobile purchases, adversely affected the home furnishings market. Whereas brides of the cut glass age had taken pleasure from collecting, using, and displaying china and glassware, many women now found dishes less appealing as symbols of prosperity, individuality, and class mobility than major durable goods acquired on credit. The compulsion of monthly or weekly payments reminded people of their financial obligations, making major installment purchases seem precious, for the threat of repossession at default enhanced the feelings of value ascribed to durable goods like radios, refrigerators, and cars. To Wells, evidence of this symbolic shift abounded: the eclipse of the china cabinet, the waning demand for hundred-piece dinner services, and skyrocketing sales of inexpensive open-stock lines like Yellowstone. Yet the excitement surrounding department stores' modern European exhibitions, which featured French, Austrian, and Swedish china and glass, also demonstrated that some shoppers still had unrequited longings for the right kind of tableware. Rhead concurred that college-educated "Lucy Rhodes" and "Sarah Hunt" frequented department store nooks in search of "anything except something in crass taste" and high school graduates "Ethyl Smith" and "May Brookes" trailed close behind, rejecting "old-fashioned" decorations in favor of "styles and types which they have been told are in good taste." With Rhead's advice, Wells planned to use styling as a tool for satisfying the unfulfilled yearnings of these middle-class department store shoppers.[29]

Wells pursued the Macy account beginning in 1928, believing himself well equipped for department store negotiations. He soon became rattled by the personnel—the ever finicky buyers and their self-possessed stylist helpmates—that staffed this consumption palace. Since the war, Macy's had built a reputation as a fashion leader, employing college-trained stylists "to study new desires" and help factories create merchandise in "good taste." The gigantic store served more than sixty thousand customers daily during holidays and boasted some 150 selling departments, including a whole floor devoted to china, glass, and other household accessories. As usual, Gaertner facilitated communication between manufacturer and retailer, working closely with Macy's china buyer, a Mr. Olsen, and the store stylist Ford Tarpley, on a forty-one-piece set ornamented with decals of great bridges, including Brooklyn's. But when a committee of Macy's "stylists and art experts," Tarpley included, rejected the proposed design—"turned it down flat"—Gaertner was "disgusted with this decision." Since Olsen and the china department's sales staff remained enthusiastic about the pattern, Gaertner refused "to be influenced by the verdict of a few young men and women, who have no commercial experience, but believe they know something about applied art!" With yet a third tunnel kiln factory, Plant No. 8, under construction and Newberry carping as usual, Wells had little time or inclination for stylistic poppycock. Throwing up his hands, Wells turned the Macy project over to the very recently hired Rhead. Whereas Gaertner had balked at the store's muscle flexing, Rhead responded by putting on kid gloves.[30]

The big difference between Gaertner and Rhead lay in their approaches to embellishment, a difference that signaled, among other things, the eclipse of a visual culture dependent on highly refined representations. Gaertner had done much to upgrade the chromolithographic aesthetic, but he remained wedded to Old World conventions—to floral sprays, stylized borders, and realistic landscapes—that had begun to lose ground to simpler fashions. In contrast, Rhead appreciated the look of simple, modernist designs. Nothing exemplified the new mode better than Charlie Sebring's Leigh line, the outgrowth of his Umbertone project. At Sebring Pottery Company, art director Joseph Palin Thorley collab-

Green Wheat dinnerware, Leigh Potters, Alliance, Ohio, 1928–1931. Salem China Company Collection, National Museum of American History, Smithsonian Institution

orated with consultant designer Gale Turnbull and stylist Dorothea O'Hara to design a series of novel shapes, forms, and decorations for Leigh ware. A promotional virtuoso, Charlie Sebring in 1928 opened a showroom at New York's Waldorf Astoria to entertain top buyers at an exclusive preview of Leigh ware, made at his pet pottery, Leigh Potters, in Alliance, Ohio. Macy's men reportedly stopped dead in their tracks upon seeing Turnbull's Green Wheat decal pattern on several Leigh shapes. Gaertner's nemesis, Macy's stylist Ford Tarpley, featured Green Wheat in a china and glass exhibition and spotlighted it in newspaper advertisements. So, when Tarpley rejected the Brooklyn Bridge pattern, he did so with Leigh ware in mind.[31]

Sebring's victory gave substance to Rhead's theories about decorative development and corporate strategy. Notwithstanding his respect for Gaertner, Rhead recognized that the design lexicon of the decalcomania tradition was almost exhausted after thirty years. By engaging the cogs of ceramic art engineering, Sebring had replaced "pretty posies" with some fifty distinctive, fashionable decorations. At the moment when Homer Laughlin earned its livelihood from nickel dishes, Macy's sold Leigh in "short sets" containing eighteen, twenty-four, thirty-two, or forty-eight items for more than seventeen dollars each. The Sebrings' successful strategy had revamped the Victorian hundred-piece dinner service into a smart, up-to-date object of desire and provided one solution to the problem of underconsumption. Rhead so admired the Leigh line and Sebring's boldness that he exalted Green Wheat as the "best modernistic tableware pattern" made in America or Europe.[32]

The appeal of the Green Wheat pattern stemmed from Turnbull's fusion of conservative and avant-garde elements. Middle-class women had responded to extreme art-moderne styling with trepidation. Some felt that ultramodern accessories, like the spotted or zigzagged pottery designed for British manufacturers by Susie Cooper and Clarice Cliff, were ill suited to conventional decorating schemes, while others objected to cups and teapots with "decided angles and sharply contrasting surfaces," finding these objects "difficult to handle comfortably." They wanted products that were different from those of their grandmothers but that fit into "interiors of every sort." Green Wheat filled the bill.[33]

More than any other cultural phenomenon, the evolution of casual dining, or easy eating, accelerated an appreciation of the modern style in table accessories. Factors such as the servant problem, the rise of apartment living, and Prohibition reconfigured cultural expectations of womanly duties, at least for the middle class. Facing shortages of suitable domestic servants, good cooking wines, and spacious pantries, middle-class women rejected the Victorian ritual of formal dining and its accessories, including elaborate cut glassware, specialized silverware, and hundred-piece dinner sets. Although a hallmark of civilization before the war, the Sunday dinner seemed like a "relic of barbarism" during the 1920s. Even the best middle-class housekeepers, who liked "nice things in the house," discarded their buffets and glass-fronted china cabinets as old-fashioned. The home furnishings director of *Better Homes and Gardens*, Christine Holbrook, lent her authority to eating in the kitchen, pantry, and dining nook, declaring that the new mode was here to stay. Although consumers continued to acquire china and glassware, enjoying these artifacts for their symbolic properties, the declining utility of enormous dinner services eroded the tableware market as it had existed for decades.[34]

Meanwhile, a chromatic revolution gripped the home furnishing trade following the introduction of new pigments, lacquers, and dyes by the American chemical industry. Before the Great War, the German chemist Wilhelm Ostwald and the American educator Albert H. Munsell had established competing systems of color theory, which achieved currency among art teachers, commercial artists, and manufacturers. Afterward, prescriptive writers like Matthew Luckiesh, an outspoken lighting engineer who eventually worked as General Electric's colorist, reminded producers that color, with its powerful sway over mood, could be used to sell goods. By the 1920s, experts in manufacturing and merchandising pooled their resources to create chromatic objects in all shapes and sizes; the four-color advertisements introduced by the *Saturday Evening Post* in 1924 constituted a visual watershed in the publishing world. Writing about color and industry in their inaugural issue, *Fortune's* editors declared the Anglo-Saxon at last released from "his chromatic inhibitions" and ready "to outdo the barbarians" in his use of brilliant hues.[35]

In the domestic sphere, color worked wonders, declared *Better Homes and Gardens,* "transforming even the simplest and least expensive interior into almost unbelievable beauty." As the locus of activity, the kitchen quickly became the focal point of the household's chromatic revolution (plate 4). Coal and oil stoves dirtied kitchens and required householders to give their kitchens frequent face-lifts. Paint hid grease and grime. New accessories offered another solution to dinginess. In 1926, New York's leading retail buyers, including those at Macy's, initiated a color-in-the-kitchen movement, stocking housewares departments with bright red, blue, green, and yellow equipment, from sponges and brooms to major appliances. Within months, chromatic fever gripped the entire retail trade, taking the "fairer sex by storm." Shoppers insisted on pots, pans, cutlery, glassware, and pottery that matched their breakfast nook sets. By the decade's end, the colored kitchen craze extended beyond Broadway and Lake Shore Drive to include "Mrs. Housewife" on Main Street. The fastidious Mrs. Shearer, a middle-class consumer in Washington, D.C., found gratification in modernizing her kitchen with color. Painting the walls a rich ivory and the woodwork jade green, she pronounced the new look "pretty good."[36]

As color became the "prima donna" of household decoration, stylists learned to fuse color theory with popular psychology in ways that appealed to manufacturers and retailers intrigued or bewildered by chromatic furor. Hazel H. Adler, who billed herself an interior decorator, color merchandiser, and president of the Taylor System of Color Harmony on Fifth Avenue, counseled clients such as Sears, Roebuck & Company, the National Lead Company, and B. F. Goodrich & Company on chromatic matters. Most notably, she advised the Ford Motor Company on color choices for its Model A. Adler also wrote promotional booklets for firms like the George W. Blabon Company, a linoleum manufacturer, advising consumers that "a colorless home" revealed "a colorless personality." She knew that colorless or dull people were out of tune with the twentieth-century "culture of personality," which prized people with strong self-images who could nonetheless relate to the crowd. While the selection, use, and display of colorful products provided women with avenues for self-expression, the acquisition of household objects made by quantity production allowed consumers to declare affinity with mass culture. The prerequisites for fitting into American culture were paradoxical, and color embodied those incongruities. Experts like Adler engaged these principles to advance their consulting firms and to promote color mania.[37]

In the tableware trade, the dual forces of informality and color initially coalesced in Fostoria's line of daintily tinted glassware, aimed at a middlebrow audience. For decades, manufacturers like Steuben Glass Works had made chromatic art ware for the "classes." In turn, pressing factories imitated Steuben's art glass palette, creating gaudy iridescent items—today known as carnival glass—for a larger portion of the market. But Fostoria's breakfast, luncheon, tea, and dinner sets in transparent hues of azure, dawn, orchid, and topaz were novel when introduced in 1925. Fostoria had a simple goal: use these modestly priced lines to wrest a share of the profitable trade in wedding present china away from American and European porcelain factories. To pique middle-class interest, Fostoria created conservative designs like Minuet, a Colonial Revival shape for "the modern hostess," who appreciated "all the grace and charm of early America." Hiring New York–based N. W. Ayer & Son to develop a national advertising campaign, Fostoria—and competitors that scurried behind—made colored glass dishes into fashionable dining services.[38]

In the crockery arena, retailers from Boston to Philadelphia picked up the chromatic gauntlet by promoting brightly colored faience. Department stores, importers, and gift shops filled their windows with so-called peasant pottery from Italy, Holland, and Czechoslovakia. Food packagers placed these bright dishes in advertisements for raisins, oatmeal, and puffed rice, which looked delicious in bowls of pink, green, and yellow. When Mildred Maddocks Bentley, director of the Delineator Home Institute, set a luncheon table for six, she chose for its centerpiece a polychrome Italian majolica bowl filled with pink tea roses. Accustomed to the refined, tight look of the decalcomania aesthetic, consumers gasped at the brightness and the looseness of these designs, which suggested cozy, cheery, and comfortable living. Fostoria glassware and peasant pottery slowly accustomed people to a new look in tableware design.[39]

By the late 1920s, Ohio potteries had jumped on the chromatic bandwagon, garnering all their resources to emulate Fostoria's pale hues and majolica's bold designs—with mixed results. Successful products like Sebring's Mayglow and Homer Laughlin's Yellowstone had demonstrated what color could do for crockery sales. When Limoges and the Edwin M. Knowles China Company initiated research on Peach-Blo and Mayglow, pink-bodied decal tableware, Homer Laughlin's sales staff pressed their art director to think pink. Rhead loathed it as the "color of fat blondes and naughty ladies" and decided to turn the pink idea upside down. To create a new decorative type for quantity production, the art director had to distinguish between transient styles and sound styles, selecting treatments from the latter group as models for development. As Leigh Potters fully understood, the design process drew upon a pottery's ornamental trinity: clay bodies, shapes, and decorations. Changes to those sacred cows could not be taken lightly. Thinking of Green Wheat, Rhead urged managers to sidestep the pink fad, proposing a long-term research project geared toward creating tableware with "color values" of "universal appeal." Why not join the fashion brigade of potters promoting short sets for easy eating? If his rhetoric sounded much like an advertisement for Fostoria or an after-dinner speech by Charlie Sebring, it also speaks of Rhead's awareness of the competition.[40]

In facilitating new decorative treatments for department stores, Rhead relied on the stylistic coaching of the crockery buyers Gerald S. Stone, who succeeded Olsen at Macy's, and George S. Ujlaki at Gimbel Brothers. Known in the crockery trade as dean of the buyers, Stone had a reputation for his smooth manners, keen eye, and creative ideas. In 1929, Rhead had positive experiences with Stone, Olsen, and Tarpley, who visited West Virginia to discuss the next year's lines. These aesthetic arbiters of Macy's wanted modern designs, but they urged Rhead to pursue "conservative development." With Leigh ware on their minds, Macy's men gently dismissed the decal world of "pretty roses" and "dicky daises." Similarly, Ujlaki, "not interested in existing patterns," urged Rhead to consider new textures and colors, including ocher and coral. Overall, these crockery buyers confirmed Rhead's belief that the time was ripe for a new look in ceramic decoration.[41]

The creation of new clay bodies and colored glazes lay at the core of Homer Laughlin's stylistic evolution, requiring team work by Rhead and the factory chemist, Albert V. Bleininger, who brought complementary knowledge to the project. Much about the development project was hit-or-miss; often, Rhead tested Bleininger's promising glazes on experimental shapes with horrendous results. By 1930, they had refined a series of art glazes in French rose, Sienna brown, and leaf green that looked good on Rhead's sculptural shapes. (Helen Ufford, associate director at the *Delineator*, praised these lines as versatile enough for every meal, illustrating the ware in her column.) Riding the success of Homer Laughlin art glazes, Rhead next year introduced Clair de Lune, a gray-blue that suggested the "pale soft, alluring color of the moonlight," and Vellum, a smooth off-white "the texture and color of old ivory." He applied these glazes to the rectilinear Century shape, embellished with modernistic decals. Department store buyers welcomed Century Vellum, ordering some twenty-four million pieces during its introductory year alone.[42]

Homer Laughlin exited the Jazz Age with a new look. By 1929, 90 percent of the firm's wares were made with ivory bodies. These off-white goods had clear, yellow, or pastel art glazes and bold modern-style decals. Consumers' changing taste preferences, as expressed through the voices of crockery buyers and in sales statistics, led the firm to reassess the decal aesthetic. Ironically, Rhead's hiring coincided closely with the peak year for decal sales. At his urging, Homer Laughlin adopted an annual model change, introducing one or two new shapes every year and eliminating older items as demand dwindled. The pottery also started to make short sets for Gimbels, Macy's, and other highly visible New York department stores. While volume customers like Woolworth and Quaker Oats continued to stock decal pottery, the appearance of those decorations changed as dime store and scheme-ware buyers also pushed for designs that were simpler, bolder, more colorful, and more modern. With these visual innovations—initiated on the urging of crockery buyers—Homer Laughlin in large measure took the first steps toward fracturing decalcomania's strong hold on pottery decoration.[43]

A New Deal for American Dinnerware

> An art director's job is to make stuff which will sell.
> —Frederick Hurten Rhead, 1936

During the Great Depression, Homer Laughlin's largest customers curbed their orders, and the firm's new general manager, Joseph M. Wells, scrambled to cope with changes in the pottery's customer base. Tightening his belt, William A. O'Grady slowly cut Quaker Oats' purchases from $1.6 million in 1930 to $500,000 in 1935. Woolworth's orders dropped from $3.8 million, or 54 percent of Homer

Laughlin's sales, in 1929 to $1 million, or 22 percent of sales, in 1935. In part, Woolworth and other five-and-tens had discovered a Depression Era golden goose: glassware in pale hues of pink, green, yellow, and blue. An ideal mass-market product, this imitation Fostoria tableware, made by midwestern factories like the MacBeth-Evans Glass Company, retailed for half the price of comparable ceramics. Showy, cheap, and plentiful, this glassware dovetailed with Woolworth's seizure of the color-in-the-kitchen idea. Chromatic household accessories, including green kitchen gadgets and pink, green, and yellow tableware, had filled dime store shelves for years. Moreover, Woolworth's retrenchment coincided with Newberry's retirement in 1930 and the hiring of P. G. Frantz as his successor. A fan of foreign chinaware, Frantz fumed when that year the USPA, represented before the Ways and Means Committee by the aging W. Edwin Wells, pressed Congress for heavy duties under the Smoot-Hawley tariff. Newberry might have tolerated his old friend's testimony, but Frantz, who enjoyed roaming around Europe in search of novelties, exploded when the Senate approved the advance. "Joe" Wells did everything to make amends, enlisting Gaertner and Rhead to turn on their charm, but nothing worked. Frantz turned his back, buying from Homer Laughlin only those goods he could not find elsewhere.[44]

In part, the younger Wells steered his firm through these hard times by piecing together sales to small customers, undercutting less competitive USPA firms and, inevitably, pushing some tottering potteries over the edge. To enlarge his share of the scheme-ware business, Wells trimmed pennies per dozen off the prices of Quaker Oats' cups, saucers, plates, bowls, sugars, and creamers, hoping to entice O'Grady into buying more goods. Emulating the Sebrings, he probed the recesses of the premium trade, answering the calls of small vendors who wanted bits and pieces of crockery for even the most minor of promotions. During the early 1930s, Frank A. Sebring Jr., who managed the Salem China Company in Salem, Ohio, built a profitable trade as purveyor to movie theaters, which gave away tableware at midweek pictures to encourage moviegoing. Few potteries lavished as much effort on "dish night" as did "Tode" Sebring, who pioneered the practice of product placement as an advertising mechanism and whose dish deliveries included fantastical display units. Other Sebrings followed suit, with movie palaces consuming much of the Depression Era output of Limoges and the Sebring Pottery Company. Wells waded into the fray and soon routinely sold dishes to some three dozen movie houses in Chicago. By 1932, one incensed Sebring salesmen became so irritated by the competition that he

LADIES !

ATTEND
THE BAYWOOD
ON

CHINA NIGHT

AND

SECURE

A COMPLETE SET

OF

THIS ELEGANT

CHINA

Dish night at a neighborhood theater, 1932. Salem China Company Collection, National Museum of American History Archives Center, Smithsonian Institution

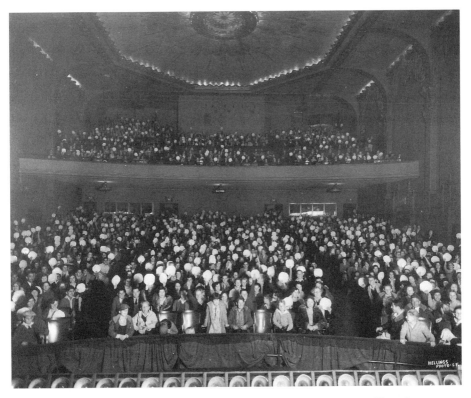

Moviegoers holding up their free plates, dish night, 1932. Salem China Company Collection, National Museum of American History Archives Center, Smithsonian Institution

condemned Homer Laughlin's output as "five-and-ten trash" in a telegram to a New York distributor catering to movie theaters. Wells went on to copy Salem's strategy of building customers among furniture stores, relying on small jobbers for distribution to this market, rich with installment sales. Still, this patchwork business hardly satisfied Homer Laughlin's capacity: five tunnel kiln factories, whose efficient operation depended on round-the-clock production.[45]

Frustrated by the state of the economy and alarmed by the Woolworth debacle, Homer Laughlin's managers evaluated their approaches to technology, design, and markets. As the Depression wore on, the dish-making colossus closed two of its plants; the company could not afford any more losses. Just as the economic crisis eroded consumer purchasing power, competition from cheap imported ceramics—"millions of dozens of cups and saucers" from Japan— threatened mass-market potteries. Concurrently, Czechoslovakian and German potteries, desperate for a nibble of the American chain store trade, developed automatic machinery that formed cups and plates—thus undercutting American prices. At the end of his long career, W. Edwin Wells solemnly announced to the National Brotherhood of Operative Potters that only "well-managed and modernly equipped factories" would pull through. The proof was in the pudding: Kresge's Mount Clemens Pottery Company reportedly operated at full capacity. The senior Wells's farewell statement to the union presaged major technical changes that would take place at Homer Laughlin during the ensuing years under his son's direction.[46]

Much like contemporary automakers, who used styling in an effort to stimulate car sales, the younger Wells engaged the triumvirate of industrial science, product design, and manufacturing technology to revive the chain store trade and to enlarge the department store business. First, he expanded the firm's decorative research program, adding in 1931 an annex to Plant No. 5 for the art department, the ceramics laboratory, and a new pilot plant. Next, Wells invested heavily in mechanical engineering, hiring in 1934 Walter Howard Emerson, a graduate of MIT who had Fordized production at Kresge's Mount Clemens. In charge of Homer Laughlin's new planning department, Emerson reorganized production in several complex stages, using mass-production methods to make the base of a product, leaving the firm's managers with a spectrum of opportunities in the realm of decorating. His mechanization projects increased throughput but did not compromise Homer Laughlin's commitment to flexible production or cramp Rhead's options in terms of product design.[47]

Meanwhile, the art department also geared up, functioning much like "a tool or a machine" that churned out some five hundred drawings, three hundred models of shapes, and three thousand decorated samples each year. As ceramic art engineer, Rhead spent an average of two hours per day in conferences with factory officials, salesmen, crockery buyers, admen, printers, materials suppliers, and decal manufacturers and another two hours supervising the work of an assistant art director, two staff modelers, some china decorators, and a few errand boys. With administrative tasks completed, he worked on new decorations for established clients or new customers, creating modernistic banded wares for Macy's and Gimbels or dreaming up syndicate patterns for W. T. Grant Company. However, his foremost responsibility was creating new lines for the mid-January trade show in Pittsburgh. At this annual spectacle, the most important department store buyers contemplated which patterns to stock in the forthcoming year. There, Wells expected the fruits of ceramic art engineering—good designs in the modern style—to inspire big-time buyers to carry Laughlin wares.[48]

As important buyers pressed Wells for novel products, their exhortations reached fever pitch, reflecting consumers' "insatiable" desires "for something new, something different, something more beautiful, something more useful, and, in particular, something cheaper." In effect, the mode for soft, casual colors had run its course by 1934, and buyers searched for a new look. To some extent, visual freshness might still be achieved by placing modernistic decals against subdued backgrounds, but the market could only bear so many Green Wheat spin-offs. At Limoges, designer Viktor Schreckengost, a native Ohioan who worked on the shop floor at various Sebring potteries before attending art school, broke aesthetic ground with Flower Shop, a flat decal design whose novelty captured the fancy of department store shoppers. As competitors imitated Limoges's bright red and green motif, prices fell so much that "flowerpot" dishes became dime store staples. In addition, European factories were hit hard by the Depression, making it difficult to procure high-quality decals on time and creating eleventh-hour delivery crises. Gaertner's death in 1932 toppled the apple cart, eroding whatever advantages Homer Laughlin had among foreign printers. The best way out of this decorating dilemma was to diversify the firm's embellishing options, breaking away from tried-and-true decal technology. Although it never disappeared from the potter's tool kit, decalcomania started surrendering its crown during the 1930s to new decorating methods, including relief molding, simple hand painting, bright chromatic glazes, and silk screening. At Homer Laughlin, the slow death of decals went hand in hand with the rise of simple shapes and colorful glazes geared toward casual dining in the home.[49]

In 1933, some industry observers argued that the repeal of Prohibition struck the final blow against formal dining; more than ever, consumers stocked their kitchens with informal accessories. Even if they did not drink, consumers living on Depression Era incomes had to cook and entertain themselves at home. Many dusted off their dining room tables and reinstated the evening meal with a twist of informality. In 1933, the Chase Brass & Copper Company targeted stay-at-home diners with the first of its "table electrics" designed for the new buffet dinner. Determined to capture the attention of easy eaters, Wells made his initial move with a dramatically different product for Homer Laughlin: baking dishes, called Oven Serve. Designing this line for Woolworth after the dime

Homer Laughlin's Oven
Serve, lowest-priced baking
ware on the market in
1933. Brochure, Homer
Laughlin China Company

store introduced twenty-cent merchandise in 1932, Rhead took his cues from
Corning Glass Works, the Crooksville Pottery Company, and the Harker Pottery
Company, which made casseroles and other baking dishes. Frantz's antipathy
began to fade when Woolworth restaurants started cooking daily specials in
Oven Serve, putting baking dishes filled with scrumptious preparations in windows to lure hungry shoppers inside. With Woolworth orders back, Wells offered Oven Serve to premium vendors, department stores, and hardware stores,

giving contest to the Pyrex monopoly on cookware shelves. The Oven Serve experiment showed Wells that Depression Era consumers were ready, willing, and able to buy decal-free crockery especially designed for easy eating.[50]

In this context, Homer Laughlin's managers took the first real steps toward creating the chromatic line that took the 1936 Pittsburgh show by storm: Fiesta. Two forces came together in the design process. In 1934, the sales manager Louis K. Friedman, in charge of the pottery's department store accounts, advocated that Homer Laughlin "imitate . . . Italian glazes." (He referred to the inexpensive, gayly colored peasant pottery from Italy, Spain, France, Mexico, Ireland, Hungary, and Germany that was being sold in quaint department store nooks called "Little Mexico" or "Normandy Kitchen.") About the same time, Wells pressed for emulation of the more costly California faience, the modernistic tableware produced by two Los Angeles structural clay-working firms, Pacific Clay Products and Gladding, McBean & Company (plate 5). (With their wild colors, West Coast ceramics embodied the uninhibited spontaneity of California's casual lifestyle, which *House Beautiful* described as "hot-off-the-griddle" like "Hollywood's own backdrops.") As Fae Huttenlocher showed in *Better Homes and Gardens,* these solid-colored dishes, created expressly for buffet dining, complemented "red apples and blush-tinted pears" in "gay table settings" for fall meals. Helen Sprackling wrote in her *Better Homes and Gardens* column that Pacific's pumpkin yellows and Apache reds could be mixed, making it ideal for "simple entertaining." To Sprackling, a hostess's success depended on "unforgettable food" and on table settings made chromatically attractive with Ohio glassware and California pottery.[51]

California colored dinnerware, which depended on low-temperature firing, was not unique. In terms of production, the Golden State had a small but well-established ceramics industry that filled the local demand for faience tiles and garden pottery. This clay tile industry took off following the 1915 Panama-California Exposition in San Diego, which popularized a Spanish Colonial style. Stemming from a confluence of Spanish, Mexican, and Native American heritages, this aesthetic depended on striking blue, green, and yellow tiles for much of its eye appeal. By the 1920s, clay workers introduced chromatic household accessories to match their architectural faience. Wells recognized that firms like Gladding McBean had neither the interest nor the capacity for making pottery on a mass-production basis. When California faience made a big splash at the 1935 Pittsburgh show, the quest to add new dimension to Homer Laughlin's product portfolio ensued.[52]

Without question, Homer Laughlin's "California" undertaking rested on the strong foundation laid by earlier research and engineering projects, with behind-the-scenes technical accomplishments making design innovation possible. When working on the Vellum glaze, Bleininger conquered the problem of application by adapting atomizers to suit continuous-flow production; and when laboring over Oven Serve, he discovered how certain percentages of talc affected the shrinkage, porosity, and durability of clay bodies. Emerson continued to fine-tune the firm's production setup, often in response to Rhead's request for small technical adjustments that made a big difference in the product's appearance. In tandem, spraying equipment, low-temperature clay bodies, and other new gizmos and concoctions became key elements in Homer Laughlin's technical repertoire. Yet it was the stunning juxtaposition of modern shapes with dramatic colors, rather than the details of glaze composition or firing temperatures, that excited crockery buyers at the 1936 Pittsburgh show. Technical ingenuity under-girded the firm's design resiliency, but stylistic precociousness still depended on a close reading of the marketplace, making the business-culture nexus the most important node in this tale about Homer Laughlin's "new deal" in dinnerware decoration.[53]

Working on the "California development" that evolved into Fiesta enabled Rhead to measure his theories about American social classes against the reality of mass markets. Consumers like Katherine Perry relished everything about California ware, using her aquamarine set "only at breakfast" for decades until all but a few pieces had broken. Perry perfectly fit Rhead's vision of a middle-class woman, with her smart quarters at the Eddystone in Washington, D.C., outfitted with Sheraton-style furniture, politely worn Asian rugs, and modern odds and ends. If he had visited Perry's four-room apartment, Rhead might have knowingly nodded at her heirloom cut glass and Bavarian china, glanced appre-ciatively at her Wedgwood dinner service, scowled at her Japanese luncheon set, and quietly sized up her California dishes. Personally, Rhead disliked the "crude appeals" of California faience, with its "greens the color of gangrene, yellows and browns the color of manure," and "equally offensive" pinks and blues. He much preferred soft art glazes, like those developed for Gimbels' Ujlaki. Still, the job of ceramic art engineering demanded suppression of personal prefer-ences for the firm's benefit. With Wells commanding him to spare no effort or expense on the California spin-off, Rhead pressed on.[54]

To capture the attention of department store shoppers who had vehemently rejected skyscraper modernism, Rhead blended the old and the new in Fiesta, endowing the line with a good deal of the commonplace and a sprinkle of novelty (plate 6). This fusion came through in the look and the name of the product, designed to trigger responses among middlebrows searching for "anything except something in crass taste." In the visual realm, Rhead crafted Fiesta's shape in the hybrid style now identified as art deco, a stylized modernism toned down with historicist references. By January 1935, Rhead's modelers had stumbled upon a "jolly and pleasant" shape with "concentric circles" that would act as a foil for "obvious and brilliant colors." The globular forms harked back to the earthy Arts and Crafts aesthetic, but the low-relief circles meant different things to different audiences. Traditionalists equated the rings with marks left by the old potter's wheel, while modernists recollected the futurist imagery from the Worlds of Progress Expositions. When managers met in the spring to select the best glazes from among those developed by Rhead and Bleininger, salesman Friedman pressed for "blatant" hues "that shouted the most." The art director held his tongue but quietly countered with a palette of four hot colors that cried out and a satiny ivory vellum that exerted a calming effect. Thus through shape and color Fiesta embodied the contradictions of modernism. Made with flexible mass-production technology, the line nevertheless remained tied to nature and tradition by virtue of its roots in California and the Spanish Colonial Revival. Rhead's equivocation ensured that Fiesta would visually appeal to audiences that otherwise rejected modern styling.[55]

In the verbal realm, Fiesta's name carried the same double meaning as its shape and palette, although much of this symbolism is lost on today's consumer. In April 1935, Rhead and Friedman contemplated appellations; names like Park Lane, Plaza, and Rhapsody had ritzy connotations; euphonious terms like Tazza, Tazza Faience, Chalte Faience, and Dashe Faience, little cultural meaning. Searching for a lively, fun-and-sun name, they toyed with Flamingo before deciding on Fiesta, the Spanish word for feast or holiday. A fabulous choice, Fiesta resonated among conservative and avant-garde audiences alike. To those versed in the Spanish Colonial Revival, the name obviously referred to California living. With Mexican tourism on the rise, some consumers took Fiesta to be a reminder of exotic vacations spent south of the border. To those who stayed at home and read Stuart Chase's 1931 best-seller, *Mexico: A Study of Two Americas,* Fiesta stirred up memories of the simple village inhabitants of Tepoztlán, who lived machineless lives and made beautiful folk crafts. Moviegoers may have recalled favorite films in fantastical Spanish settings; and tango lovers possessed by the dance marathon craze thought of their favorite Latin beat. Finally, to the party crowd and the literati, the name had a distinctive modern twist, for *Fiesta* was the alternate title of Ernest Hemingway's bullfighting novel, *The Sun Also Rises* (1926). With its multiple meanings, the name Fiesta reflected some of the fundamental tensions embodied in the design of Homer Laughlin's new object of desire.[56]

Throughout 1935, Rhead solicited opinions on the new line from buyers, who suggested this and that about shapes and colors. Having created Fiesta for department stores, Homer Laughlin's managers quickly discovered how much the line appealed to high-volume distributors. By summer, dime store crockery men admitted that they would buy—if the price was right. Although Fiesta never entered the pottery's decorating rooms, high startup costs and expensive ingredients dictated that Wells reserve the line for his carriage trade. Trying to give Gerry Stone at Macy's a run for his money, Ujlaki of Gimbels asked for exclusive control of Fiesta in December. When Wells refused, the Gimbels buyer nonetheless submitted an immense order for his New York store, a sign that portended well for the forthcoming show.[57]

At Pittsburgh, buyers' eyes popped out: "Fiesta was so outrageously different and so low in price," Rhead bragged to a colleague, "that everybody bought it whether they wanted it or not!" In reality, Fiesta's success was a matter of contrast, for other East Liverpool potteries showed copycat patterns or extreme motifs, either boring or shocking crockery men. The stylist Simon H. Slobodkin had so modernized the rooms of the W. S. George Pottery Company that buyers not dumbfounded by his avant-garde designs were put off by the ostentatious display, featuring black patent leather flooring, red shelves, blue cellophane curtains, and bright white lamps. To create Homer Laughlin's exhibits, Rhead drew on his love of Mexicana, developed during his Santa Barbara years, and created the Fiesta girl, a sensual flamenco dancer who became the line's symbol and an omnipresent figure on brochures and display units. In Homer Laughlin's rooms, buyers admired images of the senorita, whose limberness, glamor, and festivity stood in sharp contrast to the hokeyness of dish night's little Dutch girls. Fiesta not only caught show goers' attentions with its "smart rather than arty" shape and bright yet harmonious color but also sustained their interest with its potential sales appeal. Sold through the open-stock system, Fiesta epitomized casual tableware, "sport" dishes in mix-and-match colors. A shopper could decide on her own chromatic combinations, using blue plates, red cups, and yellow bowls if that selection met her fancy. The Fiesta ensemble fully embodied Hazel Adler's theories; by choosing Fiesta, a woman might de-

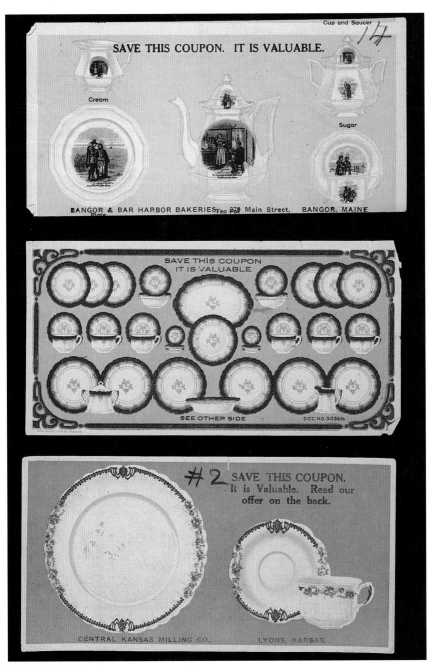

Plate 1. Coupons for pottery premiums, 1910s. National Museum of American History Archives Center, Smithsonian Institution

Plate 2. Middlebrow taste: Katherine Wicks Perry's Wedgwood china, 1937. National Museum of American History, Smithsonian Institution

Plate 3. A working woman's pride: Nellie Petrowski's tableware. Taylor, Smith & Taylor, East Liverpool, 1937. Private collection

Plate 4. Color in the kitchen. Advertisement in *Better Homes & Gardens*, 1930, Library of Congress

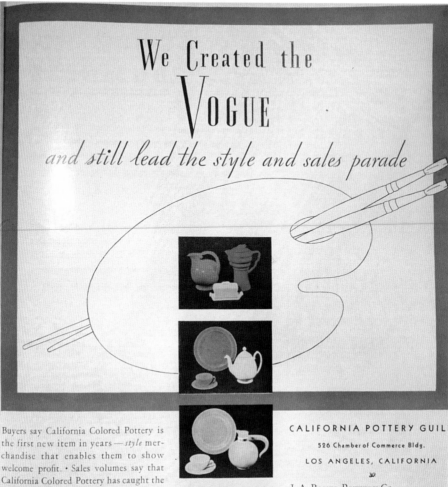

We Created the
VOGUE
and still lead the style and sales parade

Buyers say California Colored Pottery is the first new item in years — *style* merchandise that enables them to show welcome profit. • Sales volumes say that California Colored Pottery has caught the public fancy—created a demand for bright, cheerful tableware both as new equipment and as replacement — a *double* market. • California Colored Pottery is the original and has steadily maintained its leadership in style, color, quality and *saleability*. It is riding on the crest of popularity — the dominant favorite everywhere; not only because of its own superiorities, but for its California background—a background recognized as the style-center of the world.

CALIFORNIA POTTERY GUIL

526 Chamber of Commerce Bldg.

LOS ANGELES, CALIFORNIA

J. A. BAUER POTTERY CO.
415 W. Ave. 33, Los Angel

GLADDING, McBEAN & CO.
2901 Los Feliz Blvd., Los Angel

METLOX MFG. COMPANY
Manhattan Beach, Californ

PACIFIC CLAY PRODUCTS
306 W. Ave. 26, Los Angel

VERNON KILNS
2300 East 52nd St., Los Angel

CALIFORNIA COLOR  CAPTURES CUSTOMER

Plate 5. California's brilliant pottery, which inspired Homer Laughlin's managers. Advertisement in *Crockery and Glass Journal*, August 1937, clipping, Art Department Files, Homer Laughlin China Company

Plate 6. Fiesta, 1936. Brochure, Homer Laughlin China Company

Designed by Ely Jacques Kahn, Architect, New York. Plumbing fixtures, with their metal fittings, designed and executed by Kohler of Kohler

In the Metropolitan Museum of Art

—Exhibition of a modern bath and dressing room

THE new importance of the bathroom as a place of beauty in the modern home could hardly be more strikingly emphasized than it is by this room by Mr. Ely Jacques Kahn in the current Exhibition of American Industrial Art at the Metropolitan Museum, New York.

That the bathroom was chosen as one of the typical rooms to be shown in this internationally important exhibition is in itself an eloquent fact. The manner in which this room unites artistry with logical simplicity demonstrates the wisdom of the choice.

The walls are of glass. The floors are of special yielding rubber. Radiators are recessed behind tiled grilles, and over their warmth

Chromium-plated Kohler fittings in the Cellini pattern enhance the distinguished beauty of the jet black Kohler fixtures

hang the towels. Such thoughtful details throughout illustrate how comfort parallels beauty.

Into this setting are introduced a Kohler bath and lavatory of gleaming black, with chromium-plated fittings—faucets, handles, and escutcheons—also of Kohler make, in the graceful *Cellini* design. These Kohler contributions are in patterns available to all.

Kohler fixtures of modern style and beauty —in lovely color or lustrous white—are made for simplest bathrooms as well as costly ones. Write to Kohler Co., Kohler, Wis., for a free 72-page book, in color, showing fixtures for bathrooms, kitchens, and laundries, with color schemes, floor plans, and prices.

KOHLER Co. *Founded 1873 · Branches in Principal Cities · Shipping Point*, Sheboygan, Wis.

KOHLER OF KOHLER
Plumbing Fixtures

1929, Kohler Co.

Plate 7. The bathroom beautiful. Kohler's colored fixtures at the Metropolitan Museum of Art, 1929. Advertisement in *Liberty*, June 29, 1929, Kohler Company

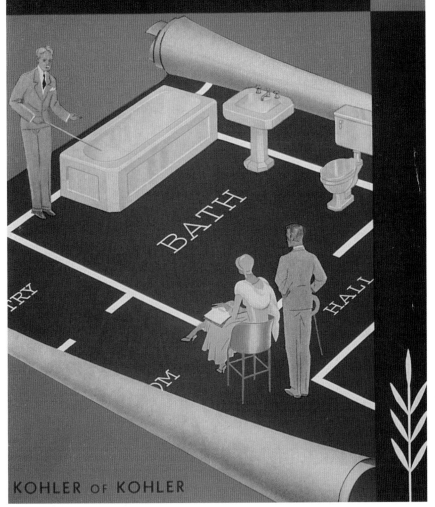

Plate 8. Tutorial on Kohler's Matched Sets, 1932. Brochure, Kohler Company

Plate 9. Fry's opalescent ovenware. Advertisement in *Good Housekeeping*, April 1922, Morris Library, University of Delaware

clare membership in mass culture, and, by mixing colors, she would display her individuality or personal taste. Recognizing this versatility, many buyers, big and small, from St. Louis's Famous-Barr to Syracuse's E. W. Edwards & Son, immediately bought Fiesta in every color; more cautious retailers went home to mull over the novelty, submitting orders during the spring. Back in Manhattan, Bloomingdale's china department showcased Homer Laughlin's Fiesta next to some California ware. Pleased with sales of the new tableware, Gimbels' Ujlaki canceled his order for Pacific Clay's faience and spotlighted Fiesta as his premier color line.[58]

As buyers flocked to Homer Laughlin's hotel rooms to see Fiesta, they encountered another novel tableware embellishment: silk screen decorations. By tradition, potters used the Pittsburgh show as a coming-out party for dish debutantes, but they also depended on the exhibit, packed with competitors, buyers, stylists, and journalists, as a vehicle for testing less mature products. In the opening days, salesmen displayed all their goods, including experimental pieces; if too many passersby snarled or scoffed, blushing salesmen stashed the new stuff under the counter and pulled out tried-and-true patterns. For designs that survived this rite, sales staff anxiously awaited the midshow arrival of wide-awake journalists like Madeline Young Love of *China, Glass and Lamps* and Fae Huttenlocher of *Better Homes and Gardens,* whom they pressed for feedback—and free press. Such was the case in 1936, with Homer Laughlin's new silk screen decorations.[59]

During the 1930s, Rhead watched the gigantic Toledo-based Owens-Illinois Glass Company introduce dime store tumblers with brightly colored silk screen motifs. Licensed to use equipment patented by Solar Laboratories in Beaver, Pennsylvania, an Owen-Illinois subsidiary, the Libbey Glass Company, silk-screened three thousand tumblers per hour at a machine attended by one operative. Recognizing the mass-production potential of this "baby," Rhead, Bleininger, and the plant manager, Harry Spore, pressed Homer Laughlin's managers to try out the technique, with Solar providing experimental decorating equipment by late 1935. At a moment when potteries sought to achieve maximum novelty at least cost, silk screening offered several advantages. In the art department, the new method provided Rhead with a fast mechanism for satisfying buyers like James Faulds, the crockery man at Kauffman's department store in Pittsburgh. Excited about the new technology, Faulds gave Friedman some fabric samples with "new designs," hoping the Rhead might use these swatches to create "something modern in dinnerware decoration" for his store. If buyers' cloth samples left him uninspired, Rhead might create borders, brushwork motifs, or banded effects: the decorative possibilities were endless; the final products, of good quality. On the shop floor, silk screening offered significant cost reductions, as four women, each working for $3.50 a day, could decorate six hundred dozen items. In comparative terms, silk screen decorations cost from two to four cents per dozen, while other embellishments cost from fifteen to twenty-five cents. The technology had several glitches—screens broke if improperly fitted, some shapes failed to accept color—but it worked splendidly once the kinks were ironed out. When Homer Laughlin showed prototypes at Pittsburgh in 1936, competitors rushed home to contact Solar. Astounded at the designs, Woolworth's new crockery buyer, H. H. Lindquist, more sympathetic to USPA potters than his predecessor, P. G. Frantz, predicted that silk screen decorations would be a "very effective weapon against anything Russian, Japanese, Chinese, Ethiopian, or otherwise."[60]

The successes of the Pittsburgh show propelled Homer Laughlin to the top of the stylistic ladder among American potteries. Fiesta and silk screen lines opened mass-market pottery to the chromatic and casual revolutions. In mid-1936 the Textile Color Card Association, an organization that established chromatic standards and predicted fashion hues for each style season, introduced a collection of "pottery tones," featuring faience blue, ceramic green, and Spanish magenta. In December, Mabel J. Stegner featured a holiday breakfast table set with Fiesta in *Better Homes and Gardens,* signaling Homer Laughlin's victory over California wares, which had appeared in this middlebrow magazine for several years. Woolworth's Lindquist pressed Wells to create a downscale version of Fiesta. As business picked up in 1936, Lindquist prepared to restock his five-and-tens with good-looking crockery that would appeal to down-and-out middle-class shoppers who browsed at Woolies. In response, Rhead designed Harlequin, a less expensive monochromatic line in an exaggerated streamlined shape. By the mid-1930s, streamlined modernism, condemned by department store shoppers, found ready buyers in the dime store trade. Style was a peculiar thing, with a trajectory nearly impossible to predict. Fiesta and its stepchild, Harlequin, challenged the fundamental rules of trickle-down fashion theory.[61]

As orders poured in for colored and silk screened lines, Homer Laughlin's tunnel kilns remained up and running during the "Roosevelt recession" of 1937. Ever watchful of costs, Rhead began to create plainer shapes compatible with silk screening, trying to balance customer expectations with the constraints the

Harlequin, a Fiesta spinoff for F. W. Woolworth & Company, 1937. Brochure, Homer Laughlin China Company

new technology imposed. Silk screening breathed new life into the casual color mode, endowing tableware with a soft, bold modernism that was difficult to achieve with chromolithography. Monochromatic lines, silk screened shapes, and gay modern decals, some depicting Mexican scenes of sombreros, cacti, and peasant vases, found niches in Homer Laughlin's product portfolio. Yet despite this revolution in decoration, Rhead continued to create lines covered with floral decals; consumers at all price levels and taste preferences continued to buy quantities of pottery decorated with "pretty posies." For decades, Homer Laughlin would continue to serve this segmented market. The decal aesthetic died a long, drawn-out death.[62]

Homer Laughlin's newfound status as style kingfish rattled the USPA's long-time aesthetic leader, Charlie Sebring. The Depression had driven Leigh Potters out of business, and the Sebring family's pottery interests coalesced around three firms that Charlie Sebring helped to manage: Sebring, Limoges, and the Salem China Company. As he tried to upgrade these firms' product lines, Charlie Sebring watched Homer Laughlin and turned greener than Green Wheat with envy. In 1937, his West Virginia rival dominated all the trade shows, and Sebring's potteries "failed to impress the buyers with the distinctiveness and unusualness" of their offerings. "We did not have," he complained to other top managers, any new lines equivalent to "Barbara Jane or Ivory Porcelain or Umbertone or Pink Body or Flower Shop or Petit Point," referring to the Sebring-Leigh-Limoges hit parade. Grasping for ideas, he and Schreckengost visited Homer Laughlin and Libbey to witness silk screen technology in action. Shortly afterward, Charlie Sebring rushed back from the home furnishings show in New York, reporting excitedly on the popularity of ceramic cookware of all shapes, sizes, and colors. The clincher came when he proposed a decorative development program that sounded like a blow-by-blow account of Rhead's accomplishments: creating colored bodies, developing a talc body, making cookwares, experimenting with banding machines, establishing a pilot plant, introducing "colored glazes of the California or Fiesta type," and adopting the silk screen process. To survive cutthroat competition from low-wage economies like Japan's and Czechoslovakia's as well as that from open shops and mechanized glassworks, the Sebrings had to develop higher-priced products, broaching big middlebrow markets like Montgomery Ward.[63]

By decade's end, the East Liverpool potteries experienced design fever, with factories searching for ways to please the eye without sacrificing utility. In many respects, Rhead had achieved his dream for the tableware industry, for most design-conscious firms had hired experienced practical men to orchestrate decorative development. At Knowles, Vincent Broomhall, an East Liverpudlian who had studied design at Pittsburgh's Carnegie Institute of Technology, worked with decal manufacturers to simplify and loosen up the look of chromolithographic designs. At Taylor, Smith & Taylor, the Staffordshire man Thorley, who had left the Sebrings, created Fiesta copies in bright and pastel colors. Pulling them-

American Modern dinnerware, Steubenville Pottery Company, 1939. National Museum of American History, Smithsonian Institution

selves together, the Sebrings made a big splash at the 1938 Pittsburgh show, where "artists and designers from other potteries were seen making notes and sketches" of Jiffy Ware, a cooking line designed by Schreckengost. When asked to revamp Salem and Limoges offerings, Schreckengost, then teaching at the Cleveland School of Art, wisely insisted on input from the firm's sales manager, who understood the competition, attended all the trade shows, and, most important, knew all the buyers. Like Rhead, these designers adopted the maxim, "keep up with the customers," and avoided "snooty decorative types" that appealed little to average consumers.[64]

The managers at Steubenville Pottery Company in Ohio took a different approach to design when they agreed to manufacture products designed by Russel Wright, a young New York consultant seeking to build a signature American line. A decorative dabbler turned designer, Wright secured a good degree of visibility when his aggressive spouse promoted his designs among Manhattan tastemakers. Introduced in 1939 as a dinnerware breakthrough, Wright's American Modern, with organic shapes, speckled glazes, and artsy-craftsy colors such as bean brown and curry green, owed much to a nascent studio pottery move-

Form follows function? Art Department Files, Homer Laughlin China Company

ment and even more to the vogue for casual color that had been unfolding for a decade. Like the leaders of the industrial design profession, Wright had little patience for prevailing mass-market fashions. Rather than creating pretty, inexpensive patterns that "Mamie Jenkins" and "Mrs. Brown" would buy, he expected to remold these women's tastes and the world in his own image through better design. Despite the celebration of Wright as an aesthetic god by curators and design historians, the truth is that he spent four years trying to find a pottery that would adopt his designs, ultimately settling for Steubenville, a small factory desperate for business during the Depression. Riding on the success of California ware and Fiesta, Wright's products achieved greater visibility in the postwar era, when growing purchasing power enabled more consumers to buy into the middle-class way of life. Even then, Steubenville's output paled next to that of mass-production factories like Mount Clemens and Homer Laughlin. Rhead shared his distaste for American Modern with one of his siblings, who sent him a cartoon mocking Wright's interpretation of easy eating and the "form-follows-function" rubric promulgated by tastemaking consultants. Addressing the USPA, Rhead described Wright's cream pitchers and sugar bowls as being modeled after "male urinals" and "infant toilets." American Modern, he argued, reflected an "elementary knowledge and appreciation of form": it was "slithery and wise-cracking rather than smart, the type of ware one would expect to be used by parlor pinks and communists."[65]

During World War II, American potters dominated the domestic market for table accessories, as hostilities temporarily curtailed imports of Czechoslovakian, German, and Japanese ceramics. Inch by inch, American ceramics regained their footholds in five-and-tens, especially after the sinking of the gunboat U.S.S. *Panay* in 1938 precipitated a boycott of Japanese products. With essential raw materials like uranium oxide reserved for military use, Homer Laughlin curtailed production of some bright glazes, such as Fiesta's yellow and red. Facing dwindling decal supplies, the firm focused on getting the most out of monochromatic, banded, and silk screen embellishments. Overall, wartime shortages forced potters' hands in terms of design, ushering new visual responses to the versatility question among USPA firms. Confronted with a scarcity of skilled labor to apply delicate handles and finials, Schreckengost introduced simpler forms and shapes. To the dismay of East Liverpool potters, popular magazines like *Life* spotlighted the accomplishments of factories like Syracuse China and Lenox China, peripheral firms whose porcelain tableware in part filled the voids in middlebrow and highbrow markets created by the hiatus in European trade. Such publicity fanned prejudices against American earthenware table accessories, with middle-class shoppers buying porcelain made by decorating shops and hotel china factories for the sake of owning "fine china."[66]

At Rhead's death in 1942, members of the USPA lamented more than the passing of the "outstanding designer in the ceramic field." They mourned the end of an era. Managers at Homer Laughlin remembered his "immense energies and broad interests," his "quick perception and vigorous . . . expression," and his abilities as a writer, critic, and innovator. When this veteran of the potteries died of cancer after a lifetime of exposure to often-hazardous materials, colleagues suspected that product design in the pottery tableware industry would never be the same. Uncannily, American potters sensed their own demise when equating Rhead's passing with the destruction of the "the mold, the case, and the block." Within two decades, the American tableware industry would be reduced to a handful of factories struggling to survive amid competition from foreign potters, plastics manufacturers, and quantity-production glassworks. No voice like Rhead's would rise above the vortex of the postwar market, offering a vision for decorative development that would liberate the stumbling industry from the nightmare of inexpensive Japanese imports, especially designed to meet the demands of American consumers.[67]

CHAPTER 5

Better Products
for Better Homes

"Why, you can't go to town in a bathtub!" These words, uttered by a rural woman whose family owned a car but no tub during the 1920s, are the stuff of legend in the history of the automobile and American life. In the interwar years, "automobility" became the surest sign of a family's social status and its aspirations for membership in the middle class. As people invested financially and culturally in consumer society, they elected to spend their durable goods dollars on transportation items rather than on household improvements, including better facilities for human waste disposal, which makes the rural woman's perceptions of the bathtub even more pertinent. According to a three-year survey completed in 1928 under the auspices of the General Federation of Women's Clubs, more than twenty million Americans—some 17 percent of the population—still lived in dwellings without bathrooms. To sanitary fixture manufacturers like the Kohler Company of Kohler, Wisconsin, such statistics marked a durable goods niche ripe for development by a firm with a sophisticated, well-oiled marketing organization.[1]

More than other firms in this study, the Kohler Company tried to stimulate desire and to "make people want things" by using three interrelated strategies of enticement: product design, national advertising, and consumer credit. The fundamental goal revolved around converting the trinity of basic bathroom fix-tures—the toilet or water closet, the sink or wash basin, and the bathtub—from producer goods bought by builders into major durable goods purchased directly by consumers. The company unfolded this plan at the peak of the so-called durable goods revolution of the 1920s, as manufacturers of cars, refrigerators, stoves, and radios all offered their alluring products to consumers on credit. In many respects, the firm fits the well-known model of the family-dominated entrepreneurial enterprise that tried to achieve economies of scope and scale through product diversification and the coordination of an extensive marketing force. During the interwar years, Kohler struggled to find a place in an oligopo-listic market dominated by Chicago's Crane Company and Pittsburgh's Standard Sanitary Manufacturing Company. In the shadows of these diversified giants, Kohler's feisty, visionary president, Walter J. Kohler Sr., developed a distinctive approach to design, innovation, and marketing.[2]

At the helm of his family's firm from 1905 to 1937, Walter Kohler expanded its manufacturing base, making the Kohler Company into a "full-line" plumb-ing supplier. Rather than emulate the practices of big business—expanding his company through horizontal consolidation, vertical integration, and the estab-lishment of bureaucratic hierarchies—Kohler embraced a corporate strategy that emphasized continuity between the family firm, its community, and its cus-tomers. An eclectic set of ideas about citizenship, consumption, and efficiency lay at the heart of his philosophy. Kohler's amalgamated ideas drew sustenance from his readings of John Ruskin and Frederick Winslow Taylor, the Ameri-canization movement that grew out of the Great War, and his financial interests in a plumbing fixture firm. At the same time, his belief in the power of the en-

Walter J. Kohler, 1928.
Kohler Company

vironment to shape character revealed his sympathies with the loosely defined progressive reform tradition. Like other civic-minded businesspeople who came of age in the Progressive Era, Kohler saw politics, economics, and society as part of a seamless web. Good citizenship rested both on the assurance of political freedom and on the guarantee of economic security and its material manifestations. In this calculus, business leaders shouldered responsibility for minding the nation's wealth-generating machine, the corporation, and for fostering loyalty to the state by ensuring that deserving citizens enjoyed higher living standards. As chief executive, Kohler saw it as his duty to fortify the status quo that nourished good citizenship through mass consumption. In his schema, the American home—the site of biological re-creation, social reproduction, and the setting for plumbing fixtures—was an object of veneration, rejuvenation, and ideological conveyance.

Kohler spent much of his time grappling with the identity and the desires of his household customers. During his thirty-two-year presidency, bathroom aesthetics passed through three stages: the age of woodwork, the age of efficiency, and the age of modernity. In the first two periods, a handful of interest groups—architects, reformers, and engineers—competed for audiences among bathtub manufacturers, lobbying for fixtures that met local sanitary specifications. By the third era, a mind-boggling cacophony had emerged, as Kohler's product mix became more complex. The big question was, Which customers really mattered—branch managers, sales promotion men, jobbers, jobbers' salesmen, architects, builders, plumbers, landlords, apartment dwellers, or home owners? In the interwar years, Kohler faced the job of identifying, understanding, and satisfying the wants of these very different customers. By the 1920s, the firm had earned the trust of some six hundred jobbers and their clients, the plumbers, on whose loyalty sales depended. Nevertheless, its president recognized that security bred indifference. When he discovered feminine purchasing power during the prosperity decade, his biggest problem became to convince the men in the plumbing trade that Mrs. Consumer was the customer who really mattered. Repeatedly, the sales organization resisted efforts to inject fashion into the fixtures market. Jobbers' sales agents scoffed at colored products, and plumbers insisted on selling the cheapest goods, even to well-heeled customers. Futilely, Kohler did everything in his power to pry open new niches; marketing expenditures grew, but sales and profits plummeted.[3]

During his three decades as president, Walter Kohler experimented with promising business elixirs, from brand-naming to national advertising, in an effort to shape consumers' perceptions of sanitary plumbing fixtures and to increase sales. In rural America, Kohler aimed to meet the basic human need for healthful sanitary equipment; in wealthier urban areas, to stimulate consumer interest in home modernization and create a replacement fixtures market. If Kohler had appreciated the great satirist Sinclair Lewis, he might have chosen a different path. When the novelist allows his quintessential middlebrow, real estate agent George F. Babbitt to luxuriate in a "curving porcelain" bathtub to the dulcet "drip, drip, dribble" of "beautiful nickel taps," he comments on a bubbly splendor that seemed decadent to many Americans. Sensuous bathing was fine for fictional characters or for movie stars; when Gloria Swanson sponged down in a mammoth tub in Cecil B. DeMille's *Male and Female* in 1919, her bath represented the epitome of Hollywood hedonism. In real life, most consumers thought sanitary fixtures should be neither seen nor heard. Perhaps embarrassed by the obvious reference to bodily functions, few cared about the style, color, or shape of fixtures. As Americans chose how to spend surplus cash in the 1920s, they satisfied their yearnings for novelty with dime store trinkets, for luxury goods with items like crystal, and for status demarcators with cars, radios, and other electrical appliances. During the Great Depression, even better-off consumers had little money to spend on installment sales. In the late 1930s, Kohler retired from his executive office possessed with new wisdom about consumers and their motivations. Although people valued certain objects as signifiers of identity, they understood plumbing fixtures in a far more utilitarian way.[4]

Cleaning Up, Branching Out

> K for Knowledge assuring success,
> O for Organization which is the best.
> H for Harmony dominating us all,
> L for Loyalty come at your call.
> E for Efficiency best of its kind,
> R for Reliability none better can find.
> C for Confidence show by our Sales,
> O for Originality which ends our tale.
> —William H. Barth, Kohler Company, 1917

Americans spent much of the nineteenth and early twentieth centuries devising new gadgets, gizmos, and concoctions to brush away, suck up, cover up, or wash away the visible and invisible manifestations of dirt. During the Progressive Era, reformers added campaigns against germs, odors, and filth to the list of causes designed to remake America in the image of the white middle class. From social workers to home economists, the new professionals spread the gospel that John Wesley, the founder of Methodism, had espoused in the eighteenth century: cleanliness was "next to godliness." Once the infrastructure of modern sewage systems was in place, architects, builders, and engineers brought bathrooms to buildings inside the homes of both wealthy Americans and the middle class. In new residences, the one-stop bathroom replaced the hodgepodge of hygiene equipment—bedroom toilet sets, stove-top washbasins, chamber pots, outdoor privies, water closets, and other makeshift expedients.[5]

This clean craze portended the expansion of the enameling and pottery trades, which supplied the fixtures. By 1901, J. M. Kohler Sons Company, a foundry operated by the brothers Robert, Walter, and Carl Kohler, in Sheboygan, Wisconsin, was making farm equipment as well as enameled fixtures, including bathtubs, washtubs, sinks, and drinking fountains. After the untimely deaths of his two siblings, Walter Kohler in 1905 assumed the presidency. With the help of his younger half brother Herbert V., he began to build the Kohler Company, incorporated in 1912, into one of the "big three" plumbing supply houses in the United States.[6]

The Kohlers approached the burgeoning sanitary-ware trade in several ways; their tactics in market research are especially pertinent to this story of manufacturers imagining consumers. During the late nineteenth century, many small and midsized enamelware manufacturers and jobbers followed associationist tactics, establishing cartels for controlling markets. In 1894, those in the Midwest, including Kohler, formed the Central Supply Association to facilitate relations with truculent regional members of the National Association of Master Plumbers. By contrast, the largest enamelware makers followed in the footsteps of the Singer Sewing Machine Company, the McCormick Harvesting Machine Company, and the National Cash Register by building impressive marketing organizations. In Pittsburgh, the gigantic Standard Sanitary Manufacturing Company, created by a merger in 1899, phased out sales to independent distributors and began to build a wholly owned network of branch offices and wholesalers. The Kohlers started to emulate parts of this model, establishing in 1905 a Chicago branch office, which within three years was selling half their products. Between 1909 and 1916, the company opened branches in thirteen cities: Atlanta, Denver, Detroit, Houston, Indianapolis, Philadelphia, Pittsburgh, London,

Los Angeles, St. Louis, St. Paul, San Francisco, and Seattle. Unlike Standard, Kohler used branch offices staffed by managers and "sales-promotion men" as platforms for catering to established distributors. The offices sold fixtures to jobbers, who in turn sold them to plumbers; as the last link in the distribution chain, plumbers dealt directly with home owners. However, selling fixtures constituted only part of a showroom's job. Top managers at Kohler also depended on display room managers as fashion intermediaries.[7]

"K for Knowledge assuring success"—a line of the jingle by William H. Barth, manager of the Kohler Company's flagship showroom on West Forty-second Street in New York City—referred to the customer feedback loop critical to the firm's product innovation formula. Branch managers had trained well for their assignments as data gatherers. Barth, a Cooper Institute graduate who could speak architectural lingo, had been a plumbing supplier for four decades; Pittsburgh's Harry E. Clark had worked for Standard; and Philadelphia's H. J. Hanna Jr. had sold fixtures for the Potteries Selling Company, a short-lived distributor for Trenton sanitary-ware factories. Born "with a plumber's ladle in his hand," Lewis Phillips, manager of the Indianapolis office, had worked for both Standard and Crane. As seasoned veterans of the plumbing supply business, such managers comprehended the technical difficulties faced by architects, builders, and plumbers. They combined this experience with the salesman's bag of tricks to size up customers. The smallest details, from vocal intonation to personal grooming, yielded vital evidence about a customer's character and truthfulness. Just as competent salesmen differentiated between shoppers and browsers, astute branch managers readily distinguished whiners from clients with legitimate concerns. Anyone could walk through the door of a Kohler showroom to praise or castigate products. Showroom managers reported anything newsworthy to Walter Kohler.[8]

By the 1910s, Kohler's reading of branch managers' reports corroborated his theory that a seismographic shift was under way in the sanitary trade. Reformers condemned the bathrooms that late nineteenth-century sanitarians had heralded as crowning achievements of the plumber's craft: ornate wainscoting, Eastlake-style cabinetry, wooden floors, concealed pipes, and marble lavatories all reportedly provided breeding grounds for germs. When Standard introduced its new lines for 1911, the "bathroom of the hour" boasted a porcelain toilet, a porcelain sink, and an enameled tub. Everything about the room—its smooth tiled walls, small window with tinted panes, exposed pipes, and stunning white fixtures—spoke to a clean, durable, and efficient sanitary ideal. This new design came on the market at an opportune moment. For decades, women from the well-to-do and comfortable classes had complained about the so-called servant problem. As more and more white working-class women opted for factory and clerical jobs, upper- and middle-class homemakers had trouble finding maids willing to work for low pay, to live in, and to perform arduous chores without grumbling. Free of nooks and crannies, the new all-white bathroom promised fewer chores than its Victorian wood predecessor, making it appealing to women who supervised difficult servants or who did their own housework.[9]

Kohler responded to this ultraclean aesthetic with the so-called apron tub, precursor to the built-in unit common today. Previously, cast-iron tubs fell into several categories, including those in wooden frames or with four feet, neither of which fit progressive notions of cleanliness. To be sure, these tubs cleansed immersed subjects effectively. Their dirt drawbacks related to construction, as bacteria lived inside dark wooden frames or between the floorboards under footed models. While some box-shaped bathtubs existed, these units, cast in multiple pieces by enameling shops, depended on a plumber's skills in fitting. At the joints, crevices harbored moisture, soap residue, and germs. Kohler's engineers overcame these problems with foundry practices that enabled the one-piece casting of large enameled items with big folded rims, or aprons. Denied a patent claim, Kohler watched other manufacturers, including Standard, adopt his methods and designs. By the Great War, several types of tub competed for consumers' bathing dollars, but the apron tub soon became the preferred unit.[10]

With the apron tub, Walter Kohler established the product development model that he favored for the next two decades. He collected information about the market through branch offices, using this customer data to design new lines, keep track of regional taste preferences, and fathom how his products compared with those of competitors. As irrational as this seems to those accustomed to late twentieth-century analysts who use computers to correlate zip codes and consumption habits, Kohler's methods for reading the market paralleled those used by Thomas Hawkes, Jesse Dean, and W. Edwin Wells. Yet Kohler operated in a market that stratified rather than segmented. As fashion intermediaries forwarded information about this layered market—composed of people with disparate preconceptions about dirt, cleanliness, and fixtures—Kohler sifted through the mass of incoming letters for useful data. In many respects, he faced a culturally more complex challenge than did Wells at the Homer Laughlin China Company, whose fashion intermediaries—retail buyers working for mass merchandisers—stood closer to the ultimate consumer. In the long run, Kohler

"Colonna" Bath, Plate No. K-64   "Bretton" Lavatory, Plate No. K-580

In this "Colonna" bathtub you buy exactly the same superior quality as in KOHLER "Viceroy" built-in tubs

We wish to emphasize as strongly as possible that there is but *one* Kohler quality—the highest. Whatever the price of the bathtub, lavatory, kitchen sink or other enameled plumbing ware you select for your home, if it is Kohler ware it is *always* the same high quality. The same workmen use the same materials and make every piece in the same way. Without regard to price, you get exactly the same quality-value in all Kohler fixtures.

Choose enameled ware made by Kohler of Kohler

No old style or sectional unhygienic patterns in Kohler Ware

Every Kohler piece is thoroughly modern. The lines are artistic. Every woman will appreciate the absence of grooved ornamentation which affords lodging places for dust and grime.

Kohler enamel has a smooth, white surface, and the color is uniform. All Kohler enameled ware is made in one factory—the largest in the world devoted exclusively to the production of enameled plumbing ware.

Sectional view of one-piece "Viceroy" built-in bath—the lightest and easiest cleaning tub of its type—Plate No. V-12-A. "Columbia" Lavatory—Plate No. K-205-F.

Your architect will tell you that Kohler designs are handsome and that Kohler enameled ware is most durable—it will last a lifetime. Your plumber is glad to install it, because he has no trouble with it—its hygienic features and its ease of cleaning always satisfy his customers. The cost of installation is no more than for cheaper, inferior ware.

Kohler Co. originated one-piece construction. Kohler baths simplify the work of installation, and eliminate unhygienic sectional features.

Kohler production

When you buy a piece of Kohler enameled ware you secure the product of the largest factory in the world devoted exclusively to the production of enameled plumbing ware, made by an enthusiastic, efficient organization imbued with high ideals.

"It's in the Kohler Enamel"

MAKERS OF
Enameled Bathtubs, Lavatories, Sinks, Etc.

KOHLER CO.

Founded 1873

Kohler, Wis., U. S. A.

BRANCHES
London   New York   Chicago
Boston   San Francisco

The classic footed tub and the apron tub. In the era of the footed tub (top), Kohler and other manufacturers perfected technologies for forming red-hot iron into massive shapes with double walls, introducing the apron tub (bottom left). Advertisement in *Saturday Evening Post*, September 18, 1915, Kohler Company

would see how long-distance communication, involving four or five nodes on the production-consumption continuum, proved a drawback in gauging consumers' tastes, desires, and outlooks.

Better Homes, Kohler Style

> Whatever helps to make the American home a better and more
> attractive place to live contributes to the physical and spiritual
> up building of the nation.
> —Walter J. Kohler, 1929

From the 1910s to the 1930s, Walter Kohler literally put his own house in order, building an industrial town that embodied his ideas of beauty, cleanliness, efficiency—and Americanism. By the turn of the century, the Kohlers had moved from Sheboygan to a new manufacturing complex some four miles west, in the hamlet of Riverside. Disturbed by the "nondescript" houses that workers hurriedly erected close to the hot, dirty, smoky foundry, Kohler undertook the project of building, piece by piece, one of the most publicized early twentieth-century factory towns: Kohler Village. Rooted in progressive visions of social perfection, Kohler Village assumed a distinctive character under the influence of 100 percent Americanism—a wartime campaign against hyphenated Americans, specifically German-Americans. As the offspring of an Austrian immigrant, Kohler hoped to make his quaint little Anglo-Saxon village the incarnation of his loyalty and nationalist sympathy. In this context, Kohler Village in the 1920s joined other communities that supported Better Homes in America, the standard-bearer of the campaign to make the detached, single-family suburban dwelling the agent of conformity, racial purification, and moral regeneration. What better home for an unwashed American-in-training than one outfitted with modern plumbing fixtures made by the Kohler Company? Even more important, what better imagery for national advertising campaigns than pictures of Kohler Village, a model company town filled with full-blooded American, colonial-style, Better Homes?[11]

Kohler Village belongs to a group of approximately forty company towns built throughout the United States between 1910 and 1929. These villages differed from nineteenth-century company towns, like Lowell, Massachusetts, and Pullman, Illinois, in significant ways, most important of which were their creators' progressive commitments to both the physical separation and the visual disassociation between spaces for living and working. The professional architects, planners, and landscape architects who designed them decried the monotony, repetition, and shoddy construction that characterized conventional industrial housing. Widely publicized as solutions to labor unrest among immigrant workers, these new company towns provided, through contract, rental, or purchase, each head of a household with the object that most symbolized middle-class status: a single-family dwelling in an idyllic suburban setting. The model villages used site plans with cul-de-sacs, curvilinear streets, shade trees, landscaped islands, pedestrian walkways, town squares, playgrounds, parks, and a variety of culturally uplifting architectural styles. In theory, the immigrant worker who owned a beautiful Colonial Revival home would absorb American ideals from his tangible surroundings, developing an appreciation for the employer and nation that made the good life possible.[12]

Shortly after moving to Riverside in 1899, Kohler embraced the potpourri of ideas that connected environmental factors to social uplift under the banner of Progressivism. With several architect companions, including W. C. Weeks and Richard Phillip, he toured Europe in 1912 to examine planned industrial communities, including world-famous model industrial villages built under the auspices or influence of Sir Ebenezer Howard, father of the English Garden City movement. Impressed, Kohler returned to Wisconsin determined to remake Riverside in the image of British beautiful. In particular, Kohler appreciated the British planner's concept of decentralization. Critical of the haphazard, unhealthful congestion of nineteenth-century cities, Howard invoked the sylvan image of the "machine in the garden," urging factories to relocate in picturesque planned communities far away from noisome urban blight. This garden idea struck a chord with Kohler, who had inadvertently initiated a decentralization plan by leaving Sheboygan. Almost a decade after arriving in Riverside, and only a few months after touring Europe, he incorporated the three-thousand-acre site surrounding his foundry as Kohler Village. A few years later, he applied the lessons of the Garden City movement to this site, where running water was at a premium and the streets unpaved.[13]

In the interim, he busily dealt with a major reorganization, recapitalization, the opening of branch sales offices, and technological improvements at the foundry. When the booming economy of the early war years temporarily stimulated construction, Kohler faced a housing crisis as his factory output tried to keep pace with demand. In 1916 he mobilized by hiring a team of housing and landscape experts, including the German-born planner Werner Hegemann, to appraise real estate holdings with the aim of laying out a new company town on the Garden City model. In collaboration with Elbert Peets, a young landscape architect from Cambridge, Massachusetts, Hegemann laid out a master plan for the "Kohler Garden City."[14]

Built in several stages between 1916 and the Great Depression, Kohler Village followed a town plan that divided the landscape into discrete industrial, commercial, and residential zones. The layout conveyed a sense of order, harmony, beauty, and affinity with nature. In contrast to new company towns built from scratch, Kohler Village integrated existing structures into the quaint landscape by modifying them to blend in, like workers melting into the pot. In Walter Kohler's description, when older houses were "painted white" and their "lawns prepared and planted," the "entire village" took on a "very interesting and prosperous appearance." Richard Phillip, the architect from Milwaukee's Brust & Phillip who had toured England with Kohler, designed most of the new structures built from 1916 through the mid-1920s. Anglo-Saxon styles became tools for conveying a distinctively American way of life. Phillip's picturesque commercial block on High Street, across from the factory, featured Tudor-style stores with arched windows, stone coping, and steep roofs and gables. His American House, which opened in June 1918, was an enormous structure with rental rooms for some three hundred male workers and resembled a large English country house in the Queen Anne style. For married men, Phillip filled neighborhoods with worker-owned houses in Colonial Revival styles. Fittingly, Kohler resided a short distance from the town's center, at Riverbend, a cloistered waterside estate designed by Phillip in the style of a lordly manor house.[15]

Like other manufacturers who sponsored new company towns, Kohler believed in the ability of the village environment to shape the stable workforce critical to steady production and potential expansion. For decades, the Kohlers had struggled to retain highly paid foundry workers whose skills were at a premium in the burgeoning iron-making and enameling trades. Even after the installation of casting machinery, the foundry still relied on skilled labor for certain operations. Artisanal knowledge of metalworking operations remained integral to the company's output, and Kohler elevated the craftsman to the status of folk hero in his corporate culture. By the mid-1920s, visitors entering the vestibule of the company's general office building, predictably bedecked by architects Brust & Phillips with a symbolic clock tower, faced seven breathtaking wall murals that exalted foundry labor. Painted by Arthur Covey, a corporate muralist whose clients included William Filene & Sons in Boston and Lord & Taylor

Muralist Arthur Covey installing *Pouring a Mold*, 1925. Kohler Company

in New York City, scenes like *Tapping a Cupola* and *Pouring a Mold* depicted muscular workers toiling amid hot, dangerous equipment, capturing what the Kohler Company described as the "dignity and nobility" of factory work. Although modeling his figures after real Kohler workers, Covey used considerable license with the machinery, juxtaposing foundry men against fantastical or antiquated devices. Through this legerdemain, Covey focused the viewer's gaze on the men, emphasizing the human element central to flexible batch production. Yet his murals hid the stark reality of high turnover rates. Lured to Wisconsin by the promise of steady employment at high wages, early workers grew frustrated with housing shortages that forced them to live miles from Riverside. When many deserted Kohler, the company faced production backlogs.[16]

From Kohler's perspective, village housing was a hedge against labor scarcity, industrial instability, and an influx of unwashed greenhorns; but it also was fodder for corporate promotions designed to build goodwill and profits. There was no better way to harness what Kohler described as the village's "sentimental advantages" than through participation in Better Homes in America (BHA), a voluntary organization backed by Herbert Hoover's Department of Commerce. The brainchild of Marie Mattingly Meloney, the reform-minded editor of the

Delineator, BHA mixed a tempered version of nineteenth-century domesticity, the progressive impulse for efficiency, and Herbert Hoover's brand of associationism to promote the detached single-family dwelling as the ideal American residence. Among supporters, BHA meant different things. To Meloney, home ownership provided an avenue for promoting family life; to Hoover, it offered a dual-purpose tool that alleviated housing problems and stabilized wages, prices, and the economy; and to the Kohler Company, it presented an unparalleled opportunity for using Kohler Village to market new products.[17]

One BHA propaganda device was the national Better Homes in America Week, which featured an annual contest for the best demonstration home. Following guidelines published in the *Delineator* and circulated by the Commerce Department, local committees—usually composed of women from civic, philanthropic, and educational organizations—set up model houses, educational programs, and home economics demonstrations, which competed for prizes and for publicity in Meloney's magazine. Model homes showcased furnishings, appliances, and fixtures donated by manufacturers, who advertised their sponsorship. The Better Homes idea spread rapidly. In 1921, there were 521 demonstration homes across the country; in 1925, 1,700; in 1930, 6,700; in 1932, 8,300. The movement gained momentum during the early 1930s, as sponsors saw the model home as the ideal family-oriented entertainment for hard times; by inference, BHA pageantry advocated family unity as a problem solver over social protest.[18]

Walter Kohler's sister, Marie Christian Kohler (1876–1943), was the driving force behind Kohler Village's participation in BHA. As a director and major stockholder in the Kohler Company, she comprehended the public relations value of Better Homes activities. Every year, beginning in 1925, she oversaw the local celebration of Better Homes in America Week, which featured a new model home that tourists could visit throughout the summer. Kohler Village's demonstration units—sold at cost by the Kohler Improvement Company and financed by the Kohler Building & Loan Company—embodied conservative ideas and the "character-building" power of domesticity. A typical model was a Cape Cod–style cottage for a family of four, outfitted with new Colonial Revival furnishings and with hand-me-downs that showed "the continuing of family life" and the "cherishing of family traditions." The houses also had "smart and modern" appointments, including the latest plumbing and heating systems, which promised efficiency and comfort. As educational devices, Marie Kohler's exhibits trained visitors to think about careful, moderated consumption. As mar-

keting tools, the homes showed how particular products—Kohler products—
could augment the consuming experience.[19]

Advertising the Kohler Way

> The whole purpose of our advertising, both in our magazines and
> our own literature, should be to induce action on the part of the
> consumer, and goodwill and cooperation on the part of the dealer.
> —L. L. Smith, Kohler Company, 1921

The Kohler Company took advantage of the celebrity accorded to its model village and Better Homes exhibits in several ways. Foremost, the firm simply basked
in the glory of newspaper headlines and magazine articles that touted Kohler
Village's virtues. In this respect, Walter Kohler emulated Henry Ford, who
smugly noted how much gratis publicity his five-dollar-a-day wage policy, initiated in 1914, had generated; however, unlike Ford, Kohler did not scoff at national advertising. With the aid of his in-house expert, L. L. Smith, Walter Kohler
learned to see how Kohler Village's spotless streets, trimmed landscape, and
quaint houses might serve as advertising leitmotifs to build dealer loyalty and
stimulate home owners' desires for his brand of fixtures. Not by serendipity had
Walter Kohler opened a corporate advertising office in 1916 nor by accident did
his firm's selling expenses steadily increase from $606,000 in 1921 to $2.4 million in 1929, from 10.1 to 15.3 percent of net sales. During the Great War, two
aspects of federal policy had encouraged American manufacturers to take advertising seriously. First, advertising men working for the federal government in
George Creel's Committee on Public Information demonstrated their prowess
by successfully mounting emotionally powerful poster campaigns that sold Liberty and Victory Bonds, rallied support for the Red Cross, urged men to become
doughboys, promoted food and resource conservation, and generally stirred
American patriotism. Once morally questionable showmen, advertising men
exited the war as confident professionals who had earned the respect of businessmen like Kohler. More important, the federal government's imposition of an
excess profits tax in October 1917 (raised in February 1918 and repealed in 1921),
which defined advertising expenses as fully deductible business costs, provided
a real economic incentive for corporations to invest in advertising. Every dollar
spent on advertising by a profitable firm translated into sixty to sixty-five cents

saved in taxes; in other words, a business could buy a dollar's worth of advertising for only thirty-five to forty cents. Needing to spend their excess profits quickly and as a legitimate business expense, manufacturers hiked promotional budgets during the war. Fully aware of the scarcity of both goods and cash in the inflationary wartime economy, many businesses in the short term embraced what *Printers' Ink* described as goodwill advertising. In anticipation of a postwar boom in consumer spending, firms like Kohler promoted themselves as worthy, patriotic, stable institutions that would again deliver the goods after the Armistice.[20]

Collaborating with Smith, Walter Kohler adopted an advertising strategy designed to foster dealer cooperation and build brand recognition. Although managers still imagined their consumer as an amorphous jobber-architect-plumber amalgam, they started seeing the benefits of sparking home owners' interests in their particular brand of fixtures. Under Smith's aegis, Kohler advertising shifted in scale, tone, and thematic focus. The firm bought space in national magazines like the *Literary Digest* for "reason-why" campaigns announcing the "superior quality" of Kohler products. With Smith on board, advertisements emphasized the benefits of Kohler-brand fixtures in the context of home-centered family values. When the reality of the new tax code hit, Walter Kohler hired a national agency, Erwin, Wasey & Company (EW), to design an enlarged consumer-oriented advertising campaign. Walter Kohler and Smith also continued to invest in dealer and trade advertising. Dependent on branch offices for the burden of product promotion, Smith upgraded the firm's "dealer helps": large plumbers' catalogues; architects' leaflets, folders, and portfolios; window units for showrooms; electrical signs for distributors; exhibits for plumbers' conventions and state fairs; booklets on Kohler Village; and a monthly house organ, *Kohler of Kohler News*. In short, Kohler typified durable goods manufacturers who took advantage of federal tax policy to continue trade advertising at a steady pace while enlarging campaigns aimed directly at consumers.[21]

Thereby, Walter Kohler joined the ranks of industrialists struggling with the great paradox of modernity. Sustained productivity required the expansion of consumer demand, but the task of stimulating self-indulgence seemed contrary to the asceticism that lay at the heart of the Kohler way. Just as the architect Richard Phillip used Anglo-Saxon motifs to teach village dwellers about American values, the advertising agency EW manipulated the printed medium to create a visual culture that encouraged consumption through participation in a clean, robust American lifestyle. Professionals knew how to get multiple audiences in focus. The EW imagery readied both the Kohler Company and the home-owning public for a durable goods revolution in plumbing fixtures. Kohler Village figured as a key variable in this equation.

When account representatives from EW's Chicago office visited Wisconsin in September 1918, their zeal for Kohler Village impressed the president. "They have outlined a policy," he excitedly wrote to his brother, "that Kohler stands not only for the Kohler Co., but for a quality, a product, a community spirit, an inspiration, etc., and the story will be told in a series of advertisements." Walter Kohler trumpeted: "They were all very much inspired by the community development, which is now sufficiently advanced to be conspicuous." EW's proposals included a new corporate seal—a bronze medallion showing a foundry man in his work clothes—to serve as both a community emblem and an icon in all of the Kohler Company's advertisements. "The publicity will be handled in a manner that the Kohler Co. will benefit, to a great extent," Walter Kohler told his sibling, "by being located in the village of Kohler." Ultimately pleased with EW's campaign proposals, he acceded to copywriters: "Kohler products," boasted a typical advertisement from the mid-1920s, "are made in a village where houses are homes and yards are gardens, where civic pride and pride of good work go hand in hand." In the firm's executive offices, advertising imagery exerted a mighty sway over managers, who came to imagine that the fantastical village depicted by the company's powerful public relations machine was the real thing.[22]

Throughout the 1920s, in-house publicists used Kohler Village to teach members of the Kohler organization—branch managers, sales promotion men, jobbers, jobbers' salesmen, and plumbers—how to promote products. Each month, the house organ, *Kohler of Kohler News,* published lively articles on village activities, chatty vignettes about production processes, and full-page magazine advertisements. Browsing through the *News,* readers learned to think about Kohler fixtures as components in a larger system for better living. Schooled in these basics, members of the company's marketing organization traveled to Wisconsin for annual conferences prepared for a high old time. They were not disappointed. For example, in August 1927, a parade of executives, branch managers, town officials, high school bands, and scout troops escorted the entourage along High Street to the American Club for breakfast and a speech by Walter Kohler. Saturday afternoon's activities included visits to factories and showrooms, a tour of Kohler Village with its Better Homes model, and a fete at Riverside, featuring a horse show, music, dancing, and movies of a recent plumbers' convention and the Lindbergh flight. On Sunday, exhausted jobbers finally got down to business. After church services, they attended a morning session devoted to product demonstrations; after lunch, bands accompanied the men, whose trunks were filled with folders, catalogues, and display units, back to their train. They left imbued with an idea of systematized living, Kohler style.[23]

Rule of Thumb

> The material progress of humanity has been brought about by
> discovering and devising more and better kinds of goods and the
> means of producing them.
> —Walter J. Kohler, *Mill and Factory*, 1940

Walter and Herbert Kohler learned important lessons during the Great War that shaped decision making over the next two decades. The ban on residential construction (housing starts fell from 421,000 units in 1914 to 118,000 in 1918) combined with the U.S. Fuel Administration's request for half-time production of enamel dampened sanitary fixture sales. Profiting from wartime contracts for shells and other metal castings, the brothers recognized that reliance on a single line of products—especially one linked to the volatile construction trade—was risky business.[24]

During the 1920s, the Kohler Company built on the legacy of other family-owned durable goods manufacturing firms that focused on product diversification and highly refined marketing organizations. The brothers aimed to build on the firm's strength in household durable goods while expanding beyond the bathtub realm. First, the Kohlers had to find a product with a demand cycle that complemented enamelware; plumbing fixtures found their largest market in urban areas, with sales peaking during warm weather when construction was under way. The brothers' initial diversification efforts targeted year-round rural, marine, and industrial markets with an electrical generator introduced in 1920 at the National Tractor Show in Kansas City. A four-cylinder gasoline-powered engine, the new Kohler Automatic Power and Light unit generated 110-volt direct current. For rural America, the timing was perfect; offered on three different installment plans, the expensive Kohler Automatic—one model cost $595 in 1921—enabled better-off isolated households to power the new electrical appliances, from sewing machines to corn grinders, then flooding the market. But the Automatic had other applications. In 1920, a U.S. Department of Agriculture extension survey found that nearly 70 percent of farmhouses, isolated from municipal water systems, were without running water. With electricity from portable generators, farm families could pump water indoors, eliminating the backbreaking chore of hauling water and replacing their cold, smelly outdoor privies with indoor flush toilets. Within the Kohler Company, the Automatic's introduction enhanced core technical competencies, as the firm hired electrical engineers to design and develop the new line.[25]

The next stage of product diversification entailed the mastery of an entirely new area—pottery manufacturing. Although the Kohler brothers had mulled over ceramics since November 1918, they delayed entry into this line for several reasons. In part, their attentions were focused on the Automatic, the village, and the Kohler organization, and their actions responded to larger trends in the plumbing supply business. As a small player in an oligopolistic market, Kohler was caught in a bind. Although the firm might introduce new lines, the success of those items was limited by the jobbers' conservative expectations and issues of volume, delivery, and price rather than design. Furthermore, Standard's chief executive, Theodore Ahrens, ruled the enamelware industry's trade association with an iron fist. Walter described him as an "erratic dictator" with "arbitrary inclinations," whose impulsive actions led enamel men down dead-end paths, such as the decision to reduce prices during the 1919 building boom—when new housing starts numbered 315,000—despite increased costs and high inflation. The president recognized that he had to find "some line of work" that developed his firm's "individuality."[26]

By early 1919, Walter Kohler contemplated the expansion of his bathtub empire with the addition of continuous-flow vitreous sanitary pottery for making sinks and toilets. When the construction business collapsed and new housing starts declined to 247,000 in 1920, he minded the store, keeping a watchful eye on Trenton's sanitary pottery trade, which, hurt by the recession and in a protracted fight with labor, eventually collapsed. Up until that point, New Jersey potteries, mostly small to midsized family firms, produced almost half of the ceramic plumbing fixtures used in the United States. They employed skilled and semiskilled union workers, organized into sanitary locals of the National Brotherhood of Operative Potters, to make fixtures under craft and batch production setups. The largest of these firms, Thomas Maddock's Sons Company, operated a twenty-one-kiln plant, with a weekly output of five thousand pieces, including sinks, toilet bowls, tanks, drinking fountains, showerheads, urinal stalls, and general bathroom accessories. With a few years, this bastion of flexible production lay in ruin, victims of overlapping battles with labor, national plumbing supply houses, and Justice Department monopoly busters.[27]

Following the trade upheaval, Standard and Crane revved up for a race to win dominance of the market as the construction business regained momentum. In 1921, new housing starts numbered 449,000; in 1923, 871,000; and in 1925, 937,000. Standard bought potteries in Ohio, Indiana, and California, gearing up for expanded ceramics production, while Crane opened a foundry in Louisiana, leaving Kohler, its major supplier of cast-iron fixtures, in the lurch. In 1924, Crane added the Trenton Potteries Company to its holdings, reorganizing production to ease skilled labor out of the picture. By mid-decade, Trenton's sanitary business was turned upside down; its only hope for salvation appeared to rest in the hands of the plumbing suppliers who were partially responsible for the ruckus.[28]

For Walter and Herbert Kohler, the bedlam in Trenton provided entry into the pottery business through the backdoor. Unable to compete, small factories looked eagerly for bailouts. In September 1925, Kohler purchased the business of Cochran, Drugan & Company, which operated a bottle kiln factory close to Trenton. One of the greatest attractions was the location, which provided ready access to major northeastern markets. Another lure was the expertise of the city's ceramists. Andrew Cochran, a veteran of the potteries, agreed to stay on to tutor Herbert Kohler. At first, Cochran-Drugan seemed a solid, low-cost investment; before long, Kohler's managers discovered that their bargain purchase was a nineteenth-century rat's nest.[29]

Kohler's managers entered the pottery business with a blank slate. Either they knew little about Cochran-Drugan's standing in the trade, or they refused to listen to local gossip and credit reports. When long-standing customers refused to buy fixtures made at the plant, Kohler began to suspect that something was rotten. Outspoken jobbers scoffed at Kohler's pottery, doubting the ironmonger could whip Cochran-Drugan into shape. Jobbers who did buy fixtures complained about quality. Architects, plumbers, building managers, and home owners—growing accustomed to high degrees of standardization in quantity-production goods—expected perfection from even the most utilitarian durable goods, including bathroom fixtures. Kohler's customers read advertisements that touted the company's commitment to exacting craftsmanship, and they recoiled from the flawed goods emerging from its Trenton factory.[30]

First and foremost, consumers objected to the color of Cochran-Drugan's fixtures, which failed to fit their ideas of whiteness. Ever since germ theory gained currency in popular culture beginning in the 1880s, sanitary reformers usurped white for their cleanliness campaigns. At the World's Columbian Exposition in

1893, whiteness bedazzled fair goers. In the new century, reformers, doctors, teachers, and manufacturers deemed white as ideal for bathrooms, a color suggestive of a clean, germ-free environment. The vermin- and disease-ridden encampments of the Great War contributed to the heightened fetish for cleanliness. In 1924, journalist Estelle H. Ries, writing for *Fruit, Garden, and Home,* the precursor to *Better Homes and Gardens,* praised the "all-white bathroom" as the apex of sanitary modernity. Like other enamelware manufacturers, Kohler pledged to endow its fixtures with "snowy purity," but challenges from technology and labor at the Trenton factory fractured that promise.[31]

Consumers accustomed to exacting standards made possible by quantity-production techniques recognized that not all whites were snowy. Minor differences in hues and tints resulted in chromatic chaos when distant factories were involved; and the job of creating uniform and matching colors, textures, and densities for glassy coatings applied to different bases—iron and ceramics—doubled Kohler's troubles. Problems were exacerbated when the firm, concerned for worker safety, abandoned the inexpensive, widely available lead fluxes that had long been used to melt enamels and glazes. As chemists developed lead-free formulas, products bore the telltale signs of their experiments—mismatched, speckled, grayish, and otherwise imperfect white coatings. Sam Wolff, president of the Wolff Supply Company, reported that one of his "best accounts" complained that Kohler pottery failed to "harmonize" with the "the snow white color of Kohler Enamelware." Compared to its tubs and sinks, the Kohler toilet tanks had "a decided grayish color."[32]

Herbert Kohler's spirits dampened by the hour. A devotee of efficiency, the vice president grew annoyed with the rule-of-thumb practices that dominated Trenton's pottery trade and with Cochran's difficulties in modernizing the plant. From Herbert's perspective, the problems stemmed from a lack of shop floor discipline. When black specks marred glazes, he blamed foremen who did not force workers to take precautions against contaminants on the production line. Although their union was broken, Trenton's sanitary potters remained fiercely independent, resisting supervision they saw as a threat to craft autonomy. The bottle kilns built in 1898 coughed up coal dust that contributed to the dirt dilemma. Within a few months, Herbert urged moving pottery production to Wisconsin, where foreman schooled in scientific management could keep tabs on manufacturing. Managers started planning a new tunnel kiln facility in early 1926.[33]

Kohler's decision to make vitreous plumbing fixtures in Wisconsin dramatically changed the firm's marketing practices. Burdened with high shipping and selling costs, Kohler could not compete with volume price leaders like Standard; hence, by necessity, the firm focused on carving a niche for high-class plumbing supplies. Kohler decided to tap into home owners' expectations for cleanliness, efficiency, and beauty and placed even greater responsibility for reading consumer tastes and pushing fixtures on branch managers. "We should not underestimate the difficulty of distribution," confided Herbert to Walter Kohler. "Our managers," he emphasized, "should be able to sell and teach others to sell." For almost a decade, Kohler used design, advertising, and public relations to help dealers break down customer resistance to sanitary ware as a consumer durable. For fixture houses, the emphasis on the style-conscious world of shoppers proved a big step, and the Kohler Company blazed the path.[34]

The Cinderella of Housework

> The time will come when people who have Chevrolets will wash their dishes mechanically.
> —J. Robin Harrison, Kohler Company, 1927

By the 1920s, most American manufacturers paid attention to women's purchasing power. Products with the greatest "she appeal" included electrical appliances—from irons to washing machines—that promised to lessen burdensome household chores. By the middle of the decade, plumbers saw appliance sales as a way to supplement income earned through installations and service. Whereas department, hardware, and electrical stores and utility showrooms stocked costly "electrical specialities" like refrigerators, plumbers needed products that allowed them to use their unique installation skills to take advantage of the prosperous Christmas season. Sears, Roebuck & Company and General Electric made complicated appliances like refrigerators; but Kohler, whose expertise lay in foundry work, was unprepared to manufacture goods that required sophisticated electrical design and labor-intensive assembly lines. The trick entailed adapting foundry skills to making relatively simple plumbers' specialities. In addition, Kohler had to refine its marketing mechanisms to help plumbers push the new durable goods to women consumers.[35]

The Kohler Company's venture into the market for consumer durables grew out of another aspect of its affiliation with BHA—the aspect that rallied behind the drives for rationalization and standardization. Within Herbert Hoover's bureaucracy, efficiency advocacy extended to matters of personal finance and industrial production. Knowing that consumers hesitated to borrow money to purchase expensive durable goods, the Commerce Department published pamphlets that explained the ins and outs of installment selling. To Walter Kohler, the urges to Hooverize and Americanize could be used to advance his firm's market position. Hoover's department gave federal priority to the rational home, and his BHA provided the ideal advertising venue for efficient home products. President Kohler decided to take advantage of all this visibility and introduce innovative durable goods that might be sold directly to consumers on the installment plan.[36]

In late 1926, the Kohler Company announced the first of its consumer durables, a plumbers specialty product designed expressly for Mrs. Consumer: the Kohler Electric Sink. A solution to the drudgery of doing dishes, the electric sink bridged the eras of hand and automatic washing. Little remembered today, electric sinks flourished briefly during the Jazz Age. Like other short-lived devices, they resolved the need of a particular moment. During the 1920s, the appliance craze combined with consumers' perceptions about the scarcity of servants into an imperative for "labor-less dishwashing through electricity." Any mechanical device that promised to save time and energy appealed to well-off women who suddenly had no dependable domestic helpers. Kohler was in a good position to respond to the demand for so-called mechanical servants. In terms of production, the firm's engineers—who designed the electric sink, maintained the factories, and worked for Kohler subsidiaries on village construction projects—possessed the requisite electrical and mechanical knowledge for creating the new line. As for distribution, Kohler's showrooms could be easily fixed up for demonstrating, promoting, and selling kitchen appliances.[37]

Other equipment manufacturers had similar devices on the market. In May 1926, Country Gentleman assessed several of these contraptions, designed for use with or without electricity. Some performed notoriously, leaving scraps of vegetables, gravy, and meat on cups, bowls, and plates; others were portable appliances, requiring the homemaker to fill and drain water by hand; still others simply consisted of a wire sink-shaped basket with a hose attachment for manually squirting soapy and clear water on the dishes. These drawbacks meant that Kohler engineers decided to design a machine that not only was easy to use but also washed dishes clean. Ultimately, the Kohler Electric Sink, available in seven models, large and small, combined the functions of a conventional sink and a dishwasher. Modeled after the Walker Electric Dishwasher Sink introduced in

A lifelong servant—yours for no more than a servant's wage for a few months

The KOHLER ELECTRIC SINK

It is economy to pay money for some luxuries. The Kohler Electric Sink is an economy. It does effortlessly, three times a day and year after year, a task that by the old way of doing costs physical fatigue, and mental weariness, and money, and time worth more than money.

Every woman knows the cost. And no American woman, in these "Electric Twenties," intends to keep on paying that cost forever. The Kohler Electric Sink is here. *Now* is the time

to stop paying tribute to the tyrant of the dishpan.

The Kohler Electric Sink washes dishes shining clean, as you would wash them. It rescues hands from harshening dishwater: saves precious china from old-time hazards of breaking and chipping Then, its easy task completed, it becomes the best of all sinks for every other use, ahead of its day in features of practical convenience.

Ask your plumber about buying the

Kohler Electric Sink on convenient payments—*installation cost included.* A servant's wage for a few months —that's all it means. The coupon will bring more information about this and other fine Kohler fixtures for modern homes.

KOHLER CO., Kohler, Wis.

Gentlemen : Please send descriptive literature as checked. □ Kohler Electric Sink
  □ Other Kohler Plumbing Fixtures

Name _____

Address _____ SEP 5-21-27

KOHLER CO., *Founded 1873*, KOHLER, WIS. · *Shipping Point,* Sheboygan, Wis. · BRANCHES IN PRINCIPAL CITIES

KOHLER OF KOHLER
Plumbing Fixtures

The Kohler Electric Sink, 1926. Kohler Company

1925, Kohler's one-piece enameled sink had a compartment outfitted with a revolving spray tower, whose openings propelled jets of soapy hot water onto silverware, dishes, and glasses in a basket. Within two minutes, dishes dirtied by five people came clean. Using the electric sink, a homemaker might save twenty-two minutes in washup time each day. A Salt Lake City woman reported that her pots and pans were "cleansed perfectly" by the appliance, while a Lexington, Massachusetts, consumer marveled at her hands, which lacked dishpan "redness and roughness," thanks to the electric sink.[38]

Anton Brotz and other Kohler engineers achieved the electric sink's final design after two years of experiments, drawing on feedback wherever they found it. Throughout 1925, housewives in Kohler Village operated prototypes in their homes, with engineers looking over their shoulders, scribbling down notes, and hurrying back to their drawing boards to make adjustments. As the release date neared, Kohler's advertising manager, L. L. Smith, asked the Good Housekeeping Institute (GHI) for an endorsement. Established in 1909, this Manhattan-based research wing of the magazine *Good Housekeeping* analyzed household equipment and other consumer products in the interest of its middle-class readers. Like many products, the electric sink failed to win a seal of approval on the first round. GHI's consulting engineer George W. Alder reported a major design flaw: silverware never got clean, primarily due to a faulty basket that bunched together knives, forks, and spoons. When long-standing customer A. W. Prescott of the Prescott Supply Company in Binghamton, New York, also complained about the silver arrangement and sent rough sketches of other possible improvements, Kohler's product developers knew they were in trouble. The next few months were frantic, as Brotz and his helpers rushed to fine-tune the electric sink for 1927.[39]

The electric sink also presented the Kohler organization with a complex marketing problem. First, Kohler had to educate consumers to accept the idea of a successful mechanical dishwasher. Despite the servant shortage, housekeepers nevertheless resisted spending money on a device that lacked a track record. Even more challenging, the firm had to convince potential purchasers to choose its electric sink over other models. Even Katherine A. Fischer, GHI's director, lamented consumers' uneven response to electrical dishwashers. Personally averse to greasy water, Fischer welcomed the day when dish-cleaning machines would be commonplace, transforming the arduous chore into a painless activity, into the "Cinderella of housework." To overcome consumer distrust, Kohler invested in a comprehensive marketing plan.[40]

J. Robin Harrison, the Kohler specialty salesman in charge of promoting the electric sink, tried to build customer confidence in several ways. Targeting the dirt-and-germ phobias of stay-at-home mothers trying to keep things clean without servants, Harrison touted the electric sink's hygienic qualities. If Americans of the Progressive Era liked to scrub away dirt, those who remembered the horrible disease and fatalities of the Great War and who survived the influenza epidemic of 1918 had become obsessed with cleanliness. The U.S. Army medical researcher James G. Cumming reported that people eating off machine-washed dishes were less likely to catch the flu than those using hand-washed utensils. Roy L. Dearstyne, a public health official from northern Virginia, corroborated Cumming's findings with data from a restaurant study. Eventually, word of these investigations trickled down to mass magazines. Nell B. Nichols, household editor for *Farm & Fireside,* warned women that improperly washed dishes harbored dangerous bacteria, as did dirty dish mops and dishcloths. All of this fueled Harrison's fires. In 1927, *The Proper Use of the Kohler of Kohler Sink,* a sales booklet for established customers, told readers that the electric sink rid the home of the dish mop, dishpan, and other "germ-infested" implements, making possible hospital-level sanitation. By 1927, the Good Housekeeping Institute, the H. J. Heinz Company in Pittsburgh, and the Aluminum Goods Manufacturing Company in Manitowac, Wisconsin, had installed Kohler Electric Sinks in their model kitchens, where visiting home economists, including businesswomen and teachers, saw the labor-saving machine as an avenue to clean living.[41]

Branch offices assiduously promoted the electric sink; showrooms installed special alcoves with dishwasher exhibits and placed cutaway models in windows, so that curious pedestrians might study the machines' mechanisms. In these showrooms, electric sink saleswomen labored to convince jobbers, architects, plumbers, and homemakers to sell, specify, or buy the Kohler dishwasher. Much like corporate home economists demonstrating for public utilities and appliance companies, these saleswomen—seen within the Kohler Company as experts on "the woman's viewpoint"—infused a technologically intimidating product with a feminine accessibility. Specially briefed by Kohler's top executives, they tried to override resistance to the dishwasher's novelty, price, and luxury status with pragmatic pitches to homemakers' worries about household sanitation and the servant problem. These intensively trained saleswomen ventured into the field ready to counter every imaginable consumer objection, from "don't need it" to "untried product." On the road, they lectured home economics classes, women's clubs, master plumbers, and jobbers' salesmen about the virtues of all Kohler fixtures. Their responsibilities also included sizing up prospective buyers to recommend appropriate colors, sizes, and models and to report back on the different likes and dislikes of potential purchasers. On the heels of Kohler demonstrators came plumbing fixture salesmen, who earned big bonuses on electric sink sales—such as they were.[42]

Even to cutting-edge architects, home economics devotees, and well-heeled urbanities, the electric sink had a major drawback: high price. In 1929, homemakers could wash dishes using a few inexpensive supplies—soaps, water softeners, rubber scrapers, mops, cloths, and drainers, or they could clean up by using basket contraptions outfitted with hoses, priced at $12 to $15. An electrical dishwasher required a more significant investment; portables cost $150, and sink models ranged from $300 to $400. The Electric Sink cost $400 plus a $40 plumber's installation fee. Its price exceeded that of a Frigidaire refrigerator, which sold on average for $350 in 1927, and came in slightly below an economy car such as the Chevrolet ($595) and the Ford Tudor Model T ($495). As a luxury durable good, the electric sink had to be sold on the installment plan. Under this system, the seller granted conditional possession of a product to a consumer who had signed a contract to pay for the item in regular monthly installments. "While it does seem wrong for manufacturers to utilize the conditional sales plan because it induces the consumer to make artificial purchases," Walter Kohler confessed to Herbert, "seventy percent of the automobiles are sold today on that basis, as are talking machines, pianos, houses, and practically everything except the bare necessities." To create a market for the electric sink, Kohler executives spent much of the late 1920s trying to teach the ins and outs of credit or budget sales to its marketing organization, including showroom managers, jobbers, and plumbers. Although the electric sink intrigued mechanically minded plumbers like the Bostonian who immediately ordered one for his "old lady," many of these small businessmen were bewildered by this expensive consumer durable good—and even more frightened of installment selling.[43]

As the electric sink sales specialist, Harrison decided that his firm would have to overcome "the many factors in the plumbing industry which make for confliction, overlapping of activities, jealousies, and even enmities" in order for the dishwasher to succeed. In an incisive critique of the distribution chain that linked Kohler to consumers through company showrooms, jobbers, jobbers' salesmen, plumbers, and plumbers' salesmen, Harrison laid out a comprehensive plan for rationalizing this antediluvian system; however, his was a voice in the wilderness, for he was a powerless middle manager. L. L. Smith advocated another approach:

color advertising. "One big advantage that the Standard Sanitary Mfg. Co. appears to have gained," Smith noted, "was through sending out color proofs, which the plumbers, who are always looking for attractive pictures, quite generally posted up in their stores or windows." Seniority won out. In 1927, Smith's office devoted 27 percent of its $1.1 million budget to electric sink advertising, the largest sum ever spent by a sanitary-ware company to promote a single fixture. The watershed campaign included full-page advertisements in mass-circulation magazines and a plethora of dealers' helps designed for jobbers, for jobbers' salesmen—and especially for plumbers.[44]

Throughout the life of the electric sink, plumbers proved unresponsive to Kohler's wooing and uncooperative partners in advancing installment sales. They distrusted multiple-party transactions, which they saw as infringing on their autonomy. Like other appliance manufacturers, Kohler had arranged for a sales finance company, CIT Financial Corporation, to handle installment contracts, and CIT could repossess an item after a buyer defaulted on one payment. As merchant-craftsmen who valued amiable customers relations, plumbers balked at the thought of becoming involved in repossession. The plumbers' nonparticipation doomed the electric sink scheme to failure. Backed by plumbing supply houses, associations like the National Trade Extension Bureau labored to make plumbers into better merchants, but to little avail.[45]

When sales of sanitary fixtures slumped during the Great Depression, the electric sink fared worse than any other product in Kohler's line. In 1934, accountants listed a $1.5 million loss on the firm's operating statement; net losses on the electric sink totaled 137 percent of the product line's net sales. The company dropped the product.[46]

Beauty Meets the Bathroom

> Color means Kohler.
> —N. W. Ayer & Son, 1930

Taking heed of ongoing marketing problems with the electric sink, Walter Kohler—like W. Edwin Wells at the Homer Laughlin China Company—began to recognize how the Jazz Age design craze fit into his goal for converting sanitary plumbing fixtures from a producer good to a consumer good. At the moment when Stuart Chase and F. J. Schlink, authors of *Your Money's Worth*, a critique of profligate consumption published in 1927, advocated product standardization as a cure for industrial waste, sanitary-ware manufacturers confronted sagging sales rooted in declining housing starts, saturated urban markets, and resistant rural markets. Looking to the auto industry, *Ceramic Industry* prodded sanitary men to embrace styling as a mechanism for stimulating demand. Why not, trade journalists argued, emulate General Motors, famous for its diversified line of automobiles, by responding to consumers' desires for variety in styles, shapes, colors, and prices? Why not add the pink bathroom to the list of desirable durable goods available on the installment plan? The risqué image of Gloria Swanson's soapy splendor had tititlated moviegoers, and DeMille continued to film exotic actresses like Myrna Loy in bubble baths. The sleek stylish tub was fast becoming one of the leading fixtures in Hollywood films; to the millions of women who attended the movies every week, sensuous bathing scenes represented the glamor, beauty, style, enjoyment, and wealth that epitomized the pinnacle of consumerism. The material world awaited the ascent of a bathtub genius, an Alfred P. Sloan Jr. of enamelware, who could give form to the fantastic bathing equipment shown on film. Theoretically, women who took delight from these fictions might willingly transfer their sensual longings to real-life objects of desire, if those bathtubs fulfilled the right promises in the right ways. With the feminine penchant for style in mind, between 1927 and 1934 Kohler's managers entered the world of fashion, stopping at the kiosks of color, modern styling, advertising, and credit sales. The outcome was the modern bathroom ensemble, the matching holy trinity of toilet, sink, and bathtub that we know today.[47]

Like Detroit's automakers, Walter Kohler aimed to use colorful, stylish designs, mass advertising, and installment sales to reorient consumers' perceptions of his product lines, converting utilitarian sanitary equipment into fashionable goods. This objective fit into his larger schemes for remaking the American house into a Better Home and for reshaping American workers into conscientious middle-class citizen-consumers. To be sure, Kohler did not try manipulate purchasers into buying sanitary fixtures by creating a need and filling it, as did the makers of soap, perfume, hand lotion, and other disposable goods. Rather, much like Wells at Homer Laughlin, Kohler created durable goods that tapped into people's nascent desires. Through Kohler Village and Better Homes activities, Kohler learned how to combine his own imperative for a dependable workforce with his target audience's greatest material longing: home ownership. What most mattered about Kohler's BHA affiliation is what it taught him about consumers: they welcomed suggestions about gender roles, the superiority of Anglo-Saxon architecture, and the importance of affluent consumption as long as the required goods were within their financial grasp. By the same token, the electric sink's uneven reception provided Kohler with a tutorial of a different sort: consumers rejected high-price durable goods of questionable utility. From these object lessons, Kohler crafted his beauty-in-the-bathroom strategy.

Building on the new fascination with the automobile as a symbol of financial security, class status, mobility, and personal taste, Kohler decided that consumers saw other durable goods as similar repositories of meaning, and he sought to tap into this perceived reality. He maintained that the family who completed monthly installment payments on a piano, radio, stove, refrigerator, or dish set felt a great financial and emotional release, and sometimes transferred this exhilaration to pride in possession. These goods represented sacrifice, discipline, and material achievement. To some, the ownership of brand-name durable goods—a Ford or Victrola purchased on credit—signified judicious spending habits. By tapping into these symbolic meanings, Kohler hoped to resolve one of the greatest problems facing fixture firms: underconsumption. If people endowed cars, stoves, and dishes with special meaning, might Kohler not use the tools of enticement—design, advertising, and credit—to direct their desires toward bathroom fixtures? After all, Americans had already shown their appreciation of the bathroom as a dual-purpose household space; it was not only a machine for clean living but also a place for sensual indulgence. From the electric sink campaign, Kohler well knew that plans for the bathroom beautiful had to include designs aimed at different income levels. Although sanitary-ware firms had always made fixtures in a hierarchy of prices, perhaps Kohler could refine this somewhat haphazard practice to create—emulating General Motors—a line of fixtures for every taste and pocketbook. If consumers upgraded their cars from Chevrolets to Buicks as their incomes grew, might they not also replace old-fashioned white fixtures with smart, up-to-date, colored bathroom accessories? What better reflected a family's upward mobility than its ability to indulge in the luxury of bathroom remodeling?

Initially, Kohler embraced color as the "style note" that would encourage Americans to take just as much pride in their kitchen sinks, laundry tubs, and bathtubs as they did in Frigidaire refrigerators, Victrola phonographs, Steinway pianos, and Buick automobiles. Like other contemporary businessmen, he perceived something magical in color that might stimulate the "more frequent" buying of sanitary fixtures. In large measure, Kohler's chromatic imagination was stirred by the immensely successful color-in-the-kitchen movement. This merchandising fervor, inaugurated by urban department stores in mid-decade, inspired the Fostoria Glass Company to create its remarkably popular pastel glassware and pushed Homer Laughlin to toy with tinted materials, leading to products like Yellowstone, Fiesta, and Harlequin. Helping to pioneer the chromatic vogue in the appliance field, enamelers introduced brightly colored stoves and refrigerators at the American Gas Association's annual trade show in 1926. Soon, several foundries and sanitary potteries—including the Universal Sanitary Manufacturing Company of New Castle, Pennsylvania, and the Eljer Company of Ford City, Pennsylvania, and Cameron, West Virginia—introduced bathroom fixtures in black, tan, green, and other colors. New Jersey's General Ceramics Company made porcelain fixtures to architects' specifications, filling requests for unusual sizes and colors if the contracts proved worthwhile. While General Ceramics had a ready market in the Northeast, small inland manufacturers like Universal suffered from high freight charges and the lack of metropolitan showrooms essential for placing speciality products in the urban limelight. Watching these firms carefully, Kohler's managers began to speculate how their customers might respond to color.[48]

Kohler broached the field of color merchandising circuitously, testing the waters during the mid-1920s by promoting brilliant faience tiles as appropriate backdrops for white bathroom fixtures. Branch offices joined the tile crusade in a major way, for color added visual appeal to showrooms. On the coasts and in the heartland, faience window displays attracted the attentions of consumers tired of the sterile look of white. Venturing into showrooms, they found even more visual delights. In Chicago, Kohler's refurbished display area in the Tribune Tower looked deliciously chromatic, with a richly painted coffered ceiling, a floor of green and purple slate, and fixtures set against faience tiles. The capacious Los Angeles showroom featured bathrooms and kitchens embellished with colorful tiles, and the small Indianapolis branch office installed faience exhibition platforms in colors that harmonized with its walls, rugs, and furnishings. Those in the know praised the dazzling bathroom dressed in color. Interior design expert Helen Koves reminded budget-conscious readers that colored tiles cost no more than white ones, while highbrow journalist Margaret McElroy of *House and Garden* reveled in the possibilities for tiling, painting, and wallpapering the bathroom in any and every color—except hospital white.[49]

The faience moment served Kohler well, for it visually accustomed potential customers, from architects to household consumers, to the chromatic bathroom while the firm geared up for pottery production. Once its Wisconsin pottery opened, Kohler's engineers pressed ahead to develop ceramic and enameled fix-

The faience moment. In 1926, Kohler transformed its Chicago showroom into a beaux arts delight with rich chromatic appointments. Kohler Company

tures in six signature shades: Autumn Brown, Lavender, Spring Green, Old Ivory, West Point Grey, and Horizon Blue. In March 1927, Standard, whose chemists had been busily working behind the scenes on a parallel development of colored glazes, used the trade press to announce its plans to introduce chromatic fixtures within a year. Immediately, Walter and Herbert Kohler gave top priority to their color project; by April, they were scrutinizing enamel and glaze trials. In August, the managers unveiled colored prototypes to visiting wholesalers, who responded enthusiastically. Adapting preview methods used by Detroit auto-makers, the Kohler brothers put samples of colored fixtures on display in their showrooms in the fall and watched consumers' reactions. Top executives cheered when branch managers reported that women in particular took pleasure from the "striking and beautiful color effects." The gendered dimension of Kohler's sales strategy appeared to be working. Following these market tests, Kohler introduced Color Ware in December 1927 through a full-page color advertise-ment in America's most widely read magazine, the *Saturday Evening Post*.[50]

Designing glazes, previewing markets, and undertaking a mass-circulation advertising campaign constituted the first steps in the drawn-out development of Color Ware. Riding on the *Saturday Evening Post* campaign, Kohler had be-come the nation's leading maker of colored sanitary fixtures by early 1928. In the following year, the architect Ely Jacques Kahn selected jet black Kohler fixtures for his bathroom installation in the Metropolitan Museum's annual Exhibition of American Industrial Art (plate 7). Acknowledgment from architects aside, Kohler soon uncovered major trouble spots in its marketing organization. Just as plumbers were the fly in the ointment of the electric sink campaign, the show-rooms proved irksome in the Color Ware project. With factory engineers labor-ing to fine-tune chromatic glazes and enamels, Kohler's managers cautioned branch offices against aggressively pushing colored fixtures. There was no sense in accumulating orders that the Wisconsin factories were unprepared to fill. In-stead, Kohler's executives urged branch offices to use lavish displays of chro-matic fixtures—sometimes accounting for half of the products in a showroom—as prestige builders, showpieces of the firm's artistic and technical skills. In this way, Color Ware could serve as an excellent talking point about Kohler's quality engineering commitment in dealing with customers primarily interested in sta-ple lines. The architects, engineers, and builders who entered the Kohler show-room fully anticipated hearing eloquent lectures from the sales staff while they pondered fixture requisitions. Although branches effectively negotiated Color Ware previews, their sales personnel seemed unable to fathom the concept of using a luxury line to create goodwill, enhance corporate prestige, and stimulate desire for stock items. Something was amiss.

Unlike the salesmen who ran retail showrooms for potteries and glass factories, Kohler's branch managers—men who had grown up in the hot, dirty, dusty foundry trade—felt ill at ease with matters of style, fashion, design, and taste. At home in the world of producers' goods, Kohler's branch managers squirmed when top executives expected them to remake the company's showrooms into stages for consumer goods and become salesmen. Their well-established selling practices, grounded in fact-based product descriptions, simple displays, and price advantages through discounts, worked fine as long as Kohler made standard lines, because jobbers, jobbers' salesmen, and plumbers understood plain talk, which also reflected the integrity of snow-white bathroom fixtures. Branch offices tolerated the fad for faience tiles, which served as props for pure white fixtures; and they endured the electric sink, which had its own team of demonstration ladies. But they never hid their distrust of Color Ware and its prestige-oriented sales plan. Trained to promote cleanliness, efficiency, and family values, branch managers felt ill at ease with fashion. While top management had evolved, branch managers had stood still. If Color Ware were to succeed, it was essential that the front line carry its banner high.[51]

Kohler executives struggled with unanticipated contingencies that upset the chromatic apple cart in the larger sanitary fixture market. By the late 1920s, fastidious shoppers exercised their veto power by objecting to variations in the hues and tints of Color Ware. Earlier in the decade, consumers had demonstrated their expectations of aesthetic and technical precision by rejecting off-quality white fixtures produced at Kohler's pottery in Trenton. As problematic as it was to ensure the purity of white glazes and enamels, the task of consistently creating uniform bright colors was even more exacting. Variations in shades of purple and green, perhaps indiscernible in factory inspection rooms, became blatant in domestic installations. Burdened with technical difficulties, Kohler warned showroom managers that its factories could not guarantee precise chromatic matches; from Wisconsin, managers urged salesmen to tell customers that fixtures, if slightly off-tint, still harmonized with each other. Consumers rejected such sales patter. Priced at from 25 to 100 percent more than white fixtures, Color Ware had to match. As consumers resisted the multiplicity of hues, tints, and shades coming out of Kohler's factories, slow turnover and excessive returns plagued the manufacturer and its distributors. Color exacerbated sales problems, rather than helping the company penetrate consumer markets with a new durable good.[52]

Kohler did not grapple with its color dilemma in a corporate vacuum. The firm's chromatic nightmare dovetailed with a riot of color that started to plague the entire sanitary fixture industry before the stock market crash of 1929. As companies large and small—Universal, Eljer, Standard, Crane, and Kohler—competed for consumers' dollars by rushing to color, they inundated distributors with a rainbow of hues. Each company produced its own purple, its own green, and so forth. Although manufacturers saw signature colors like Standard's Rose du Barry and Kohler's Spring Green as mechanisms for differentiating among their lines, nothing prevented consumers from buying fixtures made by different companies. Before long, jobbers and plumbers complained about surplus inventories of mismatched fixtures. Those initiated in the fixture trade recoiled at reports of inventory buildups, which conjured up images of the dreaded underconsumption plague. Consumer demand fit into the equation, but in less obvious ways.[53]

Within a short time, this chromatic nightmare attracted attention from the Commerce Department, dedicated to spreading the gospel of simplification through public-private cooperation. By 1929, the department's National Bureau of Standards (NBS) established a planning committee for manufacturers, distributors, builders, plumbers, architects, and home economists interested in creating standards for six sanitary fixture colors: green, orchid, ivory, blue, light brown, and black. As experts on the woman's perspective, home economists especially supported commercial standards that would "assist the homemaker who is untrained in color ensembling to combine equipment in her home more artistically." This project paralleled hundreds of similar ventures within the NBS's "simplified practice" program, designed to eliminate the excessive variety that presumably caused oversupply, industrial waste, and stagnant markets. Following Hoover's interpretation of the associationist tradition, the NBS encouraged but did not force manufacturers to comply with simplified standards. In the sanitary-ware industry, smaller factories rejoiced at the new standards, first published in 1931 and revised in 1937. Nonplussed by special orders for fixtures in "almost every conceivable shade," the Abingdon Sanitary Manufacturing Company in Illinois readily adopted the NBS hues. When customers ordered fixtures in other colors, Abingdon treated those requests as special orders, subject to a surcharge. At Kohler, managers resisted the simplified practice, decrying the prospect of joining a flock of sanitary sheep. In their minds, a firm's palette was a distinctive signature, a tool for competing in a style-conscious market. The solution to the color riot did not lie in industrywide conformity but in greater efficiency at the level of the firm.[54]

While the NBS wrestled with chromatic chaos, Kohler's managers struggled to cope with a mounting economic crisis. When housing starts fell from 753,000 in 1928 to 93,000 in 1933, Kohler's sales and profits declined. The company reduced prices to keep up with mail-order houses that sold cheap colored fixtures made by small factories like Universal and Eljer. Yet price cuts only contributed to the misery. As Walter Kohler told his executive staff in June 1929, the "tightening economic situation" made "fundamental research vitally important" to the company's welfare. Like other executives exploring industrial science, Kohler defined "fundamental research" in a pragmatic way: developing new processes to lower both manufacturing costs and retail prices and making a renewed commitment to styling.[55]

As design became a keynote in the home furnishings trade, sanitary fixture firms one by one picked up the gauntlet. As with color, smaller firms like Universal led the way; before long, the big three—Standard, Crane, and Kohler—followed suit. Design patents offered little protection, and copying became the rule of the day. Thus when Standard introduced a staple lavatory with a "square bowl," Herbert Kohler urged his brother to make a high-class sink with "a distinctly modern note." Also following Standard, Kohler created an upbeat line of plumbers' brass, the Octochrome.[56]

In the sanitary fixture trade, firms had long relied on in-house expertise to make the limited aesthetic decisions that went into creating standardized lines. Kohler's early twentieth-century products most likely stemmed from a collaboration among the firm's managers, mechanical engineers, consultant architects, and, later, pottery modelers. During the late 1920s, Standard broke away from this form-follows-function tradition of engineer-driven design by hiring industrial designer George Sakier to establish a Bureau of Design Development. Sakier had studied engineering at Columbia University, learned about art in Paris, worked as a commercial illustrator, and designed glass tableware for the Fostoria Glass Company. Rather than set up an in-house design department, Walter Kohler whetted his appetite for styling by turning to familiar fashion intermediaries—women and advertising executives—for help.[57]

Pleased by the input of GHI's home economists, consultants at the Delineator Home Institute, and his own electric sink saleswomen, Walter Kohler judged that the "woman's viewpoint" might make a difference in Color Ware development. His sister's enormous success with BHA also reinforced his appreciation for women's skills in domestic matters. Kohler's aesthetic research program included sessions with the former advice book author Hazel H. Adler, president of the Taylor System of Color Harmony, the New York consulting firm that helped Henry Ford select colors for the Model A. In September 1929, Adler and her assistants, Misses Cook and Heile, overhauled Kohler's chromatic portfolio. Blending color theory, good design principles, and the woman's viewpoint, the Adler team lectured Kohler men on chromatic facts: carefully chosen colors alleviated eyestrain among industrial workers, stirred shoppers to buy, and reduced the psychological burden of housework. On the principle that color affected mood, Adler and her assistants invented the colors Silver Green, Bisque, and Thrush Gray for kitchen and laundry fixtures. Arguing that certain colors conveyed a sense of high style, they created Tuscan, a rich golden tint that suggested "modernity and good taste," to replace dirty-looking Old Ivory in the bathroom. Adler's designer hues produced gratifying results; Tuscan became one of Color Ware's best-sellers. As the saleswoman Mildred D. Strauss reported from Massachusetts during the mid-1930s, this golden hue was the Boston showroom's "most popular color" due to its clarity, warmth, and reliability.[58]

The Kohler Company also changed advertising agencies, replacing Erwin, Wasey & Company with N. W. Ayer & Son. With Madison Avenue offices, Ayer fit the swank image that Kohler hoped to project with Color Ware. The agency's track record spoke for itself. In 1927, a nervous Henry Ford, witnessing the eclipse of his leadership in the auto industry, hired Ayer to promote his new Model A as "a smart stylish car," and its high-class campaign helped to change Ford's reputation for dowdiness. Outstripping Standard and Crane on expenditures for consumer advertising, Kohler wanted the most for its dollar—for if any piece of household equipment needed a new image, it was the bathroom fixture. Ayer knew something about bathroom styling, as its clients included Cannon Mills, the textile firm that revolutionized towel merchandising with designs for "mass" and "class" markets. Following the changeover to the new agency in January 1930, Herbert Kohler, writing to his Philadelphia branch manager, divulged his hope that Ayer, which had departments devoted to market research and design, could develop "an effective program for increasing the prestige of the company and the acceptance of our products by the public." In charge of the Kohler account from 1930 to 1944, Ayer's executives never hesitated to put in their "two cents" about design, encouraging the fixture manufacturer to switch visual gears. Color remained in the firm's design lexicon, but it became part of a larger marketing strategy for promoting "matched beauty in plumbing fixtures."[59]

The company reimagined the bathroom fixture market in feminine terms, building on earlier attempts to reach women customers with the electric sink. This time, however, Kohler avoided the wildly unfamiliar; taking heed of home furnishings trends, in 1931 it introduced the bathroom "ensemble," a philosophy that became the cornerstone of the company's Depression Era lines. At the most basic level, Kohler reached out to housekeepers, whose daily routines exposed them to "sets" of everything from tableware to bedroom furnishings. Kohler's venture into Matched Sets also reflected other factors, including the color problem. Generally, sanitary-ware vendors sold sinks, toilets, and tubs separately, doing little to encourage architects, builders, and consumers to buy fixtures made by one company, a strategy that contributed to mismatched hues and "dead" inventories. In part, producers were to blame, for they provided few financial incentives for Joe Jobber or Peter Plumber to push fixtures in threesomes, until Sears, Roebuck & Company started undercutting the market with inexpensive "bathroom outfits" costing less than $100. Kohler responded with Matched Sets at different price points, from the luxurious Mayfair at $1,150 to the modest Colonna at $98. In Kohler's case, the switch to bathroom suites took fortification from Ayer imagery that highlighted women as the important decision makers responsible for selecting the right Matched Sets (plate 8).[60]

Here, too, Walter Kohler's pet project, the Better Home, exerted special sway over his corporate strategy. In 1928, he had spearheaded the Home Modernization Bureau (HMB), a voluntary arm of the Home Industries Bureau concerned with stimulating building activity, stabilizing the labor market, and promoting prosperity. Supported by Hoover's White House Conference on Home Ownership and Home Improvement, HMB urged consumers to consider small remodeling projects that could be financed on credit. Taking inspiration from things Hooverized, HMB strove to rehabilitate or "renovize" substandard housing. In New Orleans, where more than 80 percent of residential bathrooms predated 1920, a Bathroom Beautiful Contest urged renovizers to weed out "baths with fancy claw feet, embossed toilet bowls, high wooden tanks, worn-down painted seats, [and] hopper-type toilets." *Kohler of Kohler News* urged plumbers, who now received higher discounts on ensembles than on single items, to follow the Louisiana example, touting the "unified design" of Kohler's Matched Sets to inspire renovizers.[61]

In the long run, Kohler's stylish bathroom fixtures, including the economy Matched Set models, failed to stimulate consumers' desires to "want things." More than any other stylistic feature, color suffered a big blow during the 1930s. Increasingly, landlords noted renters' negative responses to colored fixtures. Just as they refused to live in apartments with outmoded kitchens and bathrooms, people resented paying higher rents for units just because they had colored tubs, sinks, and toilets. Take, for example, the quintessential low-cost renter, "Mrs. Brown," who found herself "constantly moving" from one apartment to another as her husband migrated from job to job. Like other participants in American consumer society, she understood the ensemble concept and appreciated things that matched. Having experienced the "color epidemic," she also understood "color harmonies" much better than her working-class grandmother. About to take an apartment in 1937, Brown declined after seeing the bathroom. She found it wasteful to buy "new towels, face cloths, shower curtains, bath mats . . . [and] draperies" to go with the room's permanent color scheme. Like Mrs. Brown and other renters, home owners looking for visual variety appreciated towels in luminous lavender, but they responded negatively to large, unchangeable, and immovable fixtures in bright hues. As Christine Holbrook reminded readers of *Better Homes and Gardens* in 1934, painted wooden accessories, such as dressing tables, clothes hampers, hanging shelves, and towel racks, provided renovizers with simple, inexpensive decorating solutions to dreary bathrooms. Wallpaper, fiberboard, and linoleum counted among the favorite face-lifters of the magazine's Margaret White, who argued that these materials added "novel distinction" to "horse-and-buggy" bathrooms without burning a hole in a family's pocket. For even less, paint enabled renovators to tailor chromatic effects to individual tastes. At a time when one-third of America's homes lacked bathtubs and one-fifth had no kitchen sinks, expensive colored installations of fixtures and faience tiles found few markets below the "better class" of dwellings, including the mansions of Hollywood movie stars or high-priced apartment hotels in large cities.[62]

By the mid-to-late 1930s, the Kohler brothers reconsidered their approach to consumers. Through repeated experiments, they had learned much about people's preferences in household goods. No matter what the Kohler Company did, bathrooms remained at the bottom of Americans' list of desirable durables. Whether or not fixtures had eye appeal mattered less than their price, performance, and versatility. At Kohler, the persistent demand for the Cardinal bathtub, a built-in unit predating the apron tub, drove this point home. For several years, Kohler attempted to drop this single-shell unit from production, but consumers kept asking for it. In the late 1930s, Kohler made twenty-four models of Cardinal tubs; Standard made twenty; Crane made fourteen; and six smaller firms made from six to eighteen. Not only cheaper than apron tubs, the popular Cardinal had features that other built-in units lacked. As product engineers reported to Herbert Kohler and other top executives, "the design of the Cardinal tub permits the user to step closer to the tub and also provides a grip rim." A good deal had changed since Progressive Era sanitarians rejected Cardinal-type tubs in favor of apron units. Whereas consumers once fixated on germ-harboring crevices, they now appreciated the handy rim they used to steady themselves with while getting in and out of the slippery bath. Concern over cleanliness never disappeared; germs simply took a back seat to price, safety, and utility.[63]

In 1937, Kohler's promotional booklet, *Planned Plumbing and Heating for Better Living*, expounded on the wonders of color, but it acceded that there was "much to be said in favor of white fixtures." In a fitting acknowledgment of consumers' desires for change, the firm reminded readers that white fixtures afforded the opportunity to renovate a bathroom "at will and without restraint." Kohler's pronouncements dovetailed with snowy reawakenings among other household equipment businesses. Within a few years, tile contractors deserted faience in favor of white installations with fine accents of bright color. Appliance manufacturers like Iowa's Maytag phased out grey, brown, and green washing machines in favor of white models. In many respects, the chromatic revolution experienced a backlash: white, the darling of Progressive Era reformers, triumphed over the brilliant palette favored by modernist designers. No longer primarily a symbol of cleanliness, white became the color of choice as the consumer society matured. It provided a standardized, neutral backdrop around which housewives could construct personal statements about identity, comfort, and beauty. As Walter and Herbert Kohler discovered, there was no better testimonies to consumer power than the revival of white.[64]

When his prescription for better living fell apart during the Great Depression, Walter Kohler, dressed in a three-piece suit, a starched white collar, and a Panama hat, endured a deluge of hisses and boos as he crossed picket lines outside his factories during its 1934 strike. For several years, the Kohler Company had operated in the red, with losses totaling $2 million in 1932 and $700,000 in 1933. As the demand for sanitary fixtures fell, Walter and his brother, Herbert, took measures to assure workers of steady, if not full, employment in anticipation of a building trades recovery. When the company announced plans to adhere to minimum wages and hours approved by the National Recovery Administration (NRA), workers balked. Under the aegis of the recently formed Federal Union No. 18545, they requested more pay for less work—sixty-five cents per hour and thirty-hour weeks, instead of forty cents per hour and forty-hour weeks. These demands heightened labor-management tensions, for employees were also unhappy with the health hazards of foundry work, a company-sponsored union, speedups initiated in the name of scientific management, penalties for defective workmanship, and mandatory wage deductions for mortgages. Many complained that only managers could afford to buy houses in Kohler Village. From Walter Kohler's perspective, these complaints spoke to the cluelessness of workers, who understood little about the problems of keeping a sanitary-ware firm afloat. As economic conditions worsened, Kohler's seven warehouses grew bloated with excess inventory. In April 1933, the firm closed its branch offices in Atlanta, Indianapolis, and Omaha. While the NRA hoped codes would encourage management-labor cooperation, Walter Kohler and his workers locked horns at the feet of the agency's mascot, the patriotic Blue Eagle.[65]

When an aging Walter Kohler stepped down as president in 1937, he left behind more than a disgruntled workforce and a fractured version of the American dream. His real legacy concerned product diversification and design innovation. With six corporate divisions, the Kohler Company had become a full-line plumbing supplier making electrical generators, ceramic fixtures, enameled fixtures, brass accessories, boilers, and radiators. Indeed, the electric sink and Color Ware counted among Kohler's few failures, in part because they were products ahead of their time. With these items, Kohler had tried to reorient people's perceptions of enameled and pottery plumbing fixtures, so as to redefine and expand the category of consumer goods. Drawing on methods pioneered by Sloan at General Motors, Kohler created a bathroom for every pocketbook. Intrigued, consumers swam toward the lure, nibbled at the bait, and then hurried away in search of more tantalizing objects: autos, radios, phonographs, refrigerators. In a few decades, postwar consumers would behave differently, with the automatic dishwasher and the chromatic bathroom joining the list of desirable consumer goods. The time would come when people who drove Chevrolets actually did wash their dishes mechanically.

CHAPTER 6

Pyrex Pioneers

WHEN CORNING GLASS WORKS ventured into the housewares market with Pyrex Ovenware in 1915, the upstate New York company acted boldly, braving an entirely new frontier. Searching for applications of the remarkable new glasses created by its research laboratories, Corning hoped to capitalize on the Progressive Era efficiency craze by making shatterproof food containers that went from the refrigerator to the stove without breaking. Much like the Kohler Company, which tried to convert plumbing supplies into consumer durables, Corning chanced the domestic sphere knowing little about housewares and even less about the mechanisms for learning about women's likes and dislikes. From 1915 through the 1930s, Corning managers struggled with limited success to find the right market niche for their baking line. They wondered: Who bought Pyrex, and why? Who disliked Pyrex, and why? Were "class" consumers, that is, the top 5 percent of the urban population, the best market for Corning's new miracle glassware? Or were "mass" consumers, the 30 to 65 percent of the population that composed middlebrow America, a better target group? Consequently, Pyrex Ovenware spent most of its youth as a product without a clear-cut identity, a fact painfully apparent in poor sales.

In large measure, Pyrex's identity crisis stemmed from a disjuncture between Corning's internal and external environments, from a lack of communication between managers valuing industrial science and technology as tools for improving American living standards and consumers dissatisfied with the performance, price, and peculiar appearance of the miracle glassware. The story stands at odds with textbook accounts of modern corporations, which portray firms successfully wielding science's magic wand to invent better materials, engaging industrial designers to streamline products, and using powerful advertisements to persuade consumers. In such heroic accounts, firms rarely trip, stumble, and fall as they create materials and introduce new products. With glass bake ware, Corning tumbled along like a toddler whose desire to run surpassed its balancing ability.

Between 1910 and 1940, the white-collar professionals responsible for the baking-ware innovation—the Pyrex pioneers—struggled to take the pulse of American consumers. Compensating for the lack of well-lubricated feedback loops, they looked high and low for fashion intermediaries who could explain women's product preferences to them. Ultimately, three types of expert dominated the Pyrex project: home economists, who claimed knowledge of the "woman's viewpoint"; advertising executives, who brandished the tools of enticing copy and seductive imagery; and market researchers, who argued that statistics always told the truth. With these advisors, the Pyrex pioneers came to believe that oven ware purchasers looked remarkably like themselves: white, middle-class, and advocates of scientific housekeeping. In cities, they shopped at big department stores; in small towns, at hardware shops. Over several rather painful years, Corning's experts discovered how much their hypothetical consumers differed from their real-life counterparts, whose negative perceptions of Pyrex's looks, price, and performance circumscribed sales. Slowly but surely, Corning managers learned that they could not capture, cage, and control the consumer. They had to study, record, and analyze the butterfly of taste, so as to design products that better met women's expectations.

Laying Expert Foundations

Corning Glass Works entered the twentieth century situated in a branch of the American glass industry devoted to the manufacture of "specialties." This catchall term described a wide range of goods made by craft and batch production methods, often to detailed specifications provided by customers. For speciality orders, Corning competed against firms like the MacBeth-Evans Glass Company in Charleroi, Pennsylvania, near Pittsburgh; both companies made globes, tubes, shades, and various components for illumination; beakers, tubes, retorts, and other laboratory equipment; lenses, roundels, and lanterns for railroad, marine, and automobile signaling; crystal blanks for cutting and engraving shops; odd bits and pieces for engineering applications; and some household dishes. They capitalized on niche markets avoided by large firms like the Owens-Illinois Glass Company and the Pittsburgh Plate Glass Company, which used quantity-production techniques to manufacture, respectively, containers and flat glass. They also stayed clear of competition with firms that focused on single niches, such as the Fostoria Glass Company, the West Virginia pressing factory that achieved leadership in consumer tableware through styling and advertising.[1]

Firms like Corning and MacBeth were specialty glassmakers by choice. A firm's decision to make specialties did not testify to managerial weakness or short-sightedness. Production runs of specialty lines were small and highly profitable. The more niches carved out by a specialty glassmaker, the greater its potential earnings. Specialty production had another hidden benefit: many items were components of products made by other manufacturers, which meant that these firms or their vendors covered most selling expenses. In the railroad supply business, wholesalers that put Corning glass in signal lanterns assumed responsibility for sending out drummers and advertising the wares in railway journals. This freed Corning to focus its time, money, and energy on improving materials, technologies, and products.

The problem inherent in the specialty trade was the unpredictability of demand. Pittsburgh Plate Glass could keep its factories running year-round by stockpiling standardized window panes in anticipation of seasonal peaks in building construction, but specialists like Corning, which made highly differentiated products, filled orders as they came in. Speciality glassmakers could not second-guess how many and what kind of products customers wanted. To gain some control over markets, specialists collaborated in confidential agreements to set prices, limit output, and share patents, as did Corning, the Libbey Glass Company, and the Phoenix Glass Company in the 1890s concerning their bulb and tube business with electric lamp manufacturers. In addition, each specialist targeted niches that made use of firm-specific strengths, such as technical competency or locational advantages. Thus, for example, MacBeth-Evans developed a full range of high-quality kerosene lighting specialties, and Corning produced lead glass blanks for cutters and engravers in the Crystal City. Yet such focused production had disadvantages. When the electrical age dawned and the fad for cut glass waned, MacBeth and Corning had to scramble to find replacement lines that kept their skilled glassblowers busy.

Centrifugal forces pulled specialists in multiple directions, and Corning's

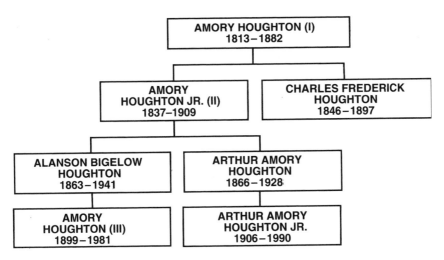

Figure 2. The Houghton managers. *Source:* Corning Incorporated

managers—several generations of the Houghton family (figure 2)—learned to keep their firm's balance by perfecting the art of producer-user collaboration. Beginning in the 1850s, the dynasty's founder, Amory Houghton Sr., invested in glass factories in Somerville, Massachusetts, and Brooklyn, New York. After the Civil War, Houghton, anxious to free himself from high fuel costs, labor unions, and persistent creditors, relocated in Corning, on the Chemung River in upstate New York. Within a few years, his Corning Flint Glass Works failed. Sons Amory Houghton Jr. and Charles F. Houghton reorganized the firm in 1875 as the specialty-oriented Corning Glass Works. Over the next decades, the second generation earned customers' respect by following their exacting demands. For Meriden Silver Plate Company in Connecticut, Corning supplied glass liners for casters, baskets, and other tableware. For Dane, Westlake, & Covert in Chicago, a "tin shop" that used glass in railroad signaling equipment, Corning glassblowers worked from samples, blueprints, and letters with detailed instructions. For Thomas Alva Edison, the firm learned to produce lightbulb envelopes, or casings. By the 1890s, Corning had strong ties to the nation's railroads and electric lamp manufacturers, customers who expected precision and quality in terms of size, weight, thickness, appearance, and performance.[2]

The third Houghton generation, which managed Corning from the 1890s through the 1910s, built on this legacy of collaborative manufacturer-customer relations. But brothers Alanson B. Houghton and Arthur A. Houghton (sons of Amory Houghton Jr.) also embraced industrial science and bulk production. In response to the railroads' demands for reliable signal lenses and lantern globes, they established the American glass industry's earliest quality-control and research laboratories. To accommodate the volume needs of lamp makers like General Electric, they raced toward mechanized production. Neck and neck, Corning engineers competed with Toledo's mechanical wizard, Michael J. Owens, to revolutionize bulb blowing. In a roundabout way, these developments had consequential ramifications for the Pyrex innovation.[3]

By the early twentieth century, Corning's managerial ranks came to be dominated by college and university graduates, highly trained experts who possessed knowledge in chemistry, physics, and engineering. Alanson B. Houghton, a Harvard College graduate who also studied in Göttingen, Berlin, and Paris, learned from his European university experience that science could benefit industry. Under his auspices, Corning placed enormous value on expertise and rewarded professional accomplishment. By the 1920s, even the built environment began to reflect the firm's orientation toward experts. Customers visiting corporate headquarters, designed by the New York architect Horace Greenley, found all of the era's executive appointments: dark paneling, plate glass partitions, capacious offices for top managers. Conspicuously absent from the entryway was the blue-collar symbol that dominated other factory office buildings—the time clock and punch cards. Managers entrusted experts to keep their own time, for self-regulation was a hallmark of professionalism. When the glassworks broached the housewares trade, members of this coddled cadre, sheltered from the sooty factories in their backyards, defined the oven ware consumer in their own image.[4]

Achieving the Perfect Product

> Said a woman of deep penetration,
> I cannot see why in creation
> You should bake in the dark
> As they did in the Ark
> When Pyrex permits observation.
> —Pyrex jingle, Colonel William C. Thompson

In 1911, the town of Corning, New York, buzzed with gossip about the latest research at Corning Glass Works, where managers contemplated a radical new venture: heat-resistant glass housewares. Responsibility for this project fell into the hands of William Churchill, a scientist who had moved to upstate New York from Yale University in 1904 to found the optical lab (which was part of the Sales Department) and labored over significant improvements to railroad signal glassware. Churchill's innovations in signal lenses and lantern globes impressed owners Alanson B. and Arthur A. Houghton, who promoted him to assistant sales manager. In this new job, he handled all products except bulbs and tubing, which fell under the purview of the company president and sales manager, Alanson Houghton. The railroad products that Churchill helped to develop, including signal lenses in standardized colors and Nonex globes made from "non-expansion" borosilicate glasses, withstood abuse so well that the glassworks witnessed a significant decline in replacement orders. Churchill and other members of Corning's Factory Committee cast about for new applications for the special formulas, hoping to find a product with "little competition." Housewares offered a world of possibilities.[5]

When news of the proposal to create heat-resistant household glassware reached the community of Corning, the quest ensued for items needed by "every family" and suited to quantity production. It seemed that everyone dreamed up an idea for the best application. Edith Hoare, the daughter of a local glass-cutting entrepreneur, and William A. Young, a glassworks employee, produced the show-stopping proposal for pots and pans. As an experiment, the twosome fried some scrumptious griddle cakes in mock pans made from eleven-inch railroad roundels. The Hoare-Young kitchen caper became the talk of the town, with the news winding back to Churchill, who believed that Corning's citizens represented a cross section of the potential housewares market, a miniature consumption community of middle-class and working-class people, whose counterparts in the "real world" might respond to unbreakable glassware in comparable ways. When these surrogate consumers caught the housewares ball and ran with it, Churchill scrutinized every one of their moves.[6]

In earlier railroad projects, Churchill perfected his method of "prestige selling," a multipronged sales and development strategy that emphasized customer feedback. Under his direction, Corning's optical laboratory had become a mecca for signal engineers, who traveled upstate to help create colors that met railroads' safety requirements. Churchill had so garnered the confidence, support, and cooperation of the engineers—the ultimate users of lenses, roundels, and lantern globes—that their professional organization, the Railway Signal Association, recommended Corning's hues as national standards. One by one, railroads abandoned their unique color systems, blamed for many fatal collisions, in favor of the new hues. This represented progressive engineering at its best, with

Churchill taking his cues from "the people"—in this case, the signalmen—to design products for the betterment of material life.[7]

In the same spirit, Churchill recognized that mastery of the housewares field meant snuggling up to domestic consumers; however, in 1911, market research remained in its infancy. The year before, the trade journal *Printers' Ink* reported that American firms collectively spent no more than $50,000 on market surveys. Experienced manufacturers of consumer products relied on feedback from fashion intermediaries such as retail buyers, but the inexperienced Corning Glass Works had no such sages. Instead, Churchill laid the foundation for the producer-user collaboration that characterized the oven-ware project under his charge by welcoming input from housewives, home economists, and traveling salesmen, learning much from these people about baking ware's performance in stores, restaurants, and homes. At the glassworks, he gave top priority to gearing up the chemical laboratory to adapt heat-resistant glasses to kitchen conditions.[8]

In 1912, laboratory researchers—Eugene Cornelius Sullivan, a chemist with a Ph.D. from Leipzig University, and his MIT-trained assistant, William C. Taylor—started with the slow, laborious task of modifying heat-resistant batch formulas to suit household utensils. Sullivan began by making casseroles from existing low-expansion formulas only to discover that these prototypes did not withstand kitchen use. He decided to combine many of the qualities of Corning's technical glasses to find a mechanically strong, chemically stable material for household products. Before long, the consumer project taxed Sullivan's patience, time, and abilities, and he petitioned the Houghton brothers for additional technical expertise. They responded by establishing a laboratory devoted to the physics of glassmaking. Jesse T. Littleton, a physicist teaching at Sullivan's college alma mater, the University of Michigan, accepted its directorship in June 1913.[9]

In July 1913, a series of events involving Bessie Cook Littleton, the spouse of the company's new physicist, focused Corning's consumer project. At dinner with the Littletons, Churchill's optics assistant, Henry Phelps Gage, relayed to the newcomers the protracted story of Corning's quest for creative applications for borosilicate glasses. Based on her knowledge of domestic accessories, "Becky" Littleton suggested that they design a liner for the fireless cooker, a time-saving kitchen appliance used for steaming food. Big wooden boxes, sometimes with legs, fireless cookers featured deep metal wells that rusted at the seams or ruptured under pressure; glass liners would render these appliances safer, more sanitary, and more appealing. Later that evening, the Littletons brainstormed about potential domestic applications for heat-resistant glass, drawing heavily on Becky's homemaking experiences. Her disappointment with ceramics, including a new Guernsey casserole that fractured during its second use, turned the couple's attentions to glass oven ware. Becky implored her husband to bring home a glass substitute for the broken dish, and he returned the next day with the sawed-off bottoms of two battery jars made from Corning's Nonex glasses. Becky cooked a sponge cake in one of them, noting the unusual uniformity and easy removal of her dessert. Back at the factory, the laboratory researchers inspected and tasted the cake—"a remarkably uniform shade of brown all over"—deeming it delicious and "very well cooked." For the next month, Becky prepared her family's meals in makeshift kitchen containers fashioned from Corning's stock of Nonex, preparing french fries, steaks, and cocoa in pans made from battery jars and custards in little rings fabricated out of the ends of lamp chimneys. Becky's well-documented tests and her culinary successes led Churchill and other managers, who had mulled over the potential appeal of household products from skillets to teapots, to concentrate on baking ware.[10]

When Becky Littleton stopped her investigations because of a family illness, the day-to-day responsibility for oven-ware research temporarily fell to the chemist Sullivan, who initiated a chain of events leading to Corning's long-standing association with home economists. Sullivan asked the New York City chemistry consultant Joseph Deghuée to study cookware prototypes. Deghuée passed on the job to a person more knowledgeable on kitchen matters: Mildred Maddocks, a nationally recognized home economist who then headed the Good Housekeeping Institute (GHI).[11]

Emerging as a cohesive group during the Progressive Era, home economists aspired, in the words of one founder, Martha van Rensselaer, "to standardize and professionalize the home," so as to ensure the propagation of "good citizenship." An early practitioner, Ellen Swallow Richards, who in 1873 became the first woman to receive a degree from MIT, summarized the movement's central tenet: "The future of our republic will be determined by the character of the American home." Combining conventional notions of femininity defined in the nineteenth century by Catherine Beecher, a fundamentally environmentalist philosophy, and the contemporary impulse to resolve pressing social problems, these college and university graduates became experts on anything and everything connected to the home: child rearing, cooking, nutrition, food, furniture, appliances, and domestic accessories. Most worked behind the scenes in reform, education, and government; some, including Maddocks, rose to highly visible positions as consumer advocates and corporate advisors. As business consultants or employees, home economists shaped the way key household tools looked and functioned. In so doing, they could reach their profession's ultimate objective, influencing "the direct effects of environment" on character.[12]

Following laborious experiments at GHI, Maddocks apprised Corning that she found glass baking utensils more efficient, more durable, and easier to clean than comparable pans made of aluminum, enamel, or pottery. "I never baked better popovers than in these cups," she wrote in late 1913, finding that batter browned more evenly in glass pans than in conventional metal utensils. When she predicted that women would appreciate dual-purpose dishes for cooking and serving, Churchill started conceptualizing a product placement strategy that befitted his promising new baby. Still knowing little about household consumers, he advocated further home economics research. Pleased with womanly advice so far, Corning's Factory Committee authorized the march into the kitchen.[13]

With prestige selling on his mind, Churchill shrewdly approached Sarah Tyson Rorer, the nation's foremost authority on domestic matters. The accomplished Rorer had experience as a nutritionist, best-selling author, editor at *Ladies' Home Journal,* columnist for *Good Housekeeping,* and founder of the Philadelphia Cooking School. Producers had long asked Rorer to endorse their lines in national advertising campaigns, for her testimonials could inspire homemakers with confidence. Initially, this seasoned veteran of the kitchen so scoffed at the idea of glass oven ware that Corning managers sat "on needles and pins waiting for her report." Rorer subjected trial utensils to "strenuous practical tests," including the preparation of a delectable Baked Alaska, and discovered that glass baking ware met her highest standards. Corning's men received the news with elation. Home economics research had confirmed Becky Littleton's culinary victories. In 1914, managers decided that heat-resistant glass utensils could fit into their product portfolio after all. Favorable female feedback redoubled Churchill's interest in household glassware and spawned an outburst of creativity among Corning's product developers.[14]

In particular, Maddocks's assertions about baking ware's apparent efficiency—"slightly quicker as a heat conductor than enamelware"—excited managers, whose preoccupation with "rationalization" had reached new heights, stimulated in part by Corning's work in the mechanization of its production. Churchill, who added "efficiency" to the list of abstractions that made items desirable, envisioned glass oven ware as a dream come true for homemakers. Efficiency seeped into the consciousness of middle-class women in part through the writings of Christine Frederick, a columnist for *Ladies' Home Journal* who promoted a loose version of scientific management for the home. Those reading Frederick's *The New Housekeeping,* published in 1913, learned to value utility and cleanliness through her prescriptions for "scientific housekeeping." Women who registered for home economics courses in high schools and colleges learned exactly how to apply the principles of efficiency to domestic life.[15]

By honing in on home economics, Corning's managers hoped to learn more about the women who were, in great numbers, taking domestic science classes. Such a woman was Amelia Worth Little of Newbury, Massachusetts, who during the 1912–13 academic year attended Boston's Simmons College. Under the rubric of home economics, she studied sewing, marketing, chemistry, biology, bacteriology, cookery, religion, and household management. In her courses, Little learned basic economic theory, which identified women as consumers. Her cryptic lecture notes reveal a good deal about home economists' self-identification as consumption coaches. "Consumer is one who decreases or uses up value," Little jotted during a lecture in February 1913. Her notes continued: "Primarily woman is the consumer in economic sense because she decreases the value rather than increases it." Here lay the great contradiction of consumer society as understood by home economists. If consumption had negative consequences, as suggested by the "uses up" concept, these experts faced the challenge of teaching women to consume goods in the most efficient manner.[16]

As Little learned, the solution to profligate consumption included the application of scientific management to commonplace activities such as grooming, budgeting, and housekeeping. "The management of one's income in order that one may be dressed well is a serious matter," read an instruction manual from William Filene's Sons Company, one of Boston's leading department stores. "It takes a prominent part in the game of efficiency. The woman who spends her money wisely is the woman who has peace of mind because she has the right things to wear and because she has money to spare." Again and again, Little's instructors stressed efficiency, whether discussing personal dress or pots and pans. They aimed to train young women, who would fall prey to fashion if their natural inclinations were left unchecked, to recognize the folly of unbridled girlish desires. From her teachers, Little discovered how to apply rational thinking to household aesthetics and the management of her material longings. She came to recognize if furniture was ill proportioned for an interior and to reject the domestic clutter enjoyed by her forebears. To home economists, few temptations superseded the impulse for overconsumption, and they taught their students to avoid "the tyranny of things."[17]

The birth of home economics training and its emphasis on rationalized consumption augured well for efficiency-minded manufacturers like Corning. In classes at Simmons College, instructors taught students the fine points of generic products such as stoneware, earthenware, glassware, and wooden ware. The marketing instructor, Miss Ebbitts, detailed the pros and cons of clay vessels. These inexpensive wares absorbed no liquids and remained impervious to acids, but they broke easily, as had Becky Littleton's casserole. Glass too remained relatively unaffected by acids and alkalies. Routinely, Ebbitts distributed promotional literature about top-quality products such as Rogers Brothers 1847-brand silver plate, stocked by Boston's leading retailers. Corning's managers realized that home economists could play a substantial role in broadcasting news of their new glass cookware.[18]

Seeking to capitalize on the efficiency craze as promoted by home economists, Corning's scientists explored how borosilicate glasses behaved in the kitchen. Sullivan supervised bread baking in his home, taking photographs to document the speed and volume of loaves' expansion in pans made from tin and from glass. Jesse Littleton subjected these pans to trials in a section of the physical laboratory outfitted with kitchen equipment, discovering that when water was placed in an oven in both kinds of utensil, it came to a boil faster in glass. The decisive experiment that showed exactly how glass and metal containers behaved in ovens entailed constructing a baking dish that was part metal and part glass by partially silvering the outside of a glass utensil. Baked in this hybrid pan, a cake cooked well where it was exposed to the bare glass but remained raw and sticky where it was exposed to the metal surface. Littleton's research led to the discovery that glass baking ware absorbed oven heat better than metal containers, making it more efficient. All of this weighed heavily in Corning's 1915 patent applications, which described Pyrex vessels as the polar opposites of old-fashioned earthenware casseroles, which cracked, retained dirt and food odors, and incubated "dangerous organisms . . . of the most virulent type." As an efficient, clean, germ-free cooking device, glass oven ware embodied progressive visions of material perfection.[19]

While scientists baked bread, boiled water, and deliberated with patent attorneys, professional home economists figured into the equation as dual-purpose consumer liaisons, with duties in public relations and market research. During the first half of 1915, Rorer publicized Corning's soon-to-be-introduced glass oven ware in retail stores and in gas and electric showrooms across the nation. "I have had such good success in this state and Indiana," Rorer wrote from Ohio, "that I am sure when you are ready to place the goods on the market you will find the ladies quite ready for them." Following Rorer's appearance at Woodward & Lothrop, a department store in Washington, D.C., Mr. R. H. Husted bought some glass baking ware that performed nicely in his cook's kitchen. Husted chortled over his unbreakable purchase, reporting an "insane desire to chuck a piece . . . on the floor" to test its durability. Her tour completed, Rorer stopped at Corning, where she met with Churchill and Arthur Houghton. In the Midwest, some women had asked for glass items that would fit into popular silver-plated serving baskets like those made by the Rochester Stamping Company; others wanted glass dishes for ramekin, a preparation containing eggs, cheese, and bread crumbs. Corning decided to retain Rorer's services and then conveyed her suggestions to the Italian-born engineer Emile Pascucci, Churchill's assistant in lens design who also labored behind the scenes on oven ware molds.[20]

The look of the glass oven ware also owed a good deal to Corning's sales staff, including Colonel William C. Thompson, who worked out of the Hotel Wolcott, a residential hotel managed by his father-in-law, at Thirty-first Street near Fifth Avenue in New York City. Being well connected in Manhattan, Thompson knew china dealers, department store buyers, restaurateurs, and hotel managers, on whom he tested products still in the "laboratory stage." At his urging, Frank Slocum, proprietor of a "small but fine and sanitary restaurant at 45 Maiden Lane," agreed to give glass baking dish prototypes a test run, deeming them just right for his eatery's beefsteak and kidney pie. After a month, Slocum reported all twenty-five dishes in good shape, having survived baking in the morning, washing in the evening, and occasional crashes to the floor. Thompson's spouse had worse luck, opening oven doors to check on a chicken fricassee only to discover fractured glass casseroles—which the salesman promptly shipped to Sullivan for analysis. Aesthetics also fell under Thompson's purview: he suggested producing oven ware that matched flow-blue china and canary yellow art glass, believing that striking designs would make excellent store displays and encourage retailers to promote the line and shoppers to appreciate its beauty. Stovetop coffeepots and teapots, he asserted, would allow homemakers to enjoy the novelty of watching the water as it boiled. From Thompson's perspective, the objective was "to make variety" so as to broaden the appeal of oven ware to consumers.[21]

In May 1915, Churchill celebrated the first sale of glass oven ware, giving the written request a special place in his files: a handwritten order from Jordan Marsh in Boston. But the strange market, filled with picky purchasers, soon dampened his jubilation. Balancing utility and aesthetics to achieve the perfect consumer product proved no easy task. Customers expected flawless glassware. While Corning's factories made high-quality wares for specialty customers, the firm had not expected similar demands from retailers. In his travels from the Pacific Northwest to New England, Thompson found store managers, who objected to glass cookware marred by shear marks, refusing to restock unless Corning guaranteed unblemished pieces. Back at Factory A, Thompson's temper flared as he insisted that Churchill improve the line's overall "quality and appearance." Glass oven ware had a high price, but irregularities caused by hand pressing made pieces look cheap. Churchill pressed the Houghton brothers: if the firm's baking ware had "a brighter, more attractive finish," he wrote, the dishes would look as if they were "worth twice the price to nearly every intelligent buyer." Churchill's formula for prestige selling involved extending the precision crusade to all aspects of design, development, production, and sales.[22]

Once the oven ware appeared in the stores, Churchill faced the difficult task of capturing and sustaining public interest. The product's greatest assets—its resistance to temperature fluctuation, chemical corrosion, and breakage—were based on its seeming liability of being made of glass. In the age of metal and enameled utensils, perhaps only fools believed that the most fragile of manmade materials might bake cakes without cracking or shattering. Churchill seized the moment by initiating a national advertising campaign that announced the new oven ware under the trade name Pyrex. (The first dish made from Corning's heat-resistant formula, G 702 EJ, was a pie plate, and Churchill suggested the trade name Py-Right, or Pie Rite. By autumn 1915, he switched the name to rhyme with Nonex.) From the very beginning, advertisements in *Good Housekeeping* and *National Geographic,* designed by the F. Wallis Armstrong agency, pushed progressive themes. Pyrex would eradicate the "drudgery of scouring and scrubbing, the fruitless and endless efforts to clean things" that resisted "all cleaning!" By 1916, the advertisements featured the first Pyrex cover girl, Catherine Huber, an unmarried Corning secretary personifying the ideal middle-class consumer as imagined by Churchill and other Pyrex pioneers. Looking at readers through a clear round pie plate, Huber assured them that Pyrex Ovenware would save "time, labor, fuel." Assuming the public relations role of live consumer liaisons

Look right through

You can see the food bake on the bottom as well as the top in a *Pyrex* dish, without taking it from the oven. And the food bakes quickly and evenly, has a better flavor, and does not burn.

All this saves time, labor, fuel. It makes the food more appetizing, and the table more inviting—for you serve in the same dish.

Pyrex will not crack, chip nor craze. The hottest oven doesn't affect it. *Pyrex* is everlastingly sanitary, durable, easy to wash, a constant source of satisfaction in the well-appointed home.

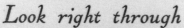

PYREX Transparent OVEN WARE

Trade mark reg.   Has the name on every piece

Many shapes and sizes from ramekins at 15c to large casseroles at $2. Sold by housewares dealers everywhere. Ask them for booklet.

CORNING GLASS WORKS, 111 Tioga Ave.
CORNING, N. Y., U. S. A. Established 1868

Corning secretary Catherine Huber personifying the Pyrex Ovenware consumer, in a national advertising campaign designed by the F. Wallis Armstrong agency. From *National Geographic*, September 1916, Corning Incorporated

like Rorer, Huber personalized Pyrex and the unfamiliar terrain of glass baking ware on behalf of potential purchasers.[23]

Meanwhile, Churchill donned his cap as sales manager and busily worked to create a sales strategy for Pyrex Ovenware. Initially, he saw department stores as its primary retailers. As the nation's palaces of consumption, these urban emporiums catered to women from the middle and upper-middle classes—Churchill's targeted "class" audience of efficiency-minded homemakers. Always on the lookout for novel goods, department store buyers responded enthusiastically to Pyrex, making it a major attraction in the housewares and kitchen equipment sections at Jordan Marsh in Boston, Kauffman's in Pittsburgh, Marshall Field in Chicago, Famous-Barr in St. Louis, and Bloomingdale Brothers in New York City. Yet Churchill soon surmised that department stores would never yield the volume necessary for significant profits. So he developed a two-tiered approach to bake-ware sales. To maintain prestige, Churchill maintained ties with "class" markets through prominent department stores; to build volume, he turned to the "mass" market served by the hardware store trade.[24]

In the opening decades of the twentieth century, hardware stores had expanded to offer more than tools and building supplies. To join the emerging consumer society, many had added sections devoted to ceramic dinnerware, cut glass, silverplate, and other quality household items suitable for wedding and holiday gifts. By the midteens, these multipurpose hardware shops buckled under the weight of competition from chain variety stores and mail-order houses, which offered gift items at lower prices. In response, proprietors reenvisioned their shops as miniature department stores, as vendors of electrical, automotive, and household goods, from forks to furniture. Ambitious hardware men combined alluring window displays, better lighted interiors, and special occasion sales with a wider variety of stock to recapture the attention of shoppers. Churchill rightly suspected that Pyrex Ovenware would appeal to hardware men looking for high-quality additions to their pots and pans counters.[25]

Linked to manufacturers through a network of wholesalers, hardware stores were accessible to new entrants like Corning only through experienced salesmen who knew the right jobbers. To penetrate this business, Churchill hired William T. Hedges, a seasoned hardware man. Hedges arrived at Corning in 1916 with fifteen years of sales experience, having worked for kitchen utensil manufacturers like Landers, Frary & Clark in Boston and the American Stamping & Enameling Company in Bellaire, Ohio. As a double ticket for success,

Churchill and Hedges paired Pyrex Ovenware with another hardware staple, Corning's Conophore lenses for automobile headlights. Hedges plowed ahead, working to situate baking ware in quality-conscious hardware stores.[26]

Top managers rewarded Churchill for his accomplishments in the oven ware startup by giving him responsibility for an enlarged Sales Department, with offices for railroad, Pyrex, and chemical ware, and put the optical laboratory under Eugene Sullivan. Churchill futilely objected on the grounds that the reorganization would distance his beloved railroad customers from Corning's signal-ware developers. Essentially, he would no longer be in charge of customer mediation. As sales manager, Churchill dived headfirst into consumer projects, drawing on home economists big and small to usher Pyrex Ovenware into general use. By 1918, Pyrex emerged as a line of some sixty items: casseroles, pudding dishes, oval bakers, pie plates, bread pans, layer cake pans, utility dishes, custard cups, bean pots, mushroom dishes, and meat platters. Successful product design and development required constant watching, and few comprehended this principle better than the Pyrex pioneers.[27]

Pyrex Problems

> One of the most time-honored traditions of the household is the belief in the fragility and aloofness of glass.
> —*House Furnishing Review,* 1920

> Women are like flowers; they must be cultivated.
> —*Hardware Age,* 1920

Despite the initial fanfare, Pyrex Ovenware limped into the Jazz Age, a pale performer compared to its siblings in Corning's product portfolio. Domestic sales peaked at $3.1 million in 1920, falling to about $1.5 million annually from 1922 to 1926; by contrast, bulbs and tubing expanding by 44 percent and laboratory glass by 115 percent during the same period (figure 3). Several factors account for this change of fortune. In part, Pyrex's performance paralleled the rise and fall of the war economy; inexpensive metal pans remained the cooking vessels of choice, and their production rebounded in the postwar period. Poor sales also reflected the problems faced by hardware jobbers. Once recognized as brand builders, these distributors were, by the 1920s, overwhelmed by brand proliferation, and they retaliated by resisting the onslaught, refusing to promote the products of specific manufacturers. Pyrex's slump also coincided with manager-

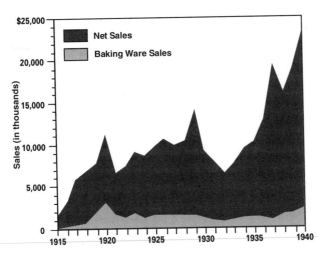

Figure 3. Corning Glass Works, net sales and Pyrex baking ware sales, 1915–1940. *Source:* Corning Incorporated and Duke University

ial shifts at Corning (figure 4). In early 1919, Alanson Houghton left the company to run for Congress, and, after a year's interim, Alexander D. Falck, an Elmira attorney who had advised the glassworks for a decade, became president. In 1919, Churchill resigned, perhaps sensing that the organizational upheaval portended ill for Pyrex. He had grown weary of watching housewares play second fiddle to other lines; in 1918, for example, he took umbrage when managers rejected as too costly Jesse Littleton's proposal for a modest home economics kitchen. With the departure of Corning's high-class efficiency engineer, Pyrex baking ware lost its most stalwart and visionary proponent.[28]

During his eight-year presidency, Falck emphasized Corning's advancement in cutting-edge technology, a sound priority that made excellent use of his legal savvy, the firm's stake in industrial engineering, and the collective experience of top management, which included research scientists. Between 1920 and 1928, annual sales for all products hovered at $9.5 million, and profits doubled, from $1.5 to $3.1 million. During these years, the demand for lightbulb components increased, especially as advertisers discovered the persuasive power of illuminated billboards and as factories ran around the clock to generate products for the prosperity decade. Corning's newly mechanized bulb business generated much of the profit. The firm's technical glass business also expanded. Chemical manufacturers like E. I. du Pont de Nemours & Company, whose growth was spurred by World War I and the 1920s business boom, demanded highly stable beakers, tubes, and retorts in all shapes and sizes. Corning's stable borosilicate formulas made ideal chemists' containers. Medical suppliers clamored for thermometer glass, while brewers and food processors, who washed, cooked, fermented, and stewed all kinds of organic ingredients, used miles of tubing, for which Pyrex glass was ideal. In chemical glassware, orders rolled in intermittently and unpredictably, and enormous retorts, bizarre beakers, spiral tubing, and other peculiar forms could only be made by craft production. In contrast, Pyrex Ovenware had a predictable demand cycle, with housewares sales peaking in June and December. When orders for technical glass diminished, foremen could keep glassblowing teams busy making pie plates, custard cups, cake pans, and other baking dishes. In short, oven ware filled out the product ensemble necessary for full employment—providing that orders were not too large or too small. From Falck's perspective, bake ware constituted a tiny but critical component of Corning's product line, whose fate was entwined with that of its more profitable borosilicate cousin, laboratory glassware.[29]

Falck also understood that Corning had more to gain from selling knowledge than from making dishes. Accordingly, he licensed other North American and European glass factories to produce oven ware under the Sullivan-Taylor dish

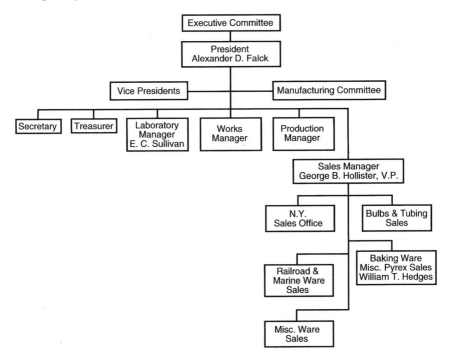

Figure 4. Corning Glass Works, organizational chart, highlighting Sales Department, 1921. *Source:* Corning Incorporated

patent, a strategy that fit his vision of how a technology-oriented firm should manage intellectual property. As dictated by licensing agreements, firms like the H. C. Fry Glass Company and the McKee Glass Company could only make a designated number of Oven Glass and Glasbake pieces per year, at the risk paying large royalties for overproduction (plate 9). As such, Corning profited from the baking-ware invention, while passing the manufacturing burden on to firms whose organizational capabilities lay in consumer products.[30]

Thus by the 1920s, Corning had expanded into radically new markets, including housewares, without adopting the multidivisional structure conducive to the management of a diverse product portfolio. Laboring within a functional Sales Department, under the vice president and sales manager George Buell Hollister, managers responsible for oven ware concentrated on selling the line through jobbers rather than on the larger marketing task of imagining consumers and adjusting products accordingly. During the early 1920s, the Sales Department's Pyrex office steadily increased its budget, with little result. An irritated Manufacturing Committee urged the Pyrex staff to add variety. Hoping to break into the drug store trade, they introduced Pyrex nursing bottles in 1922. They also tried fruit jars, teapots, coffee pots, children's tea sets, measuring cups, and refrigerator trays—to no avail. The committee's greatest frustration stemmed from the unpredictability of women's taste preferences, which sharply contrasted with the needs of electrical manufacturers, so neatly outlined in annual contracts.[31]

Jesse Littleton reiterated his idea for a domestic science laboratory, which, under the direction of a well-connected home economist, could help Corning get "in closer touch" with oven-ware users. During the 1920s, members of this booming profession increasingly specialized in gathering information about the "new type of woman in the home," whose interest in domestic efficiency had been sharpened by wartime exigencies. When the College of Home Economics at Cornell University undertook a study of household equipment, researchers canvassed rural homes, taking extensive notes on kitchen utensils like roasters, saucepans, flour sifters, mixing bowls, and baking dishes. Often, surveyors ran across Pyrex products, noting women's opinions. Elbertine Clark, a Jamestown farmwife who had married in 1924, preferred Pyrex Ovenware to metal pans, which rusted and spotted her white enamel sink. In Earlville, Mrs. W. S. Clark, an "alert, intelligent" woman interested in only "the best equipment," added Pyrex dishes to her collection of kitchen devices that would "save work." Yet none of this valuable research made its way to the glassworks. Littleton's Pyrex experience convinced him that home economics could "investigate all forms of possible appeal to customers" and "reflect the customers' attitude" back to Corning, but he could not convince his bosses to think creatively about home economics—or household consumers.[32]

Wrestling with poor Pyrex sales, the Manufacturing Committee listened to weekly progress reports by Hollister and Hedges, who were still in charge of the Pyrex baking-ware office. Lacking Churchill's vision, Hedges failed, much to Falck's dismay, to devise a "well-defined and vigorously prosecuted" Pyrex strategy suitable for the 1920s. Aggravated by resistant hardware men, Hedges let his salesmen dispose of Pyrex as they saw fit. He made little effort to get in touch with his salesman except at semiannual conferences. Oblivious to Falck's penchant for procedure, he proposed big alterations to the Pyrex line, some fifty new items, without first consulting with fellow managers in production, research, and engineering. On one occasion—on a trip to Liverpool—he disappeared from sight, failing to meet an English glassmaker interested in a baking dish deal. His decision to place Pyrex nursing bottles in hardware stores failed miserably; women preferred the antiseptic surroundings of pharmacies when looking for baby supplies. In Corning's newly professionalized corporate culture, Hedges, the seasoned hardware man turned salesman, represented a bygone era; his experience left him ill equipped for coping with managers' heightened expectations and dramatic changes in the hardware trade.[33]

By the early 1920s, hardware stores had discovered women in a big way; as a result, many blossomed into full-service home centers, whose balconies and basements brimmed with household hardware—cutlery, enameled pots, aluminum saucepans, glass baking ware, and fireless cookers. Fueled by the postwar appliance craze, these retailers, jostling utilities' showrooms for shares, opened electrical goods sections staffed by women who demonstrated irons, vacuum cleaners, chafing dishes, clothes washers, and coffee percolators. In the previous decade, hardware dealers had debated the "woman trade," admitting how little they knew about these shoppers, who by some estimates bought 80 percent of housewares. By 1919, the "woman problem" prompted *Hardware Age,* the leading trade journal, to solicit kitchen-related articles from the self-styled queen of domestic efficiency, Christine Frederick. Reiterating themes she had presented in *Printers' Ink,* Frederick offered hardware stores simple advice: think twice before stocking goods and carry items that really save labor, steps, time, and fuel. Lucile MacNaughton, advertising manager at the Bunting Hardware Company in Kansas City, Missouri, echoed Frederick, reminding fellow dealers that the trade's quality principle also applied to the "Woman's Own" department. Quick studies, hardware men heeded these suggestions. From Illinois to Mississippi, they joined the ranks of retailers courting Mrs. Consumer with creative white model kitchens filled with enamel, aluminum, and glass goods or with stunning window displays of scrumptious breads, pastries, and Pyrex dishes. And they expected manufacturers to uphold their end of the bargain, supplying household goods with woman appeal.[34]

Corning could not respond with alacrity. Nothing speaks to this more than the ongoing battle between Hedges and the factory's leading salesman, M. J. Lacey. An admirer of prestige selling, "Jack" Lacey pampered his customers for the sake of creative development. During Churchill's day, he collaborated with James Palm, a manager at Cleveland's George Worthington Company, to design metal mountings for Pyrex casseroles. These items became hot sellers in Ohio—and a big part of the oven-ware line. So when "Pyrex" Palm, as James was called at Worthington, hired local engravers to put flowers on the casserole dishes, Lacey took this idea back to upstate New York, along with a growing appreciation for customer feedback. Under Hedges, Lacey continued to coddle hardware retailers, gleaning much from these men who grew ever more conscious of women's likes and dislikes. Threatened, Hedges badgered Lacey over this, that, and the other thing. As tension mounted, Hedges appealed to top managers, but he received little sympathy and found solace in long road trips, wherein he most likely contemplated his ruin.[35]

In 1924, Falck and Hollister hired, as assistant sales director, James L. Peden, who promptly pointed out fundamental flaws in Hedges's approach. A Scottish immigrant who attended Brown University, Peden had worked as a newspaper reporter, a gun factory executive, and a valve works sales manager, lastly in Elmira, before moving to Corning on Falck's urging. Lacey, promoted by Falck to assistant sales manager, took pleasure from the Scot's agenda, which read much like prestige selling revisited. If Pyrex dishes were to compete, Peden argued, Corning's managers must discard the wholesale trade's antiquated methods. Moreover, the Pyrex sales staff must "get the facts from the real consumer," that is, "the people who actually use Pyrex ovenware." Peden's proposals included consumer surveys and promotional activities, such as home economics lectures and cooking contests, all geared toward learning more about baking-ware customers. Shaken by the stinging critique, Hedges quit in March 1925, leaving Lacey in charge of Pyrex housewares under Hollister and Peden.[36]

Together, Lacey and Peden revamped the Pyrex housewares office, placing greater emphasis on department store and china shop accounts while attempting to invigorate hardware vendors with a new zest for baking dishes. For Pyrex's tenth birthday celebration, they collaborated with Corning's in-house advertising office, part of the Sales Department, to promote a window display contest. Salesmen secured "excellent windows in large stores," and prizes went to enthusiastic retailers like the Missoula Mercantile Company and Cedar Rapids' Killian & Company; however, the displays failed to entice shoppers, so the sales staff quickly admitted defeat. Lacey and Peden licked their wounds, while other managers debated the contours of consumers' desires. In the end, Peden conceded that the problems with Pyrex Ovenware ran more than skin deep, stemming from the company's inability to imagine consumers effectively. In the lingo of the time, Pyrex baking ware had a serious "marketing problem."[37]

Thumbs Down on Pyrex

> The consuming public imposes its will on the business enterprise.
> —Paul T. Cherington, J. Walter Thompson Company, 1931

Next, Peden turned to consultants in the emerging field of market research, hiring the J. Walter Thompson Company (JWT) to evaluate the embarrassing Pyrex predicament. Primarily an advertising agency, JWT had managed Churchill's baking-ware campaigns from 1917 until 1919, when the glassworks temporarily curtailed advertising during the managerial debacle. JWT had counted Corning among its best accounts, with the glassworks ranking ninth among the agency's seventy-two clients in terms of expenditures. Churchill's willingness to spend a considerable sum on advertising, some $210,000 in 1918, meant that Corning had received JWT's best treatment.[38]

In April 1925, JWT, like other New York agencies, billed itself as a full-service firm versed in copywriting, layout, package design, and market research. Clients included such leading manufacturers as Aunt Jemima Mills; Andrew Jergens; Lever Brothers; Libby, McNeill & Libby; and Swift & Company. More important, agency president Stanley B. Resor brandished clients' sales figures as evidence of JWT's mastery. The Jergens account was a case in point. To resuscitate faltering sales of a moisturizer, Resor helped this Cincinnati manufacturer to rename, repackage, reprice, and readvertise the product as Jergens Lotion. As a result, sales increased significantly. Such achievements stemmed from Resor's pluck and the behind-the-scenes work by JWT's staff of experts. Anxious to gain competitive advantage in the cutthroat advertising world, Resor had since 1920

Pyrex Ovenware window display, Philadelphia crockery dealer Fisher, Bruce & Company, 1925. Display was to help celebrate Pyrex's tenth birthday. National Museum of American History Archives Center, Smithsonian Institution

filled the upper echelons of his agency with top-notch practitioners from various disciplines. By the middle of the decade, the all-star cast included three art directors, several commercial photographers, behavioral psychologist John B. Watson, and research director Paul T. Cherington. JWT could boast of its dedication to "sound" research techniques for getting "the facts from the real consumer," largely due to Cherington's presence.[39]

When he was with Harvard Business School, Cherington helped found its Bureau of Business Research (BOBR), a think tank that pioneered the study of industry's marketing problems, and served as president of the American Marketing Association. At JWT from 1922 to 1931, Cherington supervised a staff that investigated consumers' attitudes toward household goods, including cereal, spices, makeup, toilet paper, mattresses, silverware, and rugs. The aim was to gather information about purchasing habits that firms could use to improve product performance, augment ad copy, and design better artwork. Cherington's approach appealed to Corning's executives, who hoped through the new mechanism of market research to reestablish the dialogue with audiences that had been so important to Churchill's generation of Pyrex pioneers.[40]

Cherington's experience convinced him of the independence, resilience, and power of the consumer. He thought long and hard about the key issues that preoccupied the advertising profession, and his ideas about demand, taste, and fashion are especially pertinent to the Pyrex story. Cherington believed that demand stemmed from the "fussy and troublesome ideas" that people had about particular products. These preferences emanated from the basic human need to express individuality or taste through the careful selection, display, and use of objects. Cherington admitted that forces big and small engaged people's imaginations and, ultimately, reshaped fashion. For example, the unearthing of Tutankhamen by Egyptologists from the Metropolitan Museum of Art in 1922–23 had thrust clothing designers into a "King-Tut period," with mummy figures, hieroglyphics, and other Egyptian motifs dominating fabrics, shoes, and jewelry for seasons to come. Even in the midst of such cultural eruptions, argued Cherington, shoppers still entered retail transactions with well-formulated ideas about what they wanted. Some had appreciated the Tut fad, others had not. The challenge before the nation's new experts on consumption—its product designers, department store stylists, and advertising executives—was not to manipulate but "to please and satisfy the public." From this perspective, the "balance of power" in the marketplace rested with the "buying side," and "the measure of the manufacturer's or merchant's skill" was the degree to which the firm responded to consumers. Persuasively, Cherington spoke about consumer sovereignty, whether the product was gelatin or ready-to-wear and whether his audience was statisticians or retailers.[41]

By the mid-1920s, Cherington's strong convictions situated him squarely in the middle of two fiery debates that preoccupied the advertising business. Few advertising executives disagreed with the journalist at *Nation's Business*, who declared that "fact finding" constituted a new "economic necessity," but they hotly debated two related issues: how to get the right facts about consumers, and how to use those facts to design campaigns. The first disagreement pitted advocates of the man-in-the-street school of imagining consumers, exemplified by the Homer Laughlin China Company's Frederick Hurten Rhead, against proponents of the new field of market research, including Cherington. To learn about potential tableware consumers, Rhead visited china departments in carefully selected stores, spoke to shoppers, and formulated generalizations about tastes based on his observations. While he claimed the ability to judge a woman's social class from her clothing, hairstyle, makeup, and manners, market research advocates pointed to flaws in this tactic. From their perspective, the growth of an impersonal retailing system made it difficult to engage consumers in friendly, truthful conversation on the selling floor. Just as important, rising living standards had allowed more people to step through the portal of consumer society. Economic prosperity meant that women could easily dress beyond their station, introducing the troublesome possibility of misreading the selected shopper. To guard against these problems, market researchers lobbied for a more scientific approach: the audience survey. By the 1920s, big businesses like Procter & Gamble Company depended on this method to collect measurable data about the potential purchasers of packaged foods. These early audience surveys consisted of canvassing neighborhoods on a door-to-door basis, tallying return coupons, interviewing shoppers, and compiling demographic statistics. Cherington relied on these techniques.[42]

Under Cherington's guidance, JWT's research department developed a consumer classification system that shaped the agency's work on the Pyrex account. His ABCD system categorized households by income, occupation, and education, so as to determine what different groups wanted. Under his model, Class A referred to homes with live-in servants and $10,000-plus incomes; Class B, middle-class houses "personally directed by intelligent women"; Class C, the "industrial classes," including mechanics, mill operators, and tradesmen; and Class D, unskilled laborers, immigrants, and blacks earning less than $2,000.

Cherington aimed to get the facts about those Americans with the greatest purchasing power. In his eyes, the consumers that mattered for products like Pyrex belonged to the A category, representing the "class" audience for luxury goods, and the B-C groups, constituting a larger "mass" market.[43]

Once researchers had accumulated data about consumers' reactions to particular products, JWT executives debated the best way to use that data in advertising campaigns. Cherington supported the truth-in-advertising movement, introduced by *Printers' Ink* in 1911, endorsed by the Associated Advertising Clubs of the World in 1912, and invigorated by the efficiency drives of the Great War. In his eyes, corporate attempts to mislead consumers were unethical; responsible advertising agencies must present the hard facts.[44]

Ideologically, Cherington's commitment to truth-based, or "reason why," advertising placed him in direct opposition to fellow JWT executive John B. Watson, father of the newer practice of psychological advertising. Watson, who had joined JWT in 1920, had previously been a nationally known behavioral psychologist on the faculty of the Johns Hopkins University. Like Cherington, he believed that experts could dissect desire: "The consumer is to the manufacturer, the department stores, and the advertising agencies," he told Macy's managerial trainees in 1922, "what the green frog is to the physiologist." Beyond this point, Watson parted ways with Cherington, for he disagreed with the research director's belief in consumer sovereignty. At Johns Hopkins, Watson studied the effects of conditioning on humans, concluding that environment more than heredity influenced behavior. Watson's experiments had startling implications for advertising practitioners. If external factors alone kindled response, those who understood psychological principles could manipulate the innate emotions—fear, rage, and love—that drove all behavior. Based on emotional appeals, Watson's exploitative strategy suited disposable goods like Jergens Lotion, which promised to alleviate consumers' fears of inadequacy by improving personal appearance. Resor so liked the results of Watson's stimulus-response campaigns that the psychologist, by the middle of the decade, found himself a vice president at JWT.[45]

Buckling down to research, Cherington and his staff focused on collecting the "trustworthy facts" about Pyrex consumers. The JWT team assigned to the Pyrex project were also middle-class northeasterners, whose urban values and experiences cast long shadows over the research department's perceptions, questions, and tactics: William G. Palmer, a Columbia graduate and seasoned advertising man who knew little about the household and less about glassmaking; Helen Butler, an accomplished Vassar graduate proud of her "analytical mind" and her "vivid imagination"; William P. Meigs Jr., a graduate of New Jersey's Stevens Institute of Technology, who left engineering for advertising, a career that allowed him to fuse the arts and sciences; and Pauline Clark and Cara Vorce, recent high school and college graduates, respectively, who analyzed statistics and conducted interviews. In sum, Cherington and his staff originated in Class A and Class B households. From survey director to office helper, the Pyrex team approached their subject with the confidence, if not the self-possessed air, of those sitting atop Lexington Avenue. Between 1925 and 1937, they completed forty-plus surveys of Pyrex retailers and users, seeking to ascertain how retailers and consumers viewed and used Pyrex.[46]

Almost immediately, the surveyors confirmed Peden's suspicions that problems stemmed from Corning's disregard for consumer habits, tastes, and expectations. Efficient baking ware appealed most to middle- and upper-class women, who considered themselves heirs to the progressive tradition of scientific housekeeping. By the mid-1920s, 75 percent of consumers in Class A and Class B homes in Ohio, New York, and New England owned some Pyrex dishes, acquired as gifts for weddings, birthdays, holidays, and anniversaries. In contrast, Pyrex had barely penetrated Class C households. An ironic testimony to Churchill's dedication to prestige selling, Pyrex Ovenware remained, some ten years after its introduction, a gift item for the "class" market rather than a staple for the "mass" market.[47]

Price constituted the greatest barrier; indeed, even consumers at the upper ends of the economic pyramid found Pyrex Ovenware was too expensive to buy for themselves. Those making personal purchases of glass cookware ordered items from mail-order houses, which stocked competitively priced mock Pyrex made by Corning's baking-ware licensees. In a way, Falck's chickens had come home to roost; licensing agreements limited production through quotas but did not set prices or dictate design choices. Glassworks with organizational capabilities in consumer products undercut Corning. When the H. C. Fry Glass Company introduced a sixty-five-cent refrigerator dish in 1924, Corning halted development of a similar ninety-cent product. Even bigger competition came from rival materials: consumers remained reluctant to spend ninety cents on a Pyrex pie plate rather than "anywhere from 15 cents to 40 cents" on a metal one. Overall, women considered the kitchen a utilitarian room, which they preferred to be equipped with durable, economical, and practical products, especially when those items sat in cabinets most of the day. Although they willingly splurged on inexpensive decorative accents like colorful spatulas, buckets, and brooms, women clung to their cash rather than spend it on Pyrex Ovenware, banking spare dollars for larger products like radios and refrigerators.[48]

Starting in 1926, JWT executives applied what they learned from audience surveys to campaigns geared toward eroding consumer resistance to Pyrex. Although more women bought bread, they still baked 66 percent of their pies and 75 percent of their cakes. These cooks preferred Pyrex utensils over metal baking ware for three major reasons: 61 percent thought Pyrex baked better, 40 percent found it easier to clean, and 33 percent appreciated the oven-to-table concept. Five forms—pie plates, casseroles, bread pans, baking dishes, and custard cups—constituted 81 percent of the Pyrex Ovenware in use. Armed with this data, the copywriters used their so-called fail-safe formula for giving "new expression" to "old desires," designing a series of fact-based campaigns. While they encouraged women's fantasies about romance with every purchase of Jergens Lotion, advertising executives saw little point in trying to scare, entice, or anger potential Pyrex purchasers. Surveys revealed that women appreciated Pyrex Ovenware as a vehicle for improving their families' culinary habits and a solution to burdensome chores—and not a weapon in the game of love. Everything about Pyrex baking ware, including its durability, efficiency, and sturdiness, suggested the antithesis of Watson's stimulus-response model, for women did not buy glass baking dishes on impulse. Consumers splurged on Jergens Lotion; but they invested in Pyrex Ovenware.[49]

Pyrex presented the ideal candidate for testing the theories of female copywriters, who claimed that household products needed a particular type of advertising, that is, "reason why" copy infused with "woman appeal." At the moment when home economists touted the woman's viewpoint, they waved a similar banner, selling themselves as the best composers of gender-specific text. Good copy entailed more than nodding to feminine fancies; it addressed the shared, if not universal, concerns of women as consumers. Frances Maule of JWT's Women's Editorial Department advocated the need for solid discussions of price, quality, quantity, and service. The advertising woman Ruth Leigh agreed: homemakers expected "dollar-for-dollar value" from products and straightforward explanations in advertising copy. The JWT strategy fused Corning's predisposition to market research, Cherington's ideas about truthfulness, and advertising women's notions about "woman appeal."[50]

The initial JWT Pyrex campaigns focused on "reason why" themes: good baking, economy, speed, and versatility. In 1918, JWT's photographers snapped pictures of individual utensils brimming with food, which the art director arranged in a montage to frame the copy. To wartime consumers, the look of Pyrex Ovenware mattered less than its ability to bake quickly and thoroughly. Now, JWT included food in advertisement photographs only if it complemented the stark simplicity of Pyrex shapes. Typically, a large headline dominated each advertisement; the remaining space featured a dense narrative, a mail-in coupon, and black and white photographs of several Pyrex pieces. The text described the workmanship, appearance, price, and material of the product, generalized about the item's high performance standards, and testified to the line's unique qualities, especially its value. The realist-style photographs focused on the product, conveying an objective appearance, a look that suited Corning's self-image as a technological leader and Pyrex's identity as an efficient product for the "mass" market. In 1927, JWT's $5.15 campaign targeted middlebrows familiar with the ensemble concept, which was gaining currency. These advertisements inventoried the benefits of Pyrex bake ware in ways understood by efficiency-minded consumers of the 1920s. The text appealed to women's preferences for economy and versatility, boasting that frugal housekeepers could buy every dish they needed for baking, serving, and refrigerating food for about five dollars. With mail-in coupons, the agency conveyed Corning's goodwill with gifts and bargains: free Pyrex cookbooks and packages of pie crust, discounted custard cups. Most important, the agency's commercial photographers created images that imbued Pyrex dishes with style. Masters of realism, JWT's photographers arranged Pyrex Ovenware in asymmetrical groups, positioned their cameras at oblique angles, and focused their lenses tightly and sharply to portray the baking ware as a smart product.[51]

During the late 1920s, Corning stood as one of the nation's leading national advertisers of cooking utensils. In 1928 alone, the nation's top cookware manufacturers spent some $470,000 to publicize their aluminum, cast iron, enamel, and glass kitchen products in women's magazines circulated by the Curtis Publishing Company. Of this total, Corning accounted for $123,000. In 1927 and 1928, the glassworks' advertisements appeared in six Curtis magazines—*Woman's Home Companion, Ladies' Home Journal, Good Housekeeping, McCall's, Better Homes and Gardens,* and *Farmer's Wife*—read by women in Class A, B, and C homes. Although Pyrex coupon returns suggested that women read the advertisements, sales figures demonstrated that the JWT campaign was a failure. Women refused to buy products they did not want even when bombarded by appealing images in their favorite magazines. Between 1926 and 1929, sales of Pyrex Ovenware hovered at around $1.5 million (figure 3).[52]

Further, JWT audience surveys found two new factors circumscribing consumer appreciation. Although Pyrex came with a two-year money-back guarantee, cooks who opened their stoves and found "glass and potatoes splattered all over" declined to return their ovenware to the manufacturer; instead, they tossed the broken glass in the trash and turned their backs, exclaiming, "Thumbs down on Pyrex!" Further, style-conscious shoppers claimed boredom with Pyrex's standardized appearance, with "the same old thing year after year." Accustomed to the varieties of visual modernism, including the color-in-the-kitchen movement, these women longed for fashionable cooking utensils. They wanted more shapes, colors, and even annual model changes. Costly and plain, Pyrex Ovenware looked like a poor cousin of the stylish consumer products that flooded the home furnishings trade in the 1920s. JWT threw the ball back into Corning's court, arguing that the "the best solution" to the Pyrex problem was "a manufacturing solution." Tutored by Corning on glassmaking practices, JWT executives understood that high production costs prohibited significant price reductions to Pyrex Ovenware. If Corning were to find new ways to please Class A consumers—who were the only ones who could afford Pyrex—its designs "should be changed" to include "new features, new colors, [and] lighter-weight articles." With these factory solutions, baking glass could take its rightful place in the class market. The Pyrex team at JWT had reimagined the oven-ware consumer by looking in the mirror.[53]

How to Sell More Pyrex Dishes

> What does Lucy think?
> —Corning Glass Works, 1930s–1960s

JWT's critique of Pyrex styling came on the heels of another administrative crisis at Corning, as top managers vied for positions following Arthur A. Houghton's death in 1928. After some shuffling, Falck became chairman, and Amory Houghton, Arthur's nephew and Alanson's son, assumed the presidency (figure 2). Amory's tenure ran from 1930 to 1941, which coincided with the Great Depression and the beginning of World War II, years that saw, first, low glassware sales and, with wartime, enhanced sales. Corning's sales plummeted from a peak of $14.2 million in 1929 to $6.6 million in 1933; then rose to $19 million in 1939

A photograph of two loaves of bread baked from equal quantities of the same dough at the same time in the same oven. The Pyrex dish and the metal pan are exactly the same size

Baked in old-fashioned pan

Baked in Pyrex

Bakes bread an inch higher

Bake in Pyrex once—you will never again use an old-fashioned pan

Ice Test

"Won't it break when I put it cold into my oven?"—you ask. This photograph shows that even if you put Pyrex on ice and poured boiling water into it, it would not break

Baked in Ordinary Pan   Baked in Pyrex

Cut your Pyrex loaf—compare it with your ordinary bread. You will be amazed to see how much finer in texture, how much lighter the Pyrex bread is

THE next time you bake bread, try this test. You will scarcely believe your eyes when you see the difference in the result!

The bread baked in the old-fashioned pan — the bread you have always been proud of—will actually look shrunken and pale beside that baked in Pyrex.

Your Pyrex bread will rise usually about an inch higher! All the crusts will be evenly, beautifully browned. The texture of each slice will be finer than any you have ever seen before.

Scientists tell us there are two kinds of heat in the oven—hot air heat and the heat which radiates from the walls and bottom of the oven. Hot air heat forms only one-third of the heat in the oven. Two-thirds is radiant heat.

Only the hot air can heat a metal pan. Just as an iron shutter keeps out the sun's rays, so every metal pan keeps out radiant heat. Just as a window pane lets in the warmth of sunlight, so all the oven heat floods through Pyrex.

This is why the food inside gets all the heat instead of just one-third. This is why every food cooked in Pyrex is so thoroughly, so evenly done, why it is so much more delicious.

Patriotic women use Pyrex

Women are using Pyrex because it spares the metal the Government so greatly needs; because it saves fuel, as it requires about one-half less heat; because it helps them "Hooverize." For example, Pyrex casseroles make meat so much more tender that even the cheap cuts are delicious

Oven heat does not break it

You need not be afraid of Pyrex because it is transparent. You could set a Pyrex dish or a cake of ice and pour boiling water on it. Even this will not break it. Pyrex never chips, flakes or crazes. It never rusts, burns out or discolors. After years of use, it is clean, beautiful, exactly as good as the day you bought it.

See the many dishes

Dealers everywhere sell Pyrex. Ask to see all the Pyrex dishes. *Each one is guaranteed not to break in the oven.*

Be sure the name Pyrex is in each dish. Then buy your first dish. See for yourself how durable it is, how much better it bakes, how much easier it is to clean, how dainty it is to serve in. Like thousands of other up-to-date women, you will want to Pyrex your whole kitchen—you will never again use an old-fashioned pan.

Send for the free illustrated booklet, "New Facts About Cooking."

PYREX SALES DIVISION
213 Tioga Avenue, Corning, N. Y.

CORNING GLASS WORKS

Cake Dish

Utility Dish

Pudding Dish

Pie Plate

Casserole

Manufactured by the World's Largest Makers of Technical Glass

★ **PYREX**

TRANSPARENT OVEN DISHES

160   March Good Housekeeping

Advertisement from J. Walter Thompson's wartime campaign to promote Pyrex Ovenware. From *Good Housekeeping*, March 1918, Morris Library, University of Delaware

You can EQUIP your Kitchen with PYREX Ovenware

for $5¹⁵

Pyrex custard cups are equally useful for cup cakes, shirred eggs and for moulding salads and desserts

Everyone who bakes a pie in a Pyrex plate remarks about the unusually flaky undercrust. And lemon, rhubarb and tart berry pies never "taste of the pan"

SPARKLING baking ware that is more attractive, more efficient, longer-lasting! Enough of it for practically everything you bake!

You can have a real Pyrex kitchen—all the more important Pyrex dishes—for only $5.15.

Women who have this group of Pyrex dishes say that with it they bake and serve hundreds of everyday recipes. They say, too, that their Pyrex dishes not only fill every baking need, but they look nicer, new or old, and they actually *bake better*.

Uses heat better than metals

Scientists say that Pyrex ovenware uses heat in an entirely different way from metals. It stores up *more* heat—then gives it out far *more evenly* to the food within. That is why food

The favorite everyday Pyrex outfit—casserole, pie plate, biscuit pan, loaf pan and custard cups. With the dishes shown above, you can bake apples, vegetables, macaroni, beans, meat loaf, puddings, loaf cakes, hot breads, small roasts and scalloped dishes

baked in Pyrex ovenware is never scorched on the sides while underdone in the center.

Women say, too, that Pyrex ovenware keeps food piping hot for second helpings; never discolors food; never holds odors and needs no harsh scouring.

No wonder so many women use Pyrex ovenware for *all* their baking!

Equip your kitchen with this inexpensive modern baking outfit. Do away forever with scorched, uneven baking. Don't face another sink full of dented, discolored tins! You will find Pyrex ovenware (the $5.15 outfit, or any other pieces you like) in

housewares or china sections of department stores or at hardware stores. The following guarantee accompanies every baking dish stamped "PYREX" (Trade Mark Registered in U. S. Patent Office):

Guarantee

Any PYREX dish or part which breaks from oven heat within two years from date of purchase may be replaced by any PYREX dealer *in exchange* for the broken pieces. Corning Glass Works, Corning, New York.

For the dishes shown above, tear out this list and take to your dealer:

Covered casserole, No. 621 round, No. 653 square, No. 643 oval or No. 643 shallow
—medium size $1.75
Utility dish, No. 231—medium size 1.00
Six custard cups, No. 410—small size .... .60
Pie plate, No. 209—medium size .... .90
Loaf pan, No. 213—medium size .... .90
                                    Total $5.15
All prices slightly higher in West and Canada

Now you can g[et] Nursing Bottles neck or wide [mouth] oz., at all dru[g...]

RECIPE BOOK FREE · Clip the Coupon Now!

Corning Glass Works, Dept. 105, Corning, New York
Please send free the Pyrex Book on Better Baking with sixty delicious, easily prepared new recipes. Tells of a great cooking school's ovenware tests—shows all the Pyrex dishes.

Name..

Address.......................................

You can get handsome metal mountings wherever Pyrex ovenware is sold

Hot mince or apple pie can be brought right from oven to table in this classically graceful mounting

Advertisement from J. Walter Thompson's "$5.15 campaign" to promote Pyrex Ovenware. From *Ladies' Home Journal*, November 1927, Corning Incorporated

and $34.8 million in 1941 (figure 3). Corning's new "ribbon" machine cranked out a million bulb envelopes every twenty-four hours, while expanded research labs experimented with new glasses, from fiberglass to silicone, marketed by joint ventures: Pittsburgh-Corning, Owens-Corning, and Dow-Corning. Changes also took place in the Sales Department. In 1929, Lacey transferred to a top position in another division, and Peden became sales director, succeeding Hollister as vice president for sales in the mid-1930s. Under Peden, Corning began the slow process of going back to baking-ware basics, with the Pyrex staff striving to get "the facts from the real consumer."[54]

In 1929, Peden hired a high-profile consultant, Melvin T. Copeland, a marketing professor at the Harvard Business School, to evaluate the Pyrex situation. Corning needed a housewares plan, for the 1936 expiration of the Sullivan-Taylor patents would open the cookware trade to low-cost producers other than Corning's licensees. Formerly Cherington's collaborator at Harvard's BOBR, Copeland had completed a seminal study of the hardware business during the late 1910s, and he believed that dealers would warm up to Pyrex if Corning modified its marketing strategy. In stark opposition to JWT, he pushed quantity production, urging the glassworks to cut prices and target the mass market. Copeland's arguments drew sustenance from a report on Peden's desk by Lucy M. Maltby, a home economist at Mansfield State Teachers College in nearby Pennsylvania, whose Pyrex proposals included measures for getting in touch with mass-market consumers. With a Harvard professor and a well-qualified home economist bolstering his views, the energetic Peden pushed to remake Pyrex Ovenware into a mass-market line.[55]

Using Copeland's report as a blueprint, Peden made the task of imagining consumers integral to his division, so as to achieve the long-term goal of repositioning Pyrex. Privy to in-house engineering projects, Peden suspected that chief engineer David E. Gray, who had already mechanized production of small items like custard cups and percolator tops, would soon build automatic presses for large pieces, allowing significant price reductions. Recently, Gray had visited Detroit to learn "from the automobile builders just how to make interchangeable parts," returning to Corning infected with an enthusiasm for continuous-flow techniques. In the light of impending technological shifts, Peden tired of JWT's generalizations about consumers and hired two key employees—Charles D. LaFollette and Lucy Maltby—to stalk the mass-market consumer.[56]

In many respects, LaFollette and Maltby represented flip sides of a gendered coin, each indispensable to the housewares venture. LaFollette collected hard data on purchasing habits; Maltby gathered the softer data on consumer tastes. A graduate of the Harvard Business School, LaFollette, who heralded from the famous midwestern LaFollette family of Progressives, had worked for Copeland at BOBR. Equally qualified, Maltby, a Corning native, arrived at the glassworks with a bachelor of science in home economics from Cornell University, a master's degree from Iowa State College, and seven years of teaching experience. At Iowa, Maltby had devoted many classroom projects to glassware analysis, seeking to determine how Pyrex bake ware could be transformed from a "gift item and a novelty" into a "staple product," that is, from a "class" product to a "mass" product. Maltby's knowledge of glassware distinguished her among household equipment specialists and made her particularly attractive to Corning. With this dynamic duo, the Sales Department tackled the consumer conundrum, hoping that their research investment would pay off in more prosperous times.[57]

LaFollette began with a three-year study of markets, which included statistical analyses of sales from 1915 to 1930. Using BOBR techniques, LaFollette picked up where the JWT Pyrex team had left off. He gathered facts on household purchasing habits, considering factors such as income, nativity, and race, and cross-referenced this information with data on retailers, paying close attention to which stores did and did not order Pyrex. From vendors, LaFollette solicited feedback on prices, discounts, advertising, freight charges, and distribution practices. As the Depression worsened, hardware men begged for price cuts in the light of competition from cheap cookware by McKee, Fry, and MacBeth-Evans. When LaFollette advocated these reductions in 1931, Peden resisted on the grounds that price slashing could not function as a panacea for a poor distribution plan. With this disagreement, discord entered Peden's peaceable kingdom.[58]

While the bulls locked horns, Maltby settled in as home economics director, with offices in Corning's new executive building. To Peden, Maltby's department seemed like a good investment, an inexpensive way to improve ties to consumers. Other firms such as Kraft-Phenix Cheese, Ball Brothers, Sears, Piggly-Wiggly Stores, Aluminum Goods Manufacturing, and Curtis Publishing had demonstrated that close attention to the "woman's viewpoint" paid off. Maltby's job entailed preserving, assisting, and encouraging the flow of information from consumers to the corporation. Just as Churchill had cultivated railroaders' trust, Maltby garnered homemakers' confidence to advance Pyrex's design, development, and sales. To do so, she drew on methods and tactics used by fellow home economists in business.[59]

Working in her small customer service office, Maltby initially was disconcerted by the heap of mail that poured into the factory every week, but she soon turned this paper pile into a corporate asset. In a backhanded way, JWT's tricks worked, for magazine readers saw advertisements with mail-in coupons as invitations to report their likes and dislikes. These, Maltby summarized in inter-office memos. Women disliked Pyrex's bland looks, and they were frustrated with the lack of instruction on how to cook with, care for, and use it. Following recipes formulated for metal pans, bakers often scorched their food, as glass dishes heated faster than conventional utensils. When cooks put Pyrex on stove-top burners, direct contact with flames ruined the protective shell provided by the annealing process, resulting in a big boom. From the tedious task of answering complaints, Maltby slowly but surely discovered exactly why Pyrex had flopped.[60]

To help Corning solve these problems, Maltby established her test kitchen, a full-service domestic laboratory whose female staff collaborated with managers, salesmen, scientists, engineers, and designers to improve products. Modeled after installations at universities, publishing houses, public utilities, mail-order houses, food companies, and other consumer product firms, the kitchen evinced Maltby's commitment to the home economics profession, with its goal of using the principles of scientific housekeeping to improve material life. Lined with stoves and refrigerators, the kitchen had a corner dominated by panel of thermo-couples, devices used to measure oven temperatures. Its spic-and-span atmos-phere impressed out-of-town visitors with Corning's growing concern for women's needs. More than a public relations gimmick, the test kitchen functioned as Maltby's proving ground, a laboratory that gave concrete form to her theories about gender and design.[61]

Among the first items to benefit from Maltby's home economics program was the cake pan, one of the poorest-selling pieces in the Pyrex line. This wide shal-low dish, created in the 1910s for making layer cakes, annoyed Depression Era cooks. The pan lacked handles, so bakers often stuck their fingers into the bat-ter when holding the pan; the 9 1/2 inch width prohibited homemakers from set-ting two pans side by side in modern 18-inch ovens; and the low height did not accommodate recipes for the thick two-layer cakes popular during the 1930s. In addition, although JWT advertisements suggested ways to serve food from Py-rex Ovenware, people refused to use cake pans at the table, thinking them too ugly for words. Maltby confabulated with home economics colleagues in food companies, at *Ladies' Home Journal,* and at the Good Housekeeping Institute, all of whom verified consumers' complaints. She also heeded advice from under

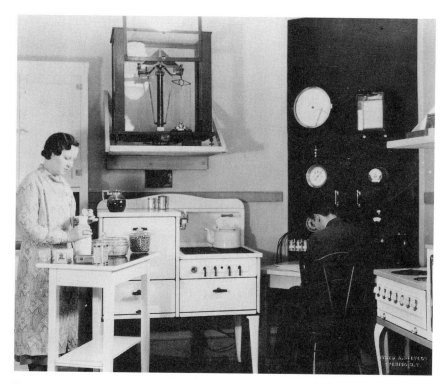

Home economist Mary Louise Linneman and researcher C. John Phillips collaborating in the Corning test kitchen, ca. 1930s. Corning Incorporated

her own roof, where her mother, a talented cook, critiqued Pyrex from the homemaker's perspective.[62]

Next, Maltby approached her superiors with recommendations for a better product: a handled, deeper, and narrower cake pan. As the new item inched toward production, test kitchen staff subjected prototypes to strenuous experiments, rushing pans from refrigerators to hot ovens, purposely burning food in them, and scrubbing them with strong soaps. Just as important, the home economists developed special recipes, which initially appeared in Pyrex recipes booklets and, later, on lively product liners. Sales of Pyrex cake pans rose following Maltby's modifications. The increase also occurred in tandem with big price reductions, which indicates that a confluence of interests and skills enabled Corning to convert Pyrex Ovenware from a product for the "classes" to one for the "masses." Over the following years, Maltby pressed managers for small changes to other Pyrex products, constantly adjusting shapes to suit evolving eating habits and fashion trends. In the long run, the specific, practical suggestions of "the girls," as Corning's home economists called themselves, culminated in big changes to the look and performance of Pyrex baking ware.[63]

Meanwhile, "the boys" at Corning grappled with the price situation; Peden finally agreed to major reductions in 1932, reluctantly accepting the premise that lower prices meant reaching a broader audience (1931 sales had plummeted to less than $840,000, nearly half of the 1929 sales [figure 3]). With price reductions, Corning's managers hoped to lure department stores back to the fold and to reassert Pyrex's leadership among small hardware retailers, whose buying practices had long irritated shoppers. To cut costs, small stores often ordered large assortments of Pyrex bake ware directly from the glassworks, sold the popular items, and failed to replenish them until all of the other items had sold. With the economic crisis, *Nation's Business* argued that companies hoping to survive the Depression needed to take greater notice of consumers' "back talk." In this context, Peden paid close attention to a key discovery by Maltby's customer service office; tired of traipsing from store to store in search of the right Pyrex dish, women started writing to the factory for particular items. Corning decided to eliminate direct sales to hardware retailers, shifting the burden of distribution and promotion to wholesalers. This tactic guaranteed a larger share of the Pyrex trade to jobbers, whose drummers encouraged stores to replenish diminishing stock. It also freed Corning's salesmen from office work, allowing them to traverse the hardware trade as missionaries of the glass gospel.[64]

During the early 1930s, Corning still found it impossible to reduce costs enough to offer large Pyrex Ovenware pieces to five-and-tens, as high-temperature melting, rare ingredients, and artisanal wages fused into a formidable price barrier. In addition, dime store display methods did not work with extensive lines like Pyrex. A chain that stocked the McKee Glass Company's Glasbake, for example, squeezed all of the items of this limited line into a display area of about fifteen by thirty inches. Such a small space was woefully inadequate for the ninety-five pieces in the Pyrex line.[65]

During the 1930s, hardware stores still constituted the best outlets for Pyrex; in fact, these retailers did better than ever with housewares. Women saw these stores as one-stop depots for all sorts of housewares, from colored glassware to fans and toasters. "Women's Own" sections had become so common that hardware trade journals stopped devoting feature articles to them, relegating notices about new departments to chatty news columns. In 1931, the *Hardware Retailer* inventoried the trade's favorite housewares, and Pyrex Ovenware received high ratings. So, as the hardware trade delved deeper into housewares, Corning's managers followed suit, hoping to benefit from the trade's new look. Little could be lost. Some observers estimated that women accounted for 60 percent of hardware store purchases, and Corning was hot on the trail of the mass-market consumer.[66]

When the 1932 price reductions failed to establish the shaky Pyrex division on a profitable basis, managers scurried to find other solutions, ultimately settling for technological and organizational fixes. The problem worsened in 1933 when F. W. Woolworth & Company introduced Oven Serve, a line of stove-to-table serving dishes made by the Homer Laughlin China Company. Designed to give Woolworth's kitchenware departments a Depression Era boost, Oven Serve gained popularity among consumers who yearned for household novelties but had little spare cash. By early 1934, Homer Laughlin had already made more than six million pieces of Oven Serve—a figure that staggered Corning executives. That year, Peden asked JWT to complete a series of retail surveys that compared the performance of Pyrex, Oven Serve, Glasbake, Wearever, Vollrath, and other enamel, tin, aluminum, earthenware, and glass products. JWT reported that consumers found Pyrex costly compared to rival products. For Corning, Woolworth's entry into baking dishes portended disaster, unless the glassworks acted swiftly.[67]

In the midst of these developments, the accountant Otto W. Hilbert collaborated with LaFollette to do some figuring that would lead to a second round of price cuts in 1937. Hilbert discovered that inexpensive custard cups and percolator tops, which accounted for 65 percent of Pyrex sales in dollars, generated little profit. Large pieces—casseroles, baking dishes, utility pans, and so forth—sat in factory warehouses and on store shelves, waiting for good homes. In his estimation, two related measures could help Corning out of this tight spot. First, the glassworks must reduce the output of small bake-ware items by 10 percent. Next, it had to discontinue all but the best-selling large pieces, offering these items at price reductions of 50 percent, so as to stimulate interest among mass-market consumers. The Hilbert-LaFollette calculations made sense to managers like Peden, who was tired of inventory buildups and feared that Corning might lose its toehold in kitchen utensils.[68]

In other parts of the company, scientists and engineers neared several breakthroughs that would aid Corning's consumer products venture. By 1934, Sullivan and other laboratory men came close to perfecting low-cost borosilicate formulas suitable for mechanical pressing. Ultimately, this advance combined with innovations in metalworking, ceramics, and refractories allowed David E. Gray and other Corning engineers to build new quantity-production equipment and a continuous-flow factory with machines to make consumer products. Two developments in 1936 preceded the opening of Corning's new press-ware plant: the introduction of a top-of-stove ware (Flameware) and the acquisition of the MacBeth-Evans Glass Company.[69]

First, Corning gave the green light to a new line of stove-top cooking utensils made of a new "strong glass," an extra-tough material that went one step beyond borosilicates. The impetus for this new product line came directly from consumers, who had written Maltby's office in frustration over Pyrex's unsuitability for range-top use. Initially, the researchers experimented with Pyrex formulas, only to find that trial pieces cracked. By 1933, the physicist William W. Shaver turned to aluminosilicate glass developed by the Corning chemist H. P. Hood. This specially treated glass had considerable mechanical strength, a high resistance to thermal shock, and tolerance of red-hot flames and electrical elements. When the press agent Leon V. Quigley visited Corning's laboratories in early 1936, he found thirty-five researchers working to perfect Flameware. Dressed in aprons, the men bent over hot stoves as they fried, scorched, and burnt potatoes in saucepans made from the new tough glass. Quigley then visited Corning's home economics department, where Maltby explained the advantages of the Flameware line, which consisted of three saucepans, two percolators, a teapot, and a small frying pan. Detachable handles enabled cooks to convert the vessels into attractive serving dishes in an instant. Flameware could go directly from refrigerator to burner, so that women could use the same containers for storing, heating, baking, and serving food. In companion literature, Maltby and her staff encouraged women to take advantage of the line's versatility.[70]

Second, president Amory Houghton took steps to protect his company's position in the oven-ware market once the Sullivan-Taylor borosilicate patents expired in 1936. Figuring it was best to declare a truce before the war erupted, Houghton negotiated for the acquisition of MacBeth-Evans, an acknowledged leader in the lighting-glass field. No slouch in consumer markets, MacBeth-Evans during the early 1930s had made inroads into five-and-tens with Fostoria spin-offs, today generally called Depression glass. But MacBeth-Evans had lost money in 1932 and 1933, while Corning's yearly profits averaged $1.2 million. So when Houghton came knocking with a consolidation proposal, George D.

MacBeth accepted. Absorbing its rival in late 1936, Corning gained additional lab expertise, factories in Pennsylvania and Indiana, and sales managers knowledgeable about consumer markets.[71]

In mid-1937, Corning laid the final cornerstone in its new consumer products strategy, opening a cutting-edge factory that put Pyrex Ovenware on "straight-line production." The press-ware plant relegated all operations, from materials melting to product packing, to some sort of belt, conveyor, or other automatic device. Rotary presses fashioned large, round, bake-ware items, such as casseroles, and sent them to annealing ovens. Mechanized production allowed Corning to initiate the LaFollette-Hilbert recommendations for a second round of price cuts. These reduction went into effect when LaFollette succeeded Peden as head of sales. Under his auspices, the firm also simplified the Pyrex line, limiting output to the thirty-six best-selling items. A pie plate that retailed for a dollar in 1920 sold for twenty-five cents in 1938; a two-dollar casserole was sixty-five cents, and so on. By the late 1930s, Pyrex Ovenware was on its way to reaching the mass market.[72]

Unlike pressing factories and crystal workshops, Corning had entered the home furnishings market unaware of established practices for imagining female consumers, and its Pyrex crisis demonstrated the folly of such an approach. The confidence that encouraged the firm to hazard entering the housewares market and to stand by its money-losing venture stemmed in part from the Houghton family's interest in laboratory research and the highly professionalized corporate culture that such a commitment spawned. The experts who created Pyrex placed a premium on efficiency, and they unequivocally believed that consumers did so too. After all, the trusted Rorer home economics research showed this to be the case. Although scientific housekeeping served Corning well during the 1910s, its influence faded during the boom-and-bust cycle of the interwar years, explaining much about Pyrex's poor reception.

Christine Frederick's high visibility notwithstanding, the gospel of efficiency found few supporters within the domestic sphere after the Great War. In many respects, little had changed since the late nineteenth century, when Thomas Hawkes bowed to consumer tastes as he designed new crystal. Frederick Rhead, the practical man, fully admitted that shoppers wanted home furnishings that expressed their individuality. For women made fashion conscious by Jazz Age culture and Hollywood glamor, costly Pyrex Ovenware looked too much like the beakers and tubing used in laboratory experiments. Using the rhetoric of efficiency to promote Pyrex only compounded the line's problem; for, as Walter Kohler learned, the idea of "one best way" stood at odds with women's expectations. Home sweet home remained a haven in a hard world, a place where consumers could escape from the forces of standardization—avoiding even its smallest material manifestations, including Pyrex Ovenware.

CHAPTER 7

Easier Living?

IN HIS WIDELY CIRCULATED *Guide to Easier Living* (1954), the industrial designer Russel Wright outlined a formula for middle-class domestic bliss that revolved around carefree suburban life and casual dining. The New York consultant urged readers to shake "free of traditionalism" and cast aside the "hard shell of snobbish convention" reflected in formal attire, afternoon tea parties, sit-down dinners, and living room suites crafted in Chippendale or Sheraton styles. As the self-appointed spokesperson for the cult of informality, Wright privately stood in stark opposition to advice columnist Emily Post, watchdog for a diminishing gentility. Whereas Post advocated "drinking tea gracefully from a fine flaring cup," Wright encouraged "more drooling, less fancy etiquette, and less housework." His stake to cultural authority rested on an idealized portrait of America as a nation free from racial strife, urban congestion, class conflict, and ethnic diversity. Wright's products expressed the postwar longing for a return to a fairy-tale normalcy, wherein the "democratization of things" ensured consensus.[1]

A student of nationally renowned industrial designer Norman Bel Geddes, Wright crafted his career as the king of casual domesticity by capitalizing on developments partially given expression by Frederick Hurten Rhead's work at the Homer Laughlin China Company. Rhead had chortled at Wright's 1939 American Modern line for the Steubenville Pottery Company: a national style seemed ludicrous to an art director whose firm catered to so many different clients and consumer groups. Yet Wright's American Modern—a dinnerware staple at department stores such as the Hecht Company in Washington, D.C., F. and R. Lazarus & Company in Columbus, Maison Blanche in New Orleans, and Foley's in Houston—prefigured a major ideological transformation of the postwar era. By the late 1940s, the notion of one American taste resounded among countless consultants, including glassware maven Freda Diamond. A graduate of the Cooper Hewitt School of Design for Women, Diamond defined herself as a great synthesizer who scanned the audience, digested what she saw, and assimilated the hodgepodge to create one best product that would appeal to everyone.[2]

Diamond's consensual outlook crystallized during the interwar years, but the Great Depression thwarted her ambitions for uplift. Spending six years as a department store stylist at Manhattan's Stern Brothers, she became exasperated with managers who clung to traditional looks: "I was sure that given the opportunity to choose and to buy better taste and fashion merchandise at moderate prices the average consumer would respond with alacrity, and this would stimulate more interest in the home and make for additional business." In 1938, she gave substance to her modernist theories with her designs for simple, Shaker-style furniture produced by the Herman Miller factory in Grand Rapids. Diamond's big breaks came during and after the war when she teamed up with businesses, big and small, that welcomed her market-shaping orientation. Then, some home furnishings producers counted her among the design profession's Olympians. She created lines for the Libbey Division of the Owens-Illinois Glass Company, Continental Can Company, Pennsylvania House Furniture, Yale & Towne, Foster Grant Company, and Window Shade Manufacturer's Association, while working as style coordinator for retailers such as Hartford's G. Fox & Company, Allentown's Hess Department Stores, and Los Angeles's May Company.[3]

Diamond's affiliation with Associated Merchandising Corporation, a national department store conglomerate, exposed her to firms eager for help with cracking the profitable home furnishings nut. She summarized: "Working with department stores as home furnishings coordinator and stylist gave me the opportunity of meeting and speaking to their customers and observing at close range what they were interested in buying. It helped me enormously in designing a product that could CREATE DEMAND. Also being involved as a consultant with the people in advertising and publicity both at the retail and wholesale level gave me a chance to help SHAPE DEMAND." The booming economy of the 1940s enabled design consultants to approach clients with the confidence of soothsayers—and to describe their subjects with comparable audacity. "Over the years," Diamond recalled, "my reputation for knowing the taste of the average American consumer grew." Although Rhead, the fashion intermediary, understood the market as stratified by class, the tastemaker saw only one customer: a middlebrow who could be taught to appreciate upscale lines. A picture of feminine elegance in tailored suits, bold jewelry, and enormous hats, Diamond impressed managers who wanted to secure the woman's perspective and the designer's eye in one neat package.[4]

During the war, Diamond established her forty-seven-year relationship with Libbey, the consumer wing of Toledo container giant Owens-Illinois. Descended from Edward Drummond Libbey's cut glass factory, the division reentered the carriage trade in 1940 with Modern American stemware, modeled to capture a business once dominated by Scandinavian and Czechoslovakian crystal. Although ill fated, this effort to create a distinctively American glassware nevertheless illustrates Libbey's budding interest in a nationalist aesthetic, which came to maturity in peacetime. When advertising executives from J. Walter Thompson predicted that backyards would become the new domestic locus, Libbey managers in Toledo hired Diamond to design casual products. With her finger on fashion's pulse, the New Yorker spiced up deadly dull sales meetings: "Pinks are the thing. Don't get into darks and blacks and dark blue. Pink." After surveying retail colleagues about patio possibilities, she created Hostess Sets, a line embodying the themes of domesticity, gaiety, and informality. Introduced in 1946, these popularly priced gift packages of machine-made tumblers featured happy motifs like Carnival, Tally Ho, and Merry-Go-Round, which promised the good life to a population tired of rations. Within eleven years, Libbey had sold more than thirty million glasses in her designs, mostly in sets of six or twelve.[5]

To be sure, Wright's and Diamond's emphasis on casual living, better design, and "good taste" suited big businesses like Owens-Illinois, whose professional managers searched for ways to cut costs, increase throughput, and conquer enormous markets. Diamond's Flair shape received the Museum of Modern Art's 1952 Good Design Award, and the Toledo men basked in the glory. "We know that fine design is essential to our high-volume business," trumpeted general manager A. M. Turner, "and recognize that many other businesses understand this truth." Yet taking this executive braggadocio as evidence of a seismic shift in design practice is problematic, for quantity-oriented Libbey did not typify home furnishings firms. For much of the postwar era, batch producers still dominated this market. Revisiting some familiar firms to see how this less-visible majority

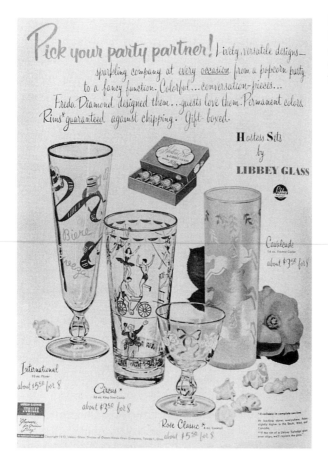

Libbey glassware designs by Freda Diamond. Advertisement in *House Beautiful*, October 1952, Libbey Inc., Toledo

responded to "multi-media" designers and to cultural prescriptions for easier living is a fitting wrap-up for this tale about imagining consumers.[6]

Coping with Consensus

When Lord & Taylor spotlighted Italian faience as a hot housewares line after World War II, New York City's most prestigious department store sent American retailers a signal: Imports *will* return. Similarly, Freda Diamond did her bit for foreign goods by spreading the word about American taste among Italian craftsman and Japanese manufacturers targeted by government economic development programs. During the 1950s and 1960s, the nation's potteries and glassworks experienced a major upheaval when foreign trade policy, including the multilateral General Agreement on Tariffs and Trades, opened the United States to inexpensive products from Europe and Asia. An explosion in melamine tableware, aggressively pushed by established molders like Boonton and new entrants such as Royalon and Lenox, exacerbated the import crisis. (Ironically for Homer Laughlin, the enormous appeal of plastic stemmed from a wide assortment of monochromatic colors; one molding compound, Plaskon, came in 11,500 hues.) In 1954, a joint envoy from the United States Potters' Association (USPA) and the National Brotherhood of Operative Potters begged Congress to raise tariffs and put quotas on ceramics. A year later Homer Laughlin's Joseph M. Wells, testifying before the Senate Finance Committee, blamed huge industrywide losses on cheap Japanese porcelain. Between 1947 and 1961, the output of the American pottery industry declined by 50 percent, and fifteen factories in the East Liverpool district of Ohio, Pennsylvania, and West Virginia filed for bankruptcy. The Steubenville Pottery, the maker of Wright's American Modern, counted among these failures. Manufacturers of pressed glass faced comparable conditions; by 1961, fifteen of the thirty-nine companies operating in 1950 shut down, with little relief in sight.[7]

While lobbying for protectionism, managers in batch production firms dealt with diminishing sales on a day-to-day basis, sometimes turning to highfalutin advisors for designs and publicity—often with regrets. Working through dealer-importers like Justin Tharaud & Son on Fifth Avenue, Russel Wright secured consultancies with potteries and glassworks tottering on the edge. Anxious to retain wartime advantages among department stores and gift shops, West Virginia's Paden City Glass Company signed a 1949 contract to produce Highlight, a complement to Steubenville's American Modern. Finding Wright's design proposals incompatible with existing setups, the faltering factory scrambled to construct a special fabrication unit before going belly-up in 1953. Similarly, managers at New Jersey's Appleman Art Glass Works, bankrupt by 1952, pulled their hair when Wright demanded textures, colors, and shapes beyond the purview of the bent glass medium. More financially stable factories in the Midwest lodged similar grievances. Indiana Glass Company's engineers tired of explaining to Wright why this or that would not fly on the shop floor. Evaluating a sketch for an hourglass tumbler with a tightly crimped waist, Indiana's Arthur Harshman reiterated the basics: "To reshape the article, it must be thrust into the fire edge first, and by the time the heavy bottom of this glass was plastic, the thin edge would have passed the liquid stage." In some instances, Wright navigated around his technical deficiencies by stationing subject specialists like the potter Doris Coutant at factories; more often, he depended on fast talk and pizzazz to save his day.[8]

Overall, industrial design offered temporary relief at best. At Imperial Glass Corporation in Ohio, Wright's Flare, Pinch, and Flame tumblers, introduced in 1950, brought the prestige associated with signature lines and masked rocky balance sheets. Similarly infected by design mania, the glassmaker A. H. Heisey & Company asked its tastemaking consultant Eva Zeisel to update handmade lines, adding Cocktail Party, Crystal Buds, and Leaf; and the Edwin M. Knowles China Company paid the California-based Virginia Hamill to create some "sure-fire Lady Bait." In contrast, more prescient managers at the Salem China Company, Homer Laughlin, and the Fostoria Glass Company steered clear of simple design solutions offered by big names and instead modified proven methods to pioneer new market niches. Some broadened the scope of scheme ware, others tapped institutional markets, and still others capitalized on love and marriage. When design fit into these factories' game plans, it played into the hands of trusted consultants and art directors who knew the technological ropes.[9]

The Sebring empire emerged from the Depression and the war with deep wounds; only its Limoges and Salem companies survived. A clan member by marriage to Frank A. Sebring's granddaughter, J. Harrison Keller joined Limoges's management in 1936. When this factory closed thirteen years later, he became Salem's president, installing labor-saving equipment to increase output by about 40 percent. For the 1950 Pittsburgh exhibit, Keller supported an industrywide initiative to battle imports with the great cure-all: casual styling. Ironically, Salem's long-standing part-time designer, Viktor Schreckengost, looked to Asian art for inspiration, creating a show-stopping lotus shape with Water Lily, Cherry Blossom, and Poppy patterns. The next year, the salesman George Weigl collaborated with Harold Krauss, the crockery man at Bamberger's department store in Newark, New Jersey, to feature Schreckengost dishes alongside matching linens and glass, all "ranch house" styled. So the story went, well into the fifties. With one eye on the competition, Keller even brought personal talents into the picture, working with the buyer from Sears, Roebuck & Company on a Harmony House exclusive, Symphony dinnerware.[10]

Yet the best casual styling, whether Keller's mail-order brainstorms or Schreckengost sensations like his Free Form shape, failed to prop up the last Sebring pottery. When Salem lost Sears's orders to Japan in the early 1950s, Keller initially relied on the family's premium heritage to keep kilns running. Since the late 1930s, East Liverpool potteries had ventured into a new giveaway field: supermarkets. New wave scheming, complete with elaborate display units oriented toward tapping feminine susceptibility to "Pretty Dishes," sustained Salem until the mid-1950s, when competition from East Liverpool rivals eroded profitability. Next, bank giveaways exhausted their course, forcing the mild-mannered Keller to take the bull by its horns: If you can't beat 'em, join 'em. By 1967, however, Salem's kilns lay idle, as the firm turned away from manufacturing and began importing flatware, silverplate, and china from Europe and Asia for resale.[11]

Meanwhile, Homer Laughlin's style-minded vice president Louis K. Friedman searched for an art director following Rhead's death in 1942. A Sebring native who had worked in local potteries throughout high school, Don Schreckengost, Viktor's sibling, filled the slot from 1945 through 1960. After studying industrial design at the Cleveland Institute of Art, "Schreck" spent the early thirties at Salem, where Tode Sebring's quest for "a different look" excited the young man's creativity. His Tricorne shape, accented with bright orange bands, presented a dramatic alternative to the decal aesthetic, paralleling Rhead's movement toward a monochrome palette. By 1935, however, Schreck moved on, accepting a design professorship at Alfred University's clay-working school. Ten years later, aggravated by the hubris of postwar consultants, he returned to the pottery district ready to wage an offensive against the notion of a single American taste. For the 1950 Pittsburgh show, Schreck embellished his new Debutante shape with eleven unique patterns—to make a point. Whereas Homer Laughlin had produced three dinnerware shapes in 1914, it made twenty-seven shapes in three clay bodies and nineteen glazes in 1953. Decorating options boggled the mind: decalcomania, underglaze transfer printing, banding, hand lining, machine lining, stamping, spray tinting, silk screening, and stenciling. Under the new art director's guidance, America's ceramics leviathan confronted consensus with what it knew best: variety.[12]

Though keeping a stiff upper lip, Homer Laughlin also suffered problems that pushed it to the brink of collapse. Once responsible for a third of USPA output, the company made 23 percent of American tableware in 1949; a decade later, 20 percent. Accompanied by an overall 50 percent reduction in USPA output, the dish colossus received "a smaller slice of a smaller pie." Many of the troubles stemmed from Japanese imports, plastics, and power shifts among American potteries. As marginal firms closed, aggressive firms like the Royal China Company in Sebring, Ohio, and Taylor, Smith & Taylor in Chester, West Virginia, attracted crockery buyers' attentions with innovative sales pitches and merchandising deals. California upstarts like Vernon Kilns became the standard-bearers of the casual

The stylistic variety that characterized Homer Laughlin's output during Don Schreckengost's tenure as art director. Promotional leaflet, 1957, Homer Laughlin China Company

mode. When Ball Stores in Muncie, Indiana, stocked Vernon's Tickled Pink, the buyer, Kathryn Petro, reported that Middletown shoppers deemed it the perfect "fit" with "their relaxed, informal way of life." To volume producers in the East Liverpool district, scheme ware looked better than ever, and desperate potteries jostled with makers of pots, pans, toys, cutlery, glass, luggage, and jewelry for shares of the $2 billion premium market. In 1949, Homer Laughlin relied on five-and-tens for 31 percent of sales. Ten years later, business fell precipitously, and premium vendors gobbled up 40 percent of the firm's products.[13]

As losses mounted, Homer Laughlin's decision makers reevaluated their century-old approach to the pottery business; in 1959, the firm began slowly converting from consumer products to institutional china for hotels, restaurants, and cafeterias. This shift, combined with a major managerial reorganization, en-sured the firm's survival. Appointed art director in 1962, Vincent Broomhall, a hometown boy with a broad range of pottery experience, marched to a different drummer than Schreck. Coming of age after the demise of apprenticeships, he nevertheless combined artistic talent and technical facility in ways that would have pleased the best practical men, including Jesse Dean and Rhead. Working as a decal designer for Palm, Fechteler & Company during the early 1930s, Broomhall shied away from detailed patterns—from "roses that you could al-most smell"—and pursued bold styling. Whether as art director at Knowles, proprietor of Continental Kilns, or freelancer for several midwestern potteries, Broomhall's propensity for "loose" designs served him well.[14]

At Homer Laughlin, Broomhall articulated a strategy that combined a respect for tried-and-true market-driven aesthetics with an imperative for technological innovation. In his worldview, the shopper, rather than the tastemaker, told the factory what to make. "Good design is what appeals to the public today, and the designer must always adjust to the present-day market." As consumers divided into discrete taste groups, importers capitalized on these differences with tradi-tional, colonial, provincial, and contemporary styling. Broomhall's talent for easy-going designs enabled Homer Laughlin to capitalize on the emerging "bolder, more modern look." Just as important, decades of factory work enabled him to back up design recommendations with plans for the requisite equipment. Under his aegis, Homer Laughlin streamlined embellishing processes in ways that cut costs yet revolutionized the appearance of the product. Whether making con-sumer lines for A&P and Montgomery Ward or institutional wares for hotel chains like Howard Johnson, the industry leader extended up-to-date informal-ity to the masses.[15]

Meanwhile, porcelain and glass factories took advantage of American diver-sity to develop more traditional markets. As cultural conservatism drew suste-nance from Cold War fears, conventional institutions—marriage, family, and home—comforted Americans seeking safe haven after despondent decades. In the twenty years after the Great Depression, the nuptial rate increased by 6 per-cent; 60 percent of the population was married in 1940, 66 percent in 1950, and 68 percent in 1960. As the number of weddings soared, so did sales of home-making necessities, both casual and formal. Manufacturers, retailers, and pub-lishers tutored the prospective homemaker, steering womanly attentions toward the bridal registry as a "clearing house through which her dreams for a perfect home" might come true. During the mid-1930s, managers at Lenox China and

Wells Drorbaugh, founder of *Bride's Magazine,* pioneered the gift registry as a merchandising device. After the war, Lenox targeted teenagers as a distinctive group; by the 1950s, advertisements in *Seventeen* tempted wishful Cinderellas with the snappy, seductive slogan, "You get the license, I'll get the Lenox." The firm also introduced a system of named patterns, making it easier for shoppers to remember and identify their favorites. West Virginia's ever adaptable Fostoria Glass Company followed New Jersey's porcelain piper, using bridal registries and mass advertising to became the nation's leading manufacturer of wedding present glassware.[16]

Situated primarily in high-end department stores and china shops, registries operated on simple principles. As magazines promoted hope chests and bridal showers, women learned to assemble household accessories piecemeal, taking advantage of others' generosity. Before her wedding shower, a bride visited a retailer, selected favorite china and glass patterns, and listed preferences with the bridal secretary, so that friends and family might buy place settings for her. At Hochschild, Kohn & Company in Baltimore, registry consultants kept abreast of home furnishing trends, including interior decorating schemes, to assist customers with tableware selections. Besides facilitating distribution, registries performed key cultural functions. Selecting from a panoply of china, glass, and silver patterns, a bride assembled a tabletop outfit that testified to her individuality, much like Cinderella's form-fitting slipper. By providing older relatives with formal gift solutions, registries also bridged the generation gap.[17]

Readers of *Seventeen* voted Fostoria the glass of choice for teenagers' hope chests, prompting the Moundsville managers to seek even more advice from a new breed of fashion intermediary: the bridal secretary. From J. L. Hudson Company, Alice Bayse reported that few Detroit brides, however sophisticated in stylistic matters, really understood the pillars of formal living, including etiquette. She encouraged tutoring. Already, Fostoria circulated classroom films such as *Crystal Clear* to expose high school home economics students to glassware's beauty and durability as well as to its utility in courtship and marriage. The film's protagonist, Mary Lee, used glassware to ensnare "the boy next door," teaching high school girls about well-appointed tables as material adjuncts to family values. Fostoria's message also reached audiences through point-of-sale aids like a 1949 countertop bridal display, which beckoned women of all ages to partake in the timeless act of enjoying fine glassware and formal meals.[18]

America's enduring batch production factories dealt with tough competition in numerous ways, but few turned to the new multimedia consultants. Especially if broaching novel product areas, they preferred to rely on well-established consumer feedback loops. When Salem pioneered supermarket premiums in 1952, its sales manager, J. A. Armstrong, relied on the Indiana grocer Henry J. Eavey to conduct a bit of research—the old-fashioned way. Setting up factory samples on a dining room table in one supermarket, Eavey's managers asked passersby to choose their favorite dishes. When customers selected Woodhue, Eavey stocked thirty-five of its supermarkets with this Salem pattern and sold more than $40,000 worth of nine-cent plates within six months. The New Ideas Committee at the Federal Glass Company in Columbus also took salesmen and retail buyers seriously, whether planning refrigerator jars or highball glasses. When the consultant designer Eva Zeisel submitted some tumbler proposals, Federal's committee decided that only one of the nine suited the factory's needs and that most of the others "did not lend themselves to decorating" or to a "volume market." Enmeshed in a production-distribution matrix with a clear-cut way of doing things, Salem's Keller and other managers in batch production firms found Madison Avenue glitter no substitute for well-established methods.[19]

Why Marketing?

As before, Corning Glass Works did things differently. Entering World War II as a mixed-output glassmaker, the firm used automatic processes to manufacture moderately priced, standardized electrical components and batch production practices to make expensive, highly differentiated technical and consumer lines. Industrial research facilities attracted military contracts, which accounted for 75 percent of wartime output. In 1941, Amory Houghton became chairman of the board; Houghton's brother-in-law, Glen W. Cole, assumed CGW's presidency until he was succeeded by William C. Decker in 1946 (figure 5). Gearing up for peacetime exploitation of its research and development laboratories, Corning had reorganized its divisions in 1943 and became a publicly traded company two years later. Under vice president Charles D. LaFollette, the Sales Department expanded its research function, providing the three product divisions with forecasts, industry analysis, and other services applicable to design and development. Meanwhile, the new Consumer Products Division, which replaced the Pyrex division of the Sales Department, devoted its full energies to Pyrex.[20]

The company's reorganization especially benefited Lucy Maltby, whose "girls" had advanced wartime development projects in ways that impressed top man-

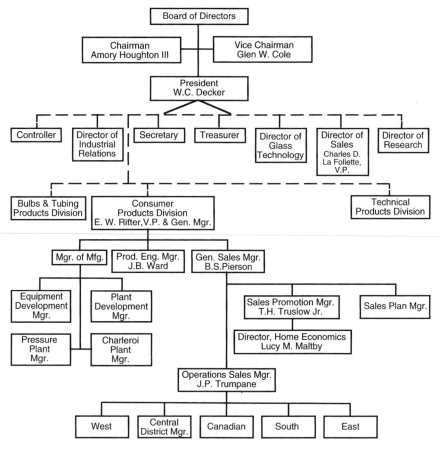

Figure 5. Corning Glass Works, organizational chart, highlighting Consumer Products Division, 1946.
Source: Corning Incorporated

agers. Executives long suspected that the heat-resistant opal glass used to make lighting products at Corning's MacBeth-Evans factory in Charleroi had broader applications. As mobilization sped up after Pearl Harbor, approximately 35 percent of the nation's war industry workers started eating meals at factory cafeterias. In response, East Liverpool potteries like Homer Laughlin churned out thousands of dozens of plain and sturdy dishes daily. Still, even tough hotel china chipped, crazed, and cracked during mass feeding. Maltby deployed test kitchen staffers Esther Rhodes and Esther K. McMurrary to determine the immediate and long-term concerns of food service managers. With space at a premium, Rhodes discovered, mess halls often stacked china plates seventy-five high, and the dishes broke from the weight. Factory, school, and government cafeterias needed enormous quantities of cups, saucers, bowls, and plates that could take such treatment, that were impervious to food stains and knife marks, and that were able to tolerate speedy handling and dishwasher compounds. When specially tempered, the Charleroi factory's white glass became the material of the hour. Cooperating with the product engineering chief John B. Ward, a wartime appointee, home economists made sure that Corning tableware met practical design requirements, providing specifications on dimensions, weight, depth, shape, surface, color, texture, finish, opacity, and stability. Through colleagues working as government procurement officers, Maltby further abetted the Opal tableware project by securing substantial military and civilian orders.[21]

Newly credentialed with a Ph.D. from Syracuse University, Maltby took charge of an enlarged Home Economics Department. Military assignments honed her understanding of how entrepreneurial spirit mattered at Smokestack University, as locals dubbed Corning. To complement LaFollette's growing market research empire, Maltby devised ways that home economics, still dedicated to the woman's viewpoint, might contribute to corporate growth. The Rhodes and McMurrary wartime investigations showed that face-to-face exchanges between household experts and other professionals yielded valuable product development data. A champion schmoozer who solicited advice from colleagues by telephone or at conferences, stores, and shows, Maltby made networking a core departmental operation. Corning's home economists still saw themselves as consumer liaisons, but they also assumed primary responsibility for promoting Pyrex among "key personnel" in manufacturing, retailing, education, and the media and among the people who had direct contact with homemakers. To advance this second aim, in 1944 Maltby hired a team of field service, or traveling, home economists, whose jobs entailed creating "a feeling-of-need" for Pyrex lines.[22]

Corning's field representatives adopted public relations models developed by agricultural extension workers and spokeswomen for utilities, food packagers, and other consumer products firms—but with one major difference: "Lucy's girls" never amused shoppers with cooking spectacles. By the late 1940s, two factors mitigated against this decades-old mainstay among business home economists. In some cities, organized workers demanded a "union card" for anyone showcasing food. Additionally, fair trade policies initiated during the Great Depression to uphold prices required equal treatment for distributors; if Corning provided one store with demonstrators, it would have to extend the service to all stores. Maltby, instead, directed her field representatives to train department store staff to conduct Pyrex demonstrations. This allowed Lucy's girls to focus on the highly professional tasks at hand: promoting products and building goodwill. The strategy worked brilliantly. Avoiding the cookie dough, so to speak, raised the travelers' status among housewares buyers, who, in turn, provided introductions to advertising, merchandise, and sales managers.[23]

While Maltby revved up her promotional machine, the Consumer Products Division remained Corning's woeful performer. Although in 1946, Pyrex sales soared (accounting for 33 percent of net sales), they fell to 22 percent in 1947 and to 12 percent in 1950 (figure 6). Using its expertise in bulb blowing, the glassworks introduced television picture tubes in 1945; within five years, contracts with TV manufacturers accounted for 44 percent of sales. As household glassware again paled next to its "high-tech" siblings, the Consumer Products Division moved to reconceptualize.[24]

Corning housewares rested on three lines marketed under the Pyrex name: Ovenware, Flameware, and Opal. Created when scientific housekeeping ruled the roost, the items still lacked casual good looks. Decades earlier, J. Walter Thompson had recommended a stylistic face-lift, but the Depression and the war postponed any action. Finally, the test kitchen work of Lilla Cortright served as a focusing device, showing how home economics ingenuity might enhance design.[25]

Shortly after joining Maltby's staff in 1946, Cortright collaborated with a team seeking household applications for Opal. Two years earlier, Corning had crafted Pyrex Color Bowls, a four-piece nesting set in hues reminiscent of "Spring Flowers," selected by Maltby from a *McCall's* interior decorating survey. Building on this success, the Consumer Products Division determined that Army-Navy glass was ideal for stacking refrigerator dishes. Since the 1930s, West Virginia's Hazel-Atlas Glass Company had sold such sets to mail-order houses, and East Liverpool potteries supplied them to appliance companies. Corning targeted a larger audience: newlyweds setting up their dream houses on the GI Bill. Perhaps tinted Opal space savers, able to go from fridge-to-oven-to-table, might appeal to brides searching for dining accessories befitting the casual lifestyle of suburbia.[26]

The project exemplified Maltby's vision of what home economics could do for Corning during peace and prosperity. As she wrote in a memo to John B. Ward, the product engineering chief: "An understanding of the importance of design changes relating to function, from the standpoint of the housewife, should not be underestimated." Revered by colleagues for her engineering bent, Maltby allowed scientific management principles to inform her wish list. The perfect kitchen glass would feature the mechanical tolerance of stainless steel, the

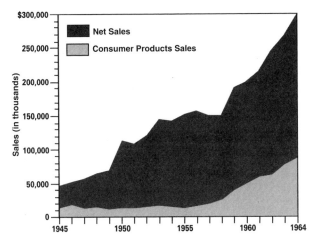

Figure 6. Corning Glass Works, total sales and consumer products sales, 1945–1964. *Source:* Corning Incorporated

heat resistance of fused quartz, and the clarity of fine crystal; and it would boast "*functional qualities* so scientifically considered that it will be possible to prove through *time and motion* studies that Pyrex dishes meet the needs of the American homemaker." If this sounded like Mildred Maddocks revisited, Maltby gave progressive rhetoric a forties twist by adding "artistic designs comparable to the best china and glass tableware."[27]

As Cortright facilitated Opal's adaptation to housewares, she cannily followed her boss's outline, step by step. Consulting with other staff, she imagined consumers and responded to their needs. When a test panel in Williamsport, an industrial city in central Pennsylvania, described their product preferences to LaFollette's team, Cortright adjusted her prototypes accordingly. She sized the butter dish to hold a pound of dairy spread while being held by an average female hand; and she created invertible covers that provided nonslip stacking and tight seals for cold storage. The new line emerged: a four-piece set in bright colors selected by Williamsport women. Cortright's work so impressed managers that they made Maltby's staff integral to other Pyrex makeovers.[28]

Corning managers admitted their fashion inadequacies by acceding to board member Arthur A. Houghton Jr.'s dream for putting design atop the corporate pedestal. A gentleman scholar with a collector's eye, Houghton—the son of Arthur A. Houghton and a fourth-generation Corning manager—had directed Steuben Glass, the firm's wayward art-glass subsidiary since the Depression. Using highbrow connections, he put Steuben Crystal in the public eye if not in the black. As his 1948 pet project, Houghton established the Corning-Steuben Design Department, a Fifth Avenue office presided over jointly by two exarchitects: Ward, who received the title Director of Corning Design, and Steuben general manager John Montieth Gates. Houghton recruited young staffers through a trainee summer camp cosponsored by Boston's Institute of Contemporary Art. By autumn, three bright-eyed, bushy-tailed designers worked under Ward in Manhattan. Their focus on visuals had an enormous effect on the Consumer Products Division.[29]

The division started upgrading its kitchen trinity, and Maltby quickly discovered that the young designers in New York remained incapable of understanding her department's full capabilities. Market research revealed that home baking and roasting had lost much of their appeal: women of the 1950s preferred to purchase commercial pastries and frozen foods and did 80–85 percent of their cooking on range tops rather than in ovens. The shift prompted Ward's staff to reevaluate Flameware, virtually unchanged since its 1936 introduction. Having had little input on Flameware's first design, Maltby gloated when the Fifth Avenue office initially asked why women disliked the line. No other Corning product, she explained, featured so many of the "annoyance factors" that drove cooks crazy. Customers' letters and remarks to her field-workers revealed a "consistent consumer demand" for percolators with capacity markings and saucepans that did not scorch food. The designers read these critiques and sent sketches for evaluation. "Looking at a drawing," Maltby patiently explained in 1951, "it is impossible for me to tell whether the spout on a Flameware dish will pour, whether the double boiler has sufficient capacity in the lower bowl," or "whether a handle is easily grasped." Clearly, New Yorkers perceived upstate as a faraway wilderness and the test kitchen as a place for baking brownies. Two years later, little had changed. When Joseph S. Knapp solicited advice on Pyrex casseroles, Maltby reminded him that she needed "actual models" for testing. From her perspective, Arthur Houghton's top-down initiative had backfired; the firm's designers considered home economics an afterthought, if at all.[30]

Meanwhile, Maltby's four to nine field representatives waved the public relations flag to stimulate interest in Corning housewares. Stationed in the West, Josephine Blanch visited Hollywood producers with Pyrex props; in the central states, Jessie Johnston supplied bake ware to home economists at Hotpoint, Norge, and other appliance companies. Starting in 1953, Ann Mikell logged in forty-five thousand air miles annually while serving the South and the Midwest. This graduate of Mississippi Southern College in Hattiesburg had spent six years as a food management specialist at the United States Department of Agriculture and seven as a home economist for General Motors' Frigidaire Division in Bal-

Lucy Maltby discussing a Flameware double boiler with a Corning product engineer, 1953. Corning Incorporated

timore. Articulate and impeccably groomed, Mikell repeatedly explained the theme that Pyrex was a time-saving, sanitary product capable of building "a higher standard of living for mankind." On the road, she gave seminars at stores and public utilities, lectured to school groups, and hobnobbed with state extension agents, magazine editors, teachers, and other corporate home economists. In Dallas, she presented Mary Carter with a "wonderful assortment of Pyrex oven and flame ware," which the TV cook promised to use *"every day"* on her show. Through Mikell's contacts in St. Louis, Pyrex dishes graced the covers of 250,000 Pet Milk cookbooks and appeared on Red Skelton's variety show.[31]

Regardless, Pyrex sales stayed unremarkable; between 1950 and 1955, the Consumer Products Division averaged $14 million, or 11 percent of net sales annually (figure 6). Corning housewares made progress at a snail's pace. Primarily, the division suffered from lack of steady leadership, for the top guard had changed several times since the war. Almost ready to give baking dishes the boot, Corning executives found their housewares savior in a physics major turned retailing executive: R. Lee Waterman. Under his direction, the venture came full circle, for Pyrex's new caretaker possessed the same vision as his predecessor of two generations ago, William Churchill. Waterman, like Churchill, succeeded partially due to circumstances beyond his control. Postwar housekeepers were ready, willing, and able to buy glass cookware—but for different reasons than their Progressive Era counterparts. By 1955, the demand for stove-top utensils, dominated by the housewares sections of department stores, exceeded the market for oven ware fourfold, but Corning's consumer durables remained lodged in hardware shops, which stacked baking dishes sky high. Waterman set two related tasks for his division: capitalize on the American penchant for easy eating and convince department stores—"the bullies of the retail business"—to treat Corning glassware as a premier line.[32]

Waterman came to Corning in October 1955 with a sophisticated understanding of merchandising, product planning, and market planning, three managerial modes that gained currency in postwar American business. He identified most with marketing, still a broadly defined field encompassing everything from product design to placement. After attending Bates College in Maine, Waterman worked for W. T. Grant Company, advancing between 1926 to 1933 from floor man to general manager in the variety chain's largest stores. He spent the rest of the thirties as a regional and national merchandise manager for Montgomery Ward & Company, returning to Grant in 1941, where he held a top post for a decade. Next, Waterman became president of Sloan-Blabon Corporation, a subsidiary of the Philadelphia carpet manufacturer Alexander Smith. Through this experience, he learned to appreciate how fluid communications among experts in all fields, from materials science to advertising, advanced creative thinking. Most important, his years at Grant infused Waterman with an indelible respect for consumers. Just as the dime store buyers Clinton Pierce Case and William F. Newberry paid close attention to Woolworth shoppers, Waterman took his cues from the marketplace, allowing the contours of demand to weigh heavily in his assessment of Corning's kitchenwares. "It is marketing's job," he stated, "to identify and satisfy wants in a creative way."[33]

Waterman's glassworks tenure coincided with a burst of antimaterialist criticism by Vance Packard, whose trilogy of best-sellers portrayed a profligate consumer culture manipulated by manufacturers, market researchers, and advertising agencies. By Packard's estimation, businesses convinced Americans to buy goods they neither needed nor wanted; market researchers developed methods for creating wasteful, compulsive consumers; and manufacturers promoted "planned obsolescence" with shoddy merchandise and outlandish styles. Waterman found Packard's diatribe so out of touch with reality that he publicly took issue. Nowhere in the housewares trade did managers collude, deliberately designing products that would soon become outdated. Rather, obsolescence arose when firms neglected to keep up with consumers' desires in terms of color, size, shape, utility, price, and packaging. "Products fail because we go out and peddle something that does not satisfy a want—or doesn't do it as well as some other product." Waterman knew this well; he had just inherited an obsolete line—Pyrex.[34]

Corning housewares needed a dramatic new look to capture two department store growth areas: range-top cookware and tableware; however, chromatic experiments aside, the glassworks tenaciously clung to the aesthetics of efficiency that fit so comfortably with its science-oriented culture. Even Maltby failed to see the transparency and colorlessness of Pyrex as a liability. "The first thing he did," recalled one of Waterman's hires, "was to get them to shake their idea that Pyrex was a clear pie plate and a measuring cup." When Pyroceram, a new family of supertough materials under study since 1952, emerged from the firm's research laboratories in 1956–57, Waterman recognized its enormous potential. The brainchild of the physical chemist S. Donald Stookey, these glass-ceramic compositions, perfected for radomes on the navy's high-speed guided missiles, withstood thermal shock far better than the borosilicate and aluminosilicate formulas used for, respectively, Pyrex and Flameware. More important, pure white Pyroceram resembled one of the household's most treasured materials: fine porcelain. Waterman advocated molding this miraculous stuff into cookware and promoting the pseudochina with all the fanfare that a top-notch advertising agency offered. If announced as a space-age material that tolerated any temperature, he hedged, consumers might appreciate glass ceramics as the embodiment of United States technical superiority over the Soviets. Zeroing in, Waterman coordinated parallel projects in technology, design, and marketing, using simultaneous programs as checks and balances.[35]

While scientists perfected compositions and engineers experimented with million-dollar melting tanks, Waterman asked Corning's home economists to contribute their two cents to space-age cookware. Blaming the gender gap between designers and consumers for innumerable product failures, he solicited Maltby's ideas. She responded by urging him to develop Pyroceram "for cooking and serving." Impressed, Waterman quickly added the test kitchen as an integral part of the design and development loop. As Corning Ware materialized in 1957–58, home economists planned its signature shape and determined specifications for the four-item line: three covered saucepans and a skillet. The "round-square" form, carefully calibrated to hold packages of Bird's Eye peas and other frozen foods, took inspiration from a competitor: stainless steel Revere Ware pans sold by Sears, Roebuck & Company. Cutting edge for its time, the curved form emphasized Pyroceram's newness, dramatized its whiteness, and highlighted its cornflower motif; the overall effect enhanced the product's tabletop appeal. Maltby's practical suggestions buttressed data gathered at the Corning Glass Center, which the firm had used as a consumer research laboratory for several years. By early 1958, polls in this ad hoc preference unit, trials from local homes, and sales experiments in Rochester, N.Y., stores determined that the target audience—urban, middle-class women, ages eighteen to thirty-four—found the line very appealing.[36]

As Waterman planned regional tests, he uncannily walked in Churchill's footsteps, initially trying out Corning Ware on conservative shoppers in Boston, Providence, Hartford, and Springfield. In Rochester, he had learned a good deal about television's ability to spread the word—and stimulate desire. Produced by N. W. Ayer & Son in Philadelphia, newsy television commercials that equated Corning's product launch with a Cape Canaveral takeoff excited so many shoppers that department store stocks vanished before newspapers even printed the follow-up ads. Waterman prepped New England wholesalers with a "person-to-person information campaign"; during the summer of 1958, a team of salesmen and home economists knocked on doors, spreading the cookware gospel. In early September, Corning Ware made its East Coast debut—accompanied by TV promotions—and sold out. In the Midatlantic and the Midwest, Waterman employed the same tactics—with enormous success. By Christmas, Corning Ware was the best-selling houseware in test markets across the country.[37]

For the 1959 national launch, Waterman hired sixteen new salesmen to promote Corning Ware with fabulous "Fire & Ice" shows. Ayer advertisements in the *Ladies' Home Journal, Reader's Digest*, and the *Saturday Evening Post* told Mrs. Consumer that Corning Ware was "Rocketing into your life!" TV commercials announced the "Cookware from the Moon" as indestructible, whether heated by flames or cooled in the freezer. Frank Fenno, a freshly minted MBA assigned to northern California, traipsed around his territory with a blowtorch, miniature refrigerator, and other paraphernalia, ready to put on demonstrations. Yet even before Corning perfected its Barnumesque tactics, Fenno found that Corning Ware had big fans. In San Francisco, he was startled when Irv Kaufmann, the buyer for Weinstein's hardware shop, submitted a $6,500 order. Siz-

Home economist Ann Mikell (right) publicizing Corning Ware on TV, 1958. Corning Incorporated

ing up the store's narrow aisles and ceiling-high displays, Fenno protested, wondering where thousands of saucepans would fit. A seasoned housewares buyer from Manhattan, Kaufmann silenced the Harvard greenhorn; the previous fall, he had been in New York and witnessed the Corning Ware shopping frenzy firsthand. In September, young Fenno and his boss nervously eyed Weinstein's windows, where other dusty cookware mountains sat. But as the Ayer-designed space ship campaign blasted across TV screens in October, Weinstein's pans sold like hotcakes. Everywhere else, the same thing happened. The subsequent Fire & Ice demonstrations gave material form to TV's black-and-white promises. Corning Ware embodied the moment's many new frontiers. "We were chasing the stars," Fenno remembered. "People grasped it," and they wanted to share in the excitement.[38]

Building on this success, Waterman searched for mechanisms to solidify his market position; a vice president since 1956, he lobbied fellow decision makers to rethink design strategies. For consumer products to succeed, Corning must relocate its design operations on site, rather than rely on ideas from Fifth Avenue. Maybe Maltby bent Waterman's ear; or perhaps he simply knew what worked.

By late 1958, he had already hired some promising young designers, including Jerry E. Wright, a University of Illinois graduate who had spent two years at Motorola Electronics in Chicago. Eager to escape urban life, Wright felt at ease in the small town of Corning, New York, and in the company's intimate environment, drawing sustenance from frequent exchanges with other professionals. Introduced in 1959, his ovoid Corning Ware teapot became an all-time bestseller. Fenno ascribed this success to good looks: "It replaced ugly on the stove for boiling water." More modest, Wright credited collaboration, including his trusting relationship with test kitchen home economists who "brought authenticity to the design process."[39]

Waterman's division flourished, expanding its share of net sales from 17 to 29 percent between 1958 and 1964 (figure 6). Sensational Corning Ware carried much of the weight, outpacing Pyrex by more than 100 percent. By the early 1960s, the line had thirty-one products and sold better than any houseware on the market. The enormous success stemmed from Waterman's ability to match consumer desires with available materials and technology. Two years before its introduction, only 2 percent of American homes had servants, part-time or otherwise. Those who loathed domestic chores welcomed labor-saving products like "boil-in-the-bag" frozen foods and attractive pots for cooking them. With one-step meals, real convenience had come to the kitchen. The home economists' dream come true, Corning Ware was a product that actually created less work for mother.[40]

The economic and cultural developments of the postwar era eroded the special position enjoyed by the nation's pottery and glass factories as manufacturers to the American people. Many plants shut down, and survivors weathered hard times by bending tradition or adapting new customs to carve market niches. Batch producers, for the most part, preferred long-standing product development strategies to consultant's fixes. Doing business as usual, these manufacturers continued to imagine women as their primary consumers. When the *Crockery and Glass Journal* urged retailers to fill managerial jobs with women, this leading trade magazine argued that the "feminine touch" could "move mountains of merchandise." Diamond's voluminous victories and Maltby's home economics program certainly seemed to substantiate the contention that the ladies, who were "thing-minded" by nature, knew "how to appeal to other women" who had "a passion for possessions." Men, in contrast, cared more about glory, prestige, and status—or so went conventional industry wisdom.[41]

Yet the age of informality rattled this decades-old gender paradigm; more and more, men participated in American materialism by collecting, cooking, and consuming. No firm understood the masculine penchant for objects better than Arthur Houghton Jr.'s Steuben Glass, which staffed its exclusive Steuben Shops with classy saleswomen trained to coddle male customers. "It's interesting how many men come in, just because they love Steuben," exclaimed Yvette Andrews, who worked as a "Steuben girl" in the flagship Fifth Avenue store: "Their enthusiasm is so genuine, it's fun to show them around." The droves of men among New York shoppers startled saleswoman Aloise O'Brien: "Way out west in Cleveland," she reported, they left "all the buying and appreciating to the women." Not since Edward Drummond Libbey's cut glass age had a factory paid such close attention to men. Modeled after Scandinavian imports, Steuben Crystal appealed to their modernist masculine tastes, as summarized by one "very calculating and scientific young man." This glassware, he explained, was "definite, clean cut, and strong—not too busy." Steuben Crystal provided the guys, who had always appreciated fine drinking and smoking accessories, with a means for enjoying a modicum of mid-twentieth-century luxury.[42]

The thousands of women who selected Fostoria glassware and the men who bought Steuben Crystal sent clear messages to American manufacturers. Brides' choices signaled the strength of the cults of domesticity and formality; men's purchases suggested that their exclusion from the consumer paradigm since the Great War had been unjustified. Overall, consumers' purchasing patterns revealed that household products that marked personal identity still mattered. Easy living had permeated American culture piecemeal, with audiences embracing the paradigm as they saw fit.

Similarly, the informality vogue penetrated the postwar pottery and glass trades and enlarged design possibilities in bits and pieces. Producers hitched their wagons to the casual modes—but not always as bid by Russel Wright and Freda Diamond. Wright advocated organic forms, Diamond brighter colors, on the grounds that Americans afraid of Cold War threats might find solace in material conformity. For quantity-production firms, consensual good looks could augment sales—if those companies, like Owens-Illinois, invested heavily in companion advertising and public relations. Although Diamond's designs helped Libbey, consultant recommendations were not prerequisites to success. Nothing demonstrated this more than Corning Ware's conquest of the market for casual housewares.

Conclusion

"QUESTION NUMBER ONE or task number one is to figure out WHAT IS THE WANT? Who will buy? Why?" Speaking to fellow Corning Glass Works executives in 1968, R. Lee Waterman summarized the major challenges facing companies that served household markets—getting the customer in focus. "This sounds very simple," Waterman remarked, "but it very seldom is." Stepping inside firms, this book probes a little-understood aspect of consumer society—the relationship between producers and their audiences. It demonstrates how the imperative for satisfying Americans' diverse tastes has contoured business strategies and tactics. Potteries and glassworks—the firms that made the household goods that men and women imbued with meaning—fostered the passage to consumerism by responding to people's material expectations.[1]

Historians often think about corporations as generic entities, which by implication fit the model of big business popularized by Alfred D. Chandler Jr. Recent scholarship in business and technology, however, acknowledges that most firms have not followed Chandler's path. In the pottery, glass, and enameling industries, manufacturers and retailers came in many shapes and sizes. Jesse Dean's china decorating workshop, staffed by highly skilled artisans, was a far cry from Corning Glass Works, which emphasized high-tech products, continuous-flow production, and scientific expertise. Among merchandisers, Richard Briggs China Warehouse, R. H. Macy & Company, and F. W. Woolworth Company each possessed distinctive managerial styles, stocks, and clients. The "big is beautiful" scheme masks the differences within corporate America and obscures the genuine relationship between the industrial economy and consumer society.

Whereas highly visible corporate giants like Procter & Gamble tried to build markets for standardized perishable goods like Crisco, few of the manufacturers discussed in this book had the desire or the wherewithal to coerce consumers. The most accomplished firms did their best to make durable goods that Americans wanted. Offering the badges of social status, gender identity, or self-assertion, they created pottery and glassware in thousands of shapes, patterns, styles, and colors. This eclectic group of manufacturers and the equally varied goods they produced operated in a corner of the industrial economy at odds with volume-oriented core firms. Like thousands of other companies in the industrial periphery, these firms eschewed emerging quantity-production opportunities in favor of batch manufacturing. More was at stake than the erosion of artisanal traditions. The Homer Laughlin China Company certainly did not become the globe's leading tableware pottery by clinging to backward technologies. During industrial America's glory years, batch practices offered the best manufacturing solutions to factories that needed flexibility in design, production, and delivery. Demand, an unpredictable force that big business tried to tame or rationalize through mass marketing, remained the lifeblood of these firms. They stood poised, ready to make whatever they thought consumers wanted: the humble cup plate, the ostentatious crystal punch bowl, and the gaily decorated dime store dish—objects as different as human faces. The batch production model conferred strength upon home furnishings manufacturers, who strove to follow to the caprices of fashion.

In terms of design, this book also departs from the reigning paradigms that emphasize elite objects and dismiss mass-market artifacts. Invented by connoisseurs, the notion of "good taste" obfuscates the diversity of Americans' material preferences and the messiness of the design process. Although academics challenge the top-down notion of "beauty," faith in a unified aesthetic still predominates among the guardians of the decorative arts tradition, notably, art museum curators. Responsible for preserving artifacts once treasured by the rich, these caretakers maintain a vested interest in highbrow culture. Deeming certain objects fit for inclusion in glitzy exhibitions, they celebrate the achievements of craftsmen, previous owners, and institutional benefactors. For students of consumerism, however, the "masterpiece" approach is inherently flawed. Its emphasis on high-class definitions of beauty denies the historical significance of commonplace items, the building blocks of popular culture.

In contrast, this book focuses on the inner workings of the industrial arts establishment, whose practitioners earned their livelihoods by creating objects for ordinary Americans. The industrial arts format has eluded scholarly scrutiny because of its atomized nature and its affiliation with batch producers, which operated outside the tastemaking realm. In those factories and workshops, the task of satisfying the multitudes required a meshing of minds, a collaboration of actors not generally associated with product design. For help in reading audiences, batch producers turned to fashion intermediaries, to men and women working at the supply-demand nexus. Factories initially depended heavily on technical specialists such as the mold maker John Oesterling, the china decorator Jesse Dean, and the decal supplier Rudolph Gaertner; but as competition accelerated, they increasingly turned to merchants, salesman, and retail buyers for advice. By the early twentieth century, a series of new professionals, from home economists like Mildred Maddocks to market researchers like Paul T. Cherington, provided housewares manufacturers with access to consumer tastes. Although these liaisons viewed the marketplace through tinted lenses, most of them fully recognized the importance of reporting consumer wants, needs, and desires with a high degree of accuracy. Distorting the evidence by peppering it with personal opinion could undermine fashion brokerage, causing the product development system to collapse.

Overall, the manufacturing firms in this book recoiled from tastemakers—outspoken aesthetes and consultant industrial designers—who tailored themselves after Oscar Wilde or Walter Dorwin Teague. Self-sanctification little impressed batch producers; nor did middlebrow beautification plans. Liberation from aesthetic bonds allowed these manufacturers to climb up and down the social ladder as they sniffed out trade. Unrestrained by prescriptions for improving taste, their factories could fiddle with a hodgepodge of visual possibilities until they hit options likely to register among their target audiences. The give and take of the established design system, wherein fashion intermediaries approved or vetoed product proposals on behalf of consumers, perfectly suited the general way of doing things among batch producers, who saw adaptability as their forte.

During and after the 1920s, batch producers avoided consultant designers, because the industrial arts tradition continued to provide its own artistic specialists, talented in-house art directors such as Frederick Hurten Rhead, whose technical skills complemented retail buyers' commercial wisdom. Although advocates of vocational education pronounced apprenticeship dead, ad hoc versions of this age-old method for transferring knowledge retained a grip on industries that valued skill. The respect accorded to practical men waned, along with factory training opportunities; but managers continued to rely on these jacks-of-all-trades, rather than on high-profile consultants from the big city, in times of stylistic crisis. If managers had to hire British immigrants—men like Rhead, who understood the Wedgwood-Bentley formula—so be it. Factory designers Rhead, Vincent Broomhall, and Viktor Schreckengost knew how to tweak the manufacturing system to get the right results.

Producer-audience relations, although not fully reciprocal, were far from coercive. Gender played a decisive role in this outcome. Batch producers did not invent the equation, "woman = consumer"; but their strategic alliances with mass merchandisers led them to accept this way of looking at the market. Late nineteenth-century retailers defined shopping as a feminine activity, and they transformed crockery emporiums, tea stores, five-and-tens, and department stores into appropriate public spaces for women and girls. As mass merchandisers like Woolworth urged producers to create durable goods with lady lure, the gears of change meshed. The process that defined consumerism as female behavior inexorably snowballed; the woman consumer, techniques for tapping into her desires, and a flurry of distinctive household artifacts emerged simultaneously. Through selective purchasing, women of all social classes voted for their favorite shapes, colors, forms, and decorations. Smart producers like Homer Laughlin, the Sebring Pottery Company, and the Fostoria Glass Company took those messages seriously. Empowered as consumers and linked to producers by fashion intermediaries, women thus shaped the design of household accessories.

There was no greater testimony to womanly influence than the ill-fated experiences of latecomers to the consumer revolution. Firms that introduced household durables during the 1910s and 1920s labored under enormous handicaps that inhibited design and development and, ultimately, limited sales. Excluded from industrial arts networks by their producer goods orientation, the Kohler Company and Corning Glass Works found themselves gasping for air after plunging into housewares. Professional fixes appealed to both companies. Each turned to home economists, advertising executives, color consultants, and market researchers, who claimed to know something about feminine taste. These experts carried weighty baggage; their middlebrow values, beliefs, and aesthetics translated into generic designs and catchy marketing slogans like the "woman's viewpoint." Abstractions like "efficiency" made sense in print but materialized as awkward glassware; although color sold cars, it did little to move sanitary plumbing fixtures. When expertise failed to deliver, the Great Depression was only partially to blame. Mostly, women accustomed to visual variety, low prices, and widespread availability rejected professional solutions and, by inference, expert intervention into domestic life.

Indeed, batch manufacturers who succeeded in household markets became so accustomed to kneeling at the feet of Mrs. Consumer that they overlooked another key audience: the male shopper. When fashion intermediaries occasionally piped up about men's purchasing power, managers enmeshed in the doctrine of separate spheres turned deaf ears. Only in the luxury trade did owner-managers, who were craftsmen or connoisseurs, admit that men took pleasure from objects. Thomas Gibbons Hawkes and Edward Drummond Libbey harnessed male tastes to push the age of cut glass; half a century later, Corning's Steuben subsidiary followed a similar path with its expensive crystal ornaments. Such ventures were unusual. It took major postwar shifts—the collapse of aging batch production industries, the refinement of quantitative market research, the rise of discount merchandisers, and the relocation of retailing to suburban malls—to correct producers' myopia, enabling them to see beyond their feminine model.

ABBREVIATIONS

Journals, Magazines, Newspapers, and Reference Works

AA	*Advertising Arts*
AD	*Arts and Decoration*
AMS	*American Men of Science*
APGR	*American Pottery and Glassware Reporter*
AR	*Architectural Record*
ASF	*Advertising and Selling Fortnightly*
BACS	*Bulletin of the American Ceramic Society*
BCR	*Brick and Clay Record*
BHG	*Better Homes and Gardens*
BMMA	*Bulletin of the Metropolitan Museum of Art*
BPGJ	*Brick, Pottery and Glass Journal*
CA	*Ceramic Age*
CGJ	*Crockery and Glass Journal*
CGL	*China, Glass and Lamps*
CI	*Ceramic Industry*
CSA	*Chain Store Age*
CW	*Clay-Worker*
DF	*Decorator and Furnisher*
ELT	*East Liverpool (Ohio) Tribune*
FGH	*Fruit, Garden and Home*
FIM	*Factory and Industrial Management*
Gaffer	*Corning Glass Works Gaffer*
GH	*Good Housekeeping*
GI	*Glass Industry*

HA	*Hardware Age*
HB	*House Beautiful*
HE	*Home Economist*
HFD	*Home Furnishings Daily*
HG	*House and Garden*
HR	*Hardware Retailer*
JACS	*Journal of the American Ceramic Society*
JC	*Jewelers' Circular and Horological Review*
JHE	*Journal of Home Economics*
JIEC	*Journal of Industrial and Engineering Chemistry*
JWTNB	*J. Walter Thompson News Bulletin*
JWTNL	*J. Walter Thompson News Letter*
KN	*Kohler of Kohler News*
KTJ	*Keramic Tile Journal*
LHJ	*Ladies' Home Journal*
MP	*Modern Plastics*
NB	*Nation's Business*
NCAB	*National Cyclopedia of American Biography*
PGBS	*Pottery, Glass and Brass Salesman*
PGR	*Pottery and Glassware Reporter*
PH	*Potters Herald* (East Liverpool, Ohio)
PHE	*Practical Home Economics*
PI	*Printers' Ink*
PIM	*Printers' Ink Monthly*
RHF	*Retailing Home Furnishings*
TACS	*Transactions of the American Ceramic Society*
USPA *Proc.*	*Proceedings of the United States Potters' Association*

Archival Material

AO-RF	Reference Files, American-Olean Tile Company, Lansdale, Pa.
APS-EUC	Edward U. Condon Papers, American Philosophical Society, Philadelphia, Pa.
CF	Carl U. Fauster Collection, Toledo, Ohio
CHC	Cambridge Historical Commission, Cambridge, Mass.
CI	Department of Archives and Records Management, Corning Incorporated, Corning, N.Y.

CI-AAH	Arthur A. Houghton Papers
CI-AMF	Ann Mikell Files
CI-BF	Biographical Files
CI-CPD	ARV 7: Consumer Products Division Files
CI-EF	ARV 25: Executive Files
CI-ENG	ARV 8: Engineering Files
CI-FD	ARV 14: Finance Division (Corporate Accounting) Files
CI-HFP	Houghton Family Papers
CI-LF	ARV 15: Legal Files
CI-MF	Lucy M. Maltby Files
CI-SP	ARV 17: Steuben Glass Papers
CI-VF	Vertical Files
CI-WF	Jerry E. Wright Files
CMG	Juliette K. and Leonard S. Rakow Research Library, Corning Museum of Glass, Corning, N.Y.
CMG-NAPBGM	National Association of Pressed and Blown Glass Manufacturers Papers
CMG-SG	Steuben Glass Works Collection
CMG-TC	Trade Catalogues
CMG-TGH	T. G. Hawkes & Company (Hawkes Rich Cut Glass Company) Archives
CMG-VF	Vertical Files
CU	Department of Manuscripts and University Archives, Olin Library, Cornell University, Ithaca, N.Y.
CU-HPG	Henry Phelps Gage Papers
ELMC	East Liverpool Museum of Ceramics, East Liverpool, Ohio
ELMC-VF	Vertical Files
HBS	Baker Library, Graduate School of Business Administration, Harvard University, Boston
HBS-MC	Melvin T. Copeland Papers
HBS-PTC	Paul T. Cherington Papers
HBS-RB	Reed and Barton Papers
HBS-RGD	R. G. Dun & Company Collection
HBS-RH	Ralph M. Hower Papers, R. H. Macy & Company Series
HL	Homer Laughlin China Company, Newell, W. Va.
HL-ADF	Art Department Files
HL-CLF	Ceramics Laboratory Files
HL-EC	Executive Correspondence

HL-ED	Engineering Department Files
HL-EF	Executive Files
HL-M	Minutes of the Meetings of the Boards of Directors
HL-SF	Sales Department Files
HML	Hagley Museum and Library, Wilmington, Del.
HML-AS	Francis Gurney du Pont Papers, Alice F. Simons letters
HML-BC	Bartley Crucible Company Papers
HML-CA	Color Association of the United States Papers
HML-OR	Office of the Registrar
HML-TC	Trade Catalogues
HSP	Historical Society of Pennsylvania, Philadelphia
JWT	J. Walter Thompson Company Archives, Special Collections Department, William R. Perkins Library, Duke University, Durham, N.C.
KA	Communications Department, Kohler Company, Kohler, Wisc.
KA-ECA	Daily Conference of Executives, Approvals with Production Conference Minutes
KA-HVK-DF	Herbert V. Kohler, Departmental Files
KA-HVK-OF	Herbert V. Kohler, Office Files
KA-KFP	Kohler Family Papers
KA-LLS	L. L. Smith Files
KA-WJK-OF	Walter J. Kohler Jr., Office Files
KSU-NBOP	National Brotherhood of Operative Potters Papers, Kent State University Archives, Kent, Ohio
MAG	Museum of American Glass, Wheaton Village, Millville, N.J.
MHS	Massachusetts Historical Society, Boston
MHS-OND	Otis Norcross Diaries
MIT-TG	Thomas Gaffield Collection on Glass and Glassmaking, Institute Archives and Special Collections, Massachusetts Institute of Technology, Cambridge
NJSM	Department of Cultural History, New Jersey State Museum, Trenton
NJSM-AP	Anchor Pottery Company Files
NJSM-VF	Vertical Files
OHS	Archives-Library Division, Ohio Historical Society, Columbus
OHS-BM	Brush-McCoy Pottery Records
OHS-EO	Edward Orton Jr. Papers
OHS-FED	Federal Glass Company Records
OHS-FOS	Fostoria Glass Company Records

SI	Archives Center, National Museum of American History, Smithsonian Institution, Washington, D.C.
SI-DS	Dorothy Shaver Collection
SI-FD	Freda Diamond Collection
SI-NWA	N. W. Ayer & Son Collection
SI-PC	Product Cookbook Collection
SI-SC	Salem China Company Archives
SI-W	Warshaw Collection of Business Americana
SICG	Ceramics and Glass Collection, Department of Social History, National Museum of American History, Smithsonian Institution, Washington, D.C.
SIL	Smithsonian Institution Libraries, Washington, D.C.
SIL-BF	Books of the Fairs Collection
SPNEA	Society for the Preservation of New England Antiquities, Boston
SPNEA-VF	Vertical Files
SU	Industrial Design Collections, George Arents Research Library, Syracuse University, Syracuse, N.Y.
SU-EA	Egmont Arens Papers
SU-RW	Russel Wright Papers
TA	Tiffany Archives, Tiffany & Company, Parsippany, N.J.
TPL	Local History & Genealogy Section, Trenton Public Library, Trenton, N.J.
UD-ML	Morris Library, University of Delaware, Newark
VB	Vincent Broomhall Papers, East Liverpool, Ohio
WL	Winterthur Library, Winterthur, Del.
WL-DC	Joseph Downs Collection of Manuscripts and Printed Ephemera
WL-TC	Trade Catalogues

NOTES

Introduction

1. Paul T. Cherington, *People's Wants and How to Satisfy Them* (New York: Harper & Brothers, 1935), 173 ("things"). Readers interested in the historiographical debates that inform this book should consult the secondary works discussed in the Essay on Sources.

2. Joel Mokyr, *The Lever of Riches: Technological Creativity and Industrial Progress* (New York: Oxford University Press, 1990), chaps. 5, 10; Neil McKendrick, "Josiah Wedgwood: An Eighteenth-Century Entrepreneur in Salesmanship and Marketing Techniques," *Economic History Review*, 2d ser., 12 (April 1960): 408–33; Neil McKendrick, "Introduction: The Birth of a Consumer Society: The Commercialization of Eighteenth-Century England" and "The Consumer Revolution of Eighteenth-Century England," in *The Birth of a Consumer Society: The Commercialization of Eighteenth-Century England*, edited by Neil McKendrick, John Brewer, and J. H. Plumb (Bloomington: Indiana University Press, 1982), 1–6, 9–33; Gervase Jackson-Stops, *The Treasure Houses of Britain: Five Hundred Years of Private Patronage and Art Collecting* (Washington, D.C.: National Gallery of Art, 1985).

3. Martin Schönfeld, "Was There a Western Inventor of Porcelain?" *Technology and Culture* 39 (October 1998): 716–32; J. H. Plumb, "The Royal Porcelain Craze," in *In the Light of History* (Boston: Houghton Mifflin, 1973), 57–69; John E. Wills Jr., "European Consumption and Asian Production in the Seventeenth and Eighteenth Centuries," in *Consumption and the World of Goods*, edited by John Brewer and Roy Porter (London: Routledge, 1993), 133–47; Neil McKendrick, "Josiah Wedgwood and the Commercialization of the Potteries," in McKendrick, Brewer, and Plumb, *The Birth of a Consumer Society*, 99–144.

4. McKendrick, "Josiah Wedgwood and the Commercialization of the Potteries"; Regina Lee Blaszczyk, "Ceramics and the Sot-Weed Factor: The China Market in a Tobacco Economy," *Winterthur Portfolio* 19 (Spring 1984): 7–19; Regina Lee Blaszczyk, British Ceramics in Maryland, gallery in After the Revolution: Life in America, installed

1985, National Museum of American History, Smithsonian Institution, Washington, D.C.; Wolf Mankowitz, *Wedgwood* (New York: Spring Books, 1966), chap. 1; Robert Copeland, *A Short History of Pottery Raw Materials and the Cheddleton Flint Mill* (Staffordshire: Cheddleton Flint Mill Industrial Heritage Trust, 1972).

5. Adrian Forty, *Objects of Desire: Design and Society from Wedgwood to IBM* (New York: Pantheon, 1986), chap. 1; Mankowitz, *Wedgwood*, chap. 1.

6. Forty, *Objects of Desire*, chap 1; McKendrick, "Josiah Wedgwood and the Commercialization of the Potteries"; Barbara Wedgwood and Hensleigh Wedgwood, *The Wedgwood Circle, 1730–1897* (London: Studio Vista, 1980), chap. 3.

7. Josiah Wedgwood to John Wedgwood, London, June 17, July 6, 25[?], 1765; JW to Thomas Bentley, Sept. 8, 1767, in *The Selected Letters of Josiah Wedgwood*, edited by Ann Finer and George Savage (New York: Born and Hawes, 1965), 34–40, 58–59 ("alias Queensware"). On creamware copycats, see Geoffrey A. Godden, *An Illustrated Encyclopedia of British Pottery and Porcelain* (New York: Bonanza Books, 1965), 337–39.

8. On Thomas Bentley, see Finer and Savage, *Selected Letters of Josiah Wedgwood*, 11–12; Neil McKendrick, "Josiah Wedgwood and Thomas Bentley: An Inventor-Entrepreneur Partnership in the Industrial Revolution," *Transactions of the Royal Historical Society* 14 (1964): 1–33.

9. JW to TB, Nov. 8, 1767, in Finer and Savage, *Selected Letters of Josiah Wedgwood*, 45–47 (45, "taste"). Neil McKendrick noted the importance of the merchant to the promotion of luxury consumption in "The Cultural Response to a Consumer Society: Coming to Terms with the Idea of Luxury in Eighteenth-Century England" (paper presented at Colonial Williamsburg, Williamsburg, Virginia, 1985).

10. Jackson-Stops, *The Treasure Houses of Britain*, 322–53.

11. Wedgwood and Wedgwood, *The Wedgwood Circle*, chap. 6; JW to TB, Dec. 26, 1772, in Finer and Savage, *Selected Letters of Josiah Wedgwood*, 141–42 (142, "white hands").

12. On "Herculaneum," see JW to TB, Dec. 1, 1769, cited in McKendrick, "Josiah Wedgwood and the Commercialization of the Potteries," 137. For JW to TB, see Finer and Savage, *Selected Letters of Josiah Wedgwood*, Aug. 23, 1772 (131, "Middling"), Aug. 18, 1772 (128, "violent").

13. On batch production, see Charles F. Sabel and Jonathan Zeitlin, *Worlds of Possibility: Flexibility and Mass Production in Western Industrialization* (New York: Cambridge University Press, 1997).

14. Neil McKendrick, "Josiah Wedgwood and Factory Discipline," in *The Rise of Capitalism*, edited by David S. Landes (New York: Macmillan, 1966), 65–81; Forty, *Objects of Desire*, chap. 2 (39, "workmanship").

15. Forty, *Objects of Desire*, chap. 2; JW to TB, Aug. 18, 1772, in *Selected Letters of Josiah Wedgwood*, 129 ("machines"). For the school, see Nancy Koehn, "Josiah Wedgwood and the First Industrial Revolution," in *Creating Modern Capitalism: How Entre-*

preneurs, Companies, and Countries Triumphed in Three Industrial Revolutions, edited by Thomas K. McCraw (Cambridge: Harvard University Press, 1997), 44.

16. Philip B. Scranton, "Diversity in Diversity: Flexible Production and American Industrialization, 1880–1930," *Business History Review* 65 (Spring 1991): 27–90 (28, "other").

Chapter 1: Cinderella Stories

1. Countless versions of "Cinderella" have appeared in the West over the centuries; this analysis draws on Joanna Cole, *Best-Loved Folktales of the World* (Garden City, N.Y.: Doubleday, 1982), 3–8; and Wanda Gág, *Tales from Grimm* (New York: Coward, McCann, and Geoghegan, 1936), 99–120.

2. Richard L. Bushman, *The Refinement of America: Persons, Houses, Cities* (New York: Knopf, 1992), xiii ("vernacular").

3. HGO to SFO, Jan. 22, 1800 ("china"; "give"), Feb. 4, 1800 ("comfortable"; "entitled"), Otis Papers, MHS, transcription, Federal Boston Research Project, SPNEA.

4. Lowell Innes, *Pittsburgh Glass, 1797–1891: A History and Guide for Collectors* (Boston: Houghton Mifflin, 1976), chap. 8; Arlene Palmer Schwind, *Glass in Early America: Selections from the Henry Francis Du Pont Winterthur Museum* (New York: Norton, 1993), 132, 154–55, 185.

5. Joseph D. Weeks, "Report on the Manufacture of Glass," in *Report on the Manufactures of the United States at the Tenth Census (June 1, 1880)*, vol. 2 (Washington D.C.: Government Printing Office, 1883), 58; Pearce Davis, *The Development of the American Glass Industry* (Cambridge: Harvard University Press, 1949), 82–85; Kirk J. Nelson, "Progress under Pressure: The Mechanization of the American Flint Glass Industry, 1820–1840" (master's thesis, University of Delaware, 1988); HGO to SFO, Feb. 8, 1800; Rodris Roth, "Tea-Drinking in Eighteenth-Century America: Its Etiquette and Equipage," in *Material Life in America, 1600–1860*, edited by Robert Blair St. George (Boston: Northeastern University Press, 1988), 439–62; Jane Shadel, "Documented Use of Cup Plates in the Nineteenth Century," *Journal of Glass Studies* 13 (1971): 128–33; Kenneth Wilson, *American Glass, 1760–1930: The Toledo Museum of Art* (New York: Hudson Hills Press and Toledo Museum of Art, 1995), 1:275 (Leslie).

6. Dennis Michael Zembala, "Machines in the Glasshouse: The Transformation of Work in the Glass Industry, 1820–1915" (Ph.D. diss., George Washington University, 1984), 80–81; George Wallis, "New York Industrial Exhibition, Feb. 6, 1854," in *The American System of Manufactures*, edited by Nathan Rosenberg (Edinburgh: Edinburgh University Press, 1969), 201–307 (287–90, glassmaking); Innes, *Pittsburgh*, 26–27.

7. Davis, *Glass Industry*, 83, 90–91; Deming Jarves, *Reminiscences of Glassmaking*, 2d ed. (New York, 1865), 3; Raymond E. Barlow and Joan E. Kaiser, *The Glass Industry in Sandwich* (Windham, N.H.: Barlow-Kaiser, 1983), 1:64–65.

8. *Yarmouth Register and Barnstable County Weekly Advertiser,* Dec. 20, Dec. 27, 1838, cited in Barlow and Kaiser, *Glass Industry in Sandwich,* 1:42–43 (Kerr); Leigh Schmidt, *Consuming Rites: The Buying and Selling of American Holidays* (Princeton: Princeton University Press, 1995), 150 ("cups").

9. Wallis, "New York Industrial Exhibition," 288.

10. "Now and Then," *CGJ* 16 (Dec. 14, 1882): 10 ("taste"); "The Manufacture of Tableware," *PGR* 11 (June 26, 1884): 16, 19 ("attention").

11. Innes, *Pittsburgh,* chaps. 14, 16, 17.

12. "Glass Notes," *APGR* 2 (Jan. 22, 1880): 4; "J. Ernest Miller, Dean of Glass Makers, Dead," *Pittsburgh Post Gazette,* Jan. 20, 1930; U.S. Design Patent 10,727, John Ernest Miller, June 18, 1876; Union Glass Company, Somerville, Mass., to Charles Yockel, Philadelphia, Sept. 13, 1895, Yockel Papers, WL-DC; Johns Brothers, Fairmont, W. Va., to Charles Yockel, Feb. 18, 1896, Yockel Papers, HSP.

13. Gary Everett Baker, "The Flint Glass Industry in Wheeling, West Virginia: 1829–1965" (master's thesis, University of Delaware, 1986), 119–23; Weeks, "Report," 79; Davis, *Glass Industry,* 151–53; Zembala, "Machines," 199–200, 253; "Death of a Prominent Glass Manufacturer," *CGJ* 14 (Nov. 10, 1881): 31–32.

14. "Western Manufactories," *CGJ* 1 (March 6, 1875): 6; "Death of John Oesterling," *CGJ* 18 (Nov. 22, 1883): 22; "Mr. Oesterling's Death," *PGR* 10 (Nov. 29, 1883): 19; Baker, "Flint Glass," chap. 4; Jane Shadel Spillman, *American and European Pressed Glass in the Corning Museum of Glass* (Corning, N.Y.: Corning Museum of Glass, 1981), 269–70; *Illustrated Catalogue of Glass Ware, Manufactured by McKee & Brothers* (Pittsburgh, 1871), 2, CMG-TC; *Catalogue and Price List of Glassware, Manufactured by Adams & Company* (Pittsburgh, 1871–72), 8, CMG-TC.

15. "Letter from Wheeling," *APGR* 4 (Feb. 10, 1881): 18; WL to TG, March 3, 1886, vol. G 666.1 G3, MIT-TG.

16. "The Manufacture of Tableware," *PGR* 11 (June 26, 1884): 16, 19; "New York," *PGR* 17 (Oct. 13, 1887): 10; "New York," *PGR* 17 (July 28, 1887): 9; Montgomery Ward & Company, *Catalogue* (1884): 152–53, HML-TC; Montgomery Ward & Company, *Catalogue No. 42* (1887–88), 204, SIL; "New York," *PGR* 17 (July 28, 1887): 9.

17. Schmidt, *Consumer Rites,* chap. 3; U.S. Patent 342,743, H. Franz, "Glass Mold," May 25, 1886; U.S. Patent 351,197, John Ernest Miller, "Manufacture of Glass Shoes or Slippers," Oct. 19, 1886; Neila M. Bredehoff, George A. Fogg, and Francis C. Maloney, *Early Duncan Glassware: Geo. Duncan & Sons, Pittsburgh, 1874–1892* (Boston: Privately printed, 1987), 143–52.

18. "Business Memoranda," *APGR* 5 (July 14, 1881): 12; "Business Memoranda," *PGR* 12 (Feb. 19, 1885): 12; *By-Laws of Associated Glass and Pottery Manufacturers,* folder 4, box 5, OHS-BM; "The Glass Trade: Pittsburgh," *CGL* 1 (Jan. 21, 1891): 20–21; "Glass Notes," *APGR* 4 (March 3, 1881): 8 ("mania"); Shirley P. Austin, "Glass," in *Report*

on the *Manufactures of the United States at the Twelfth Census (June 1, 1900)*, vol. 9 (Washington D.C.: Government Printing Office, 1902), 33.

19. "The Crockery Trade," *NYMG*, April 4, 1871 ("public"); OS file 23, CMG-VF; "New York Letter," *PGR* 15 (Sept. 9, 1886): 6 ("Italian"; "beautiful"); "New York Letter," *PGR* 16 (Dec. 2, 1886): 9, 11; "New York," *PGR* 17 (July 28, 1887): 9.

20. "Glass Cutting and Engraving," *PGR* 12 (April 16, 1885): 14 ("angles"); "Price and Art," *CGJ* 16 (Nov. 16, 1882): 27; "Great American Industries, VIII: A Piece of Glass," *Harpers New Monthly Magazine* 470 (July 1889): 247–64 (261, "inferior"); Davis, *Glass Industry*, 162; "Glass Manufacture in the United States," *Scientific American* 21 (Oct. 23 1869): 263.

21. Annette Blaugrund, *10th Street Studio Building: Artist-Entrepreneurs from the Hudson River School to the American Impressionists* (Southampton, N.Y.: Parrish Art Museum, 1997), 99; *Clayton, the Pittsburgh House of Henry Clay Frick: Art and Furnishings* (Pittsburgh: Helen Clay Frick Foundation, 1988); William Hosley, *Colt: The Making of an American Legend* (Amherst: University of Massachusetts Press, 1996).

22. *Gems of the Centennial Exhibition* (New York, 1877), 21, reel 53, SIL-BF; Thomas Westcott, *Centennial Portfolio: A Souvenir of the International Exhibition at Philadelphia, Comprising Lithographic Views of Fifty of Its Principal Buildings, with Letter-Press Description* (Philadelphia, 1876), 46, reel 50, SIL-BF; J. S. Ingram, *Centennial Exposition, Described and Illustrated* (Philadelphia, 1876), 283–87, reel 49, SIL-BF. On Scott, see ["Documentation for Francis E. Peters's Donation"], 79.21, and "Donations to the Hagley Foundation," Oct. 14, 1980, 80.30, HML-OR.

23. William T. Dorflinger, "The Development of the Cut Glass Business in the United States" (paper read before the annual meeting of the American Association of Flint and Lime Glass Manufacturers, Atlantic City, N.J., July 25, 1907); Davis, *Glass Industry*, 159–60.

24. On Hawkes's background, see Jane Shadel Spillman, *The American Cut Glass Industry: T. G. Hawkes and His Competitors* (Woodbridge, England: Antique Collectors' Club, 1996).

25. "Cutting and Engraving Glass," *CGJ* 27 (Jan. 11, 1883): 21; Ovington Brothers, *Blue and White China* (Brooklyn, 1883), 50–51, box: Pottery 4, SI-W; "The Art of Cutting Glass," *Harper's Weekly* 34 (Jan. 25, 1890), reprinted in *Glass Club Bulletin* 159 (1989): 15–16; "American Cut Glass, How Manufactured, and Who Manufactured It," *JC* 21 (Nov. 1890): 33–34, 37–40; "The Sparkle of Cut Glass," *CGL* 10 (July 31, 1895): 20; "The Art of Cutting Glass: Prismatic and Beautiful Ornaments and Pieces of Tableware," *CGL* 11 (April 15, 1896): 15–16; "Art of Making Cut Glass," *CGL* 13 (April 7, 1897): 16–17; Day Allen Willey, "The Process of Cutting Glass Dishes," *Scientific American Supplement* 53 (June 28, 1902): 22141–42; J. J. Vallely, "Craftsmanship Exhibited in Fine Cut Glass," *JACS* 3 (Feb. 1920): 149–51.

26. "American Cut Glass," *JC* 25 (March 3, 1893): 55; Jane Shadel Spillman and

Estelle Sinclaire Farrar, *The Cut and Engraved Glass of Corning, 1858–1940* (Corning, N.Y.: Corning Museum of Glass, 1977), 38–39, 47, 39 ("jewels," from 1882 newspaper).

27. "The Art of Cutting Glass," *CGL* 11 (April 15, 1896): 15; "Bachelor's Combination Cabinet and Details," *DF* 3 (Dec. 1883): 83; "Dorflinger's American Cut Glass," advertisement in *Commercial and Financial Chronicle* 53 (Jan. 9, 1892): 90. A thoughtful analysis of male consumerism in the Gilded Age is Mark A. Swienicki's article, "Consuming Brotherhood: Men's Culture, Style and Recreation as Consumer Culture, 1880–1930," *Journal of Social History* 31 (Summer 1998): 773–808.

28. Sampson to [Charles F.] Houghton, Sept. 3, 1887; Crocker to TGH, Oct. 28, 1889; Brewer to TGH, Nov. 24, 1885 ("RR"), CMG-TGH.

29. "Executor's Sales, Estate of Moses LaRue, Oct. 31, 1905," WL-DC; "Inventory of the Property of Edward Orton Jr.," Feb. 1915, folder: "Estate papers," box 1, OHS-EO.

30. Matthew Smith to George and John Smith, Liverpool, Dec. 16, 1826, Matthew Smith Letterbook, Maryland Historical Society, Baltimore.

31. John Wanamaker, advertisement in *Scribner's Magazine* (April 1881): 16, clipping in folder: "Dry Goods, Bills of Sale and Advertisements," SPNEA-VF.

32. "Trade Items," *PGR* 17 (Aug. 25, 1887): 12, 20; "A Brief History of an Ancient Firm" (Boston: Richard Briggs, 1926), folder: "China and Glass," SPNEA-VF; "Recent Deaths: An Old Boston Merchant," *Boston Evening Transcript,* July 31, 1893. On Norcross, see "The Crockery Dealers of Boston in the Forties," *CGJ* 24 (April 30, 1886): 32–34; Otis Norcross diary, book 4, Otis Norcross & Co., Net Profits [1848–1857], MHS-OND; *In Memoriam: Otis Norcross* (Boston, 1883); "Hon. Otis Norcross," *CGJ* 16 (Sept. 14, 1882): 25–26; "Obituary," *APGR* 7 (Sept. 14, 1882): 19–20. For the associations, see "Boston Earthenware Association," *CGJ* 20 (May 20, 1875): 11, 14; "Boston Crockery Merchants," *CGJ* 8 (July 11, 1878): 5–6; "Boston's Crockery Trade," *CGJ* 18 (Aug. 30, 1883): 40–42 (40, "mercantile class"); Otis Norcross diary, book 1, July 11, 1863, and book 3, July 1, 1871, Jan. 25, 1872, MHS-OND; Minute book, 1883–1906, Earthenware and Glassware Association of Boston Records, MHS.

33. JMS, "India China Vase," trade cards, 1882, folder: "China and Glass," SPNEA-VF; "Correspondence," *APGR* 6 (March 9, 1882): 4 ("India"; "costly").

34. "Boston Reports," *CGJ* 19 (May 28, 1884): 20 ("flocks"); Karl Baedeker, *The United States with an Excursion into Mexico: A Handbook for Travelers* (1883), cited in Herbert A. Kenny, *Newspaper Row: Journalism in the Pre-Television Era* (Chester, Conn.: Globe Pequot, 1987), 8.

35. James T. Fields, *A Conversational Pitcher* (Boston, 1877), 9 ("admire"); HWL to My Dear Girls, *The Letters of Henry Wadsworth Longfellow,* 6 vols., edited by Andrew Hilen (Cambridge: Belknap Press of Harvard University Press, 1966–82), 5:3272.

36. Fields, *Conversational,* 7–8; Elder Brewster teapot, 1983.0802.10, and Longfellow jug, 1980.0858.01, SICG; Jean McClure Mudge et al., *Ceramics and Glass at the Essex Institute* (Salem, Mass.: Essex Institute, 1985), 46–47.

37. RB to TGH, Aug. 25, 1883 ("attractive"); Aug. 20, 1883 (salt); Oct. 12, 1885 (candlestick); June 13, 1887 (decanter); July 12, 1888 (bottle), CMG-TGH; Howard to Reed & Barton, March 13, 1903, letterbook, vol. 101, HBS-RB.

38. Harriet Beecher Stowe [Christopher Crowfield, pseud.], *House and Home Papers* (Boston, 1865), 118–19, 158, 118 ("wild-flowers"); *Catalogue of Articles for Sale by Richard Briggs* (Boston, n.d.), 2, 31, Rare Book Room, Library of Congress, Washington, D.C. Both consumers and culture critics relished Briggs's china-decorating practices, as did judges for the Massachusetts Charitable Mechanic Association, who rewarded his displays of innovative designs with praise and prizes; "Exhibition Awards," *CGJ* 1 (Jan. 9, 1875): 6; *The Tenth Exhibition of the Massachusetts Charitable Mechanic Association* (Boston, 1865), 106; *Eleventh Exhibition of the Massachusetts Charitable Mechanic Association* (Boston, 1869), 131; *Twelfth Exhibition of the Massachusetts Charitable Mechanic Association* (Boston, 1874), 109.

39. RB to TGH, Sept. 25, 1884; Jan. 24, 1885; Feb. 12, 18 ("paper"), 1887; Jan. 26, 1887; May 6, 1882; Jan. 14, 1880; April 7, 1887 ("life"); Nov. 26, 1883 ("class"), CMG-TGH.

40. RB to TGH, March 15, 1882; Aug. 15 ("meat"), Oct. 13, 1885; Jan. 1, 1886; July 7, 1884; Jan. 26, 1885; Dec. 6, 1888; April 19, Oct. 22, Nov. 27, 1885; Washington customer to RB, Nov. 24, 1885 ("effective"), CMG-TGH.

41. Fields, *Conversational*, 9.

42. Davis, *Glass Industry*, 153–54, 162; ["Of the eight flint glass factories"], *PGR* 13 (June 11, 1885): 25.

43. "The United States Glass Company," *CGJ* 34 (Aug. 13, 1891): 26, 29; ["A good deal of misapprehension"], *CGL* 1 (March 18, 1891): 22; ["The annual meeting"], *CGL* 4 (Aug. 24, 1892): 22–23; "Business Memoranda," *PGR* 13 (April 23, 1885), 12–13; "Business Memoranda," *PGR* 12 (Dec. 4, 1884): 12–13; Ohio, State Geologist, *First Annual Report of the Geological Survey of Ohio* (Columbus, 1890), 140–41, 152, 187–90, 267–68; S. W. McKee & Company to TG, March 4, 1886, vol. G 666.1 G13, pt. 2, MIT-TG; Warren Candler Scoville, *Revolution in Glassmaking: Entrepreneurship and Technological Change in the American Industry, 1880–1920* (Cambridge: Harvard University Press, 1948), 80.

44. Davis, *Glass Industry*, 154; Zembala, "Machines," 199–200; Austin, "Glass," 979; Jay William Blum, "National Collective Bargaining in the Flint Glass Industry" (Ph.D. diss., Princeton University, 1934), 217; U.S. Bureau of Labor Statistics, *Productivity of Labor in the Glass Industry*, Bulletin 441 (Washington, D.C.: Government Printing Office, 1927), 95.

45. "Originality in Design," *PGR* 4 (Jan. 27, 1881): 10; Sears, Roebuck & Company, *Catalogue* (1895), 518–20, SIL; Richard H. Slavin, "The Development of Current Economic Problems in the Pressed and Blown Glass Industry" (Ph.D. diss., University of Pittsburgh, 1961), 101.

46. Sears, Roebuck & Company, *Catalogue 113X* (1903), 690, SIL; S. B. Reed,

House-Plans for Everybody (New York, 1879), 62–65 (62, "comfortable"); Ella Rodman Church, *How to Furnish a Home* (New York, 1881), 35–46; Thomas E. Hill, *Hill's Manual* (Chicago, 1881), 151 ("snowiest"); Marion Harland, *House and Home: Complete Housewife's Guide* (n.p., 1889), 41 ("sip").

47. Harriet Edwards, "Present Fashions in Glass," *Harper's Bazaar* 33 (Nov. 3, 1900): 1714–15; Lu Ann De Cunzo, "A Future after Freedom," *Historical Archeology* 32 (1998): 42–54.

48. "American Cut Glass, How Manufactured, and Who Manufactured It," 33 ("middle"); "Cut Glass Making," *New York Tribune*, Nov. 23, 1902 ("Vanderbilts"), clipping, Historical Memo Notebook 7, CI; *Trade Press Opinions on Rich Cut Glassware, Manufactured by L. Straus & Son* [New York, 1892], CMG; U.S. Department of Commerce, Bureau of Foreign and Domestic Commerce, *The Glass Industry: Report on the Cost of Production of Glass in the United States*, Miscellaneous Series 60 (Washington, D.C.: Government Printing Office, 1917), 47, 73, 220; William S. Blake, Union Glass Company, Somerville, Mass., to Charles Yockel & Sons, Philadelphia, Feb. 24, 1904, box: "Glass," SI-W; "Cut Glass Association Meets in Convention," *GI* 3 (Aug. 1922): 149–51; C. L. B. Tylee, Arcadia Cut Glass Company, Newark, N.Y., to O. B. Greene, New York City, Jan. 8, 1902 (Altman), Arcadia Cut Glass Company Records, WL-DC.

49. "Dorflinger's American Cut Glass," advertisement in *Century Magazine*, Nov. 1889, clipping, Advertising Files, MAG.

50. "Novelties in Glass by an Old-Established House," *Manufacturers' Gazette*, reprinted in *CGJ* 24 (Oct. 21, 1886): 23; "Wonders of Glass-Making: Visit to the New England Glass Works, and What Was Seen There," *Boston Evening Transcript*, Jan. 1, 1884, and "The Glass Workers: A Partial Strike at the New England Works—An Interview with the Proprietor" [1885], clippings, Scrapbook of Articles on Glass, vol. 3, MIT-TG; Susan E. Maycock, *Survey of Architectural History in Cambridge: East Cambridge*, rev. ed. (Cambridge: MIT Press, 1988), 176–88; Wilson, *American Glass*, 2:587; "Corning, N.Y.," *CGL* 1 (March 4, 1891): 19; "The Late Strike at Corning, N.Y.," *CGL* 1 (May 6, 1891): 23.

51. For a full account of the Owens-Libbey story, see Scoville, *Revolution*.

52. Gillinder's legacy is described in "Correspondence," *APGR* 6 (March 9, 1882): 4. On Libbey, see "An Exposition of Glass Making," *JC* 27 (Oct. 11, 1893): 1 ("diamonds"); *Libbey Glass Company, World's Fair, 1893* (Toledo, 1893), box: "Glass," SI-W; *The Book of the Fair: An Historical and Descriptive Presentation of the World's Science, Art, and Industry, as Viewed through the Columbian Exposition in Chicago in 1893* (Chicago, 1895), 843 ("room"), reel 99; "The Great Libbey Glass Company at the World's Fair," *The Illustrated World's Fair* 4 (April 1893): 502, reel 110; *Harper's Weekly* 37 (May 13, 1893): 437–60, reel 121, SIL-BF; Department of Commerce, *The Glass Industry*, 218.

53. *Reports of the United States Commissioners to the Universal Exposition of 1889 at Paris* (Washington, D.C., 1890), 424, reel 91, and *Official Catalogue of the United States Exhibit* (Paris, 1889), 124, reel 86, SIL-BF; Wilson, *American Glass*, 2:831; "Rem-

iniscences of Our Trip to the Columbian Exposition," Aug. 1893 ("prettiest"), WL-DC; *The Best Things to Be Seen at the World's Fair* (Chicago, 1893), 175, reel 99, SIL-BF; *The Century World's Fair Book for Boys and Girls*, 222–23; Scoville, *Revolution*, 94–96; *Libbey Glass Company, World's Fair, 1893*, 9 ("Eulalia"). For Mower and Scott, see "Documentation for Items Donated by Frances E. Peters," Nov. 18, 1976, 76.46, and "Donations to the Hagley Foundation," Oct. 14, 1980, 80.30, HML-OR.

54. "Fine Cut Glassware," *CGL* 11 (April 22, 1896): 16–17; Department of Commerce, *The Glass Industry*, 219; Davis, *Glass Industry*, 245–49.

55. Carl U. Fauster, *Libbey Glass Since 1818* (Toledo: Len Beach, 1979), chaps. 2, 3; Kate Field, *The Drama of Glass* (Toledo, 1893).

56. Photograph, "Yale Class of 1899," folder: "Yale classes," drawer: Interiors, SPNEA-VF; *Things Beautiful* (Toledo: Libbey Glass Company, 1902), 18–23, CF.

57. Harvey Green, *The Light of the Home* (New York: Pantheon, 1983), chap. 5; Ellen K. Rothman, *Hands and Hearts: A History of Courtship in America* (New York: Basic Books, 1984), chap. 5; "Trade Items," *PGR* 17 (May 12, 1887): 12–13; "The Glass Trade: Pittsburgh," *CGL* 1 (Dec. 31, 1890): 13.

58. "The Earthenware Trade: Trenton, N.J.," *CGL* 1 (Feb. 4, 1891): 17; Frank Haviland, "Haviland China at First Hands," advertisements in *Century Magazine*, Nov. 1889, n.p., Jan. 1890, 15; C. Dorflinger & Sons, "Ice Cream Sets," advertisement in *Century Magazine,* June 1897, 29; C. Dorflinger & Sons, "Wedding Gifts," advertisement in *Century Magazine*, June 1898, 23; Higgins & Seiter, "Fine China, Rich Cut Glass," advertisement in *Century Magazine*, 1895, clippings, Advertising Files, MAG; J. Walter Thompson, folder: Libbey Glass Company, photographs of advertisements, 1896–1910, Account files, box 12, JWT; *Things Beautiful*; *American Beauty* (Toledo: Libbey Glass Company, 1904); *The Gentle Art of Giving* (Toledo: Libbey Glass Company, 1905), all in CF.

59. J. R. Sprague, "What Is the Future of the Retail Store?" *PIM* 10 (Feb. 1925): 22–24, 98–100, (23, quotations); "How to Inaugurate and Operate a China and Glass Department," *CGJ* 62 (Dec. 14, 1905): 91–92.

60. Tylee-Greene letters, Jan.-March 1902, Arcadia Cut Glass Company Records, WL-DC (department stores); "A Fellow Craftsman Discusses Some of His Business Methods," *JC* 47 (Dec. 2, 1903): 74–75 (jewelers); Louise Schoenberger Conway, "Wedding Present List," Chicago, June 1, 1908, WL-DC. The Conways received 170 gifts, including thirteen glass items: six came from men, five from women, and two from couples.

61. "Our Artistic Glass Equal to Europe," *New York Times,* May 13, 1926, cited in Wilson, *American Glass*, 2:643; Higgins & Seiter, advertisements in *New York Times*, May 14, 21, 1893; *Fine China—Rich Cut Glass, Catalogue No. 10* (New York, ca. 1898), 11, boxes: Pottery, SI-W; Bawo & Dotter, "June Weddings," advertisement in *CGJ* 51 (April 26, 1900): 10; F. Scott Fitzgerald, "The Cut-Glass Bowl," in *Bernice Bobs Her Hair and*

Other Stories, edited by Barbara H. Solomon (New York: Signet Classics, 1996), 237–56, 237 ("presents"); Pauline Condon, Wedding Present List, 1919, Condon Collection, SPNEA; "Brilliant Church Wedding Today," *Newburyport [Mass.] Daily News,* June 12, 1919 ("multitude"); Christine Terhune Herrick, "New Cut Glass and China," *Harper's Bazaar* 38 (Feb. 1904): 198–200. On china cabinets, see Maria Parloa, *Home Economics* (New York, 1898), 37; "The Sparkle of Cut Glass," *CGL* 10 (July 31, 1895): 20.

62. Robert Grant, "The Art of Living: House-Furnishing and the Commissariat," *Scribner's Magazine* 177 (March 1895): 305–15, (313–14, quotations).

63. Fitzgerald, "The Cut-Glass Bowl," 237–56 (238, "huge").

64. Frank A. DePuy, *The New Century Home Book* (New York: Easton and Mains, 1900), 85; Condon, Wedding Present List.

Chapter 2: China Mania

1. "Correspondence," *APGR* 5 (June 16, 1881): 12; "Correspondence," *APGR* 6 (March 30, 1882): 22 ("champion"). Unless otherwise noted, this chapter draws on *CGJ's* Trenton column, 1875–1895, written by an unidentified china decorator who had lived in the city since 1868.

2. On moss rose's popularity, see "Correspondence," *APGR* 5 (Sept. 8, 1881): 24, 26.

3. George M. Coates, account book, 1824–37, WL-DC; "Boston Crockery Merchants," *CGJ* 8 (July 11, 1878): 5–6; Moses Yale Beach, *Wealth and Biography of the Wealthy Citizens of New York City* (New York, 1845; reprint ed., New York: Arno Press, 1973), 21, 25; N.Y. vol. 192: 505, 600, HBS-RGD.

4. Marc Jeffrey Stern, "The Potters of Trenton, New Jersey, 1850–1902: A Study in the Industrialization of Skilled Trades" (Ph.D. diss., State University of New York at Stony Brook, 1986), chap. 1.

5. For the Coxons, see Francis Bazley Lee, *History of Trenton, New Jersey: The Record of Its Early Settlement and Corporate Progress* (Trenton, N.J., 1895), 320; N.J. vol. 45: 351, HBS-RGD. On Davis, see N.J. vol. 46: 21, 110, 194, 233, and vol. 47: 384, HBS-RGD; "Obituary," *CGJ* 34 (Sept. 3, 1891): [35–36]. On Bloor, see "Death of William Bloor, Sr.," *CGJ* 5 (June 7, 1877): 14; N.J. vol. 44: 92, and vol. 45: 461, HBS-RGD; E. M. Woodward and John F. Hageman, *History of Burlington and Mercer Counties, New Jersey, with Biographical Sketches of Many of Their Pioneers and Prominent Men* (Philadelphia, 1883), 745–46; "Obituary," *CGL* 11 (Jan. 22, 1896): 26 (Ott). On Vodrey, see Jabez Vodrey, diary, ELMC.

6. Geoffrey A. Godden, *The Illustrated Guide to Mason's Patent Ironstone China* (London: Barrie & Jenkins, 1971), 11; Jean Weatherbee, *A Look at White Ironstone* (Des Moines: Wallace-Homestead Book Company, 1980), 12–15.

7. N.Y. 192:513, 595 (Collamore), 510, 581 (Haviland), 511, 544 (Rees), HBS-RGD. On New York's growth, see M. Christine Boyer, *Manhattan Manners: Architecture and*

Style, 1850–1900 (New York: Rizzoli International, 1985); Edward K. Spann, *The New Metropolis: New York City, 1840–1857* (New York: Columbia University Press, 1981).

8. On Leigh and Maddock, see "Obituary [for William Leigh]," *CGJ* 10 (March 8, 1900): 32; ["Mr. Maddock"], USPA *Proc.* 10 (1886), 10; "Obituary [for Thomas Maddock]," *CGL* 18 (June 22, 1899): n.p; Woodward and Hageman, *History of Burlington and Mercer Counties*, 202; N.J. 44:40, 110n, 46:61, HBS-RGD; "Trenton Has Oldest Pottery Salesman," *Trenton Sunday Times Advertiser*, June 28, 1931. On Haughwout, see *Annual Report of the American Institute of New York* (1850), 52; (1851), 58; (1858), 76; George Wallis, "New York Industrial Exhibition, Feb. 6, 1854," in *The American System of Manufactures*, edited by Nathan Rosenberg (Edinburgh: Edinburgh University Press, 1969), 293; Margot Gayle and Edmund V. Gillon Jr., *Cast-Iron Architecture in New York: A Photographic Survey* (New York: Dover Books, 1974), 142. On Shaw, see ["The death of Mr. James Shaw"], *CGJ* 37 (Jan. 17, 1889): 20; "Obituary," *CGJ* 37 (Jan. 17, 1889): 24; ["We chanced to pass"], *CGJ* 18 (Nov. 1, 1883): 21; N.Y., vol. 191, 499, HBS-RGD. For Vaupel, see H. F. Louis Vaupel, "Kurze Biographie Meiner Selbst, 1860–1900," translated by Rosemarie C. Sauerman, 88 ("drawing"), CHC.

9. For Trenton's output, see U.S. Manufacturing Census for Mercer County, N.J. (June 1, 1860), Products of Industry in First Ward, City of Trenton, 5; Second Ward, 5; Third Ward, 2; Fifth Ward, 1; Sixth Ward, 7, EM; and U.S. Manufacturing Census for Mercer County, N.J. (June 1, 1870), Products of Industry in First Ward, City of Trenton, 5–7; Third Ward, 1, 8; Fifth Ward, 1; Seventh Ward, 1, EM; Alfred Day, "Secretary's Report," USPA *Proc.* 14 (1890), 9–12 (CC was introduced in 1853; WG in 1856). On "Trenton goods," see House Committee on Ways and Means, *Arguments before the Committee of Ways and Means on the Morrison Tariff Bill*, 48th Cong., 1st sess., 1884, 298. For tariffs, see Herman John Stratton, "Factors in the Development of the American Pottery Industry, 1860–1929" (Ph.D. diss., University of Chicago, 1929), 301, 312.

10. "Correspondence," *APGR* 1 (Aug. 21, 1879): 691; Woodward and Hageman, *History of Burlington and Mercer Counties*, 747; Richard Edwards, *Industries of New Jersey. Part I: Trenton, Princeton, Highstown, Penning, and Hopewell* (New York, 1882), 190; "Jesse Dean Has Added Much to Trenton's Pottery Fame," *Trenton Evening Times*, March 22, 1910, clipping, Dean file, NJSM-VF ("how"); *Trials and Confessions of an American Housekeeper* (Philadelphia, 1854), 9–18 (ornaments); Catherine E. Beecher and Harriet Beecher Stowe, *The American Woman's Home* (New York, 1869; reprint, Watkins Glen, N.Y.: Library of Victorian Culture American Life Foundation, 1979), 84; Eliza Leslie, *The House Book; or, A Manual of Domestic Economy for Town and Country* (Philadelphia, 1841), 233 ("white crockery"); "Decorating for the People," *CGJ* 22 (Oct. 8, 1885): 25 ("no money").

11. "Where Do All the Fine Goods Go?" *CGJ* 24 (Nov. 11, 1886): 2 ("all classes"); Pair of vases, Arita, Japan, nineteenth century, 1997.211–212, and John Singer Sargent, "The Daughters of Edward Darley Boit," oil on canvas, 1919.19.124, Museum of Fine

Arts, Boston; ["Philadelphia prides itself on its china"], *PGR* 13 (June 4, 1885): 17; "Individual Beer Mugs," *CGJ* 24 (Aug. 26, 1886): 24; C. G. Ellis mug, 89.94.6, Sandwich Glass Museum, Sandwich, Mass.; "Decorating for the People"; "The Old Moss Rose," *CGJ* 23 (April 22, 1886): 22.

12. On the fair, see U.S. Centennial Commission, *International Exhibition, Fairmount Park, Philadelphia, 1876* (Philadelphia, 1875), SIL-BF; John Maass, "The Centennial Success Story," in *1876: A Centennial Exhibition,* edited by Robert C. Post (Washington, D.C.: National Museum of American History, Smithsonian Institution, 1976), 22. For ceramics, see *The Illustrated Catalogue of the Centennial Exhibition* (New York, 1876), 110, 115, 146, 302, 382; J. S. Ingram, *The Centennial Exposition* (Philadelphia, 1876), 404–10, 459–60, 561–62, SIL-BF.

13. John Hart Brewer, "Report of the Secretary," USPA *Proc.* 3 (1877), 6–9; Brewer, "Report of the Secretary Centennial Committee," USPA *Proc.* 3 (1877), 15–19 (18, "ladies"); Alice Cooney Frelinghuysen, *American Porcelain, 1770–1920* (New York: Metropolitan Museum of Art, 1989), 37–43, 166–69.

14. *Gems of the Centennial Exhibition* (New York, 1877), 52–54 (54, "lack"); Susan H. Myers, "Ceramics," in Post, *1876,* 108–13 (111, *Herald*).

15. Frank Henry Norton, ed., *Frank Leslie's Illustrated Historical Register of the Centennial Exposition, 1876* (New York, 1877), 120–21, SIL-BF; William Hosley, *The Japan Idea: Art and Life in Victorian America* (Hartford, Conn.: Wadsworth Atheneum, 1990), chap. 2.

16. For Walters, see Alice Cooney Frelinghuysen, "Aesthetic Forms in Ceramics and Glass," in *In Pursuit of Beauty: Americans and the Aesthetic Movement,* edited by Doreen Bolger Burke (New York: Metropolitan Museum of Art, 1986). On Childs, see Hester M. Poole,"The City Residence of Geo. W. Childs, Esq.," *DF* 14 (June 1889): 69–70; "Private Offices of Geo. W. Childs, Philadelphia," *DF* 8 (April 1886): 6–7; Arnold Lewis et al., *The Opulent Interiors of the Gilded Age: All 203 Photographs from "Artistic Houses" with a New Text* (New York: Dover, 1987), 176–77.

17. Alfred T. Goshorn, "Effects of the Centennial Exhibition," in *The World's Fair in Retrospect* (1893), 423–29, SIL-BF.

18. John Trowbridge, "Imaginary Dialogue on Decorative Art," *CGJ* 7 (June 13, 1878): 5–6 (*Atlantic Monthly*); Clarence Cook, *The House Beautiful* (New York, 1878), 235–46.

19. George W. Oliver, "Secretary's Report," USPA *Proc.* 6 (1880), 6–9 (7, "Art"); Tiffany & Company, ["Blue Book for 1890–1"] (New York, 1890), TA.

20. William Leach, *Land of Desire: Merchants, Power, and the Rise of a New American Culture* (New York: Pantheon, 1993), 55–61 (Baum).

21. Isidor Straus to Mr. Mandell, May 10, 1892 ("must buy"), and Interview with Percy S. Straus, Feb. 15, 1933, both in folder: L. Straus & Sons, case 1, HBS-RH; Ralph Hower, *History of Macy's of New York, 1858–1919: Chapters in the Evolution of the*

Department Store (Cambridge: Harvard University Press, 1943), 104–5, 144–45, 222–23; "Obituaries: Nathan Straus," *CGJ* 109 (Feb. 1931): 58.

22. "Decorative Devices," *New York Press,* cited in "Decorative Devices," *CGJ* 32 (Nov. 27, 1890): n.p. ("new"). On JMS, see John Connelly, *A Century-Old Concern: Business of Jones, McDuffee & Stratton Co., Founded by Otis Norcross, the Elder, in 1810* (Boston: George H. Ellis, 1910), 20 ("woman's"; "acceptable"); Otis Norcross diary, bk. 1, Feb. 14, 1863; bk. 3, April 16, 1874 (buying excursions), MHS-OND; "An Old Boston Concern," *CGJ* 1 (April 17, 1875): 14; "Correspondence," *APGR* 1 (Sept. 4, 1879): 14; "Business Memoranda," *PGR* 9 (June 28, 1883): 12; JMS, "India China Vase," 2 trade cards, 1882, folder: "China and Glass," SPNEA-VF; "Correspondence," *APGR* 9 (March 9, 1882): 4 ("India").

23. For women and display, see "Tasteful Arrangement of Store," *APGR* 3 (July 15, 1880): 8–9 (9, quotation). On JMS, see *King's Hand-Book of Boston* (Cambridge, 1878), 284; "Boston," *CGJ* 2 (Dec. 2, 1875): 18; "Correspondence," *APGR* 6 (March 9, 1882): 4 ("pitchers"); "Business Memoranda," *APGR* 8 (March 1, 1883): 14; "Progressive Cost of Production of Pottery," *CGL* 11 (March 4, 1896): 21–22.

24. Stowe, *House and Home Papers,* 118–19, 158.

25. "Pottery Decoration," *CGJ* 6 (July 5, 1877): 14 ("train up"); "Domestic Decorations," *CGJ* 10 (Dec. 18, 1879): 16 ("bread"); "The Development of China Decoration," *CGJ* 24 (Nov. 4, 1886): 25; "Enamel Colors and Amateurs," *CGJ* 26 (Dec. 15, 1887): 20, 23.

26. Walter Smith, *Art Education, Scholastic and Industrial* (Boston, 1873), 166, 172; "Pottery Decoration," *CGJ* 6 (July 5, 1877): 14 ("feminine mind"); Nina de Angeli Walls, "Educating Women for Art and Commerce: The Philadelphia School of Design, 1848–1932," *History of Education Quarterly* 34 (Fall 1994): 329–55; "Business Memoranda," *PGR* 8 (Feb. 1, 1883): 12.

27. "Pottery Decoration," *CGJ* 6 (July 5, 1877): 14; "Cincinnati Potteries," *CGJ* 10 (April 28, 1879): 19; "Cincinnati Exhibition," *CGJ* 10 (Oct. 2, 1879): 5; "Pottery at the Cincinnati Exhbition," *CGJ* 10 (Oct. 9, 1879): 19; Benn Pitman, *A Plea for American Decorative Art* (Cincinnati, 1895), cited in Carol Macht, introduction to *The Ladies, God Bless 'Em* (Cincinnati: Cincinnati Art Museum, 1976), 7–13 (10, "women"); Mary Louise McLaughlin, *China Painting: A Practical Manual for the Use of Amateurs in the Decoration of Hard Porcelain* (Cincinnati, 1877); McLaughlin, *Pottery Decoration under the Glaze* (Cincinnati, 1880); Mary Gay Humphries, "The Cincinnati Pottery Club," *Art Amateur* 8 (Dec. 1882): 20–21; "Cincinnati Art Pottery," *Harper's Weekly* (May 28, 1880): 341–42; Elizabeth William Perry, "Decorative Pottery of Cincinnati," *Harper's New Monthly Magazine* 62 (May 1881): 835–45.

28. "Suggestions to Amateurs," *China Decorator,* reprinted in *CGJ* 26 (Aug. 11, 1887): 19; George Ward Nichols, *Pottery: How It Is Made, Its Shape and Decoration* (New York, 1878), 38–39 (38, "business").

29. "Suggestions to Amateurs"; "Enamel Colors and Amateurs," *CGJ* 26 (Dec. 15, 1887): 20, 23; "A Plate," *CGJ* 18 (July 26, 1883): 27–28; "The Spirit of the Amateur," *CGJ* 27 (June 7, 1888): 27; Mass. vol. 90, p. 289, HBS-RGD (Walter); "Chicago Trade Reports," *CGJ* 14 (Nov. 24, 1881): 22 (Phillips); "Society of Decorative Art," *CGJ* 7 (May 15, 1878): 20; *Catalogue of Strictly First Class White and Decorated French China, and White English Porcelain Dinner, Tea, and Chamber Sets* (New York, [1885]), Special Collections, UD-ML.

30. *Good Form Dinners: Ceremonious and Unceremonious,* 4th ed. (New York, 1890), 51–60; Susan H. Myers, "Aesthetic Aspirations: Baltimore Potters and the Art Craze," *American Ceramic Circle Journal* 8 (1992): 25–54 (Haynes); Nina de Angeli Walls, "Art, Industry, and Women's Education: The Philadelphia School of Design for Women, 1848–1932" (Ph.D. diss., University of Delaware, 1995), 226–27 (Sartain).

31. "Miss A. F. Simons," business card [1881]; Alice F. Simons to Elise du Pont, May 16, 1875 (New York); Jan. 21, 1879, Jan. 6, 1880 (Paris); Nov. 14 ("editress"), Nov. 16, 1881 (nunnery); Jan. 24 ("pupils"), May 10 (Wilde), June 26, 1882, all in box 15, HML-AS.

32. Simons to du Pont, Nov. 7, 1881 ("music"); March 24 ("Japanese"), April 7 ("lambrequin"), May 9 ("table"), May 10, ("barrel"), May 12, 1882, box 15, HML-AS.

33. Frances Elizabeth Peters, "Documentation for Items Donated by Frances E. Peters," Nov. 18, 1976, 76.46 (Scott), HML-OR; "Fashion Rules," *CGJ* 21 (Feb. 5, 1885): 21; "The Development of China Decoration"; ["It was just nine years last Sunday"], *CGJ* 21 (May 14, 1885): 20; "Enamel Colors and Amateurs," and "China as a Work of Art," *DF* 25 (Dec. 1894): 95–96; *Exhibition of American Art Industry of 1889* (Philadelphia, 1889), 22 ("appreciation"), TPL.

34. *Thirteenth Exhibition of the Massachusetts Charitable Mechanic Association* (Boston, 1878); *Fourteenth Exhibition of the Massachusetts Charitable Mechanic Association* (Boston, 1881); ["The American Institute"], *CGJ* 12 (July 8, 1880): 16; *Report of the Board of Commissioners of the Eleventh Cincinnati Industrial Exposition* (Cincinnati, 1883), 152–53 (152, "brightness"; 153, "tasty"); Simons to du Pont, Aug. 19, 1882, HML-AS.

35. U.S. Manufacturing Census, Schedule 3, Products of Industry in Trenton, Mercer Country, N.J., May 31, 1880; Earthenware Trade of New York City, *The Tariff on Earthenware* (New York, 1872), 5; Mercer Pottery Company, letters from Illinois, Michigan, Ohio, and Indiana, 1875–80, boxes: Pottery, SI-W; Tariff Hearing before Tariff Commission, in *Annual Report of Commission for 1882* (Washington, D.C.: Government Printing Office, 1882), 1:754, 1978; John Hart Brewer, "Report on Statistics," USPA *Proc.* 11 (1887), 13–15.

36. John Hart Brewer, "Report of the Secretary," USPA *Proc.* 5 (1879), 5–7 ("masses"); N.J. 45:176 ("good"), 45:534 (struggled), HBS-RGD; "Correspondence," *APGR* 1 (Aug. 1, 1879): 10; U.S. Manufacturing Census, 1880; H. Leonard & Sons to Mercer Pottery Company, Feb. 7, 1879, and Ott & Brewer to W. L. Tucker & Son, Jan. 26, 1874 (delays),

both in boxes: Pottery, SI-W; "Pottery and Potteries," *Evening Argus* (Trenton), Jan. 3–21, 1873; *Daily State Gazette,* Dec. 5, 1878; "The American Crockery Company," *CGJ* 2 (Dec. 2, 1875): 19; Kiln notebook (Nov. 1877–July 1878), Ott & Brewer Papers, WL-DC; J. H. Goodwin, "Secretary's Report," USPA *Proc.* 9 (1885), 7–8.

37. Woodward and Hageman, *History of Burlington and Mercer Counties,* 694; F. A. Wilbur, "Report on Clays," in *Mineral Resources of the United States, 1883 and 1884,* 49th Cong., 1st sess., 1885, H. Misc. Doc. 36, 699; Progressive Manufacturing Company, Advertising leaflet (Trenton, N.J., c. 1881), 1 ("taste"), box 3: Pottery and Glassware, Miscellaneous Advertisements Collection, WL-DC. On printed and filled decorations, see W. S. Harris, *The Potter's Wheel and How It Goes Round* (Trenton, 1886), 45–58, WL-TC; William Evans, *Art and History of the Potting Business, Compiled from the Most Practical Sources for the Especial Use of Working Potters* (Shelton, Eng., 1846), 35–50; Ernest Albert Sandeman, *Notes on the Manufacture of Earthenware* (London: H. Virtue & Company, 1901), 287–326; Alfred Day, "Report of the Committee on Statistics," USPA *Proc.* 9 (1885), 11–12.

38. "The Potteries: Trenton," *CGJ* 19 (April 10, 1884): 34 ("if").

39. "Economical Home Decoration," *DF* 3 (Dec. 1883): 89.

40. Sandeman, *Notes,* 325–26; "Decalcomania," *Scientific American Supplement* 55 (May 30, 1903): 22931–32; George H. Stapleford, "The Manufacture of Ceramic Decalcomania," *BACS* 15 (Nov. 1936): 383–91; "Trenton Earthenware Manufactories," *CGJ* 6 (Oct. 25, 1877): 25–26 (Ott & Brewer); House Committee on Ways and Means, *Arguments before the Committee of Ways and Means on the Morrison Tariff Bill,* 298; Barbara Himmelfarb, *Official White House China: A Presentation from the National Museum of History and Technology, Smithsonian Institution* (Washington, D.C.: National Museum of History and Technology, Smithsonian Institution, 1979), 18–20; "Native Ceramics at the American Institute Fair," *CGJ* 10 (Oct. 9, 1879): 20.

41. *Daily State Gazette* (Trenton), May 1, 1879 ("never"). For the full account of the Lenox-Ulrich decal experiments, see Regina Lee Blaszczyk, "The Aesthetic Moment: China Decorators, Consumer Demand, and Technological Change in the American Pottery Industry, 1865–1900," *Winterthur Portfolio* 29 (1994): 121–53. When the French at midcentury went crazy over the sticky colored pictures known as *decalquer,* they coined a term that described the madness: *decalcomanie.* When Americans adopted the product and the mania, they changed the French term to *decalcomania,* or *decals* for short.

42. John J. Cleary, "Trenton in Bygone Days," *Trenton Sunday Times-Advertiser,* Sept. 14, 1930, clipping in Cleary Scrapbook of Trenton History, 4:27, TPL.

43. A fuller discussion of photoceramics appears in Blaszczyk, "Aesthetic Moment." Simons to Elise du Pont, May 16, 1875, box 15, HML-AS; U.S. Patent 260,065, Auguste Tournoux and François Schmalz, "Process of Producing Indelible Photographs on Porcelain," June 27, 1882 ("helio-ceramic"). Schmalz assigned half of his rights to Dean.

44. Jesse Dean, advertisement in *CGJ* 13 (March 31, 1881): 25; Katherine C. Grier,

Culture and Comfort: People, Parlors, and Upholstery, 1850–1930 (Amherst: University of Massachusetts Press, 1988), 129–62; Miles Orvell, *The Real Thing: Imitation and Authenticity in American Culture, 1880–1940* (Chapel Hill: University of North Carolina Press, 1989), 73–102.

45. House Committee on Ways and Means, *Arguments before the Committee of Ways and Means on the Morrison Tariff Bill*, 231–45, 297–99; House Committee on Ways and Means, *Duties on China, Porcelain, and Stoneware*, 47th Cong., 1st sess., 1882, 6–15.

46. "Correspondence," *PGR* 8 (April 12, 1883): 20 ("crockery"), and *PGR* 9 (Sept. 27, 1883): 23, 26 (26, "white"); "Business Memoranda," *PGR* 9 (May 3, 1883): 14, and *PGR* 10 (Jan. 17, 1884): 12.

47. "Business Memoranda," *PGR* 14 (Jan. 7, 1886): 13 (Straus); Poole, "The City Residence of Geo. W. Childs, Esq."; Haviland & Company to Rogers L. Barstow, invoice, Aug. 16, 1881, folder: Glass and Ceramics, Rogers L. Barstow Collection, WL-DC.

48. Stratton, "Factors," 310; Alfred Day, "Report of the Secretary," USPA *Proc.* 11 (1888), 9–10; John Hart Brewer, "Report of the Committee on Statistics," USPA, *Proc.* 12 (1889), 16–19 (18, "know"). For decades, retailers profited from the snob appeal of imported china by taking high markups on these lines. See William Burgess, "Report on the Wholesale Selling Price of Foreign-Made Pottery in the Country of Manufacture, Compared with the Wholesale Selling Prices of Similar Pottery Ware Produced and Sold in the United States," [1910], 2, box 10, William Burgess Papers, Seeley G. Mudd Manuscript Library, Princeton University Archives, Princeton, N.J.; U.S. Department of Commerce, *The Pottery Industry: Report on the Cost of Production in the Earthenware and China Industries of the United States, England, Germany, and Austria*, Miscellaneous Series 21 (Washington, D.C.: Government Printing Office, 1913), 623–44.

49. "A Dinner Service of China: How It Found Its Way into an East Side Tenement," *CGJ* 25 (June 30, 1887): 25–26; "Phew! Read This, Potters," *CGJ* 34 (July 30, 1891): [26].

50. For more on Dean's incorporation, see Blaszczyk, "Aesthetic Moment," 146–47.

51. Alfred Day, "Report of the Secretary," USPA *Proc.* 11 (1887), 9–10, and "Secretary's Report," USPA *Proc.* 12 (1888), 9–11; Thomas Maddock, [Banquet Address], USPA *Proc.* 12 (1888), 26–30; ["The United States Potters' Association"], *CGL* 2 (Nov. 11, 1891): 22; State of Ohio, Bureau of Labor Statistics, copy of questionnaire completed by the Homer Laughlin China Company, Aug. 11, 1892, box 111, HL-EC; "Jesse Dean Company Troubles," *Daily State Gazette* (Trenton), Nov. 22, 1892.

52. HLCC, *Catalogue and Price List of Semi-Vitreous China* (East Liverpool, Ohio, 1896), [9], HL-EF; W. Edwin Wells, "President Wells's Address," USPA *Proc.* 17 (1905), 10–15; "Display of Choice and Novel Line of English Decals Win Much Praise Here," *PH*, Oct. 2, 1924; "Everything Decorated Nowadays," *CGJ* 72 (Nov. 10, 1910): 22–23.

53. "Decalcomania," *Scientific American Supplement;* "The Gallery of Colour and Transfers: A History of Decorative Processes for Pottery in the Nineteenth Century,"

Exhibition guide, City Museum & Art Gallery at Stoke, Stoke-on-Trent, Staffordshire, Eng., n.d. (typescript, SICG).

54. Ernest Mayer et al., "Report of the Committee on Machinery," USPA *Proc.* 20 (1896), 42–46 (44, decals); Aaron Hamilton Chute, *Marketing Burned Clay Products, Including an Analysis of Location, Importance, and Development of the Industry* (Columbus: Ohio State University, 1939), 300.

55. William Burgess, "Address of President," USPA *Proc.* 19 (1895), 7–9; John N. Taylor to J. E. Norris, Dec. 20, 1897, NJSM-AP.

56. For Mountford, see Blaszczyk, "Aesthetic Moment," 150–52.

57. "Trenton," *CGL* 14 (Aug. 18, 1897): 11–12 ("odd"); "Jesse Dean," *Daily State Gazette* (Trenton), July 31, 1897, clipping in Scrapbook of Trenton Industries, vol. 1, TPL; W. Edwin Wells–JD letters, Aug. 10, 11, 1900, box 319; Clarke–JD letters, Nov. 14, 16, 1899, box 259, HL-EC.

Chapter 3: Beauty for a Dime

1. CPC-WEW letters, Dec. 1899 ("good"), Feb. 6, 1900, box 247, HL-EC.

2. Cherington, *People's Wants and How to Satisfy Them*, 173 (quotation); "W. E. Wells," *BACS* 10 (Oct. 1931): 326–28; "W. E. Wells Retires as General Manager of Homer Laughlin," *PH*, Jan. 23, 1930; "Citizens of Pottery District Pay Homage to Its Dead Leader," *PH*, Sept. 24, 1931; "W. E. Wells Passes On," *CGJ* 109 (Oct. 1931): 23, 45.

3. HLCC, *Catalogue and Price List, April 1, 1901*, 8 ("People"), HL-EF.

4. Joe Dickey, "Industrial Welfare Department, Homer Laughlin China Company," *PH*, April 30, 1931 ("beauty").

5. Thomas Maddock, [President's Address], USPA *Proc.* 13 (1889), 5–8 (5, "rich"); Thomas Maddock, [Banquet Address], USPA *Proc.* 13 (1889), 28–30; "The Potteries: East Liverpool," *CGJ* 18 (Nov. 29, 1883): 14; Alfred Day, "Secretary's Report," USPA *Proc.* 16 (1892), 14–20 (18, "poor").

6. "East Liverpool," *APGR* 3 (April 29, 1880): 10–11 ("purely"); "Kiln Record of U.S. Potters' Association," USPA *Proc.* 13 (1889), 22–23; "East Liverpool Potteries," *CGJ* 6 (Dec. 20, 1877): 12; "The Banquet," USPA *Proc.* 35 (1913), 87.

7. Chute, *Marketing Burned-Clay Products*, 54–56; T. Rigby & Co., Order Book, 1878–80, ELMC-VF; "White Granite," Sept. 20, 1890, folder: Knowles, Taylor & Knowles, ELMC-VF; Sebring Pottery Company, advertisement in *CGJ* 34 (Dec. 3, 1891): 89. On salesmen's duties, see Timothy B. Spears, *100 Years on the Road: The Traveling Salesman in American Culture* (New Haven: Yale University Press, 1995).

8. James C. Shaw to Homer Laughlin, March 4, 20, 22, 27, and 31, 1888, box 30, HL-EC.

9. Lucille T. Cox, "When First Woman 'Crashed' Pottery Office," *ELT*, March 23, 1942

("man"); GWC to HLCC, Jan. 13, 1891, box 46, Feb. 1, 1897 ("kicks"), box 175, HL-EC; HLCC, *Catalogue and Price List of Semi-Vitreous China*, [12–13] (Golden Gate).

10. "Route, George W. Clarke," [1897]; GWC to HLCC, March 14, 1897, box 175; July 24, Sept. 26, 1900, box 302, HL-EC.

11. GWC-HLCC letters, boxes 45, 143, and 173, HL-EC.

12. GWC-HLCC letters, Feb. 28, June 7, 1898, box 175; April 14, 1905, box 670, HL-EC.

13. GWC-HLCC letters, Feb. 1, 8, July 4 ("every"), 1897, box 175; July 24, 30 ("strong"), Sept. 7, 20, 1900, box 302, HL-EC.

14. "Regular Crockery vs. Gift Tea Dealers," *APGR* 9 (Oct. 4, 1883): 29 ("mine"); GWC to HLCC, April 21, 1897, box 175, HL-EC [Sketches by the Field's buyer do not survive.]; Tylee-Greene letters, March 1902, Arcadia Cut Glass Company Records, DC-WL; Herbert A. Gibbons, *John Wanamaker*, 2 vols. (New York: Harper, 1926), 2:206.

15. "The Crockery War," *CGJ* 18 (Oct. 11, 1883): 29 ("red"); "A Dinner Service of China: How It Found Its Way into an East Side Tenement," *CGJ* 25 (June 30, 1887): 25–26; "Gift Enterprises and the Crockery and Glass Trades," *PGR* 13 (Oct. 8, 1885): 14, 17; "Crockery Dealers Aroused," *CGJ* 10 (July 24, 1879): 28; "Tea, Baking Powder et al.," *CGJ* 26 (Aug. 18, 1887): 18; "The Teapot Upset," *CGJ* 33 (May 14, 1891): 26, 29; William I. Walsh, *The Rise and Decline of the Great Atlantic & Pacific Tea Company* (Secaucus, N.J.: Lyle Stuart, 1986), 22.

16. Acme Tea Company, Great Atlantic & Pacific Tea Company, and Union Pacific Tea Company, trade cards, file: Tea and coffee, SPNEA-VF.

17. Andrew McGeorge Lamb, "A History of the American Pottery Industry: Industrial Growth, Technical and Technological Change and Diffusion in the Generalware Branch, 1872–1914" (Ph.D. diss., London School of Economics, 1984), 25–26; Ladies' Home Journal, *Premium Catalogue and Mail-Order List* (Philadelphia, 1891), n.p.; Eastern State Tea Company, [Catalogue of Products and Premiums Prizes] (New York: Eastern State Tea Company, 1900), both in UD-ML; Lincoln, Seyms & Company to HLCC, Jan. 30, 1902 ("woman"), box 366, HL-EC; Violet Altman and Seymour Altman, *The Book of Buffalo Pottery* (New York: Crown, 1969), chap. 1 (Larkin); 77.30 (Peters), HML-OR. Some Trenton potteries made scheme goods; see London Needle Company, NYC, to James E. Norris, Anchor Pottery Company, June 3, 1903, NJSM-AP.

18. "Sebrings!" advertising flyer for grocery store, [1880s], file: Sebring, ELMC-VF; Ohio, vol. 32, 432 ("pushing"); 452, 750, HBS-RGD; "Necrology: F. A. Sebring," *BACS* 16 (Jan. 1937): 23–24 ("modern"), and "Frank A. Sebring, Pottery Builder, Dead," typescript, 1936, file: Sebring, ELMC-VF; "Sebring Brothers," *Genealogical and Family History of Eastern Ohio* (Sebring: Lewis Publishing, 1903), 669; Joseph G. Butler Jr., *History of Youngstown and the Mahoning Valley, Ohio* (Chicago: American Historical Society, 1921), 1:539–43; "Forty-Nine Years of Enterprise," *PGBS* 54 (Aug. 1938): 12–13, 28; *Sebring, Ohio: A Brief History of the Town, Its Founding Industries, and Institutions*

(Sebring: Anniversary Committee, 1949); 14–20; "Six Sebring Boys Founded International Pottery Hub," *Alliance (Ohio) Review,* Aug. 31, 1949; Jana Theis, "The Home of 'Dish Night,'" *Western Reserve* (July/Aug. 1983): 59–61; "A Thriving Pottery Town," *CW* 38 (Nov. 1902): 433–34; Sebring Bros. & Co., advertisement in *CGJ* 33 (Jan. 15, 1891): 44 ("bulk"); Sebring Bros. & Co., advertisement in *CGL* 1 (Dec. 17, 1890): 39; "The Earthenware Trade: East Liverpool," *CGL* 1 (Jan. 21, 1891): 16; Sebring Pottery Company, "One Dollar Assortments" and "War Plaques," advertising circulars [1898], folder: Sebring, ELMC-VF.

19. WEW et al., "Art and Design Committee," USPA *Proc.* 24 (1902), 17–18; Joseph G. Lee, "President Lee's Address," USPA, *Proc.* 26 (1904), 12–15; House, *Eleventh Special Report of the Commission of Labor: Regulation and Restriction of Output,* 11th special report, 58th Cong., 2d sess., 1904, H. Doc. 734, 682; Marc Jeffrey Stern, *The Pottery Industry of Trenton: A Skilled Trade in Transition, 1850–1929* (New Brunswick: Rutgers University Press, 1994), 112–13 (speedups); Will A. Rhodes et al., "Report of the Art and Design Committee," USPA *Proc.* 26 (1904), 21–24 (22, "crudity").

20. Louis I. Aaron, "Statistics Committee," USPA *Proc.* 25 (1903), 23–25 (24, "cereal"); Union Pacific Tea Company to HLCC, Feb. 8, 1902 ("trifle"), box 370, HL-EC.

21. WEW to American Cereal Company, Nov. 21, 1900, box 301; George Everett Clapp, Union Pacific Tea Company, to WEW, Feb. 26, March 2 ("advertising"), 6, 1902, box 370; Murkland to WEW, Jan. 2, 25, 29, 1909, box S-112; C. W. Kress, S. H. Kress & Company, to WEW, May 29, 1899, box 251, HL-EC; Sears, Roebuck & Company, dinnerware circulars, box: Pottery, folder: Sears, SI-W.

22. Lamb, "A History of the American Pottery Industry," 54, 63–66.

23. "W. E. Wells"; "Resolutions on the Death of Louis I. Aaron," USPA *Proc.* 41 (1920), 3–4; *NCAB*, s.v. "Aaron, Marcus"; "Homer Laughlin Sr.," *CGJ* 14 (Dec. 12, 1897): 12; HL-M; *Price List and Illustrations, Plain White Wares Made by the Homer Laughlin China Company, Newell, West Virginia, January 1, 1907,* HL-EF; Lamb, "A History of the American Pottery Industry," 57–60.

24. "Personal," *CGJ* 24 (Oct. 28, 1886): 27; "The Potteries: Trenton," *CGJ* 33 (Feb. 19, 1891): 26; "The Potteries: Trenton," *CGJ* 34 (Aug. 6, 1891): 25; "The Potteries: Trenton," *CGJ* 34 (Aug. 27, 1891): 33; William C. Gates Jr., "Arthur Mountford: Pictorialist of the Upper Ohio," *Timeline* 4 (Feb./March 1987): 40–48; HL-M.

25. "Arrangement between Nathan-Dohrman Co., San Francisco, Cal., and Homer Laughlin China Co., East Liverpool, Ohio, for the Marketing of Their Goods in California," Feb. 1, 1901, box S-138, HL-EC; "Trade Items," *PGR* 17 (May 12, 1887): 12–13; GWC to HLCC, July 30, 1900 ("Pittsburgh"), WEW to GWC, July 26, 1900 ("weeks"), box 302, HL-EC.

26. John K. Winkler, *Five and Ten: The Fabulous Life of F. W. Woolworth* (New York: Robert M. McBride, 1940); Daniel J. Boorstin, *The Americans: The Democratic Experience* (New York: Random House, 1973), 113–18; William R. Taylor, "The Evolution of

Public Space in New York City: The Commercial Showcase of America," in *Consuming Visions: Accumulation and Display of Goods in America, 1880–1920*, edited by Simon J. Bronner (New York: Norton, 1989), 287–309.

27. Frederick Hurten Rhead, "Chats on Pottery," *PH*, Aug. 11, 1932 ("shawl"); CPC to WEW, Dec. 1899 ("strictly"); Winkler, *Five and Ten*, 118 ("upper-crusters"); "Selling the Slav in Your Town," *HA* 105 (Jan. 5, 1920): 105–6 ("foreign trade").

28. "The Teapot Upset," *CGJ* 33 (May 14, 1891): 26 ("families"), 29; Elaine S. Abelson, *When Ladies Go A-Thieving: Middle-Class Shoplifters in the Victorian Department Store* (New York: Oxford University Press, 1989), 31 ("shawl trade").

29. Ned Mitchell, "Some Things I Have Learned about Window Decorating," *CSA* 1 (July 1925): 25–26, 29–30; CPC to WEW, April 19, 1909, box 94-S, HL-EC.

30. FWWC, Fitchburg, Mass., to HLCC, Aug. 19, 1908 ("great"), box 69-S, HL-EC; Chute, *Marketing Burned-Clay Products*, 138. For manager-customer relations, see WEW to FWWC, York, Pa., Feb. 8, 1910; FWWC, Springfield, Ill., to HLCC, Feb. 19, 1919, box S-110, HL-EC. On market testing, see CPC-WEW letters, April 20, 22, 1908, box 69-S; Jan. 9, 16, 19, 1909, box S-80, June 8, 10, 15, 1909; Case, notice to store managers, June 24, 1909, box 94-S, HL-EC. For positive feedback, see WEW to Turner E. Howard, FWWC, Holyoke, Mass., Feb. 2, 1909; Howard to HLCC, Feb. 5, 1909, box S-80; CPC to WEW, Sept. 27, 1909, box 94-S; H. P. Smith, FWWC, South Norwalk, Conn., to HLCC, Oct. 15, 1910; WEW to Smith, Oct. 18, 1910, box S-136, HL-EC. For kicks, see H. King, FWWC, York, Pa., to HLCC, Jan. 20, 1909; WEW to King, Jan. 23, 1909, box S-90, HL-EC.

31. CPC-WEW letters, Jan. 20, 1909, box S-80, and March 9, 1910, box S-110; J. U. Troy, FWWC, New York, Feb. 18, 1911, box S-140; Rudolph Gaertner, New York, to WEW, July 3, Aug. 22, 1913, box L-323, HL-EC.

32. W. T. Grant, "The Function of the Chain Store: Why the Distributive System Which Serves the Public Best at Least Cost Is Bound to Survive," *CSA* 3 (Jan. 1927): 19, 90 (90, "cost"); Lloyd S. Graham, "Some Chain Store Executives I Have Met," *CSA* 3 (Aug. 1927): 16, 50, 53–54, 67–68; William F. Newberry to WEW, May 14, 1914 ("Customers"), box S-311, HL-EC.

33. Winkler, *Five and Ten*, 118 ("poorer").

34. FHR, "Chats on Pottery," *PH*, Oct. 13, 1932 ("Rudy"); I. Bentley Pope et al., "Art and Design Committee's Report," USPA *Proc.* 29 (1907), 42–46; Henry Brunt, "Report of Historian," USPA *Proc.* 33 (1911), 26–28; "Report of Art and Design Committee," USPA *Proc.* 37 (1915), 24 ("directors"); RG to WEW, Aug. 22, 1913, box L-323 (Kress); CPC to WEW, Dec. 12, 1908, box S-80, HL-EC.

35. FHR, "Chats on Pottery," Oct. 13, 1932 ("confessor"); "Decalcomania Manufacturer Dies Abroad," *CGJ* 112 (Oct. 1932): 38; "Death of Rudolph Gaertner Lamented by Pottery Industry," *PH*, Sept. 23, 1932; RG to WEW, Dec. 7, 1912, box L-323; WEW to CPC, March 18, 1908, box S-69, HL-EC.

36. USPA *Proc.* 29 (1907), 45; RG to WEW, Dec. 16, 1910, box L-211; Nov. 29, 1912, box L-323, HL-EC; Stapleford, "The Manufacture of Ceramic Decalcomania," 391.

37. Michael J. Ettema, "Technological Innovation and Design Economics in Furniture Manufacture," *Winterthur Portfolio* 16 (Summer/Autumn 1981): 197–223.

38. Henry Brunt, "Report of the Historical Committee," USPA *Proc.* 28 (1906), 27–31; HB, "Report of the Historical Committee," USPA *Proc.* 29 (1907), 20–23 (21, "slip-shod"); "Memorial to Henry Brunt," USPA *Proc.* 38 (1916), 2–3.

39. E. Samuel Hilton, Trenton, to James E. Norris, Anchor Pottery Company, Feb. 25, 1900 ("stock"), NJSM-AP; WEW to RG, April 14, 1910, box L-117, HL-EC; "Edward L. Carson, 70, Retired Decorating Manager at Laughlin's, Dies Here Suddenly," *PH,* May 31, 1934.

40. WEW to FWWC, Chicago, March 9, 1905, box 591; CPC-WEW letters, Dec. 23, 28, 1908, box S-80; WEW to Charles McDevitt, FWWC, Milford, Mass., Aug. 4, 1911, box S-180, HL-EC.

41. PAM-WEW letters, Sept. 19, 1910, Feb. 11 ("blind"), April 22, May 4, 6, 8, 1911, box S-185, HL-EC; Norbert Elias, *The Civilizing Process,* vol. 1, *The History of Manners,* translated by Edmund Jephcott (1939; New York: Pantheon, 1978).

42. CPC, circulars of HLCC lines, Jan. 27, 1911 ("lily"), box S-140; Jan. 27, 1904, Jan. 28, 1905, box 591; WEW to FWWC, Willimantic, Conn., May 6, 1914, box S-311; JUT to CPC, March 26 ("pink"); WEW to CPC, March 4 ("brick"), 7, 16, April 1 ("treacherous"); WEW to FWWC, Lancaster, March 30; JUT to WEW, March 31; CPC to WEW, March 31, 1908, box S-69, HL-EC. On the bone dishes, see WEW to CPC, July 18; CPC to WEW, Aug. 6, 1908, ("ladies"), box 69-S, HL-EC.

43. Ohio, Bureau of Labor Statistics questionnaire completed by HLCC; HL-M; HLCC, *Daintily Decorated Table and Toilet Wares from the World's Largest Potteries* (Newell, W. Va.: HLCC, 1908), HL-EF; USPA *Proc.* 33 (1911), 30.

44. GWC to HLCC, Dec. 20, 1911, box 1815, HL-EC; Bernice L. Thomas, *America's 5 & 10 Cent Stores: The Kress Legacy* (New York: Wiley, 1997), chap. 2.

45. House Committee on Ways and Means, *Hearings on the Pottery Schedule,* 60th Cong., 2d sess., 1908, 20, 59–60.

46. D. F. Haynes, *Report of Committee of Award on Designs Prepared for the United States Potters' Association* (Baltimore, 1890); DFH, "Report of the Committee on Design," USPA *Proc.* 14 (1890), 17–21 (20, "female"); House Committee on Ways and Means, *Hearings on the Pottery Schedule,* 47 ("women"); [West End Pottery Company], *Columbia China Company, East Liverpool, Ohio, Manufacturers of Semi-Porcelain Specialties for Premium and Advertising Purposes, Dinner Ware and Toilet Ware, White and Decorated* (East Liverpool: West End Pottery Company, [1910]), n.p. (Epstein).

47. Winkler, *Five and Ten,* 172–75; Godfrey M. Lebhar, *Chain Stores in America, 1859–1962,* 3d ed. (New York: Chain Store Publishing, 1963), 41; WEW to WFN, May 17, 1923, box S-769, Jan. 6, 1917 ($1 million), box S-484; WEW to Charles M. Doll, Aug.

7, 1916, box L-528 (W. S. George), HL-EC; HLCC, *Price List and Illustrations, Plain White Wares Made by the Homer Laughlin China Company, Newell, West Virginia, and East Liverpool, Ohio, January 1, 1916*, 1, HL-EF; USPA *Proc.* 37 (1915), 11; R. N. Logan, "Resolutions on the Death of William Shaw George," USPA *Proc.* 48 (1925), 4–5.

48. Montgomery Schuyler, "Towers of Manhattan and Notes on the Woolworth Building," *Architectural Record* 33 (Feb. 1913): 98–112; WEW to CPC, Nov. 17, 1911, box S-180, HL-EC.

49. "A. T. Newberry Passes Away," *Wilkes-Barre (Pa.) Record* Oct. 12, 1923, clipping, HL-EC; Winkler, *Five and Ten*, 138.

50. WFN to WEW, Sept. 27, 1921 ("prestige"), box S-697; April 1, 1914 ("deterioration"), box S-310; RG to WEW, July 3, 1913 ("decal girls"); Nov. 11, 1912 ("patterns") box L-323, HL-EC. For Gaertner's meetings with Newberry, see RG-WEW letters: Nov. 27, Dec. 16, 1912, Jan. 4, 1913, box L-323; April 11, 18, 28, 29, May 5, June 15, July 23, 29, 1914, box L-415, HL-EC.

51. Stratton, "Factors," 310–11, table 39; Charles Ashbaugh, "President's Address," USPA *Proc.* 39 (1917), 12–14; WEW to WFN, April 13, 1920, box S-640; Oct. 7, 1921, box S-697, HL-EC; Sears, Roebuck & Company, *Catalogue 125* (Fall 1917), 694–718; Sears, Roebuck & Company, *Catalogue 138* (1919), 905–17.

52. Marcus Aaron, "President's Address," USPA *Proc.* 40 (1919), 15–19, discusses wartime problems. For Kirkman, see RG-WEW letters, Sept. 26, 28, 1925, box L-1035, HL-EC. On decals, see Charles F. Goodwin, "Report of Historian," USPA *Proc.* 39 (1917), 37–39; Ernest Mayer, "Report of Materials Committee," USPA *Proc.* 39 (1917), 42–44; RG-WEW letters, Dec. 1915–Sept. 1918, boxes L-497, L-591; June 4, 1921, box L-784, HL-EC. For Mt. Vernon proposals, see WEW-WFN letters, 1915, boxes S-359, S-360, L-415; Feb. 9 ("larger"), box S-359, HL-EC. On Woolworth's orders, see WEW-WFN letters, March 24, box S-484; Nov. 5, 10, 1917, Feb. 6, 1918 ("Jewish"), box S-517; WEW to RG, Nov. 30, 1917, box L-591, HL-EC. For pressed glass, see Department of Commerce, *The Glass Industry*, 348.

53. Stratton, "Factors," 301, table 35; Ashbaugh, "President's Address"; Mayer, "Report of Materials Committee"; "Report of War Service Committee," USPA *Proc.* 40 (1919), 65–69; Marc Solon, "Report of Machinery Committee," USPA *Proc.* 40 (1919), 73–75; Charles Goodwin, "Report of the Historian," USPA *Proc.* 40 (1919), 87–89.

54. "President Wells's Address," USPA *Proc.* 28 (1906), 10–18; "Banquet," USPA *Proc.* 38 (1916), 58–59.

55. "Splendor of Medieval Venice the Background for Exhibiting American Pottery," *PGBS* 25 (Feb. 16, 1922), clipping, courtesy of Ellen Paul Denker; "The Manufacture of Dinnerware," *CW* 81 (April 1924): 452–55; Joseph M. Wells Jr., conversation with author, and field notes by author, Homer Laughlin showroom, Newell, W. Va., Aug. 1993.

56. Lebhar, *Chain Stores in America*, chaps. 2, 3. Although Woolworth dwarfed regional competitors, these five-and-tens also enjoyed commensurate growth. In 1920,

Kresge ran 184 stores west of the Mississippi River; by 1930, 678 stores. Dixie's Kress entered the decade with 45 stores and exited with 212. The experience of smaller limited-price variety chains, including Murphy, McLellan, and Newberry, was much the same.

57. WEW-WFN letters, May 17, 25 ("full"; "more"), 1923, box S-769, HL-EC. The full story of tunnel kilns and technological innovation at Mount Clemens and Homer Laughlin is recounted in Regina Lee Blaszczyk, "'Reign of the Robots': The Homer Laughlin China Company and Flexible Mass Production," *Technology and Culture* 36 (Oct. 1995): 863–911.

58. WFN to WEW, Sept. 27, 1921 ("prestige"); Sept. 6 ("appropriate"), Nov. 17, 1925, box S-858, HL-EC.

59. Hazel T. Becker, "Four Dining-room-less Houses," *BHG* 4 (June 1926): 14–15; Harvey A. Levenstein, *Revolution at the Table: The Transformation of the American Diet* (New York: Oxford University Press, 1988), chaps. 12–14.

60. D. William Scammell, "President's Address," USPA *Proc.* 46 (1924), 19–22; Lucille T. Cox, "Modern Pottery Pioneers," ca. 1938, newspaper clipping, folder: Sebring, HL-ADF; Blanche Naylor, "Leigh Potters Blaze Modernist Trail," *PGBS* 40 (Dec. 19, 1929): 116–19; Alden Welles, "Leigh Ware," *CGJ* 107 (April 1929): 27–29, 85; "Ivory Bodies Use More Domestic Clay," *CI* 8 (April 1929): 428; Berdan Company, promotional leaflet for Chef Coffee, n.d., HL-ADF; Sebring Pottery Company, Advertisement No. 459 A, "We Will Pay You Five Dollars for Your Old Dinnerware!" ("old"), and Advertisement No. 2, "Sensational Offer Stirs Up Amazing Interest!" box L-1210, HL-EC; Frank A. Sebring to Marcus Aaron, Dec. 21, 1927, box L-1276, HL-EC ("line"); "Potters to Combat Foreign Competition by Advertising," *CI* 6 (Jan. 1926): 45–46 ("yellow").

61. WFN to WEW, Nov. 17; WEW to WFN, Nov. 19, 1925, box S-858; Dec. 23, 1925, Jan. 16, 20, 21, 1926, box S-904, HL-EC.

62. WFN to WEW, Nov. 3, 11 ("stimulate"), 12 ("drift"); WEW to WFN, Nov. 17, 1925, box S-858, HL-EC.

63. RG to WEW, June 12 ("jazz"), 17, 19, 1925, box 1035; Dec. 21, 1927, box L-1242, HL-EC.

64. Albert V. Bleininger, "Technical History and Development of the Homer Laughlin China Company, Newell and East Liverpool, Beginning with November 1, 1920," vol. 1, entries from Sept. 19, 1924, to Feb. 18, 1926, HL-CLF.

65. WFN to WEW, Feb. 18, 1926 ("pattern"), box S-904, HL-EC; Minutes, Creative Staff Meeting, Dec. 14, 1932, JWT; FHR, "Chats on Pottery," *PH*, Aug. 11, 1932 ("Woolies"); Melvin T. Copeland, *The Principles of Merchandising* (Chicago: A. W. Shaw, 1927), 98.

66. FHR, "Chats on Pottery," *PH*, March 31, 1933 ("Tiffany").

67. Morris L. Beard, "What Buying 'Right' Means to Me: Successful Chain-Store Merchandising as Seen from the Manufacturers' Angle," *CSA* 2 (June 1926): 14–15.

Chapter 4: Fiesta!

1. "Homer Laughlin China Co.: The New Fiesta Line a Radical Departure for the Concern," *PGBS* 51 (Dec. 1935): 59; "1936 Pottery Exhibit Opens," *Pittsburgh Post-Gazette,* Jan. 11, 1936; Claire Rothenberg, "Right Out of the Kiln," *CGJ* 114 (Jan. 1936): 52–53; "Pittsburgh Glass and Pottery Show Most Successful in Years," *PGBS* 52 (Feb. 1936): 5–7, 17; "Homer Laughlin China Company: Fiesta Combined with Regular Dinnerware Most Attractively," *PGBS* 52 (May 1936): 22; Edward H. Sykes, "Pottery and Glass Exhibits in Pittsburgh," *CI* 26 (Feb. 1936): 118–21; FHR, "Good Taste in Ceramic Art Is Fundamental," *PGBS* 52 (Jan. 1937): 23, 38; "Homer Laughlin Ware," sales brochure [1937], ELMC-VF.

2. FHR, "Develop Ceramic Types Suitable to American Conditions," *CI* 35 (Nov. 1940): 35–36.

3. Joe Dickey, "Industrial Welfare Department, Homer Laughlin China Company," *PH,* Jan. 22, 1925 ("Housewife"); "A Giant among Dishes," *CI* 14 (April 1930): 408–17.

4. Roland Marchand, *Advertising the American Dream: Making Way for Modernity, 1920–1940* (Berkeley: University of California Press, 1985), 4 ("tempo"); *Annual Report of General Motors Corporation for 1925* (Feb. 24, 1926), 7 ("every"), cited in David A. Hounshell, *From the American System to Mass Production, 1800–1932: The Development of Manufacturing Technology in the United States* (Baltimore: Johns Hopkins University Press, 1984), 278. For hosiery, see H. W. Davis, "Get Your Facts—Then Advertise," *PI* 138 (Feb. 3, 1927): 149, 152, 153, 156; Paul W. Huston, "How Ipswich Met New Market Conditions," *PI* 138 (Feb. 24, 1927): 41–42. On Fostoria, see Olga Clark, "Serve It in Colored Glass," *BHG* 8 (Sept. 1929): 36. For the turn away from imitation crystal, see "Getting Back to Normalcy," *PGBS* 22 (Dec. 16, 1920): 87.

5. On trade conditions, see "When West Meets East," *CGJ* 107 (Sept. 1929): 28–29, 77; Joseph M. Wells, "Memorandum on the Pottery Industry of the United States," Oct. 6, 1929, 2–6, 10, box: JMW correspondence, HL-EF; JMW to FHR, Feb. 6, 1942, HL-ADF; Fredonia Jane Ringo, *China and Glassware* (Chicago: A. W. Shaw, 1925,) 48–49 (Homer Laughlin; Knowles, Taylor & Knowles; Taylor, Smith & Taylor; and the Edwin M. Knowles China Company were East Liverpool's "Big Four" at middecade). On credit, see Martha Olney, *Buy Now, Pay Later: Advertising, Credit, and Consumer Durables in the 1920s* (Chapel Hill: University of North Carolina Press, 1991), table 2.6B; "Potters to Combat Foreign Competition by Advertizing"; D. William Scammell, "President's Address," USPA *Proc.* 46 (1924), 19–22; WEW, "Report of the Labor Committee," USPA *Proc.* 46 (1924), 30–37; WEW, "Report of the Labor Committee," USPA *Proc.* 47 (1925), 29–36 (33, "mortgaged"). On Yellowstone, see HLCC, "Yellowstone Dinner Service," advertisement in *PGBS* 35 (Feb. 3, 1927): 6 ("Harlem"); HLCC, *Price List and Illustrations, Undecorated White and Ivory Wares Manufactured by the Homer Laughlin China Company, Newell, West Virginia, and East Liverpool, Ohio* (Newell, W. Va., 1929), 3,

HL-EF; WEW to WFN, Nov. 8, 1927, box S-1052; Nov. 26, 1927, box S-1070, HL-EC.

6. Paul Nystrom, *Retail Selling and Store Management* (New York: Appleton & Company, 1925), 56; WEW, "Report of the Labor Committee," USPA *Proc.* 45 (1923), 21–26 (22, "better dishes"). According to one weekly, women bought 49–98 percent of the merchandise, depending on the product. See James H. Collins, "Has Your Business Sex Appeal?" *NB* 16 (Dec. 1928): 23–25.

7. On buyers' demands, see "The Dramatic Story of an American Pottery," *PGBS* 40 (Aug. 1, 1929): 11–12; WEW to WFN, April 6, 1923, box S-757, and Nov. 24, 1924, box S-810, HL-EC; J. Harrison Keller, interview by author, tape recording, Salem China Company, Salem, Ohio, May 24, 1988. On Quaker Oats, see RG to WEW, June 18, 1927, box L-1175, HL-EC. On Kirkman, see RG to WEW, Sept. 26, 1925 ("excellent"), Oct. 1, 1925, Nov. 12, 21, 1925, box L-1035, HL-EC. On J. J. Newberry, see WEW to RG, May 15, 1925 ("gaudy"); RG to WEW, June 12, 15, 1925, box L-1035, HL-EC.

8. RG-WEW letters, Jan. 28, 31, 1920, box S-703; Feb. 14, June 4 ("cheaper"), 1921, box L-784; Oct. 27, 1923, April 7, 1924, box L-935; June 18, 1927, box L-1175; RG to WFN, May 23, 1923, box L-935; WEW to WFN, April 28, 1925, box S-844; April 27, 1926, box S-917, HL-EC; "Potters Predict Labor Crisis," *CI* 10 (Jan. 1928): 70–76.

9. Thomas Alexander Shegog, "The Story of Ivory Porcelain by Sebring," brochure [1923], box: JMW correspondence, HL-EF; Sebring Pottery Company, "Color! Color! Color!" advertisement in *PGBS* 37 (Feb. 2, 1928): 12; B. E. Harris, Columbus Furniture Company, to HLCC, March 23, 1928, box L-1276; Salem China Company, "Friendly Warning!" mail circular, 1928, box L-1276; RG to WEW, Oct. 1, Nov. 12, 21, 1925, box L-1035, HL-EC; "A Blazer of New Trails," *CGJ* 108 (Aug. 1930): 31–33, 48, 50.

10. RG to WEW, June 18, 29, 1927, box L-1175, HL-EC; "Art Director Is Guest Speaker at Weekly Luncheon of East Liverpool Lions Club," *PH*, Sept. 24, 1934 ("coming"); Rhodes et al., "Report of Art and Design Committee"; Will A. Rhodes, "Report of Art and Design Committee," USPA *Proc.* 27 (1905), 23–27; Frank R. Haynes et al., "Report of Art and Design Committee," USPA *Proc.* 28 (1906), 48–57; Pope et al., "Art and Design Committee's Report"; John D. Thompson, "Report of the Art and Design Committee," USPA *Proc.* 46 (1924), 69–70; "American Dinnerware Manufacturers Giving Decorations More Attention," *CGJ* 105 (Nov. 3, 1927): 17; "Rhead Goes to Laughlin's," *PGBS* 36 (Aug. 4, 1927): 9; "Homer Laughlin Employs Stylist," *CGJ* 105 (March 1928): 92; WFN to WEW, Aug. 8, 1927 ("move"), box S-1027, HL-EC.

11. FHR, "Chats on Pottery," *PH*, April 20, May 11 ("evangelists"), Aug. 17, Oct. 19, Nov. 16, 1933.

12. FHR, "Good Taste in Art Is Fundamental," 38 ("potter"); FHR, "Chats on Pottery," *PH*, May 11, 1933; Charles R. Richards, *Art in Industry* (New York: Macmillan, 1923), 217–26. On Dana, see Shelley Kaplan [Nickles], "From Arts and Crafts to Industrial Design: John Cotton Dana and the Industrial Arts Movement, 1912–1929," seminar paper, University of Virginia, Charlottesville, April 22, 1992 (5, "apostle"); FHR, "Chats

on Pottery, *PH* Aug. 24, 1933; "Chain Store Merchandise Exhibited in Museum," *CSA* 5 (Aug. 1929): General Merchandise Section [hereafter, GMS] 55, 70.

13. [Nickles], "From Arts and Crafts to Industrial Design," 13 ("industrialist"). For Bach, see Richard H. Bach, "What Is the Matter with Our Industrial Art?" *AD* (Jan. 1923): 14–15; RHB, "American Industrial Art at the Metropolitan Museum," *AR* 55 (March 1924): 304–6; RHB, "Design as a Merchandising Factor," pts. 1 and 2, *Merchandise Manager* 1 (July 1931): 17–18, 73; (Aug. 1931): 29–30, 65; RHB, "Quality Production," *BACS* 11 (June 1932): 149–52; *BMMA* 13–35 (1918–1940): passim.

14. FHR, "Chats on Pottery," *PH*, Jan. 28, Dec. 15, 1932, Nov. 23, 1933, Jan. 4, 1934; "Death Recently Claimed Notable Figure in Field of Ceramics in Staffordshire," *PH,* June 11, 1933; FHR, autobiography, ca. 1939 ("tree"), and FHR, autobiography, ca. 1940, ELMC-VF; "Frederick Hurten Rhead," *BACS* 21 (1942): 306–7; A. A. Wells and John D. Thompson, "Resolutions on the Death of Frederick Hurten Rhead," USPA *Proc.* 64 (1943), 4; Vincent Broomhall, "Report of the Art and Design Committee," USPA *Proc.* 64 (1943), 52.

15. FHR, "Chats on Pottery," *PH*, Feb. 4 ("Dutchman"), 25, March 3, 10 ("gangrene"), 17, 24, 31, April 7, 14, July 7, 14, 21, 28, Aug. 4, 1932, March 23, 1933; FHR, "Developing a New Process in a Commercial Art Pottery," *Potter* 1 (1917): 55–58; FHR, autobiography, ca. 1939.

16. FHR to George E. Roberts, March 1, 1923, HL-ADF; Winifred Rhead to Paul E. Cox, March 22, 1942, VB; FHR, "Research in Ceramic Decorative Processes," *JACS* 4 (May 1921): 326–34; "Fall Meeting Proves a Big Success," *CI* 1 (Oct. 1923): 235; AETCO, *A Modern Tile Factory: From Clay to Tiles* (Zanesville: AETCO, n.d.), 38, AO-RF; Regina Lee Blaszczyk, "'This Extraordinary Demand for Color': Léon Victor Solon and Architectural Polychromy, 1912–1936," *Flash Point: The Quarterly Bulletin of the Tile Heritage Foundation* 6 (July-Sept. 1993): 1, 10–16.

17. FHR, "The Organization of a Decorative Ceramic Research Department," *PGBS* 26 (Dec. 14, 1922): 95–113 (99, "czarist"; "patina"); FHR, "Notes on Shape Construction," *PGBS* 35 (June 23, 1927): 13–16, 33 (33, "engineering"); FHR to Roberts ("large-scale"); *JACS* 3–5 (1920–22): passim; *BACS* 2–5 (1922–26): passim; Earnest Elmo Calkins, "The Job of the Consumption Engineer," *Merchandising and Selling* 15 (May 18, 1930): 28, 60–62; EEC, "What Consumer Engineering Really Is," introduction to Roy Sheldon and Egmont Arens, *Consumer Engineering: A New Tool for Prosperity* (New York: Harper, 1932), 1 ("tool"), 2 ("pace"), 6 ("adapt"); Eugene S. Ferguson, *Engineering and the Mind's Eye* (Cambridge: MIT Press, 1992), 37.

18. "Art Director Is Guest Speaker at Weekly Luncheon at East Liverpool Lions' Club"; FHR, "Chats on Pottery," *PH*, June 25, 1931, Dec. 15, 1932, July 27, Aug. 17, 1933, and Jan. 4, 1934.

19. FHR, "Chats on Pottery," *PH*, June 23, 1931, Sept. 15, 1932, Feb. 8, 1934 ("man-

ner"); FHR, "Notes on Shape Construction," 33; FHR, "Suggestions on Ceramic Art Education," *BACS* 5 (Nov. 1926): 410–26.

20. Robert S. Lynd and Alice C. Hanson, "The People as Consumers," in *Recent Social Trends in the United States: Report of the President's Research Committee on Social Trends* (New York: McGraw-Hill, 1933; Westport, Conn.: Greenwood, 1970), 857–911. For the quotation, see FHR, "Chats on Pottery," *PH*, Feb. 8, 1934. On research, see Jean M. Converse, *Survey Research in the United States: Roots and Emergence, 1890–1960* (Berkeley: University of California Press, 1987), chaps. 1, 3.

21. FHR, "Chats on Pottery," *PH*, Sept. 25, 1932.

22. FHR, "Chats on Pottery," *PH*, June 23, 1931, Aug. 11, 1932, May 18 ("Mrs. Van Demon"), Jan. 19, Nov. 2, 1933 ("religious beliefs"), Feb. 8, March 8, ("propaganda"), April 19, 1934; FHR, "Notes on Shape Construction."

23. FHR, "Chats on Pottery," *PH*, May 4, 18 (quotations), 1933, Aug. 11, 1932.

24. Arthur A. Houghton Jr.–Tiffany & Company, Sept. 25, 26, folder 10: Tiffany, 1928–29, box 3, CI-AAH; Katherine Wicks Perry, interview by author, Washington, D.C., March 3, 1988; Nellie [Petrowski] Blaszczyk, conversation with author, Lawrence, Mass., July 1997; "Calling on the Housewife," *PGBS* 40 (Jan. 2, 1930): 17.

25. FHR, "Chats on Pottery," *PH*, Feb. 8, 1934; FHR, "Notes on Shape Construction."

26. FHR, "Good Taste in Ceramic Art Is Fundamental"; FHR, "Chats on Pottery," *PH*, May 11 ("what to make"), Sept. 7, Nov. 23 ("pooling"), Dec. 21, 1933, Jan. 11, Feb. 3, 1934 ("exceptional"); FHR, "A New Deal in Decoration on American Dinnerware," *PGBS* 51 (Dec. 1935): 45–52 (52, "organizational"); FHR, "How Can American Potters Maintain Their Gains in the Domestic Market?" *CI* 37 (Nov. 1941): 58–61; FHR, ["Talk Shop"], lecture delivered in Staffordshire, ca. 1938, 18–21, 38, 52, HL-ADF.

27. "The Wave of Modernism Sweeps the Country," *PGBS* 37 (March 29, 1928): 15 (quotation); G. A. Seaburg, "Style Trends: The Glass of Fashion and the Mode in China," *CGJ* 107 (March 1929): 41. For glassware in women's magazines, see Carnation Milk Products Company, advertisement in *Delineator* 112 (March 1928): 72; "Glass and Silver—and Tables in the Sun" and "Three Confection Fruits," *Delineator* 113 (July 1928): 29. Like Fostoria, Heisey invested heavily in national advertising. See A. H. Heisey & Company, "Selling for You," advertisement in *PGBS* 37 (Mar. 24, 1928): 4.

28. Blaszczyk, "'Reign of the Robots'"; FHR, "Chats on Pottery," *PH*, May 18, 1933 ("something").

29. Boorstin, *The Americans*, 552–55 (552, "ladder"); FHR, "Chats on Pottery," *PH*, May 18, 1933 ("Hunt"); FHR, "Notes on Shape Construction," 33 ("Smith").

30. For Macy's expansion, see notes on *Dry Goods Economist* [hereafter, *DGE*] (Feb. 18, 1922): 32; and on *DGE* (Sept. 20, 1924): 20, both in case 1, folder: store, HBS-RH. On styling, see Walter Hoving to unknown addressee, Jan. 28, 1926, folder: styling; notes on *DGE* (June 2, 1928): 75, and on *DGE* (July 21, 1928): 9, both in folder: styling; "Mer-

chandising Style," handwritten notes, June 3, 1938, folder: styling ("good taste"); *I've Seen the Largest Store in the World!* (New York: R. H. Macy & Company, 1939), 16, folder: printed matter; notes from interview with Hazel Condy, Aug. 22, 1940, folder: control, all in case 1, HBS-RH; "Stylist Plays Important Part in the Modern Store," *CGJ* 107 (March 1929): 99, 105; G. A. Seabury, "Buyer vs. Stylist," pts. 1 and 2, *CGJ* 107 (May 1929): 21–22 ("desires"), 74; (June 1929): 25, 33; "Manufacturers Should Hire Stylists," *CGJ* 107 (Oct. 1929): 21. On Macy and HL, see RG to WEW, Feb. 15, 1929, box L-1311 (quotations); RG-WEW letters, Nov. 1928–Feb. 1929, boxes L-1242, L-1311, HL-EC.

31. Naylor, "Leigh Potters"; "Macy's Make Special Exhibit of Modern China and Glass," *CGJ* 106 (Dec. 1928): 100, 173; "New Sebring Product Announced," *CI* 12 (Feb. 1929): 244; J. Palin Thorley, "Design . . . Its Importance to the Ceramic Industry," *CI* 12 (May 1929): 554–55; Welles, "Leigh Ware"; "The Green Wheat Pattern," advertisement in *CGJ* 107 (April 1929): 73; "Fiftieth Anniversary Pottery Show Opened in Pittsburgh," *PH*, Jan. 16, 1930; "Designs by the Dozen and All of Them Good!" advertisement in *PGBS* 40 (Jan. 16, 1930): 2; Cox, "Modern Pottery Pioneers."

32. FHR, "Chats on Pottery," *PH*, Sept. 28 ("best"), Dec. 7, 1933, Jan. 11, 1934 ("posies"); FHR, "What the Industries Want," 159; FHR, ["Talk Shop"], 31–32.

33. Seaburg, "Style Trends," 41 ("angles"); Naylor, "Leigh Potters," 119 ("interiors"); Gordon Sterling, "Style Isn't Static," *CGJ* 108 (March 1930): 37, 61; "Art Schools and Industry: II. Stoke-on-Trent," *Studio* 103 (May 1932): 275–83; "Novelty and Good Taste," *PGBS* 49 (Feb. 1, 1934): 6; "Buyers Talk about Modern Dinnerware," *CGJ* 114 (April 1934): 14–17, 34.

34. Elizabeth Mayo Sowards, "What of Modernism?" *CGJ* 106 (March 1928): 29–30, 103 (29, "modern style"); Bertha Averille, "What Shall I Do?" *FGH* 1 (Nov. 1922): 40; Becker, "Four Dining-room-less Houses," 14 ("barbarism"); Christine Holbrook, "Breakfast Corners That Are Bright and Gay," *BHG* 9 (Nov. 1930): 28; Mrs. Shearer to Walter L. Shearer, Aug. 22, 1931 ("nice things"), folder: Mother, 1923–31, box: Walter L. Shearer, Personal papers, HML-BC.

35. Frederick P. Keppel, "The Arts in Social Life," in *Recent Social Trends*, 979–80; Faber Birren, ed., *The Color Primer: A Basic Treatise on the Color System of Wilhelm Ostwald* (New York: Van Nostrand Reinhold, 1969); Matthew Luckiesh, *Light and Color in Advertising and Merchandising* (New York: D. Van Nostrand, 1923), 15; "Color in Industry," *Fortune* 1 (Feb. 1930): 85–94 (85, quotations).

36. John Lynn Grey, "Adventuring in Color," *BHG* 4 (Feb. 1926): 55 ("beauty"); Genevieve A. Callahan, "Bringing Color to Your Kitchen," *BHG* 3 (June 1925): 16, 52; Ross Crane, "The Right Use of Color," *BHG* 6 (July 1928): 14; "'Color in the Kitchen' Is the Latest Note in Good Housefurnishings," *CGJ* 105 (Dec. 15, 1929): 144–45; "Kitchenware Color Idea Spreads," *PGBS* 26 (Sept. 29, 1927): 27; "The Movement for Colored Kitchen Utensils Is Spreading," *PGBS* 36 (Oct. 6, 1927): 15; "More and More Colored Wares," *PGBS* 36 (Nov. 24, 1927): 33; "Colored Kitchen Wares," *PGBS* 36 (Dec. 15,

1927): 167; "Color Sells," *PGBS* 36 (Jan. 12, 1928): 33 ("Mrs. Housewife"); "Color, and Still More Color," *PGBS* 36 (Jan. 12, 1928): 33; "Color," *PGBS* 37 (Feb. 9, 1928): 32; "The Color Craze," *PGBS* 37 (Feb. 23, 1928): 33; "Color Vogue Keeps Up," *PGBS* 39 (May 2, 1929): 33; "Color in the Kitchen Still Widening Extent," *PGBS* 37 (June 14, 1928): 31; "Color in the Kitchen," *PGBS* 40 (Dec. 19, 1929): 179; "Why Not Standardize on Coloring Materials?" *CI* 10 (April 1928): 393 ("fairer"); Mrs. Shearer to Walter L. Shearer, June 1, 1932 ("good"), folder: Mother, 1923–31, box: Walter L. Shearer, Personal papers, HML-BC.

37. Helen Ufford, "May Days Urge Color for the Home," *Delineator* 114 (May 1929): 16 ("prima"); Mary Crocker, "'Sell Style, Not Price' Says Hazel H. Adler," *CGJ* 106 (June 1928): 17–18, 77; Hazel H. Adler, *Planning Color Schemes for Your Home* (Philadelphia: George W. Blabon Company, 1923), HML-TC; HHA, *The New Interior, with Modern Decorations for the Modern Home* (New York: Century, 1916); Warren I. Susman, "Personality and the Making of Twentieth-Century Culture," in *Culture as History: The Transformation of American Society in the Twentieth Century* (New York: Pantheon, 1984), 271–85.

38. Fostoria Glass Company, "The Exquisite Minuet," n.d., ("charm"), box 7, folder: old leaflets, OHS-FOS; "Potters Seek to Fight Competition," *CI* 14 (Jan. 1930): 66–70; Regina Lee Blaszczyk, "Cinderella Stories: The Glass of Fashion and the Gendered Marketplace," in *His and Hers: Gender, Consumption, and Technology,* edited by Roger Horowitz and Arwen Mohun (Charlottesville: University Press of Virginia, 1998), 139–64.

39. Lord & Taylor, "Small Things That Count in the Summer Home," advertisement in *HG* 48 (July 1925): 9; Fisher, Bruce & Company, "A Positive Leader for Your Store," advertisement in *CGJ* 110 (Aug. 1932): n.p. ("peasant"); "Attractive Italian Pottery," *CGJ* 109 (Dec. 1931): 99; Carbone, Inc., *The Shard* (Boston, 1928), 20; Carbone, Inc., "Dinner Services from Century-Old Fires of Italy's Art," advertisement in *HG* 57 (May 1930): 27; "A Page of Decorative Pottery," *HG* 48 (Dec. 1925): 127; Sun Maid Raisins, advertisement in *Delineator* 112 (Jan. 1928): 97; Quaker Oats Company, advertisements in *Delineator* 114 (Jan. 1929): 59; (April 1929): 55; and (June 1929): 53; Mildred Maddocks Bentley, "The Institute Entertains at Lunch," *Delineator* (Feb. 1929): 37.

40. "Fiftieth Anniversary Pottery Show"; Edwin M. Knowles, "Mayglow," advertisement in *PGBS* 41 (Feb. 20, 1930): 27; FHR, ["Talk Shop"], 39 ("fad"); FHR, "Color—A Designer Speaks," *CGJ* 120 (May 1937): 13; FHR, "Chats on Pottery," *PH*, Dec. 15, 1932, Aug. 3, 16, 1933 ("ladies"); [FHR], "Homer Laughlin's New Century Vellum Causes Much Favorable Comment," *CGJ* 109 (Feb. 1931): 50 ("universal"); Art Department Log [hereafter, ADL], "Art Division Program," [1929], HL-ADF; "Will Demand for 'Old Time' Sets Return?" *CGJ* 104 (Feb. 13, 1927): 14; "Domestic Pottery," *PGBS* 36 (Dec. 15, 1927): 85; "Promoting Starter Sets," *PGBS* 37 (April 26, 1928): 15; "Looking Back over '28, Peering into '29," *PGBS* 38 (Dec. 13, 1928): 57–69.

41. Gerald S. Stone, "We Must Have Better Designs," *CGJ* 110 (March 1932): 19, 43;

GSS, "We've Lost a Great Deal of Money by Being What-Is-New Buyers," *CGJ* 112 (Aug. 1934): 12, 18; GSS, "Fish That Look Like Flowers and Flowers That Look Like Fish," *CGJ* 113 (Jan. 1935): 77, 91; ADL, Nov.[?], 1929 ("conservative"), March 30–June 30, 1931 (March 31, "existing"), HL-ADF; FHR, "Chats on Pottery," *PH*, Sept. 15, 1932 ("daisies"), Dec. 21, 1933 ("roses"), March 2, 1934; Florence L. Luman, "An Analysis of the China and Glassware Department in a Department Store" (master's thesis, University of Pittsburgh, 1931), 34–60.

42. ADL, 1928–29, 1931, HL-ADF; Helen Ufford to Louis K. Friedman, Oct. 30, 1930, Louis K. Friedman Files [hereafter, LKF Files], HL-EF; HU, "Table Notes," *Delineator* 117 (Nov. 1930): 32; Vincent Broomhall, "The Work and Influence of Fred Rhead in the Dinnerware Industry" (lecture presented at the annual meeting of the Art & Design Division, American Ceramic Society, n.p., 1943), 3, VB; HLCC, "The Light of the Moon," advertisement in *PGBS* 42 (Dec. 17, 1931): 101; "Laughlin China Will Feature New Jade Shape at the Show," *PH*, Jan. 7, 1932; HLCC, "Century Vellum," advertisement in *CGJ* 109 (March 1931): 66; FHR, ["Talk Shop"], 39; "Homer Laughlin China Co. Introduces New Ware," *CA* 15 (April 1930): 226.

43. "Should Concentrate on Development Program, Says Rhead in Report," *CGJ* 128 (Jan. 1931): 58, 68; JMW to P. G. Frantz, May 11, 1931, box S-1438, HL-EC; "Matt Glazes for Gimbel Brothers," Dec. 9, 1929, LKF Files, HL-EF.

44. "Quaker Oats" and "F. W. Woolworth Company," HL-SF; "Bright Colors for Kitchen Fixtures," *CSA* 4 (April 1928): 168; "Color Fad Growing in Kitchenware," *CSA* 5 (May 1929): GMS-86; Dunbar Flint Glass Corporation, "New! Dunbar Modernistic Cutting," advertisement in *CSA* 5 (Feb. 1929): GMS-109; "Woolworth Plays up Color in Kitchen Utensils," *CSA* 5 (June 1929): GMS-100, 106; Norma E. Tobias, "Use of Color in the Home," Memorandum to Miss Holmes, March 21, 1930, reel 38, JWT; "Green Kitchen and Household Supplies Express Modern Demand for Color," *CSA* 6 (Oct. 1930): GMS-90, 93; "Utensils for Pantry and Kitchenette Shown in Green and Cream Combination," *CSA* 6 (Sept. 1930): GMS-83, 84, 86; Hubert T. Parson, "All Ready for 1932," *CSA* 8 (Jan. 1932): 24, 48; "Heavy Demands for Glass Tableware Anticipated by Buyers; to Drive for Volume at Lower Profit," *CSA* 8 (Feb. 1932): GMS-56; "Topaz Glassware Sales Gain, Crockery Gains, Buyers Find," *CSA* 8 (March 1932): GMS-54. On pink tableware, see WFN-WEW letters, July 20, 23, 1928, box S-1123, HL-EC. On Frantz's attitude, see JMW to PGF, Aug. 14, 1934, box S-1741, March 26, 1930, box S-1317, HL-EC. On Woolworth's foreign chinaware, see "Varied Toy Novelties Fashioned of China, Glass, and Celluloid," *CSA* 6 (Sept. 1930): GMS-24.

45. ["Quaker Oats Cost Analysis"], [ca. 1931], LKF Files, HL-EF; "China Breaks into the Movies," *CGJ* 109 (Dec. 1931): 83, 89; Rudy Linder, interview by author, tape recording, Salem, Ohio, Aug. 27, 1991; Floyd W. McKee, "Dinnerware as Premiums," [1955], box 5, folder: Salem History; Salem China Company, Sales Bulletins, box 3, folder: Sales Department Bulletins, 1930s-1940s; Limoges China Company, Executive

Committee Minutes, Sept. 8, Nov. 10, 1937, March 25, 29, 1938, and Salem China Company, Executive Committee Minutes, Sept. 29, 1937, all in SI-SC; Sales data for Chicago theaters, HL-SF; JMW to Charles Leigh Sebring, Aug. 26, 1932 ("trash"), box L-1582, HL-EC.

46. Charles Leigh Sebring to Reed Smoot, Senate Finance Committee, June 15, 1932, box L-1582, HL-EC; "Potters Review Progress Made in Their Industry," *CI* 18 (Jan. 1932): 34–38; "Pottery District Humming with Activity," *CI* 21 (Dec. 1933): 263–64; "Meeting of the Joint Conference Committee of the USPA and NBOP," transcript of proceedings, Aug. 12–15, 1930, 11–15, 221–32 (11, "millions"; 231–32, "factories"), box 47, folder 1, KSU-NBOP; Albert V. Bleininger, monthly laboratory reports, Dec. 7, 1931, Sept. 8, 1932, HL-CLF; Blaszczyk, "'Reign of the Robots.'"

47. Blaszczyk, "'Reign of the Robots'"; Bleininger reports, July 5, 1934, HL-CLF; Homer Laughlin China Company (W. Va.), Minutes, April 20, 1934, HL-M.

48. FHR, ["Talk Shop"], 22–26, 35–39 (25, "machine"); ADL, March 23–July 21, 1931 (Gimbel), May 15–21, 1931 (Grant), HL-ADF; B. G. Twitchell, "Profit and Volume in Chain-Store Merchandising," *CGJ* 112 (July 1934): 27, 48.

49. JMW, "Buyers' Ideas Create 90 Percent of New American Dinnerware," *CGJ* 114 (Feb. 1934): 25, 38 ("something"); John W. Wingate, "The Buyer Must Be a Statistician, Economist, Teacher, [and] Psychologist to Understand Customers' Viewpoint," *CGJ* 114 (Aug. 1934): 13–17, 20; "Potters' Convention Reflects Optimism," *CI* 24 (Jan. 1935): 16–19; Egmont Arens, "Report on Pottery and China Market," 1936, folder: Sebring Pottery, Design and Marketing Report, box 27, SU-EA; Viktor Schreckengost, "What Is the Future of American Ceramic Design?" *RHF*, July 12, 1937.

50. "Buffet Entertaining," *PGBS* 48 (Dec. 7, 1933): 7; Arthur J. Hogan, "We're Cooking at the Table Now!" *Chase News* 2 (July 1937): 3; Sayre-Robeson Co., "The Homer Laughlin China Company, Oven Serve, Proposed Campaign," [1934], HL-EF; ADL, Jan. 13–Dec. 30, 1933, HL-ADF; Bleininger, reports, March 2–Nov. 6, 1933, Jan. 8, 1934, HL-CLF; JMW-PGF letters, March 28, 1931, Feb. 22, April 21, 1932, May 19, 1933–Feb. 13, 1934, April 21, July 12, 1934, boxes S-1417, S-1500, S-1614, S-1626, S-1634, S-1660, S-1677, S-1726, S-1741, HL-EC; Hubert T. Parson, "Woolworth Goes to 20 Cents," *CSA* 8 (March 1932): GMS-5, 32; "Public Response to 20-cent Lines Exceeds Woolworth Estimate," *CSA* 8 (April 1932): GMS-9, 28–32; "Woolworth Invades Dinnerware Field," *CGJ* 110 (March 1932): 17, 38; J. Walter Thompson, "Competitive Ovenware Prices Compared to Pyrex," Aug. 1934 and Oct. 1934, reel 38, JWT; JMW to George S. Ujlaki, July 19, 1934, box L-1735, HL-EC; John D. Thompson, HLCC, to Sedalia China & Glass Store, Sedalia, Mo., Oct. 6, 1933, box L-1687, HL-EC. Wells offered each volume vendor a distinctive Oven Serve variation. Woolworth sold Oven Serve decorated with boldly painted green flowers; Kress, without any embellishment; department stores, with special glazes in either orange or ivory.

51. FHR, "More about Color," *CGJ* 120 (June 1937): 13, 38; "Peasant Ware Reaches

New Heights," *CGJ* 112 (June 1934): 15, 24; Carl B. Sharpe, "Keep Your Eye on Mexico," *CGJ* 112 (Oct. 1934): 15–16; "Mexican Ware—Losing or Gaining Public Favor?" *CGJ* 113 (May 1935): 18, 37; "Two Structural Products Firms Make Success at Pottery," *CI* 25 (Aug. 1935): 71–72; "California Sun-Kissed Pottery Made in Modern Plant," *CI* 25 (Sept. 1935): 131–32; "Originality Is Key to Success of California Potters," *CI* (June 1936): 432, 434; "California Creates," *HB* (Nov. 1934) ("griddle"), quoted in Susan E. Pickel, *From Kiln to Kitchen: American Ceramic Design in Tableware* (Springfield: Illinois State Museum, 1980), 7; "Gay Table Settings for Colorful Autumn Meals," *BHG* 13(Sept. 1934): 30 ("apples"); Helen Sprackling, "We Set the Table in Fashion," *BHG* 14 (Oct. 1935): 20–21, 48–49, 60–61 (21, "simple"); "The Roving Reporter on the West Coast," *CI* 29 (Dec. 1937): 462–64; Bleininger reports, Sept. 4 ("imitate"), Oct. 5, Dec. 10, 1934, Jan. 12, 1935, HL-CLF; JMW to GSU, March 16, 1934, box L-1735, HL-EC.

52. Rufus B. Keeler, "The Use of Clay Products in Modern Homes," *BACS* 4 (July 1925): 310–20; Joseph A. Taylor, "Creating Beauty from the Earth: The Tiles of California," in *The Arts and Crafts Movement in California: Living the Good Life,* edited by Kenneth R. Trapp (Oakland, Calif.: Oakland Museum, 1993): 103–27.

53. Bleininger reports, Dec. 7, 1931, Jan. 4, June 5, 1932, Jan. 7, March 2, 1933, HL-CLF; FHR, "A New Deal," 45–52.

54. John Talmadge, "Fine China Goes Modern," *Keystone* 58 (Feb. 1931): 127–29; Perry interview; Regina Lee Blaszczyk, "Gift of Ceramics and Glass," memo to Collections Committee, NMAH, Dec. 29, 1987, and RLB, Survey notes on Perry apartment, both in accession 1988.0014, SICG; FHR, "Good Taste in Ceramic Art Is Fundamental," 38 ("crude"); JWM-GSU letters, July 26, Oct. 17, 1934, box L-1735, HL-EC; GSU, "Concentrate on Re-Order Items," *CGJ* 110 (Feb. 1932): 25, 59; ADL, March 23, 1935 ("California"), HL-ADF.

55. Richard Striner, "Art Deco: Polemics and Synthesis," *Winterthur Portfolio* 25 (Spring 1990): 21–34. Robert W. Rydell discusses the modernist imagery of the 1930s in *World of Fairs: The Century-of-Progress Expositions* (Chicago: University of Chicago Press, 1993). Unless otherwise noted, this discussion of Fiesta's development in 1935 is based on FHR, "Pottery Design Moving toward Modernistic," *CI* 25 (Sept. 1935): 123; FHR, "Color—A Designer Speaks"; FHR, "More about Color," 13, 38 (38, "jolly"); FHR to A. S. Newsom, Bristol Pottery, Bristol, Eng., Feb. 25, 1936 ("blatant"), HL-ADF; ADL, Jan. 30 ("circles"), Feb. 14, March 12, 19, 22, 23, 25, April 1, 5, 13, 25, 26, May 14, June 17, Oct. 15, 29, Nov. 21, 1935, HL-ADF; Bleininger reports, April 8, May 6, June 12, July 12, Sept. 9, Nov. 9, 1935, HL-CLF.

56. Warren I. Susman, "The Culture of the Thirties," in *Culture as History*, 150–83; Jeffrey Meikle, "Domesticating Modernity: Ambivalence and Appropriation, 1920–1940," in *Designing Modernity: The Arts of Reform and Persuasion, 1885–1945*, edited by Wendy Kaplan (New York: Thames & Hudson, 1995), 142–57; Helen Delpar, *The Enormous Vogue of Things Mexican: Cultural Relations between the United States and Mexico,*

1920–1935 (Tuscaloosa: University of Alabama Press, 1992); James Oles, *South of the Border: Mexico in the American Imagination, 1914–1947* (Washington, D.C.: Smithsonian Institution Press, 1993).

57. Homer Laughlin's white clay body cost $0.77 a pound; the Fiesta talc body, $0.71 a pound; and the ivory body, $0.66 a pound; see Bleininger, laboratory notebook, May 20, 1937, HL-CLF. The pottery's regular white glaze cost $0.0277 a pound; Fiesta red, $0.373 a pound; Fiesta blue, $0.1577 a pound; Fiesta green, $0.117 a pound; Fiesta yellow, $0.1087 a pound; Harlequin pink (introduced for Woolworth in 1936), $0.171 a pound; see Bleininger, laboratory notebook, March 10, April 20, May 15, Aug. 13, 1936, HL-CLF.

58. FHR to Newsom ("outrageously"); "Homer Laughlin's Fiesta Ware Brings Business—Result of Long Experiment," *CI* 26 (June 1936): 434 ("sport"), 446 ("smart") Customer records, HL-SF; Arens, "Report on Pottery and China Markets," SU-EA.

59. Susan B. Nevin, "Editor is Consultant on China and Glass," *Pittsburgh Post-Gazette,* Jan. 17, 1936; Vincent Broomhall, interview by author, tape recording, East Liverpool, Ohio, June 3, 1988; Viktor Schreckengost, interview by author, tape recording, Cleveland, Ohio, June 8, 1992.

60. Owens-Illinois Glass Company, *Annual Report,* 1936, 5; Bleininger reports, June 8, 1934, HL-CLF; ADL, 1936–37, HL-ADF; George H. Stapleford, "Silk-Screen Printing and Its Application to the Dinnerware Industry," *BACS* 16 (May 1937): 188–95; FHR to Newsom; FHR to Jean C. Vollrath, Sheboygan, Wisc., June 29, 1936; FHR to Mr. Sidebottom, Owens-Illinois, Huntington, W. Va., Feb. 15, 1936; FHR to Gordon Forsyth, Burslem School of Art, Staffordshire, Eng., May 6, 1937; R. S. Giese, Fort Pitt Glass Company, to FHR, May 8, 1937, all in HL-ADF; FHR, "Good Taste in Ceramic Art," 38; FHR, "A New Deal," 49–50; FHR, "Art and Design in Dinnerware," *CI* 28 (Jan. 1937): 78–79; "Silk-Screen Manufacturing Dept., Cost," [Sept. 1936], folder: Silk-screen manufacturing department cost, HL-ED. On Faulds, see ADL, May 26, 1936, HL-ADF; FHR, "Chats on Pottery," *PH,* Feb. 16, 1933. For Woolworth, see H. H. Lindquist to JMW, Feb. 18, 1936, box S-1945, HL-EC.

61. "Premium Ware Going Well—New Fall Colors Include Pottery Tones," *CI* 26 (June 1936): 410; Mabel Stegner, "Latchstring's Out—Larder's Full!" *BHG* 15 (Dec. 1936): 48; HHL to JMW, May 27, 1936, box S-1971, HL-EC.

62. JWM to HHL, Feb. 5, 1937, box S-2143, HL-EC; "All American Theme Brings Pottery Sales," *CI* 32 (Feb. 1939): 27–29; "What's Coming in Color in Postwar Ceramics," *CI* 43 (Sept. 1944): 52–54.

63. Edward H. Sykes, "Pittsburgh Spotlights Pottery and Glass," *CI* 28 (Feb. 1937): 127–29; Limoges minutes, March 8, June 4, July 23, Sept. 8 (5, "Barbara Jane"; 6 "Fiesta type"), 16, Nov. 10, 16, 1937, SI-SC; "Japanese Pottery Imports Slow U.S. Production," *CI* 29 (Sept. 1937): 175–76; "Tariff Adjustment Only Relief for Potters," *CI* 27 (Oct. 1936): 245.

64. Limoges minutes, Jan. 22 (3, "artists"), Aug. 10, Nov. 3, 1938, Feb. 6, 1939, SI-SC; Gordon Forsyth, *20th Century Ceramics* (London: The Studio Limited, 1936), 28; Salem minutes, Aug. 8, 1939, SI-SC; "Trends in the Dining Room," *CGL* 56 (Sept. 1936): 31–32; Broomhall interview; "China 1937" and Yorktown designs, trade journal clippings, late 1930s, Vincent Broomhall Scrapbook, VB; "Vistosa" (East Liverpool: Taylor, Smith & Taylor Company, 1938); "Lu-Ray Pastels for Modern Charming Tables" (East Liverpool: Taylor, Smith & Taylor, [1939]), in file: Taylor, Smith & Taylor, ELMC-VF; Schreckengost, "What Is the Future of American Ceramic Design?"; Household Finance Corporation, *Better Buymanship, no. 18, Dinnerware,* rev. ed. (Chicago: Household Finance Corporation, 1938), 26; "New Tonal Glaze Base Is Shown by Designer," *RHF,* Nov. 27, 1939; "The Designer Knows Your Customer," *RHF,* Aug. 19, 1940; FHR, "Report of the Art and Design Committee," *USPA Proc.* 60 (1939), 45–46 ("snooty"); "How Far Are We Buying American?" *RHF,* April 28, 1941 ("keep up"). Fiesta knock-offs appeared soon after the 1936 Pittsburgh show; see "Caliente: Whether in Spain or in Paden City—It Still Means Hot," *CGL* 56 (Sept. 1936): 40–41.

65. Pickel, *From Kiln to Kitchen,* 10–11; William J. Hennessey, *Russel Wright: American Designer* (Cambridge: MIT Press, 1983); Regina Lee Blaszczyk, "The Wright Way for Glass: Russel Wright and the Business of Industrial Design," *Acorn: Journal of the Sandwich Glass Museum* 4 (1993): 2–22; "Can American Ceramics Establish a Market That Will Last?" *CI* 35 (Dec. 1940): 7; FHR, "Art and Design Report, USPA," typescript, 1940 ("urinals"), HL-ADF.

66. "Launch Jap Boycott at East Liverpool," *CI* 30 (Jan. 1938): 23–24; "Retail Chain Stores Adopt Jap Boycott," *CI* 30 (Jan. 1938): 24; "How War May Affect U.S. Ceramic Plants," *CI* 33 (Oct. 1939): 29–33; "Can American Ceramics Establish a Market That Will Last?" *CI* 35 (Oct. 1940): 5–7; "World War II and Ceramics," *CI* 35 (July 1940): 21–22; "Now Is the Time to Develop True American Design," *CI* 35 (Aug. 1940): 19–20; "Dinnerware Imports Almost Stopped," *CI* 36 (Jan. 1941): 74; *Sterling Book, Listing the Products of the Taylor, Smith & Taylor Company* (East Liverpool: TST, 1942), cat. no. H3413, ELMC-VF; J. Palin Thorley, "The Ceramic Designer in Wartime," *CGJ* 131 (July 1942): 46; Pickel, *Kiln to Kitchen,* 12 (Schreckengost); "What American Women Do Know about American Ceramics," *CI* 38 (June 1942): 62–64; "Largest Promotion in History Skyrockets Dinnerware Sales," *CI* 39 (Oct. 1942): 42–44; "War Has Serious Effects on 1943 Color Situation," *CI* 40 (Jan. 1943): 11–12; Eleanor Vatcher, "Wartime Style and Design Trends in China and Glass," *CGJ* 133 (July 1943): 48; "Wartime Position of Pottery Outlined; Substitutes for Strategic War Materials," *CGJ* 133 (Sept. 1943): 38; Vincent Broomhall, "Design Simplification a Wartime Measure," *CGJ* 134 (Jan. 1934): 43–56; "American Dishes: Home Product Fills Gap Made by War and Boycott," *Life* 9 (Sept. 9, 1940): 76–79.

67. Broomhall, "Report of the Art and Design Committee," 52 ("outstanding"); JMW and JDT, "Resolutions on the Death of Frederick Hurten Rhead," 3 ("mold"); Ephraim

Friedman, "The Plastic Blitz Is On," *CGJ* 135 (Nov. 1944): 32–58; Beryl Kent, "Factors in Japanese Pottery Comeback," *CI* 52 (March 1949): 95, 120.

Chapter 5: Better Products for Better Homes

1. Kenneth T. Jackson, *Crabgrass Frontier: The Suburbanization of the United States* (New York: Oxford University Press, 1985), 173 ("can't"); Joseph Interrante, "'You Can't Go to Town in a Bathtub': Automobile Movement and the Reorganization of Rural American Space, 1900–1930," *Radical History Review* 21 (Fall 1979): 151–68; "4,000,000 Homes Have No Bathroom Facilities," *CI* 10 (June 1928): 607.

2. "Making People Want Things," *KN* (March 1928): 20; "Total Sales of All Products by Months, 1873–1930," box: Auditors' reports, KA; *President's Report to the Shareholders of the Standard Sanitary Manufacturing Company, for the Year 1925* (Pittsburgh, 1926), [2].

3. "[Sales] Summary," March 8, 1939, folder: Miscellaneous factory-related materials, box: Miscellaneous, KA.

4. Sinclair Lewis, *Babbitt* (New York: New American Library, 1980), 80 ("drip"); "The Rise and Fall of the Bath," *Screen Guide* (Sept. 1934): 32–33.

5. Suellen Hoy, *Chasing Dirt: The American Pursuit of Cleanliness* (New York: Oxford University Press, 1995), chap. 4; Maureen Ogle, *All the Modern Conveniences: American Household Plumbing* (Baltimore: Johns Hopkins University Press, 1996); May N. Stone, "The Plumbing Paradox: American Attitudes toward Late Nineteenth-Century Domestic Sanitary Arrangements," *Winterthur Portfolio* 14 (Autumn 1979): 283–309.

6. Trudi James Eblen, "History of the Kohler Company of Kohler, Wisconsin, 1871–1914" (master's thesis, University of Wisconsin at Madison, 1965), outlines the firm's early chronology.

7. HVK, "Selling Recommendations," Nov. 3, 1924 ("promotion"), folder: HVK, 1920–24, KA-WJK-OF.

8. William H. Barth, ["Kohler Co."], *KN* (June 1917): 19 ("success"); "Branch Office," *KN* (Dec. 1916): 6–7; (Jan. 1917): 9; "Boston," *KN* (Feb. 1917): 8; "Philadelphia," *KN* (June 1917): 18; "Indianapolis Office," *KN* (Dec. 1917): 16–17 ("ladle").

9. Standard Sanitary Company, *The Evolution of the Bath Room, 1875–1911* (Pittsburgh, 1911), n.p., Design P65.

10. Advertising Dept., Kohler Company, "Notes on the History of Plumbing, 1900–1940," April 1942, 2–4, folder: Notes on the history of plumbing, KA; WJK to HVK, Oct. 14, 1922, folder 154B: HVK, 1920–24, KA-WJK-OF; George G. Gallatti, ["Notes on Kohler Pottery"], n.d., 28–29, folder: Full-line manufacture, 1925–27, KA; H. F. Staley, "The Manufacture of Enameled Iron Sanitary Ware," *TACS* 8 (1906): 172–79.

11. Eblen, "History," chap. 2 ("nondescript"); Walter H. Uphoff, *Kohler on Strike: Thirty Years of Conflict* (Boston: Beacon, 1966), chap. 1; John Higham, *Strangers in the*

Land: Patterns of American Nativism, 1860–1925 (New York: Atheneum, 1978), chaps. 8, 9.

12. Margaret Crawford, *Building the Workingman's Paradise: The Design of American Company Towns* (New York: Verso, 1995).

13. WJK to Arthur J. Mertzke, Oct. 2, 1931, folder: White House conference on home building and home ownership, 1930–32, KA-KFP; WJK to George L. Geiger, Nov. 4, 1931, and GLG to William B. Powell, New York, Nov. 9, 1931, all in folder: Village development and future plans, WJK, 1920–39, box 2: Village development, KA; Uphoff, *Kohler on Strike*, 6. On Howard and garden cities, see Crawford, *Building the Workingman's Paradise*, chaps. 4, 6; M. Christine Boyer, *Dreaming the Rational City: The Myth of American City Planning* (Cambridge: MIT Press, 1983), chap. 3 and 191–94.

14. [Hegemann Survey], 1916 ("Kohler Garden City"), and WJK to Werner Hegemann, Jan. 16, 1917, both in folder: Village development—Hegemann and Peets, box 2: Village development, KA; Arnold R. Alanen and Thomas J. Peltin, "Kohler, Wisconsin: Planning and Paternalism in a Model Industrial Village," *Journal of the American Institute of Planners* 44 (April 1978): 145–59. After a brief association, Hegemann and Kohler parted ways; when nativists labeled the firm "Kohler von Kohler," Walter Kohler may have decided to cut off colleagues whose national origins might hurt business prospects. See WJK to HVK, Nov. 30, 1918, folder 154A: HVK, 1917–19, KA-WJK-OF. By late 1917, Kohler secured the first of several government contracts for weapons components: iron castings for mine anchors, dummy hand grenades, and proofing shells. See WJK to HVK, Dec. 22, 1917, Jan. 17, Feb. 2, 1918, folder 154A: HVK, 1917–19, KA-WJK-OF.

15. WJK to HVK, June 15 ("white"), 29, Aug. 30, 1918, folder 154A: HVK, 1917–19, KA-WJK-OF; WJK to Richard Philipp, Sept. 5, 9, 1916, in folder: Village development, early plans, 1916–17, box 2: Village development, KA; "A Group of Houses at Kohler," *KN* (April 1917): 12–14; "The Proposed American Club," *KN* (June 1917): n.p.; ["Kohler Co."], [ca. 1934], folder: Village development and future plans, WJK, 1920–39, box 2: Village development, KA; Alanen and Peltin, "Kohler, Wisconsin."

16. "Tapping a Cupola," *KN* (April 1925): cover; "Notable Architectural Exhibit," *KN* (April 1925): 18; "Arthur Covey: Distinguished American Muralist," *KN* (Oct. 1948): 12; "The Town of Kohler, Wisconsin: A Model Industrial Development," *Architecture* (April 1925), clipping, and L. L. Smith to Lisa Dougherty, *Fortune*, Dec. 16, 1929 ("dignity"), both in folder: Murals, KA-LLS.

17. "Dedication of the American Club," *KN* (July 1918): 2; WJK, "The Story of Kohler" (address presented at the annual dinner meeting of the Massachusetts Sanitary Club, Boston, Nov. 10, 1920), 10; WJK to Thomas R. Adams, May 16, 1927 ("sentimental"), both in folder: Village development and future plans, WJK, 1920–39, box 2: Village development, KA.

18. Janet Anne Hutchison, "American Housing, Gender, and the Better Homes Movement, 1922–1935" (Ph.D. diss., University of Delaware, 1989), chaps. 4, 5.

19. In 1928, the Kohler Village model home attracted 15,000 tourists; in 1932, attendance peaked at 16,000. For the rest of the decade, visitation seesawed with the economy. In 1934, there were 3,600 visitors; in 1935, 8,100; in 1936, 7,600, with the number dwindling to 1,300 at Marie Christian Kohler's death during World War II. Visitation also paralleled the fortunes of BHA nationally. The movement collapsed after Hoover's presidential defeat in 1932 and finally disintegrated as a national force during the Great Depression. For 1928–58 attendance, see A. Oehl to Armond W. Grube, July 2, 1959, folder: Better Homes Week, 1929–70, box 2: Village development, KA. For Marie Kohler's BHA activities, see *KN* (1925–43): passim; "Marie Christian Kohler," *KN* (Nov. 1943): 19 ("character"); Kohler Company, *Kohler Village: A Town-Planned Wisconsin Industrial Community, American in Spirit and Government* (Kohler, Wisc.: Kohler Company, 1928), 4 ("smart"); James Ford–MCK letters, July 12, 1930, May 13, 1931, both in folder: Kohler Village, Better Homes Awards, 1925–43, box 2: Village development, KA.

20. "Selling Expenses," June 20, 1932, folder: Miscellaneous factory-related materials, box: Miscellaneous, KA; "Advertising Men to Cooperate with the Government," *PI* 98 (March 29, 1917): 97; "Government Accepts the Aid of Advertising Men on War Problems," *PI* 99 (April 5, 1917): 28–32; Bruce Bliven, "Uncle Sam's Megaphone: What the Committee on Public Information Really Is and Does," *PI* 105 (Oct. 24, 1918): 3–6; Olney, *Buy Now, Pay Later*, chap. 5; Paul Studenski and Herman E. Krooss, *Financial History of the United States* (New York: McGraw-Hill, 1963), 295–98, 310.

21. L. L. Smith, "Advertising Budget for 1922: Comparisons and Comments," Dec. 21, 1921, folder: Advertising estimates and budget figures (1922), KA-LLS. Plumbers' trade papers containing Kohler advertisements included *Plumbers Trade Journal, Domestic Engineering,* and *Metal Worker;* architectural papers, *Architectural Record, Architectural Review, Architectural Forum,* and *Journal of the American Institute of Architects.* Consumer-oriented campaigns appeared in *House and Garden, House Beautiful, Good Housekeeping, Literary Digest, American Magazine, McClures, Harpers' Magazine, Country Life, Harpers' Bazaar, Country Life,* and *Saturday Evening Post.* See "Approximate Advertising Material Cost for 1917," Aug. 1, 1917; "Cost per Inquiry on National Mediums," Nov. 6, 1917; "Mediums Used in the First Six Months of 1918"; "Advertising Budget for 1920," Nov. 15, 1919, folders: Advertising Estimates and Budget Figures (1917, 1918, 1920), KA-LLS. Advertising expenses also covered ephemeral materials such as streetcar posters; exhibits at trade shows such as the New York Hotel Men's Exposition and the National Plumbers' Convention; and advertisements in yearbooks and program leaflets for organizations such as the State Fireman's Association, Nowiny Polskie, Wisconsin Bowling Association, Wisconsin Banker & Manufacturer, and the American Legion. See "Analysis of Miscellaneous Advertising," Nov. 13, 1919, folder: Advertising estimates and budget figures (1919), KA-LLS.

22. WJK to HVK, Sept. 6, 1918 ("inspiration"), folder 154A: HVK, 1917–19, KA-WJK-OF; "The Things We Grow up With!" advertisement reprinted in *KN* (Feb. 1925): 20

("houses"); "Those Who Know about Such Things," advertisement reprinted in *KN* (Jan. 1925): 24; "A Tiny Garden," advertisement reprinted in *KN* (March 1925): 20; "When Little Children," advertisement reprinted in *KN* (Oct. 9, 1925): 23.

23. "Report of Committee on Enameled Ware Sales Promotion," Jan. 16, 1925; "Outline of Discussion on Sales Promotion Conference," Jan. 28, 1925; "Report of Committee on Enameled Wares Sales Promotion," March 30, 1925; LLS to Oscar A. Kroos, Sept. 16, 1926, all in folder: Sales conferences, KA-LLS; "Wholesalers' Convention Held at Kohler," *KN* (Sept. 1927): 2–8.

24. WJK to HVK, April 24, June 15, July 27, Aug. 12, 30, 1918, folder 154A: HVK, 1917–19, KA-WJK-OF; HVK to T. Harry Thompson, Jan. 23, 1934, folder: N. W. Ayer & Son, KA-HVK-OF; U.S. Department of Commerce, Bureau of the Census, *Historical Abstracts of the United States, Colonial Times to 1957* (Washington, D. C.: Government Printing Office, 1961), Series N 106–15. David M. Kennedy, *Over Here: The First World War and American Society* (New York: Oxford University Press, 1980), and Ronald Schaffer, *America in the Great War: The Rise of the War Welfare State* (New York: Oxford University Press, 1991), provide overviews of the war economy.

25. On executives' role in design and development, see Daily Conference of Executives [hereafter, DCE], June 25, 1928, KA-ECA. For the Automatic, see "Establishing Dealerships," May 24, 1921; OAK and LLS, "Advertising Kohler Power-Light," May 23, 1921; "Establishing Dealers Mainly Thru the Plumbing Industry," May 22, 1921; "Lower Prices on Kohler Automatic Power and Light Unit," May 11, 1921; Bulletin 68-OAK, "Kohler Automatic," May 16, 1921, all in KA-ECA; "Electricity—Without Storage Batteries," advertisement reprinted in *KN* (Jan. 1921): 6; "Kohler Automatic on Exhibition," *KN* (Feb. 1921): 14; "Think What You Could Do with Kohler Electricity," advertisement reprinted in *KN* (March 1925): 6; Commercial Investment Trust, New York, to Kohler Company, Oct. 30, 1926; HVK to Paul Fitzpatrick, CIT, Dec. 10, 1926, both in folder: Commercial Investment Trust, KA-HVK-OF; "The Private Electric Plant and Its Relation to Comfort and Health on the Farm," *KN* (May 1927): 6; *Bold Craftsmen* (Kohler, Wisc.: Kohler Company, 1973), 16–17.

26. WJK to HVK, Nov. 30, Dec. 21 (Ahrens), 1918, Jan. 4 ("arbitrary"), 18, 1919, folder 154A: HVK, 1917–19, KA-WJK-OF; "Theodore Ahrens," *BACS* 17 (Aug. 1938): 368.

27. On Kohler and Trenton, see WJK to HVK, Jan. 27, 1919, folder 154A: HVK, 1917–19, KA-WJK-OF; Kohler Company, Board of Directors Minutes, Jan. 29, 1919, cited in Gallatti, ["Notes on Kohler Pottery"], 6; ["Notes on Sales Convention, 1919"], folder: Sales conferences, KA-LLS. For Trenton, see LeRoy Minton, "The Sanitary Ware Industry in America," *Ceramist* 4 (Sept. 1924): 337–50; "Who Began Vitrified Porcelain Sanitary Ware Making?" *BACS* 16 (Sept. 1934): 384–86; W. A. Darrah, "The Vitreous Sanitary Ware Industry," *BACS* 4 (June 1935): 261–82; "Thomas Maddock's Sons Company Acquired by American Radiator & Standard Sanitary Corporation," *CA* 14 (Aug.

1929): 59, 62; "Expert Analyzes Ruling in Sanitary Pottery Case," *PGBS* 35 (March 10, 1927): 27, 31; Stern, *The Pottery Industry of Trenton*, chap. 10.

28. A. F. Haack to George C. Gallatti, "History of Vitreous China Plumbing Fixtures at the Kohler Company," April 12, 1971, folder: Kohler expansion to full-line manufacturing, KA; "Largest Single Pottery for Sanitary Earthenware Production: New Plant of the Thomas Maddock's Sons Co., Trenton, N.J.," *Ceramist* 6 (June 1926): 565–611; Stern, *The Pottery Industry of Trenton*, chap. 11.

29. "Agreement between the Kohler Company, Andrew C. Cochran, Walter F. Drugan, and Cochran, Drugan & Company," May 18, 1925; "Settlement Sheet of Sale of Cochran, Drugan & Company to the Kohler Company, as of Sept. 1, 1925"; "Copy of Agreement between the Kohler Company and Andrew C. Cochran," June 16, 1925, all in folder: Trenton, General data, box: Pottery, KA; "Pottery," Nov. 11, 1925, folder: Trenton, Manufacturing data, box: Pottery, KA; "Kohler Company Becomes a Major Full-Line Plumbing Products Manufacturer," Aug. 20, 1971, 7–21, folder: Kohler Company expansion, KA; "Kohler Buys Pottery Plant," *KN* (Sept. 1925): 14; WJK to HVK, Sept. 29, 1925, folder 154C: HVK, 1925–29, KA-WJK-OF.

30. HVK to Andrew C. Cochran, Nov. 2, 6, 1925, folder: Trenton, ACC files, 1925, box: Pottery, KA.

31. Ogle, *All the Modern Conveniences*; Robert W. Rydell, *All the World's a Fair: Visions of Empire at American International Expositions, 1876–1916* (Chicago: University of Chicago Press, 1984), chap 2; James Gilbert, *Perfect Cities: Chicago's Utopias of 1893* (Chicago: University of Chicago Press, 1991), chap. 4; Matthew Luckiesh, *The Language of Color* (New York: Dodd, Mead, 1918), 26; Estelle H. Ries, "Getting the Most from Your Bathroom," *FGH* 2 (Feb. 1924): 11–12, 52 (11, "all"); "The Manufacture of Kohler Ware," *KN* (July 1917): 9–11, 15–16; "Kohler of Kohler Enameled Plumbing Ware," advertisement reprinted in *KN* (Jan. 1925): 24 ("snowy").

32. HVK to ACC, Nov. 2, 1925 (Wolff), folder: Trenton, ACC files, 1925, box: Pottery, KA.

33. HVK-ACC letters, Oct. 24, Dec. 1–3, 7, 1925, folder: Trenton, ACC files, 1925; HVK to ACC, March 16, 1926, folder: Trenton, ACC files, 1926; "Program of Reorganization for Cochran, Drugan & Company Plant," June 18, 1925, folder: Trenton, General data, all in box: Pottery, KA; Darrah, "The Vitreous Sanitary Ware Industry"; "The Manufacture of Vitreous China at Kohler," *KN* (March 1928): 3–6, and (April 1928): 4–7.

34. HVK to H. H. Held, Kohler Company, Philadelphia, April 4, 1927, folder: Philadelphia correspondence, box: Branch correspondence and advertising, 1930s-50s, KA; HVK to WJK, Sept. 30, 1925 ("underestimate"), folder 154C: HVK, 1925–29, KA-WJK-OF.

35. "How to Build up a Profitable Business with the Kohler Electric Clotheswasher," *KN* (Oct. 1928): 21–23; "How to Increase Christmas Business by Selling Kohler of Kohler Electric Clotheswashers," *KN* (Nov. 1928): 19; "Selling Kohler of Kohler Electric Clotheswashers," *KN* (Nov. 1928): 20–21; "What Is Selling?" *KN* (Dec. 1928): 19; "An Outline

for Selling Kohler of Kohler Electric Sink-Dishwashers," *KN* (Dec. 1928): 20–21; "Planning Next Year's Business," *KN* (Jan. 1929): 19–21.

36. Karen Dunn-Haley, "The House That Uncle Sam Built: The Political Culture of Federal Housing Policy, 1919–1932" (Ph.D. diss., Stanford University, 1995), chap. 5, esp. 147.

37. "Announcing the Kohler Electric Sink," *KN* (Nov. 1926): 2–7 (4, "laborless"); "Until We Throw Dishes Away," *New York Herald Tribune*, Nov. 15, 1931, clipping in folder: Electric Sink data, KA-LLS.

38. Clara Woolworth, "Making Dishwashing Endurable," *Country Gentleman* (May 1926), clipping; "Kohler Publicity Story," [1926]; A. E. Mallman to J. H. Deeley, "Report on Studies Taken Washing Dishes with Electric Sink and by Hand," May 3, 1927; "Solves the Dishwashing Problem," Boston, Nov. 1925, and "Dishwasher Lightens Task," clippings on Walker model, n.d., all in folder: Electric Sink, KA-LLS; Kohler Company, *Now—The Kohler Electric Sink Will Wash the Dishes* (Kohler, Wisc.: 1926), KA; "Announcing the Kohler Electric Sink"; "Yes, Times Have Changed," advertisement reprinted in *KN* (Nov. 1927): 23 (testimonials).

39. "Announcing the Kohler Electric Sink"; *The Story of Good Housekeeping Institute* (New York: Good Housekeeping Institute, 1923); *The Story of Good Housekeeping Institute: A Record of Twenty Years of Service to Homes of America* (New York: Good Housekeeping, 1929), 28–29; George W. Alder to LLS, Nov. 12, 1926; A. W. Prescott to Joseph Worscheck, Dec. 14, 1926; J. B. Bray to LLS, Dec. 6, 7, 1926, all in folder: Electric Sink data, KA-LLS; HVK to Frank Brotz, Jan. 7, 1927, folder 154C: HVK, 1925–29, KA-WJK-OF; "Outline for Demonstration of Electric Sink," n.d., folder: Sales—Electric Sink, KA-HVK-DF.

40. R. C. Angelbeck to Oscar A. Kroos, "Suggestions for Marketing the Kohler Dishwasher," Nov. 25, 1925, folder: R. C. Angelbeck; HVK to J. Robin Harrison, Feb. 22, 1927, folder: Sales—Electric Sink, both in KA-HVK-DF; "Notes Regarding Kohler Electric Dish Washer Sink," Jan. 18, 1926; "Sales Analysis of Kohler Electric Sink-Clotheswasher," n.d.; Katherine A. Fischer to Herbert E. Fleming, Conover Company, Chicago, Feb. 17, 1927 ("Cinderella"), all in folder: Electric Sink data, KA-LLS.

41. J. Robin Harrison to HVK, "A More Forceful Advertising Appeal," March 7, 1927, folder: Sales—Electric Sink, KA-HVK-DF; Louise Stanley, Chief, Bureau of Home Economics, U.S. Department of Agriculture, to Joseph Worscheck, Kohler Company, March 20, 1926; James G. Cumming, "Influenza-Pneumonia as Influenced by Dishwashing in 370 Public Institutions," *American Journal of Public Health* 10 (July 1920), typescript; Roy L. Dearstyne, "Comparison of the Bacterial Counts from Machine and Hand-Washed Dishes and Their Significance," *American Journal of Public Health* 10 (Nov. 1920), typescript; Herman N. Bundesen, "The Disinfection of Eating and Drinking Utensils," *Chicago's Health* (Feb. 22, 1927): 54–55; HNB, "Rules for the Washing and Cleansing of Dishes and Eating Utensils," *Chicago's Health* (Feb. 22, 1927): 56, clip-

pings; Nell B. Nichols, "How I Take the Hate out of Dish Washing," *Farm and Fireside* (Feb. 1927), clipping; "The Kohler Electric Sink," n.d., all in folder: Electric Sink data, KA-LLS; *The Proper Use of the Kohler of Kohler Sink* (Kohler, Wisc.: Kohler Company, 1927), 3 ("germ"), KA. On home economists, see "Kohler Electric Sinks Installed in Model Kitchens," *KN* (Nov. 1927): 11; DCE, March 14, 1927, KA-ECA.

42. "Kohler Co. Has Fine New Seattle Showroom," *KN* (Dec. 1926): 16–17; WJK to R.C. Angelbeck, March 4, 1927, folder: Advertising and showrooms, 1926–38, KA-HVK-DF; "Kohler Electric Sink Demonstrating Saleswomen," *KN* (Feb. 1927): 8; HVK, "Selling Program for the Electric Sink as Given to the Demonstrating Saleswomen" ("viewpoint"; "need"), Dec. 1, 1926, folder: Sales—Electric Sink, KA-HVK-DF; "Two New Folders Ready for Distribution," *KN* (Nov. 1929): 20; Bulletin OAK-166, "Electric Sink Sales Bonus for Plumbing Fixture Salesmen," March 8, 1927, and Bulletin OAK-167, "Electric Sink Sales Bonus for Plumbing Fixture Supervisors," March 8, 1927, KA-ECA.

43. "A New Day for Dishes," *Delineator* (Jan. 1929), clipping, folder: Electric Sink data, KA-LLS; WJK to HVK, May 26, 1922 ("sales plan"), folder 154B: HVK, 1920–24, KA-WJK-OF; T. J. Hines to Paul Fitzpatrick, Memoradum on Kohler Company, Boston, Nov. 22, 1926, and HVK to PF, Feb. 14, 1927, both in folder: Commercial Investment Trust, KA-HVK-OF. For prices, see HVK, "Selling Program for the Electric Sink as Given to the Demonstrating Saleswomen," Dec. 1, 1926; Richard S. Tedlow, *New and Improved: The Story of Mass Marketing in America* (New York: Basic Books, 1990), 313 (refrigerator); Alfred P. Sloan Jr., *My Years with General Motors,* edited by John MacDonald and Catherine Stevens (New York: Doubleday, 1963; New York: Doubleday Currency, 1990), 162 (cars).

44. On distributors, see folder: Kohler Company, branches, policy making; WJK to HVK, Jan. 10, 1930, folder 154D: HVK, 1930–34, KA-WJK-OF; J. Robin Harrison, "Kohler Electric Sink Specialty Sales Plan" ("jealousies"), April 7, 1927, folder: Sales—Electric Sink, KA-HVK-DF; LLS to OAK, March 12, 1923 ("advantage"), March 21, 1927, folders: Advertising estimates and budget figures (1923, 1927), KA-LLS.

45. Bulletin OAK-68, "Kohler Automatic," May 16, 1921, KA-ECA; JRH to HVK et al., "Plan for Utilizing Specialty Sales Methods in Selling Kohler Electric Sinks," April 4, 1927; JRH to HVK, "Outline of Sales Manual for Plumbers Dealing with Kohler Electric Sink," Feb. 14, 1927, both in folder: Electric Sink data, KA-LLS; "Planning Next Year's Business Success," *KN* (Jan. 1929): 19–21.

46. "Operating Statement for the Year 1934," box: Auditors' reports, KA.

47. "Pink Bathrooms!" *CI* 10 (Feb. 1928): 193; "Pink Bathrooms Again," *CI* 10 (March 1928): 285; Stuart Chase and F. J. Schlink, *Your Money's Worth: A Study in the Waste of the Consumer's Dollar* (New York: Macmillan, 1927), chaps. 9, 10; "The Rise and Fall of the Bath."

48. "Kohler Entertains 325 Wholesalers," *CI* 9 (Oct. 1927): 500 ("more frequent"); "Colored Enamels Vogue Discussed at Heating Appliance Convention," *CI* 7 (Nov. 1926):

463; "Making People Want Things"; Norman J. Radder, "Beauty and Distinction in the Modern Bathroom," *KTJ* 6 (Dec. 1934): 14–17; WJK to HVK, Nov. 16, 1926, March 31, 1928, both in folder 154C: HVK, 1925–29, KA-WJK-OF; "Necrology: C. J. Kirk," *BACS* 16 (July 1937): 309–11; Investigating Committees of Architects and Engineers, "White and Colored Glaze Solid Porcelain Plumbing Fixtures, Acid Proof Chemical Ware, Manufactured by General Ceramics Company," May 21, 1927, folder: Factory—color, KA-HVK-DF.

49. "Kohler of Kohler and Tile: Tiles Used Extensively as Background in Magazine Advertising," *Tiles and Tile Work* 1 (Nov. 1928): 44–45; *New Ideas for Bathrooms* (Chicago: Crane Company, 1926); "Kohler of Kohler in the Tribune Tower," *KN* (March 1926): 3–5; "Kohler Co. Los Angeles Showroom Opened," *KN* (Oct. 1926): 16–17; "Indianapolis Showroom," *KN* (Dec. 1925): 5; WJK to HVK, Jan. 27, Dec. 12, 1927, folder 154C: HVK, 1925–29, KA-WJK-OF; R. C. Angelbeck to OAK, "Display of Colored Ware in Showrooms," Oct. 5, 1927, folder: Advertising showrooms, 1926–38, KA-HVK-DF; Helen Koves, *On Decorating the Home* (New York: Tudor, 1928); Margaret McElroy, "The Decoration of Bathrooms," *HG* 45 (Feb. 1924): 80–81, 116. On the faience moment generally, see "Boom for Faience Tile Seen," *CI* 6 (May 1926): 500.

50. Investigating Committee of Architects and Engineers, "White and Colored Glaze Solid Porcelain Plumbing Fixtures"; HVK to LLS, "A Series of Announcements to the Trade," March 14, 1927; WJK, "Colored Ware," April 1, 1927, folder: Factory—color, KA-HVK-DF; HVK to WJK, April 11, 1927, folder 154C: HVK, 1925–29, KA-WJK-OF; "Another Kohler Achievement—Kohler Plumbing Fixtures in Color," *KN* (Dec. 1927): 3–4 (3, "striking"); "Kohler Fixtures in Color," advertisement reprinted in *KN* (Oct. 1927): 24; "1873–1930," *KN* (Jan. 1930): 19.

51. DCE, Sept. 30, 1927, KA-ECA; "Sales Program for Colored Ware," Sept. 9, 1927, folder: Factory—color, KA-HVK-DF; WJK to HVK, March 27, 1928; WJK to HVK and OAK, Jan. 31, 1928, both in folder 154C: HVK, 1925–29, KA-WJK-OF.

52. OAK to JRH, Sept. 6, 1927, folder: Factory—color, KA-HVK-DF; DCE, Sept. 5, 1927, Jan. 9, 1931, and A. J. Wesener to OAK, "Proposed Vitreous China Lavatory Development for K-39 Catalogue," July 22, 1937, all in KA-ECA; "Sales Program for Colored Ware."

53. "Manufacturers of Sanitary Ware Should Standardize Colors," *GI* 10 (May 1929): 122.

54. Bess M. Viemont, Division of Textiles and Clothing, to Louise Stanley, chief, Bureau of Home Economics, U.S. Department of Agriculture, April 2, 1931, folder: Stanley, Louise, 1924–31, box 551, Record Group 176, National Archives and Records Service, Washington, D.C.; U.S. Department of Commerce, National Bureau of Standards, *Staple Vitreous China Plumbing Fixtures*, Simplified Practice Recommendation 52 (Washington, D.C.: Government Printing Office, 1927); U.S. Department of Commerce, *Colors for Sanitary Ware: Commercial Standard CS30–31* (Washington, D.C.:

Government Printing Office, 1932), 6; "Simplified Practice as Applied to the Ceramic Industry," *CA* 11 (June 1928): 211–13, 224; F. W. Reynolds, "Recommended Commercial Standard for Colors for Bathroom Accessories," and "Recommended Commercial Standard for Colors for Kitchen Accessories," April 30, 1937, folder: 1937–38, Colors for kitchen and bathroom, box 8, HML-CA; "Difficulties in Delivering Colored Ware," *CA* 16 (Sept. 1930): 166.

55. HVK to WJK, Feb. 4, 1928, folder 154C: HVK, 1925–29, KA-WJK-OF; HVK to John E. Frazer, Jan. 23, 1934, folder: N. W. Ayer & Son, KA-HVK-OF; DCE, Sept. 13, 1930, KA-ECA; WJK, "Conclusions of Research Conference on June 4, 1929" ("research"), folder 154C: HVK, 1925–29, KA-WJK-OF.

56. "The Kohler Octachrome Line," *KN* (July 1928): 19–21; "The Manufacture of Plumbing Brass at Kohler," *KN* (July 1928): 8–11, and (Aug. 1928): 6–9; HVK-WJK letters, Feb. 4 ("note"), April 21, 28, May 5, June 23, 1928, folder 154C: HVK, 1925–29, KA-WJK-OF; DCE, Aug. 26, Sept. 27, 1927, KA-ECA.

57. Jeffrey L. Meikle, *Twentieth-Century Limited: Industrial Design in America, 1925–1939* (Philadelphia: Temple University Press, 1979), 40 (Sakier). Thanks to Standard's aggressive publicists, George Sakier's designs eventually appeared in business journals such as *Advertising Arts* and women's magazines such as *Delineator.* See Marion Murphy to HVK, Nov. 26, 1934, folder: N. W. Ayer & Son, 1929–53, KA-HVK-OF; George Sakier, "Hot and Cold," *AA* (March 1932): 10–14; "Primer of Modern Design," *AD* 40 (Nov. 1933): 36–37; "Bathroom Design Contest Conducted by Standard Sanitary," *CA* 16 (Sept. 1930): 168; "The Bathroom in a New Guise," *CI* 16 (April 1931): 356–57.

58. WJK to HVK, "Delineator Cooperation," April 23, 1928, folder 154C: HVK, 1925–29, KA-WJK-OF; HVK, "Color Policy Established Sept. 10, 1929"; HVK to Hazel H. Adler, "New Color Policy," Sept. 12, 1929; Mildred D. Strauss to HVK, Dec. 17, 1934 ("popular"), all in folder: Factory—color, KA-HVK-DF; "Kohler Presents a New Color: Tuscan," *KN* (Oct. 1929): 19–20 (20, "modernity"); "Tuscan—A Livable Color," *KN* (Nov. 1929): 19–20.

59. "New and Enlarged Program for 1930 Kohler Advertising," *KN* (May 1930): 19–23; Marchand, *Advertising the American Dream,* 120–27, 133, 157 ("smart"), 212, 343; "Stimulus," *AA* (July 1932): 24–25; HVK to H. H. Held, Jan. 10, 1930 ("program"), folder: Philadelphia correspondence, box: Branch correspondence and advertising, 1930s–50s, KA; HVK to EW, Nov. 19, 1929, folder 153: Erwin, Wasey & Co., 1925–29, KA-HVK-OF; HVK to John Hansel, N. W. Ayer & Son, Chicago, Nov. 13, 1929; A. J. Hatfield to HVK, Oct. 31, 1930; William B. Clark to HVK, Dec. 4, 1936, Aug. 15, 1944, all in folder: N. W. Ayer & Son, 1929–53, KA-HVK-OF; "Matched Beauty in Plumbing Fixtures," *KN* (Jan. 1931): 18–23. On the agency, see Ralph Hower, *The History of an Advertising Agency: N. W. Ayer & Son at Work, 1869–1939* (Cambridge: Harvard University Press, 1939); for its advertisements, see SI-NWA.

60. "The Best Salesman We Ever Had," advertisement reprinted in *KN* (June 1930):

24; "The Metropolitan Set," advertisement reprinted in *KN* (Jan. 1931): 24; "Matched Beauty in Plumbing Fixtures"; "Sell Fixtures in Matched Sets," *KN* (Oct. 1931): 13–15; "Sell Matched Sets," *KN* (Feb. 1931): 19–21; "Now You Can Sell Bathroom Fixtures in Matched Groups," advertisement reprinted in *KN* (Feb. 1931): 24; "Practical Features as Well as Matched Beauty," *KN* (March 1931): 20–22.

61. "How Is the Building Business in Your City?" [1928]; HVK, "What Home Modernizing Means to the Plumbing Industry," [June 1928]; "Kohler Urges Coordinated Home Modernizing Campaign as Aid to Recovery in Building Industry," [1933] ("renovize"), all in folder: Home modernizing correspondence and minutes, KA-LLS; "Typical Bathrooms of Three Distinct Periods," *KN* (Sept. 1933): 11 ("claw"); "A Billion Dollar Market: Home Modernizing," *BCR* 78 (1931): 334–35.

62. "Thru a NHA Loan You May Install a New Bathroom," *KTJ* 6 (Nov. 1934): 10–11; Wilkins, "Is Underglaze a Solution to Sanitary Ware Problems?"; "Potential Possibilities of White Tile," *KTJ* 11 (March 1937): 7 ("Mrs. Brown"); "What a Market for Sanitary Ware," *CA* 23 (Feb. 1934): 45; Christine Holbrook, "What! Can This Really Be the Bathroom?" *BHG* 12 (Jan. 1934): 22; Margaret White, "Exit Horse-and-Buggy Bathrooms," *BHG* 16 (Oct. 1937): 55 ("distinction"); "Sunset Manufacturing Makes Colored Ware," *CI* 10 (June 1928): 660; "At Cliff Towers," advertisement reprinted in *KN* (March 1930): 24.

63. H. K. Degen and A. G. Zibell to HVK, "Cardinal Tubs," Jan. 12, 1937, KA-ECA.

64. "Design Gives New Appearance to Sanitaryware," *CI* 27 (July 1936): 11–12; WJK, "The Further Development of Kohler Village," Dec. 15, 1939, folder: Village development and future plans, WJK, 1920–39, box 2: Village development; WJK, "Instructions for the Manufacture of Kohler Products," March 1, 1935, folder: Pottery, box: Archives miscellaneous; Kohler Company, *Planned Plumbing and Heating for Better Living* (Kohler, Wisc.: Kohler Company, 1936), 9 ("favor"), folder: Historic plumbing literature, box: Advertising booklets, all in KA; "Potential Possibilities of White Tile"; "Production, White Model 18 and 19, 1938," and "Monthly Recapitulation of Production, 1918–1964," Maytag Archives, Maytag, Newton, Iowa.

65. "A Statement by Kohler Company," Aug. 9, 1934, National Labor Relations Board, "Case No. 115: Decision in the Matter of Kohler Company and Federal Labor Union No. 18545," March 26, 1935; OAK, [Letter responding to charges by Federal Union No. 18545], [1935]; "A Statement by Kohler Company," Nov. 23, 1936, folder: 1934 Strike, Bulletins and statements, all in G. E. Ryan Papers, KA; Uphoff, *Kohler on Strike*, chaps. 1, 2; WJK, "Reduced Time Operations," Feb. 6, 1931, KA-ECA; Board of Directors, Minutes of Meetings (transcriptions), April 24, 1933, KA.

Chapter 6: Pyrex Pioneers

1. Unless otherwise noted, this section, "Laying Expert Foundations," draws on Regina Lee Blaszczyk, "Imagining Consumers: Manufacturers and Markets in Ceramics

and Glass, 1865–1965" (Ph.D. diss., University of Delaware, 1995), chap. 7, which in part outlines the early history of the Corning Glass Works, including industrial research.

2. George Buell Hollister, "Historical Records of the Corning Glass Works, 1851–1930" (typescript, 1951; rev. 1960); 8–10, 27–30; memorandum, Meriden Silver Plate Company, Oct. 18, 1875, and DWC–Corning Flint Glass Company letters, Feb. 16, 1870, file: Railroad, airport, and marine ware, CI-VF; John Hoxie, conversation with author, Corning, N.Y., May 13, 1992 ("tin"); GBH, "Manufacture of Early Incandescent Lamp Bulbs at Corning," BACS 15 (April 1936): 194–95.

3. Arthur A. Bright Jr., The Electric-Lamp Industry: Technological Change and Economic Development from 1800 to 1947 (New York: Macmillan, 1947), 133, 152–53.

4. NCAB 31, s.v., "Houghton, Alanson Bigelow"; George S. Maltby, interview by author, Corning, N.Y., Oct. 6, 1992.

5. AMS, 2d ed., s.v., "Churchill, Dr. William"; "Dr. William Churchill, Former Optical Engineer," New York Herald Tribune, Aug. 14, 1949; "Letters to the Editor," Corning (N.Y.) Evening Leader, clippings, file: William Churchill, CI-BF; William Churchill, "Signal Glass," Official Proceedings of the New York Railroad Club 24 (Feb. 1914): 4–27; D. L. Killigrew, "A Century of Signal Glass Developments," Railway Signaling and Communications (May 1949), clipping, file: Railroad, airport, and marine ware, CI-VF; Eugene C. Sullivan, "Minutes of the Meeting of the Manufacturing Committee," May 20, 1911, box S&E 84, folder: unmarked, CI-HFP ("competition"). On sales, see P. M. Smith, "Summary of Corning Glass Works' Earnings, 1871–1955," 1956, CI-EF; "Total Sales, Daisy [Corning Glass Works], 1902–1910," file: Railroad, airport, and marine wares, CI-VF.

6. Henry Phelps Gage, "A Third of a Century of Glass in the Kitchen," Aug. 11, 1947, box 7, CU-HPG ("family").

7. John Hoxie, interview by author, tape recording, Corning, N.Y., Oct. 6, 1992 ("prestige selling"); "These Eyes Must Tell the Truth," Gaffer 5 (March 1947): 3–5, 21; GBH, "Historical Records," 55.

8. Converse, Survey Research, 88–89.

9. P.W.S., "Nursing Bottles and Signal Lights," July 27, 1955, Historical Memo Notebook (hereafter, HMN) 13, CI; ECS, "Development of Low-Expansion Glasses," JIEC 8 (1916): 399–400; ECS, "The Many-Sidedness of Glass," JIEC 21 (Feb. 1929): 177–84; ECS, "Accomplishments of the Industrial Physicist in the Glass Industry," Journal of Applied Physics 8 (Feb. 1937): 122–28; Otto W. Hilbert, "Housewares Identification, Period of Manufacturers," April 19, 1975, HMN 13, CI; AMS, 5th ed., s.v., "Sullivan, Dr. Eugene Cornelius," s.v., "Littleton, Dr. Jesse T."; ["Memorandum on Trade Name for New Consumer Glassware"], July 9, 1912, box S&E 66, folder BA, CI-HFP.

10. Corporate legend at Corning holds that the Littletons invented Pyrex baking ware in their kitchen and overlooks earlier experiments. See [Jesse T. Littleton], "Report on the History of the First Pyrex Baking Dish," [Nov. 1917]; Catherine D. Mack, "Infor-

mal Notes Taken from Dr. Sullivan about the History of Pyrex Baking Ware," n.d.; ECS to Vernon M. Dorsey, July 29, 1919 ("brown" and "cooked" attributed to JTL, Nov. 1917); OWH to Amory Houghton Jr. II et al., "Memorandum on Baking Ware," Jan. 12, 1968, with "Notes Written by Dr. Sullivan, Nov. 6, 1957," (typescript); OWH to Amory Houghton Jr. II et al., Sept. 11, 1974, all in HMN 13, CI; "The Battery Jar That Built a Business: The Story of Pyrex Ovenware and Flameware," *Gaffer* 4 (July 1946): 3–18, CI. On the Littletons, see Frank W. Preston, "In Memoriam: Jesse Talbot Littleton, 1887–1966," reprint from *GI* (Dec. 1967), file: Jesse T. Littleton, CI-BF. On fireless cookers, see Mildred Maddocks, "Cooking by Fireless," *GH* 70 (April 1914): 472–76; Mabel Hennessy, "Fireless Cookers Salable the Year Round," *HA* 105 (April 1, 1920): 105–6.

11. *AMS*, 2d ed., s.v., "Deghuée, Dr. Joseph Albert"; William C. Thompson to Arthur A. Houghton, Dec. 5, 1914, box: S&E 3, folder 18, CI-HFP; ECS to VMD, July 29, 1919.

12. Martha van Rensselaer, "President's Address," *JHE* 7 (Nov. 1915): 464 ("citizenship"); Ellen Swallow Richards, "Wanted, a Test for Man Power," *JHE* 6 (Feb. 1913): 60 ("future"); "Ellen H. Richards (1842–1911)," *PHE* 20 (June 1942): 207; Eva W. White, "The Home and Social Efficiency," *JHE* 6 (April 1913): 125 ("environment").

13. MM to Deghuée, July 15, 1914 ("popovers"); MM, "Report on Glass Utensil Ware," Dec. 23, 1913, folder: Baking Ware, box P1, CI-VF. On GHI, see George W. Alder, "Is It Approved by Good Housekeeping Institute?" *GH* 90 (Jan. 1930): 82–83, 183; "Pyrex Glass Cooking Dishes," *GH* 61 (Sept. 1915): 404; Ida Cogswell Bailey-Allen, "Testing and Approving Recipes," *GH* 61 (Sept. 1915): 396–99, 402.

14. Mack, "Informal Notes" (quotations); "Who's Who in Home Economics: Sarah Tyson Rorer," *PHE* 12 (Jan. 1934): 13; Emma Seifrit Weigley, *Sara Tyson Rorer: The Nation's Instructress in Dietetics and Cookery* (Philadelphia: American Philosophical Society, 1977).

15. ECS to VMD, July 29, 1919 (Maddocks's remarks); Christine Frederick, *The New Housekeeping: Efficiency Studies in Home Management* (Garden City, N.Y.: Doubleday, Page, 1913).

16. Amelia W. Little, Notebook for Household Management, Feb. 10, 1913 ("consumer"), Amelia Worth Little Papers, SPNEA.

17. *Filene's How I Best Utilize My $—a Year for Dress?* (Boston: William Filene's Sons, 1913), back cover ("efficiency"); Little Notebook, March 10, 1913 ("tyranny"), both in Little Papers, SPNEA.

18. Miss Ebbitts, "Marketing Outline," 7–8; Rogers Brothers, *Spoons, Knives, Forks, Etc.*, no. 108 (Meriden, Conn.: Meriden Britannia, [1913]); Jordan Marsh Company, ["Kitchen and Pantry List"]; Hopkinson & Holden, *Illustrated Catalogue of Woodenware, Enamel, and Tinware* (Boston, 1906); B. F. Macy, "Kitchen Pantry List," all in Little Papers, SPNEA.

19. ECS and William C. Taylor, "A New Glass and an Application of the Low Reflectivity of Glass for Radiant Heat," *JIEC* 7 (Dec. 1915): 1084–85; "Notes Written by Dr.

Sullivan, Nov. 6, 1957"; ECS, handwritten notes, 1914–21, folder: Baking ware, box P1, CI-VF; W. H. Curtis, "Pyrex: A Triumph for Chemical Research in Industry," *JIEC* 14 (1922): 336–37; U.S. Patent 1,304,622, ECS and WCT, assigned to Corning Glass Works, "Heating Vessel," May 27, 1919 ("virulent"); U.S. Patent 1,304,623, ECS and WCT, assigned to CGW, "Glass," May 27, 1919.

20. WC to ABH, May 29, 1915, HMN 13, and July 16, 1916, HMN 16, CI; R. H. Husted to ABH, Oct. 21, 1915 ("chuck"); ABH to Husted, Nov. 6, 1915, folder: HU 1911–19, box: S&E 73, CI-HFP; Rorer to WC, Jan. 26, 1915, folder 6, box: S&E 3, CI-HFP; WC to ABH, Aug. 17, 1915, HMN 16, CI. On the "ladies," see Rorer to WC, Jan. 23, 1915, folder 10, box: S&E 3, CI-HFP. For Rorer's visit, see AAH to WCT, Feb. 10, 1915, folder 18, box: S&E 3, CI-HFP. On her continuation, see "Pyrex Conference, Corning, N.Y.," Dec. 29–30, 1915, folder 6, box: S&E 3, CI-HFP. For serving baskets, see Rochester Stamping Company, "A Novelty in Casseroles," advertisement in *HA* 91 (June 19, 1913): 37.

21. Mack, "Informal Notes"; WCT-AAA letters, Dec. 5 ("sanitary"; "variety"), 8 ("laboratory") 1914, Jan. 4, 9, Feb. 10, 1915, folder 18, box: S&E 3, CI-HFP.

22. WCT to AAA, Aug. 20 ("quality"), Nov. 14, 1915, March 5, 1916, folder 18, box: S&E 3, CI-HFP; WC to AAA, Aug. 17, 1915 ("buyer"), folder 14, box: S&E 2, CI-HFP; WC to ABH, Aug. 17, 1915; WC, "Report of Sales Department for Week Ending Sept. 2, 1916," folder: Management Committee meetings, 1914–20, box G6, CI-VF.

23. CW to ABH, July 22, 1916 (Armstrong), folder: Baking ware, box P1, CI-VF; CGW, "Bake in Glass," advertisement in *GH* (Oct. 1915); CGW, "Looking Right Through," advertisement in *National Geographic* (Sept. 1916); CGW, "A New Material," advertisement in *GH* (May 1916), clippings, CI-WF; "Mrs. Catherine Huber Weickgenant," clipping, obituary, [1934], folder: Baking ware, box P1, CI-VF.

24. OWH, "B.W." handwritten notes, n.d.; WC to ABH, July 12, Aug. 17, 1915, folder: Baking ware, box P1, CI-VF; "Chicago Notes: Behind the Counter," *JWTNB* 43 (April 16, 1917): 1–3.

25. "Odell Hardware Company's Windows," *HA* 96 (Sept. 30, 1915): 43–46; Walter C. Grace, "The Passing of the Scrambled Show Window," *HA* 98 (Aug. 17, 1916): 41–43; "Hardware Stock That Sparkles and Sells," *HA* 98 (Nov. 25, 1916): 68–70.

26. "Will T. Hedges Resigns," *HA* 96 (Dec. 16, 1915): 51; CGW, "When They See It, They Buy It!" advertisement in *HA* 98 (Aug. 3, 1916): 107; CGW, "Mr. Hardware Man," advertisement in *HA* 89 (Aug. 24, 1916): 95; "Memorandum on Conaphore Account," March 31, 1917, folder: CGW, 1917–25, box 5, Account histories, JWT; Stanley Resor, "Corning Conophore Campaign Underway," *JWTNB* 29 (Dec. 19, 1916): 2–3; "Conophore Portfolio," *JWTNB* 31 (Jan. 17, 1917): 5–6.

27. On the managerial shift, see folder: Organization, box G7, CI-VF; "Glass Works Laboratory," *Cullet* 4 (Dec. 1922): 16–30, CMG. On home economists, see JTL to ECS, "Pyrex Cooking Efficiency," Jan. 24, 1921, folder: Baking ware, box P1, CI-VF; Lilla

Cortwright Halchin, interview by author, tape recording, Mansfield, Pa., Oct. 7, 1992; Pyrex Sales Division, "How to Sell More: A Manual of Sales Points," [ca. 1918], back cover, folder: Consumer price lists prior to 1920, CI-CPD; WC to ABH, July 12, 1915. For the line, see "Pyrex Transparent Oven Dishes" (Corning, N.Y.: CGW, 1918), boxes: Glass, SI-W. Churchill consulted "Miss Cook" at Columbia University, probably Rosamond C. Cook, a home economist at Teachers College; see Chase and Schlink, *Your Money's Worth*, 84.

28. Judith Lavin, [interview with Otto W. Hilbert], Feb. 17, 1976, HMN 13, CI (Pyrex sales); V. V. Lawless, "Why Jobbers Are Slow to Take on New Lines of Merchandise," *ASF* 3 (May 7, 1924): 24, 80–82; JTL, "Proposed Experimental Kitchen Laboratory," Feb. 4, 1918; WCH to JTL, Feb. 7, 1918; J. Frazier Shaw to WC et al., [Response to "Proposed Experimental Kitchen Laboratory"], Feb. 12, 1918, all in CI-MF.

29. ADF to AAH, May 1, 1922, folder: Falck correspondence, CI-EF; GBH to AAH, Feb. 28, 1924, folder: Hollister correspondence, 1918–25, CI-EF; Minutes, Sept. 12, 1928, 7, Minutes of the Representatives' Meetings (hereafter, MRM), JWT.

30. ADF to AAH, July 29, 1919; VMD to ADF, Sept. 3, 1919; VMD, "License Agreement," 1st draft, Sept. 3, 1919; ADF to AAH et al., "Pyrex Dish Licenses," Sept. 10, 1919; GBH to ADF, "Suggestions Regarding Baking-Ware Licenses," Sept. 11, 1919, all in Falck correspondence, CI-EF. Corning licensed Fry in 1920, McKee in 1921; see contracts, box 16–2–3, CI-LF.

31. "Sales Turnover" and "Breakdown of Turnover in Different Divisions," [1927], folder: Manufacturing Committee—Misc., box G6; folder: Minutes of the Manufacturing Committee, 1914–29, box G6; ECS, "New Types of Baking Ware," Nov. 6, 1924, folder: Baking ware, box P1, all in CI-VF. On bottles, see R. F. Merrick, CGW, to William G. Palmer, JWT, Aug. 25, 1925, folder: CGW, Account histories, JWT.

32. JTL, "Domestic Science Laboratory," March 4, 1924, CI-MF ("in touch"); H. T. F. Husted, "The Effect of the War on Characters in Adland," *PI* 104 (July 4, 1918): 31–32; Data sheets, Household equipment survey, 1925, box 9, Papers of the New York Home Economics Extension Service, CU (quotations on consumers).

33. ADF to ABH, March 2 ("well-defined"), 15, 1923, folder: Falck correspondence, CI-EF; ADF to WCH, Sept. 12, 1924, and WCH to ADF, Sept. 15, 1924, folder: Baking ware, box P1; [GBH?], "Notes on Sales Organization and Policy," 1921, folder: Organization, box G7; ADF to C. S. Izant, April 4, 1921; ADF to Executive Committee, "Some Data of Interest," April 26, 1921, folder: Manufacturing Committee meetings, 1920–21, box G6; ADF to GBH and WCH, "Baking Ware Division—Organization," March 5, 1923, folder: Organizational memos, box G7; M. J. Lacey, "For Consideration of President Falck," Sept. 10, 1924; MJL to ADF, Sept. 10, 1924; ADF to MJL, Sept. 13, 1924, folder: Baking ware, box P1, all in CI-VF; "The Organization of the Pyrex Sales Force," *Cullet* 2 (Jan. 1919): 9–11, clipping in HMN 16, CI; "Pryex Men Hold Semi-Annual Con-

ference," *HA* 98 (July 20, 1916): 50. On Hedges, see William A. Bailey, London, to AAH, Sept. 19, 1919, Falck correspondence, CI-EF; Merrick to Palmer.

34. On Frederick, see *HA* 105–108 (1920–21): passim. "How Women Buy House-hold Goods," *HA* 106 (July 22, 1920): 76–77 ("trade"; "problem"); "Teach Women What Advertising Does," *PI* 111 (June 10, 1920): 177–82. For MacNaughton, see "The Women's Labor Problem," *HA* 106 (Aug. 5, 1920): 94, 128 (128, "Woman's Own"); "Moving the Stock via the Housewife," *HA* 108 (Oct. 27, 1921): 185–87. On Pyrex, see "Proving the Case for Glass Baking Ware," *HA* 108 (Dec. 22, 1921): 65–66.

35. "Minutes," March 1, 1923, folder: Manufacturing Committee Minutes (hereafter, MCM), 1923, box G5, CI-VF; A. C. Palm to James H. Bierer, Aug. 17, 1964, HMN 16, CI.

36. File: "James L. Peden," CI-BF; JLP to GBH, "Functional Study of Sales Organization," Nov. 1, 1924, 43 ("facts"), folder: Baking ware, box P1, CI-VF.

37. "Minutes," March 5, May 15, June 20, 1925, folder: MCM, 1925; April 7, Nov. 25, 1927, folder: MCM, 1926–28, box G6, CI-VF; "Pyrex Anniversary Window Display Awards," *HA* 116 (July 23, 1925): 35–38; "Company Secures Corning Glass Works Account," *JWTNL* 81 (May 21, 1925): 1 ("marketing"); "Window Display Contest Depends upon Dealer Enthusiasm for Success," *JWTNL* 94 (Aug. 20, 1925): 3; "J. Walter Thompson Will Advertise Steuben Art Glass: Secures Remainder of Corning Account," *JWTNL* 85 (June 18, 1925), 1; "Results of Pyrex Anniversary Window Display Contest," *JWTNL* 98 (Sept. 17, 1925): 4; Minutes, Oct. 18, 1927, 2, 6, MRM, JWT.

38. George D. Selden, "Corning Glass Works," Dec. 14, 1925, and "Account Histories: Corning Glass Works," Dec. 16, 1925, folder: CGW, 1917–25, box 5, Account histories; "JWT Accounts, 1918," Stanley B. Resor Papers, Corporate History Files, box 7, folder: Client lists, 1916–64; JLP to JWT, April 5, 1925; JWT to CGW, April 25, 1925, reel 87, all in JWT. From 1919 to 1925, Federal Advertising served as Corning's agency. Under Churchill, JWT handled the campaign for CGW's Conophore automobile headlights. See "Corning Conophore Campaign Underway" and "Conophore Portfolio." On Pyrex baking ware, see "New York Note," *JWTNB* 23 (Nov. 6, 1916): 5–6; "Correction to Bulletin 23," *JWTNB* 24 (Nov. 14, 1916): 23.

39. "Partial List of J. Walter Thompson Company Clients," [ca. 1920], Information Center Records, box 1, folder: Case studies, 1920s, JWT; Roy Durstine, "The Machine That Creates Desire," *NB* 16 (June 1928): 29–30, 70; "Mr. Palmer Addresses Production Club of Corning Glass Works," *JWTNL* 105 (Nov. 5, 1925): 1 ("sound").

40. On Cherington, see Marianne Keating to Sidney Bernstein, May 6, 1964, folder: Chapter Files 4—The Salad Years, box 9, Sidney Bernstein files, JWT; *Who Was Who in America*, 2, s.v. "Cherington, Paul Terry."

41. PTC, *People's Wants and How to Satisfy Them*, 173; PTC, "The Consumer Looks at Advertising" (paper presented to the Retail Distribution Conference, Boston, Sept. 1930), 3 ("fussy"); PTC, "Place of Market Surveys in Distribution Plans," draft of essay

for *JWTNB,* [1930], 6–7 ("power"; "measure"); PTC, "Distribution in a Buyers' Market" (paper presented to the New York Section of the American Statistical Association, April 14, 1930); PTC, "Some Principles Underlying Retail Specialty Store Advertising," May 13, 1931, in Paul T. Cherington Pamphlets, HBS; Harry Botsford, "Buying Habits in the Making," *NB* 11 (Aug. 1923): 32–34; Irving S. Paull, "Trade Ethics and Style Stealing," *NB* 14 (April 1926): 26–27; Arthur C. Mace, "The Egyptian Expedition, 1922–1923," pt. 2, *BMMA* 18 (Dec. 1922), 5–11.

42. On the two approaches, see William J. Reilly, "What Should Fact-Finding Cost?" *NB* 14 (Nov. 1926): 36 ("fact finding"); Harry Tipper, "Measuring Mass Buying Habits by Probing the Individual," *ASF* 4 (Dec. 17, 1924): 26, 52–53. For the man-in-the-street method, see Converse, *Survey Research,* 93.

43. On the ABCD system, see "Families with Incomes of under $2,000 Number 79% of the Total," *JWTNL* 129 (April 23, 1926): 105; PTC, "Business Management as Human Enterprise: The Human Attitude of Management as Manifested by Advertising," Feb. 5, 1931, folder: Speeches and articles, 1929–31, box 2, HBS-PTC; PTC, "Putting the American Market under the Microscope," *ASF* 3 (July 15, 1924): 15, 60–61; PTC, "Statistics in Market Studies," *Annals of the American Academy of Political and Social Science* 115 (1924): 130–35 ("intelligent"), cited in Converse, *Survey Research,* 93.

44. Charles Austin Bates, "The New Type of Advertising Man Contrasted with the Old Type," *PI* 98 (Feb. 8, 1917): 17–19; Daniel Starch, "Greatest Weakness in Advertising Is High Sounding Phrases and Puffery," *Associated Advertising* 11 (May 1920): 11, 72–73; Frank S. Spahr, "Facts! The Basis of Indisputable Advertising," *PI* 117 (Oct. 6, 1921): 85–88; PTC, "The Place of Advertising in Modern Marketing," *PI* 121 (Nov. 9, 1922): 130–32.

45. John B. Watson, "The Ideal Executive" (speech to Macy's graduating class of young executives, April 20, 1922), John B. Watson Papers, Manuscripts Division, Library of Congress, Washington, D.C., cited in Kerry W. Buckley, *Mechanical Man: John Broadus Watson and the Beginnings of Behaviorism* (New York: Guilford, 1989), 137; Patricia Johnston, *Real Fantasies: Edward Steichen's Advertising Photography* (Berkeley: University of California Press, 1997), 154–57, 230.

46. Frances Maule, "The 'Woman Appeal,'" *JWTNB* 105 (Jan. 1924), 2 ("facts"); Helen Georgette Butler, box 3; William P. Meigs Jr., box 18; Cara H. Vorce, box 27; Pauline Clark, box 4; William Palmer, box 20, employment applications, Personnel Files, JWT; "How Well Do You Know Your JWT'ers?" "Thumbnail Sketch No. 28: William Palmer," box 2, Thumbnail sketches, JWT.

47. Minutes, Oct. 18, 1927, MRM; JWT Research Dept., consumer surveys, June–Sept. 1925, reel 38, JWT.

48. Minutes, Oct. 18, 1927, 3; July 23, 1929, 2–3 (2, "cents"), MRM, JWT; Sears, Roebuck & Company, *Catalogue No. 150* (Spring/Summer 1925), 574, SIL; "Retail Prices, 1925 to 1954," HMN 13, CI. On refrigerator dishes, see "Minutes," March 27, 1924,

folder: MCM, 1925, box G6, CI-VF; JWT Research Dept. to Ruth Waldo, "Refrigerator Dishes, Office Investigation," Aug. 10, 1925, reel 38, JWT.

49. "Market Studies," *JWTNL* 184 (July 15, 1927): 330–31 (331, "Baking Habits of Housewives"); James D. Woolf, "The Problem of Creating Desire," *JWTNB* 85 (April 1922): 3 ("desires"); Ruth Waldo, "Combining Personal and Mail Investigations," *JWTNL* 109 (Dec. 3, 1925): 2; RW, "Long Questionnaires versus Short Ones: Experience on Pyrex," *JWTNL* 111 (Dec. 17, 1925): 3; "Use of Advertising Survey Doubles Pyrex Inquiries," *CI* 7 (Sept. 1926): 253; R. F. Merrick, "This Survey Led to Copy That Doubled Pyrex Inquiries," *PI* 149 (July 8, 1926): 25–28; Minutes, Oct. 18, 1927, 1–6; Feb. 7, 1928, 7–8; Sept. 12, 1928, 7; July 23, 1929, 1–4, MRM, JWT.

50. Maule, "'Woman Appeal'"; FM, "How to Get a Good 'Consumer Image,'" *JWTNB* 84 (March 1922): 9–11; Ruth Leigh, "Over-Feminizing the Feminine Appeal," *PI* 129 (Dec. 11, 1924): 99–102 (99, "dollar").

51. "Pyrex Profits by Price Appeal," *JWTNB* 191 (Nov. 1, 1927): 461. On JWT's realist imagery, see Johnston, *Real Fantasies,* chaps. 3, 4; Pyrex ads, *LHJ*, 1927.

52. *Leading Advertisers, Showing Advertising Investments of Advertisers Spending $20,000 or over in 32 Leading National Publications for the Calendar Year 1927* (Philadelphia: Curtis, 1928), 141.

53. Minutes, Oct. 18, 1927, 1–6; July 23, 1929, 1–4 (3, "same," "new"; 4, "thumbs"), MRM, JWT.

54. On the ribbon machine, see F. W. Preston, "New Lamps for Old," *GI* 12 (Aug. 1931): 159–65; "The Bubble That Didn't Burst," *Gaffer* 5 (Feb. 1947): 3–5, 17, CI; American Society of Mechanical Engineers, *The Corning Ribbon Machine for Incandescent Light Bulb* (n.p.: American Society of Mechanical Engineers, 1983). On Lacey, see Sullivan, "Day Books, 1924–1939," March 8, 1929, CI-VF.

55. Melvin T. Copeland, "Report on Corning Glass Works," June 5, 1929, 9, folder: Baking ware, box P1, CI-VF; Halchin interview. Copeland contributed to the BOBR's bulletin, *Operating Expenses in the Retail Hardware Stores in 1919* (Cambridge: Harvard University Press, 1920).

56. "Minutes," Feb. 26, 1925, folder: MCM, 1925, box G6, CI-VF; CGW, "To Wholesale Distributors," advertisement in *HA* 121 (April 5, 1928): 28, reel 4, JWT; E. H. Wellech, "Historical Sketch" ("interchangeable"), 1960, HMN 12, CI.

57. For CDL, see Copeland-LaFollette letters, May 24–July 7, 1924, folder: LaFollette-Longley, box 2, series 2: correspondence, HBS-MC; "C. D. LaFollette Dies, Retired CGW Official," *Corning (N.Y.) Leader,* Feb. 2, 1982; Robert L. Edwards, "Professional Crystal Gazers," [1954], clipping, folder: Baking ware, box P1, CI-VF. On Maltby, see Winifred Maltby Nixon, interview by author, Sept. 1, 1993, Hammondsport, N.Y.; Delores Ferrante and Charles Ferrante v. City Stores Company, Inc., and CGW, Trial Testimony of Lucy M. Maltby, Painted Post, N.Y., Dec. 7, 1979, 1–12 ("staple"; "mass"), CI-MF.

58. CDL to MTC, Nov. 20, 1931, folder: Baking ware, box P1, CI-VF; CDL, "Jobber

Letter—U.S.," Oct. 8, 1932, folder: Pyrex Ware policy; [CDL], "New Price and Promotion Plan for Pyrex Brand Ovenware," Oct. 1932, folder: Pyrex Ware policy—General, both in box 17–5–12, CI-CPD; JLP and CDL, "Entire Line Is Repriced: More Advertising; Sales Jump," *PI* 161 (Dec. 1, 1932): 3–5, 77–79.

59. Merle Higley, "When a Woman Searches for the Sales Angle," *PI* 129 (Oct. 2, 1924): 119–25 (119, "woman's"); "Home Economics in Business: How an Expert Home Economist Helps Industry to Function Effectively," *HE* 5 (Dec. 1927): 208–9, 220–24; Marjorie M. Heseltine, "Home Economics Women in Business," *HE* 6 (March 1928): 66, 80; Frances Weedman, "Home Economics and the Manufacturer: Home Economics Work with an Electrical Appliance Company," *HE* 6 (June 1928): 159, 169–70; "Home Economics and the Manufacturer: The Home Economics Department of the Kraft-Phenix Cheese Company," *HE* 6 (Aug. 1928): 223, 232–34; Helen Robertson, "Home Economics Women in Business: The Home Cookery Department of the Piggly-Wiggly Stores of St. Louis," *PHE* 7 (June 1929): 170–72; "Household Department of Curtis Publishing Company Establishes a New Test Kitchen in Philadelphia," *JWTNL* 13 (Feb. 7, 1924): 5; "Test Kitchen Is Established by Aluminum Goods Manufacturing Co.," *HA* 120 (Sept. 22, 1927): 97.

60. Lucy M. Maltby, interview by Corning staff member, transcript, Corning, N.Y., n.d., CI-MF; George S. Maltby interview.

61. C. J. Phillips and Mary J. Nordberg, "Ovenware and Fuel Efficiency," *JHE* 26 (Jan. 1934): 37–41.

62. LMM, "Duties of the Home Economics Department," Nov. 6, 1947, 16–19, CI-MF; George S. Maltby interview.

63. LMM to F. C. Stebbins, "No. 221 Round Cake Dish," April 3, 1953; LMM to T. H. Truslow, "Cake Dish Sales," April 8, 1957; CDL to Frederick Carder, "Round and Square Cake Dishes," Aug. 26, 1931, CI-MF; "Where Mrs. Homemaker Is Never Forgotten: Consumer Products Division's Proving Grounds for Corning Glassware," *Gaffer* 4 (Oct. 1946): 5–6, CI; Halchin interview; Jerry E. Wright, interview by author, tape recording, Corning, N.Y., Oct. 5, 1992.

64. JWT Research Dept., "Corning Glass Works, Facts on Price Reduction Policy," March 1932, reel 38, JWT; CGW, "Down Go Ovenware Prices," advertisement in *HA* 130 (Oct. 27, 1932): 19–22; CGW, "Pyrex Ovenware Down in Price Up in Profit," advertisement in *HA* 130 (Nov. 10, 1932): cover; CGW, "Reduced as Much as ½," advertisement in *HA* 130 (Dec. 22, 1932): 3; "Corning Launches Promotional Campaign after Years of Research," *CI* 20 (Jan. 1933): 38–40; William J. Reilly, "What Customers Can Tell You," *NB* 20 (Dec. 1932): 50 ("back").

65. JLP to Amory Houghton III and Glen W. Cole, "Proposed Plan for Ovenware Line," May 3, 1938, folder: Baking ware, box P1, CI-VF; Minutes, Feb. 7, 1928, 7–8, MRM, JWT.

66. "How Volume Is Being Maintained," *HR* 41 (Oct. 1931): 53–55; "Variety Depart-

ment," *HR* 41 (Oct. 1931): 96–97; Harold J. Asche, "How Honeywell Keeps 'Busy as a Bee,'" *HR* 41 (Dec. 1931): 72–74; Harold W. Bervig, "Best Sellers in Housewares," pts. 3, 4, 6, 7, *HR* 41 (Aug. 1931): 49–54; (Sept. 1931): 58–63; (Nov. 1931): 70–77; (Dec. 1931): 42–47. For the percentage, see FHR, "Chats on Pottery," *PH*, March 1, 1934.

67. On Oven Serve, see J. M. Wells to Mrs. Francis Christopher, Fort Worth, Tex., Feb. 13, 1934; JMW to P. G. Frantz, Feb. 16, 1934, both in box S-1677, HL-EC; JMW to PGF, Aug. 20, 1933, box S-1626, HL-EC. For JWT's 1934 surveys, see reel 38, JWT.

68. ECS, "Notes on the Baking Ware Situation," Aug. 14, 1934; OWH, "Baking Ware," Sept. 6, 1934; ECS, "Conference on Low-Cost Baking Ware," Sept. 13, 1934; OWH, "Baking Ware Mould Expense," Sept. 21, 1934; Cost Dept. to ECS, "Annual Production and Cost for Year 1934, Baking Ware Feeder," Jan. 14, 1935; OWH, two memoranda on "Baking Ware," Jan. 8, 16, 1935, folder: Baking ware; box P1, CI-VF.

69. "The Houghtons of Corning," *Fortune* 32 (July 1945): 129–32, 253–60.

70. On aluminosilicate glass, see WCT to John C. Hostetter, Aug. 5, 1931, folder: MacBeth correspondence, 1929–36, CI-EF. For Shaver, see *AMS*, 5th ed., 6th ed., s.v., "Shaver, Dr. William Walker." On Flameware, see H. R. Kiehl, "A Historical Summary of the Development of Tempered Top-of-Stove Ware," Memo M-6532-HK, June 1, 1965, folder: Top-of-Stove, box P8, CI-VF; Leon V. Quigley, "Information on Top-of-Stove Glass Ware, Jan. 14, 1936," HMN 13, CI; "The Battery Jar That Built a Business: The Story of Pyrex Ovenware and Flameware," *Gaffer* 4 (July 1946): 4, 18, CI; Lucy M. Maltby, "Glass Utensils," in *Handbook of American Glass Industries* (Brooklyn: Brooklyn Museum, 1936), 65–68; W. W. Shaver to G. P. Smith, "Some Corning Developments, 1924 to 1972—An Expanded Review," Nov. 24, 1972, file: W. W. Shaver, CI-BF.

71. "Corning Glass Works Acquires MacBeth-Evans Glass Company," *BACS* 15 (Dec. 1936): 445–46; "Confidential Memorandum for Mr. Lindsay Bradford," Aug. 12, 1936, files: Consolidation of CGW and MacBeth Evans; "Net Income after Federal Income Taxes," [Oct. 16, 1936], both in CI-LF; "Glass Merger," *The (Pittsburgh) Bulletin Index* (Nov. 19, 1936): 26, clipping, George D. MacBeth Papers, CI-EF.

72. CDL to Mr. Badt, Levenson Co., San Francisco, Aug. 15, 1938, HMN 13, CI; "Gaffer Goes to Pressware," *Gaffer* 5 (Jan. 1947): 11–13, CI; "Corning Glass Works: Build the Plant around the Process," *FIM* 97 (April 1937): B48–B51; CGW, "Now See What $1.00 Buys," advertisement in *BHG* 17 (April 1939): 73; CGW, "New Pyrex Sets at New Savings!" advertisement in *BHG* 18 (April 1940): 111.

Chapter 7: Easier Living?

1. Russel Wright and Mary Einstein Wright, *Mary and Russel Wright's Guide to Easier Living*, rev. ed. (New York: Simon & Schuster, 1954), 1–10; Russel Wright to Henry R. Luce, Aug. 20, 1946 ("snobbish"), box 2, SU-RW. For Wright's background, see Blaszczyk, "The Wright Way for Glass"; Hennessey, *Russel Wright*.

2. "Traditional or Modern: Russel Wright American Modern," advertisement in *HB* 93 (April 1951): 1; "Russel Wright American Modern," advertisement in *HB* 93 (Sept. 1951): 11; "Exciting New Shapes in Russel Wright American Modern for Living-Room Dining," *HB* 93 (Dec. 1951): 2; "Russel Wright American Modern," *HB* 94 (Jan. 1952): 5; "Russel Wright American Modern," *HB* 94 (Aug. 1952): 1.

3. "Interview with Freda Diamond Based on a Meeting with Regina Blaszczyk," typescript, 1995 ("better taste"), author's possession; "This Diamond Is a Girl's Best Friend," *Hartford Courier,* Aug. 9, 1964; Kay Elliott, "The Name Is Freda Diamond," (Toledo) *Blade,* sec. C, Jan. 30, 1966; "The Coordinators," *HFD,* Feb. 25, 1968; Freda Diamond, "Three Home Fashion Winners for 1960," *Curtain and Drapery Department Magazine* (Dec. 1959), clippings; United States Plywood Corporation, *Famous Designers Do-It-Yourself Plans* (New York: Unites States Plywood Corporation, 1955), all in SI-FD.

4. "Interview with Freda Diamond"("SHAPE"; "average"); Freda Diamond, conversation with author, New York, N.Y., March 20, 1992.

5. Regina Lee Blaszczyk, "'We Must Create Demand by Advertising': Carl U. Fauster, Libbey Glass, and Postwar America," *Glass Club Bulletin* 170 (1993): 3–8; Edwin W. Fuerst, "ABC of Modern American Glassware," June 14, 1940, CF; *Modern American Glass: The Renaissance of a Fine American Art* (Toledo: Libbey Glass Company, 1940); J. Walter Thompson, "Owens-Illinois Glass Company, 'Kitchen Predictions' Tabulation," May 1944; JWT, "Owens-Illinois Glass Company, Nationwide Survey among JWT Consumer Panel Families," May 1944, reel 712, JWT; Carl U. Fauster, interview by author, tape recording, Toledo, Ohio, May 12, 1988 ("pinks"); CUF, "Libbey Glass— 1947 December Sales Meeting: Advertising, Merchandising, and Publicity," CF; Owens-Illinois Glass Company, Libbey Division, advertisements in *HB* 88 (July 1946): 20; *HB* 88(Dec. 1946): 110; *HB* 93 (Oct. 1951): 217; *HB* 94 (Oct. 1952): 170; *HB* 97 (April 1955): 67; "Design for Everybody: Millions of U.S. Homes Profit by Her Good Taste," clipping from *Life,* ca. 1957, SI-FD.

6. Don Schreckengost, interview by author, tape recording, East Liverpool, Ohio, May 31, 1988 ("multi-media"); Doris Burrell, "Taste Essential to Expanding Economy," *CGJ* 159 (July 1956): 5 ("fine design").

7. Alice Hughes, "Italian Fashion Booster Receives 'Star of Italy,'" clipping, folder 3: Awards J-Z, box 9, SI-DS; "This Diamond Is a Girl's Best Friend," *Hartford Courant,* Aug. 9, 1965, clipping, SI-FD; Robert Pastor, *Congress and the Politics of U.S. Foreign Economic Policy, 1929–1976* (Berkeley: University of California Press, 1980), table 3; William C. Gates Jr., *The City of Hills and Kilns: Life and Work in East Liverpool, Ohio* (East Liverpool: East Liverpool Historical Society, 1984), chap. 9; Keller, interview; "Success Story: Melamine Dinnerware," *MP* 31 (June 1954): 166–67, 344–52; Lynn Scott, "Color Sells Plastics," *MP* 31 (July 1954): 73, 172; "How the New Material Won a Substantial Place in Tablewares ($60 Million at Retail) in Less than Ten Years," *CGJ* 159 (Nov.

1956): 26–27; "Plastic Tablewares Reach Consumers through Many Retail Channels," *CGJ* 159 (Nov. 1956): 28–29; "Royal Subsidiary Produces Melmac Ware," *CGJ* 161 (July 1957): 91; "Lenox Acquires Branchell Company," *CGJ* 162 (Feb. 1958): 53; "High Style for Plastic Ware," *CGJ* 164 (Jan. 1959): 28; Ann Kerr, *The Steubenville Saga* (Sidney, Ohio: Privately printed, 1979), 2; J. Raymond Price, "Impact of Imports and Exports on the Hand-Made Glassware Industry," [1961], folder: "Impact" paper, box 9, CMG-NAP-BGM; Trundle Consultants, "Final Report on the United States Hand Glass Industry" (Society for Glass Science and Practice, Clarksburg, W. Va., 1982, photocopy), v, CMG.

8. Russel Wright to Justin Tharaud, Nov. 15, 1948, folder: Contracts, Paden City; box 68, series 2; RW-JT letters, April 13, June 15, 1949, April 8, 1954; "Notes to Lee Epstein on Tharaud Discussion," Jan. 19, 1953; Francis Johnson–JT letters, Feb. 17, 1951, Jan. 22, 25, 1952, all in folder: Paden City, box 68, series 2; RW-Appleman contracts, letters, and memos, 1947–52, folders: Appleman Art Glass; Appleman Art Glass, 1947–48; Appleman Art Glass Factory Drawings, 1948; and Appleman Art Glass Tiles, box 6, series 2; Arthur Harshman to RW, Feb. 15, 1946 ("reshape"), folder: Century Craft—Glasses, box 13, series 2; Doris Coutant–RW letters, 1948, folder: Sterling glazes, box 9, all in SU-RW.

9. Carl Gutskey to RW, Oct. 14, 1949; "Agreement between Russel Wright and Imperial Glass Corporation," Nov. 28, 1949, folder: Imperial, box 65, series 2, SU-RW; "Imperial . . . Handcrafted Glassware by Russel Wright" and "Imperial . . . Flare, Pinch, Flame," leaflets, [1950], Imperial Glass Corporation, Photographic Notebooks, microfiche T417–17, CMG-TC (Imperial made Flare until 1956, Pinch until 1967); Eva Zeisel, "Notes from a Designer's Diary," *China, Glass, and Decorative Accessories* 73 (March 1954): 12, 37; Midhurst China Sales Corporation, "Hallcraft's New Century Shape by Eva Zeisel," advertisement in *CGJ* 160 (Feb. 1957): 33; "Potters Hold Forth at Annual Meeting," *HFD*, Dec. 16, 1949 ("Bait"), clipping, VB.

10. Keller interview; Ester Hamilton, "Salem China's Keller Has Proven Pottery Business Isn't Washed Up," *Youngstown Vindicator*, Aug. 18, 1957; Broomhall interview; Edwin M. Knowles China Company, "Knowles Utility Ware Serves Best," brochure, 1940, VB; "Style in Dishes: Dinnerware Makers Count on New Design to Reverse '48 Slump," *Wall Street Journal*, Jan. 13, 1950, clipping, Keller Scrapbook, SI-SC; "Big Response Won by Color Coordinated Promotion," *CGJ* (Oct. 1951): 32, clipping, Keller Scrapbook, SI-SC; Linder interview; J. Harrison Keller, conversations with author, Salem, Ohio, Jan. 23, 24, 1989; Sears, Roebuck & Company, *Catalogue No. 200* (Spring/Summer 1950): 698–99.

11. Keller conversation, Jan. 24, 1989; Keller and Linder interviews; Salem China Company, "The Sales Promotion That Sells Dinnerware by the Carload," circular, [1953], J. A. Armstrong, Sales Department bulletin, "Premium Highlights," May 27, 1953, all in box 2, Rudy Linder files, SI-SC. For bank giveaways, see folder: Achievement reports, 1963–65, box 3, Rudy Linder files, SI-SC.

12. Melvin Herbert Bernstein, *Art and Design at Alfred: A Chronicle of a Ceramics*

College (Philadelphia: Art Alliance Press, 1986), 107; "Shreckengost Appointed Art Director," *CI* 45 (Oct. 1945): 52; *Who's Who in American Art* 4 (1940–47): 5 (1953), s.v., "Shreckengost, Don"; Don Schreckengost interview ("look"); Shirley Howard, "Ohio Valley Dinnerware: American Styled for American Taste," *CGJ* 156 (April 1955): 26–28; "Report of the Decorating Committee," folder: Decorating Committee report, 1950, HL-ED; "Notes on Ware Inventory," Dec. 7, 1953, box: Inventory data, HL-EF; Lewis K. Urquhart, "Acres of Dishes," *FIM* 113 (Feb. 1955): 84–91.

13. Ebasco Services, "General Business Study for the Homer Laughlin China Company, Newell, West Virginia," Jan. 1960 (16, "pie"); Ebasco Services, "Comments on Homer Laughlin's Domestic Dinnerware Line," [Jan. 1960], both in HL-EF; Philip A. Bennett, *Trends and Prospects in the American Dinnerware Industry,* business information service bulletin prepared for the Department of Commerce (Washington, D.C.: Government Printing Office, 1949), 11; "Noritake Expands Line, Showroom," *CGJ* 157 (Sept. 1955): 44; "The Market for Plastic Dinnerware," *CGJ* 157 (July 1955): 86; "Selling Trends in American Tableware," *CGJ* 158 (April 1956): 25–33 (32, "life"); "The Non-Retail Picture," *CGJ* 152 (Jan. 1958): 32–36. In 1958, china, crockery, and glass accounted for 15 percent of premiums; housewares totaled 40 percent; toys and novelties, 31 percent; and cutlery, 21 percent.

14. HL-M; Broomhall interview ("loose"). Broomhall's designs appear in Edwin M. Knowles China Company, "Carribean Colors in Pastel Shades," "Deanna in Festive Colors," and "Knowles Utility Ware," n.d.; Continental Kilns, "American Beauty Rose," n.d.; Harker Pottery Company, "Harker Engraved Patterns," "New! Lemon Tree," "Harker's Heritage Paneled Ware," and "Shellridge Translucent China for Every Day Dining," n.d.; Sterling China Company, *Sterling Sixties* (East Liverpool: Sterling China Company, 1959); Steubenville Pottery Company, "Economy Plan to Introduce Verve Dinnerware," 1961, VB.

15. Broomhall, "Dinnerware," *Ceramic News* (March 1965): 12 ("public"); Betty Morgan, "Sees More Emphasis on Bold Modern Look," *HFD*, Dec. 17, 1962 ("bolder"); Ronald K. Mason, "Dinnerware," *Ceramic News* (March 1964): 17, 26; J. & H. International Corporation, "Lustrous Provincial Dinnerware by Sheffield," advertisement in *Pittsburgh Press,* April 12, 1969; Montgomery, Ward & Company, catalogue page, ca. 1964, clippings, VB; "Decorating Has Gone MOD," *CI* 96 (June 1971): 34–36; *CI* 97 (Nov. 1971): 26, 37–38; *CI* 98 (April 1972): 78–80.

16. Elaine Tyler May, *Homeward Bound: American Families in the Cold War Era* (New York: Basic Books, 1988), 6, 20. On Lenox, see John Tassie, interview by author, tape recording, Princeton, N.J., Sept. 24, 1992; Robert Sullivan, interview by author, tape recording, Princeton, N.J., Oct. 15, 1992; "Aristocrat of Tableware," *CI* 29 (July 1937): 42–48; "Lonely Lenox: An Idyl in Fine China," *Fortune* 19 (April 1939): 60–61, 120–26; Lenox Incorporated, *1963 Annual Report,* 4–5; Ellen Paul Denker, *Lenox China: Celebrating a Century of Quality, 1889–1989* (Trenton, N.J.: Lenox and New Jersey State

Museum, 1989), 70 ("license"). On registries, see "Dreams Come True," *CGJ* 159 (Sept. 1956): 36–37 (37, "clearing"); "Top Ten Patterns in Tablewares Registered by Brides," *CGJ* 163 (July 1958): 56–58; *CGJ* 165 (July 1959): 27–31. For more on Fostoria in the postwar years, see Blaszczyk, "Cinderella Stories," in *His and Hers,* 139–65.

17. A place setting consisted of all the china or glass used by one person in a formal meal, including dinner, salad, bread, and dessert plates, fruit bowl, and cup and saucer. Lee M. Chapman, "The Hope Chest: A Service for Brides," *GH* 130 (Jan. 1950): 26–27; James Mayabb, "The Hope Chest: A Service for Brides," *GH* 130 (Feb. 1950): 26–27; JM, "The Hope Chest: A Service for Brides," *GH* 130 (April 1950): 26–27; [Lucy Goldthwaite et al.], "At Home with Young American Brides," ca. 1953, 10–11 (showers), folder: American brides, *McCall's* magazine, box 1, series 4, SU-RW; "Bridal Registry Helps Promote Domestic Tableware," *CGJ* 158 (April 1956): 34–35.

18. On *Seventeen,* see David B. Dalzell, factory letter 217, Nov. 14, 1946, folder 10, box 5; on Bayse, see Bayse to Dalzell, Nov. 30, 1949, folder 3, box 2, in OHS-FOS. For home economics, see Merlin DuBois, factory letter 182, Dec. 9, 1944, folder 6; DuBois, factory letter 186, March 26, 1945, folder 7; DuBois, factory letter 204, March 27, 1946, folder 8; Dalzell, factory letter 233, March 5, 1947, folder 10; DuBois, factory letter 238, Nov. 22, 1947, folder 9; Helen Hunscher and Blanche Harvey, "Crystal Clear: A Teacher's Guide" (Moundsville, W. Va.: Fostoria Glass Company, 1947), 7 ("boy"), folder 9, all in box 5, OHS-FOS. On the bridal display, see Dalzell to Norval Slater, Chicago, [1949]; Letter A to Stores, "Fostoria Helps You Step up Bridal Sales," [1949], folder 11, box 2, OHS-FOS.

19. For Eavey, see J. A. Armstrong, Sales Dept. bulletins, "A Sales Promotion Plan for Super Markets That Really Clicks," May 27, 1953; JAA, "Highlights Woodhue Dinnerware Promotion," July 15, 1953, box 2, Rudy Linder files, SI-SC. On Federal, see "Resume of Meeting," June 21 ("volume"), July 28, Sept. 7, Oct. 28, 1960, all in folder 14: New Ideas Committee, box 8, OHS-FED.

20. T. J. Thompson, "Glass Goes to War," *Chemical Industries* (July 1942), clipping in CMG-SG; CGW, *Annual Report for the Year Ended December 31, 1945,* 3–6, CI; "1941," "1943 Organization," and "1946," all in folder: Organizational charts, box G-7, CI-VF; Robert L. Edwards, "Professional Crystal Gazers," offprint, 1954, folder: Baking ware, box P-1, CI-VF.

21. Esther Rhodes to Lucy M. Maltby, "Interviews Concerning Institutional Tableware Models," Jan. 10, 1944; Esther K. McMurrary to LMM, "Institutional Tableware," Feb. 7, 1944; LMM, "Tentative Suggestions on Sizes and Shapes of Institutional Tableware," Feb. 15, 1944; LMM to B. S. Pierson and James P. Trumpane, "Progress Report on Tableware," Feb. 15, 1944; LMM to Alfred Horn, March 15, 1944; LMM to Pierson et al., "Preliminary Survey on Nine-Inch Institutional Plate," July 1944; LMM to John B. Ward, "Institutional Tableware," July 13, 1944; William J. Belknap to Charles D. LaFollette and Pierson, Memorandum on food service conference, July 10, 1944; LMM to

Pierson, "Preliminary Interview on Industrial Feeding, War Food Administration, Washington, D.C.," Aug. 3, 1944; LMM, "Government Cafeterias in Washington," Aug. 8, 1944; LMM to Ward, Memorandum on institutional tableware specifications, Oct. 13, 1944; Rhodes to LMM, "Institutional Tableware," July 15, 1945, CI-MF.

22. LMM, "Suggested Place and Extent of Nutrition Education in the Public Schools in Grade I through XII" (Ph.D. diss., Syracuse University, 1945); Halchin interview; George S. Maltby, conversation with author, Corning, N.Y., Oct. 5, 1992 ("Smokestack"); Lucy E. N. Walbridge, interview by author, tape recording, Hammondsport, N.Y., Sept. 1, 1993; "Dealers Ask Return Visits of Home Economists to Promote Sale of Consumer Products Ware," *Gaffer* 3 (Jan. 1946): 8, CI; LMM, "Duties of the Home Economics Department," Nov. 6, 1947 ("key";"feeling"), CI-MF.

23. LMM, "Duties of the Home Economics Department" ("union"); "Dealers Ask Return Visits of Home Economists."

24. Corning Glass Works, "Report on Financial Statements," 1946 and 1947, folder: Corning reports, 1947, box 15–4–5, CI-FD; CGW, "Comments on Financial Statements, for the Year 1951," C-218, box 02584, CI-FD.

25. R. Lee Waterman, Lecture notes, folder: Stanford University, Feb. 19, 1965, box 13–3–8, CI-EF.

26. Corning Glass Works, "Now! Pyrex Ware in Color!" advertisement in *Saturday Evening Post* (Nov. 1945); "New! Pyrex Bowls in the Colors of Spring Flowers . . . Only $2.50," advertisement, source unknown, 1946, clippings, CI-WF; LMM to J. H. Bierer, "Work of the CGW Home Economics Department," Aug. 10, 1961, 9, CI-MF; Sears, Roebuck & Company, *Catalogue no. 150* (Spring/Summer 1925): 574; Hazel-Atlas Glass Company, Educational Department, *A Book of Recipes and Helpful Information on Canning* (Wheeling: Hazel-Atlas Glass Company, [1930s]), 64, SI-PC; Mabel J. Stegner, "These Make a Lot of Difference and They Keep Your Refrigerator Serving You Well," *BHG* 12 (July 1933): 21, 34–35; Anna Joyce Olson, "Fall Roundup for Better Kitchens," *BHG* 15 (Oct. 1936): 108–12; General Electric, "The Beautiful New Triple-Thrift Refrigerators," promotional leaflet, ca. 1939, SI-W.

27. LMM to John B. Ward, "Pryex Housewares-Design Requirements," Dec. 29, 1944, CI-MF.

28. Halchin interview; Halchin to author, Dec. 2, 1993; Edwards, "Professional Crystal Gazers," 9; "Something New Has Been Added," *Gaffer* 5 (Oct. 1947): 3–5, CI.

29. For Arthur A. Houghton Jr. at Steuben, see Blaszczyk, "Imagining Consumers," chap. 8. On the design department, see Arthur A. Houghton Jr., *Design Policy within Industry as a Responsibility of High-Level Management* (New York: Steuben Glass, 1951); Don Wallace, *Shaping America's Products* (New York: Reinhold, 1956), 56–64; Institute of Contemporary Art, "Curriculum: The Corning-Steuben Pilot Program for Design Development," June 25, 1948; *The Corning-Steuben Design Development Program, First Interim Report* (Boston: Institute of Contemporary Art, 1949); J. B. Plaut to

J. B. Ward and J. M. Gates, "Report on Participation of the ICA in the Corning-Steuben Design Development Program," Oct. 15, 1948, all in folder: Corning-Steuben Design Dept., box 6–4–2, CI-SP; "1953 Organization," folder: Organizational charts, box G-7, CI-VF.

30. Jerry E. Wright, letter to author, Feb. 8, 1994; J. R. Blizard, "Product Development, Consumer Products," Jan. 20, 27, Feb. 17, 22, March 28, April 6, May 19, 1949, folder: Consumer products, box 7–3–5, CI-ENG; LMM to John Carter, "Your Suggestions Regarding a Five-Year Plan, and How the Home Economics Group Can Cooperate," Dec. 18, 1953; LMM to JC, "Suggestions Regarding Future Planning," Dec. 30, 1953; LMM to Joseph S. Knapp, "Casserole Set," Sept. 14, 1953; LMM to T. H. Truslow, "Functional Qualities of New Pyrex Housewares Lines," May 10, 1949 ("annoyance"); LMM to F. C. Stebbins, "Comments on Sketches of Proposed Flameware Designs" ("pour"), Dec. 17, 1951, all in CI-MF; Corning Glass Works, *Pyrex Prize Recipes* (New York: Greystone Press, 1953), SI-PC.

31. "Cooks Tour on Television: CGW's Traveling Home Economists Guest on Video Programs," *Gaffer* 8 (Feb. 1950): 8–9, 22, CI; "They Spread the Pyrex Ware Story," offprint from *Corning Glassmaker* (June-July 1953), CI; LMM to J. H. Bierer, "Work of Corning Home Economics Field Representatives and Test Kitchen," April 8, 1955, CI-MF; "If You Like to Travel, Try This Job," *Casper Morning Star*, Sept. 23, 1959; Jannita Luthi, Kansas City, Mo., to Ann Mikell, March 17, 1959; Margaret K. McDonald, Fort Worth, Tex., to AM, Feb. 9, 1954; Mary Carter to AM, Feb. 26, 1954; Thelma R. Lison, Gardner Advertising Company, St. Louis, to LMM, Feb. 7, 1955; "Foods Go from Freezer Directly into the Oven," *Wichita Beacon*, Jan. 31, 1954 ("mankind"), in CI-AMF.

32. CGW, "Comments on Financial Statements for the Year 1955," exhibit 12, box 02584, CI-FD; RLW, lecture notes, folder: American Management Association, "Fundamentals of Marketing for Non-Marketing Executives," New York City, Oct. 13, 1960, box 8–4–3, CI-EF; Frank Fenno, interview by author, tape recording, Corning, N.Y., July 4, 1994 ("bullies"); "Waterman President, Houghton Board Chief in Major CGW Officer Changes," *Corning (N.Y.) Leader*, April 14, 1964, file: Waterman, CI-BF.

33. R. S. Latham to John M. Gates, "Product and Market Planning," folder: Buck Hill Falls meeting, box 2573, CI-FD; "R. Lee Waterman," July 10, 1959, folder: Junior Woman's Club, box 8–4–3, CI-EF; "R. L. Waterman Dies at 71," *Leader* (Corning, N.Y.), April 19, 1978; "Services Held for Waterman, Ex-Head of Corning Glass," *HFD*, April 24, 1978, clippings, file: R. Lee Waterman, CI-BF. On "marketing's job," see RLW, "Marketing Strategy—New Product Introduction" (speech made at Conference on Guidelines for Marketing Policy: A Seminar for Management, sponsored by the Container Corporation of America, Arlington, Tex., May 24, 1960), box 8–4–3, CI-EF.

34. RLW, "Research and You" (speech given at the Pacific Coast Wholesale Hardware Conference, Pebble Beach, Calif., Feb. 12, 1959); RLW, "Discount Houses and Discount Merchandising" (speech given to Pacific Coast Wholesale Hardware Confer-

ence, Pebble Beach, Calif., Feb. 17, 1961); RLW, "Consumer Durable Goods" (speech given at the American Management Association's Annual Sales Forecasting Forum, New York City, Oct. 2–4, 1961); RLW, "Marketing Strategy—New Product Introduction" ("fail"), all in box 8–4–3, CI-EF; Daniel Horowitz, *Vance Packard and American Social Criticism* (Chapel Hill: University of North Carolina Press, 1994).

35. LMM to T. H. Truslow, "Proposed New Pyrex Saucepans and Skillet," Jan. 3, 1956, and LMM to RLW, "Comments on Consumer Products Line Memorandum of Oct. 7, 1955," April 11, 1957, CI-MF; Fenno interview ("shake"); S. Donald Stookey, *Journey to the Center of the Crystal Ball* (Columbus, Ohio: American Ceramic Society, 1985); M. G. Britton, "Case History of the Development of Pyroceram Brand Glass-Ceramics," Research report L-481, Research & Development Laboratory, Technical Staffs Division, Feb. 1, 1966, and G. P. Smith, "A History of a Research Project: Glass-Ceramics at Corning Glass Works," Research report L-1701, Research & Development Laboratory, Technical Staffs Division, June 20, 1975, both in HMN 3, CI; William Armistead, interview by author, tape recording, Corning, N.Y., July 1994; RLW, Lecture outline, folder: American Management Association, "Fundamentals of Marketing for Non-Marketing Executives," New York City, Oct. 13, 1960, box 8–4–3, CI-EF.

36. RLW, "Designing for [the] American Housewife" (speech given to Junior Woman's Club, Jan. 1, 1960), box 8–4–3, CI-EF; LMM to T. H. Truslow and RLW, Oct. 7, 1955 ("cooking"); Truslow, "Consumer Products Division—New Products Program," Nov. 2, 1955; LMM to Bierer, "Work of the CGW Home Economics Department, ("round-square"), all in CI-MF; June Packard, interview by author, tape recording, Corning, N.Y., Oct. 8, 1992; Jerry E. Wright, letters to author, Feb. 8, April 4, 1994; CGW, "New Beauty, New Convenience When You Cook and Serve with New Corning Ware," promotional leaflet, [1958], folder: CGW annual report, 1957, box 12–5–1, CI-SP. At busy times in the Glass Center, skillful interviewers could record 600 opinions daily, compiling sufficient data about models within a week. See Edwards, "Professional Crystal Gazers," 8–90; Wright interview, 1992; Jerry E. Wright, interview by author, tape recording, Corning, N.Y., July 8, 1994; RLW, lecture notes from Stanford; RLW, "Stanford Marketing Club, Suggested Outline of Remarks," folder: Stanford University, Feb. 19, 1965, box 13–3–8, CI-EF; Fenno interview; John Gilkes, "'Keen Competition' Upgrades Dinnerware Design," *CGJ* 156 (Jan. 1955): 57.

37. RLW, "Some Observations on Marketing in Today's World" (paper presented to Sales Meeting, Dow-Corning Corporation, Midland, Mich., July 7, 1959); RLW, "Stanford Marketing Club" ("person"); RLW, Address to the New York Daily Newspaper Association, May 18, 1959; RLW, Outline for AMA speech at Conference on Fundamentals of Marketing for Non-Marketing Executives, New York, Oct. 13, 1960, box 8–4–3, CI-EF.

38. RLW, "New Dimensions" (speech given at the Housewares Show, July 1959) ("Moon"), box 8–4–3, CI-EF; CGW, advertising circular for "New Corning Ware," 1959

("rocketing"); CGW, miscellaneous circulars for Corning Ware, 1959, all in Corning Ware Advertising Collection, 1950s, CI; Fenno interview.

39. LMM to Bierer, "Work of the CGW Home Economics Department"; Fenno interview; Wright interview, 1992 ("authenticity").

40. [Sales Summary, 1960–1961], box 8–4–3, CI-EF; RLW, Outline of Stanford remarks; Freda Diamond, "Today's Consumer . . . She's More Style-Conscious," *Tufted Textile Manufacturers Association Directory* (1956): 112–18; *HFD*, July 15, 1965 ("boil"), clippings, SI-FD; Fenno interview.

41. "Passion for Possession," *CGJ* 167 (July 1960): 167 ("women").

42. "Visits, Week Ending November 6, 1954" ("men"; "Cleveland"), folder: Salesgirls' reports, box 10–4–7; "Visits, Week Ending April 9, 1955" ("busy"), folder: Salesgirls' reports, 1955, box 8–4–2, CI-SP.

Conclusion

1. R. Lee Waterman, "Tactics for Corning Glass Works," April 25, 1968, folder: Management conference, box: C752—Corning 6, APS-EUC.

ESSAY ON SOURCES

Primary Sources

Historians often use cultural evidence, from trade cards to advice books and women's magazines, as they study the demand side of consumer society. *Imagining Consumers* takes a less-traveled path. Covering more than a century, it compares several leading companies in three industries to consider how home furnishings producers learned about their audiences. Using firms and their products as the principle units of analysis, this book draws heavily on supply-side evidence, such as trade journals, industry publications, business records, and managerial oral histories.

The ideal starting point for understanding any aspect of the home furnishings industries is a thorough review of the trade journals. Although historians of business and technology have long depended on these periodicals (which appeared during the late nineteenth century with the exponential growth of American industry), few scholars of culture and consumption use them. From the mid-1870s through the 1960s, several major weeklies published in New York City and Pittsburgh—*Crockery and Glass Journal; China, Glass and Lamps; American Pottery and Glassware Reporter; Pottery, Glass and Brass Salesman;* and *China, Glass and Decorative Accessories*—provided distributors with updates on fashion, styles, technology, new entrants, failures, and job moves. Columnists in Boston, Chicago, Cincinnati, East Liverpool, New York City, Philadelphia, and Pittsburgh kept tabs on local firms. Between 1875 and 1895, the unidentified china decorator who worked as the Trenton correspondent for the *Crockery and Glass Journal* contributed notes on current events, historical sketches, and trade biographies. His detailed column highlighted the careers of Jesse Dean and other entrepreneurs for whom no business records survive. By the twentieth century, the focus of these journals shifted to sales strategies, display techniques, and fashion reports. The *Industrial Arts Index* does not list these periodicals, and there is no substitute for diligently reviewing each volume, page by page.

Another group of publications—industry-oriented weeklies, trade association proceedings, and professional journals—illuminate economic concerns and technical change. *Ceramic Industry, Glass Industry, Keramic Tile Journal*, and *Tiles and Tile Work* catered to managerial audiences preoccupied with competition, trade policy, and technology. Published annually from 1875 through the 1960s, the *Proceedings of the United States Potters' Association* feature committee summaries on the tariff, labor relations, shipping rates, raw materials, and machinery. Beginning in 1889, the *Proceedings* included the Art & Design Committee's reports, which outline concerns with decorating costs, labor shortages, consumer taste, and the fashion system. The *Transactions of the American Ceramic Society*, succeeded by the *Journal of the American Ceramic Society* and the *Bulletin of the American Ceramic Society* between 1918 and 1922, focuses on engineering matters such as the evolution of tunnel kilns. Following the Design Division's founding in 1920, the *Journal* often published articles by Frederick Hurten Rhead, Léon Victor Solon, Vincent Broomhall, and other art directors. Eugene Ferguson wrote a thoughtful introduction to such publications: "Technical Journals and the History of Technology," in *In Context: History and the History of Technology: Essays in Honor of Melvin Kranzberg*, edited by Stephen Cutcliffe and Robert C. Post (Bethlehem, Pa.: Lehigh University Press, 1989).

Government documents complemented this extensive run of periodicals. For general statistical references, one publication proved indispensable: U.S. Bureau of the Census, *Historical Statistics of the United States: Colonial Times to the 1970*, 2 vols. (Washington, D.C.: Government Printing Office, 1975). The unpublished federal manufacturing censuses for Massachusetts, New Jersey, New York, Ohio, and Pennsylvania provide firm-specific information for the nineteenth century. Charged with monitoring trade, the Bureau of Foreign and Domestic Commerce at the U.S. Department of Commerce produced comprehensive surveys that document manufacturing during prosperity and decline, including *The Pottery Industry: Report on the Cost of Production in the Earthenware and China Industries of the United States, England, Germany, and Austria*, Miscellaneous Series 21 (Washington, D.C.: Government Printing Office, 1913); *The Glass Industry: Report on the Cost of Production of Glass in the*

United States, Miscellaneous Series 60 (Washington, D.C.: Government Printing Office, 1917); and Philip A. Bennett, *Trends and Prospects in the American Dinnerware Industry,* Business Information Service Bulletin (Washington, D.C.: Government Printing Office, 1949). Similarly, special reports by the U.S. Department of Interior's Census Office are vital for tracing economic change: see Joseph D. Weeks's essay in *Report on the Manufactures of the United States at the Tenth Census (June 1, 1880),* vol. 2 (Washington, D.C.: Government Printing Office, 1886); and Shirley P. Austin's essay in *Census Reports,* vol. 9: *Twelfth Census of the United States, Taken in the Year 1900, Manufactures,* pt. 3, *Special Reports on Selected Industries* (Washington, D.C.: Government Printing Office, 1902). Finally, the voices of manufacturers and retailers resound loudly in the tariff hearings before the U.S. Congress; see, for example, House Committee on Ways and Means, *Duties on China, Porcelain and Stoneware,* 47th Cong., 1st sess., 1882; and Senate Committee on Finance, *Tariff Act of 1921,* vol. 2, *Schedule 2: Earths, Earthenware, and Glassware,* 67th Cong., 2d sess., 1921–22.

Corporate archives were the lifeblood of this study. In many instances, business records function as valuable correctives to published sources. Serving New York–based distributors, weeklies like the *Crockery and Glass Journal* present a skewed picture of the china and glass business, especially since the crockery wars bifurcated the trade into pro-European and pro-American factions. After 1900, editors rarely conceded that most consumers acquired their pottery and glassware as premiums or from five-and-tens, and they published articles on the imported goods appreciated by retail buyers in department stores and china shops. In contrast, business archives from firms in the industrial heartland shed light on mass-market products.

The corporate archives of the Homer Laughlin China Company are a dream come true for the historian. The collection's centerpiece is a complete run of executive correspondence, consisting of millions of incoming and outgoing letters, relating to three generations of general managers: founder Homer Laughlin, W. Edwin Wells, and Joseph M. Wells. Dating from the 1880s through the 1950s, exchanges with major customers—mass retailers such as F. W. Woolworth & Company, American Cereal Company, S. H. Kress & Company, Sears, Roebuck & Company, and Kirkman & Sons—speak of the crockery buyer's role in design and development. Similarly, communications with the factory salesman James C. Shaw, the sales chief George Washington Clarke, and the decalcomania supplier Rudolph Gaertner demonstrate how these men figured into design and innovation. Sales and financial records dating back to 1915 put the customers in context.

Homer Laughlin's departmental records are another remarkable source. In the art department, the papers of Frederick Hurten Rhead include his reference books, files on competitors, and logbook. This desktop diary, which contains comprehensive notes on development projects, gives insight into the operations of a factory art department. Rhead's published oeuvre, including his "Chats on Pottery" column that appeared in the union newspaper, *Potters' Herald* (East Liverpool), from 1931 to 1935, fills gaps in these office files. In the laboratory and engineering departments, a wide array of sources, including notebooks, blueprints, and interoffice reports, reveal how materials science and technology affected design practice. This wealth of sources allowed me to extend the stylistic analysis in Sharon Dale's fine artistic biography, *Frederick Hurten Rhead: An English Potter in America* (Erie, Pa.: Erie Art Museum, 1986), and to write a cultural history of design practice.

At the Kohler Company, the Communications Department houses the firm's corporate archives and the family papers. The files of half brothers Walter J. and Herbert V. Kohler, including their correspondence, shed light on the decisions of top managers between the 1910s and 1930s and complement the stories told in the official organ, *Kohler of Kohler News.* The *News,* the Marie Christian Kohler papers, and an archival series on town development chronicle the creation of Kohler Village. Using this evidence, I built on Janet Anne Hutchison's research ("American Housing, Gender, and the Better Homes Movement, 1922–1935" [Ph.D. diss., University of Delaware, 1989]; and "The Cure for Domestic Neglect: Better Homes in America," in *Perspectives in Vernacular Architecture,* vol. 2, edited by Camille Wells [Columbia: University of Missouri Press, 1986]) to draw parallels between Walter Kohler's welfare capitalism and his business tactics. The files of the advertising executive L. L. Smith describe the Kohler Electric Sink. Written in 1963 at the University of Wisconsin, Trudi Jennes Eblen's master's thesis, "A History of the Kohler Company of Kohler, Wisconsin, 1871–1914," is a helpful guide to the firm's early years, for which few records exist.

Corning Incorporated's Department of Archives and Records Management cares for the firm's records and the Houghton family papers. Located on the Chemung River, the city of Corning has suffered several devastating floods, the most recent in 1972, with Hurricane Agnes. Following that disaster, the company established an archival program, with a mandate to retrieve and preserve records and to make them available to scholars. No professional historian had taken advantage of Corning's resources when I started my research on the company in January 1990. The business analyst Joseph P. Morone drew on published sources and oral histories for *Winning in High-Tech Markets: The Role of General Management* (Boston: Harvard Business School Press, 1993). The kitchenware buffs Susan Tobier Rogove and Marcia Buan Steinhauer used archival holdings of photographs, public relations releases, internal histories, and sales catalogues to write *Pyrex by Corning: A Collector's Guide* (Marietta, Ohio: Antique Publications, 1993). Earl Lifshey's *The Housewares Story: A History of the American Housewares Industry* (Chicago: National Housewares Manufacturers Association, 1973) recounts the official story as detailed in the trade press. Most press releases and publications maintain that Jessie and Becky Littleton invented Pyrex during a "eureka moment" in their kitchen. To debunk this myth and retell the history of Pyrex and Corning Ware as marketing ventures, I spent several months in the archives, poring over the family papers and the executive, home economics, and consumer products files.

Even small collections of business records yielded valuable information about producer-audience relations. The Archives Center at NMAH, SI, contain records from the Salem China Company. At Duke University, the J. Walter Thompson archives hold that advertising agency's records, which describe the Corning and Libbey accounts. Many of the letters from Josiah Wedgwood to his partner Thomas Bentley are housed in repositories in Staffordshire, England; they are also accessible in two publications: Ann Finer and George Savage, eds., *The Selected Letters of Josiah Wedgwood* (New York: Born and Hawes, 1965); and Katherine Euphemia Farrier, ed., *Letters of Josiah Wedgwood*, 3 vols. (Manchester: E. J. Morten in association with the Trustees of the Wedgwood Museum, 1973). At the Corning Museum of Glass, the 1880s records of T. G. Hawkes & Company contain letters from major retailers in Boston, New York, and Philadelphia. The Thomas Gaffield Collection at MIT also has correspondence for this decade, in which William Leighton Jr., the general manager at Hobbs, Brockunier & Company in Wheeling, West Virginia, outlines trade conditions for his Boston colleague. The 1890s–1900s letters to the Quaker City mold maker Charles Yockel are scattered throughout the Northeast: Corning Museum of Glass, Historical Society of Pennsylvania in Philadelphia, Museum of American Glass in Millville, New Jersey, and Winterthur Museum in Delaware. Smaller correspondence collections include those of the Anchor Pottery Company at the

New Jersey State Museum in Trenton, Arcadia Cut Glass Company at Winterthur, and Mercer Pottery Company at the NMAH Archives Center. At the Ohio Historical Society, the Federal Glass Company Records contain the minutes of the New Products Committee, which detail managerial decisions for the 1960s and 1970s. Several major archives, such as the United States Glass Company Records (Bowling Green State University, Bowling Green, Ohio), the Taylor, Smith & Taylor Collection (ELMC), and the Gillinder Records (SI), consist primarily of account books that identify customers but tell little about the negotiations at the demand-supply nexus.

Although most repositories with business records welcomed me as a professional researcher, some organizations were protective of their resources or constrained by internal and external factors. The public relations guru at one firm did not believe in collegial reciprocity, refusing my request to visit the archives even though as a Smithsonian staffer I had collaborated with the company on reproductions. Some collectors' groups devise barriers to scare researchers away. One glass club, whose members secretly removed a firm's records from its West Virginia factory during bankruptcy proceedings in the 1980s, would grant me access to the purloined papers only if I agreed to work in a locked garage and pay a dollar per page for photocopying. Even promising collections in public repositories, such as William Leighton's letters at the Metropolitan Museum of Art and the extensive Kohler Family Papers at the State Historical Society of Wisconsin, are off limits because of staff shortages and donors' restrictions.

Finally, this project relied on approximately thirty oral histories that I recorded between 1988 and 1994. During these interviews, managers, salesmen, engineers, home economists, mold makers, scientists, and designers spoke about their careers, which collectively spanned the years between the 1930s and the mid-1990s. In the Ohio River valley, Marcus Aaron II, Vincent Broomhall, David Conley, Frank Fenton, Willis G. Gaston, Robert Hill, J. Harrison Keller, Rudy Linder, Carl C. Mooney, Lynn Russi, Donald Schreckengost, Viktor Schreckengost, Joseph M. Wells Jr., and Joseph M. Wells III talked about their experiences at regional potteries and glassworks. Those with personal papers generously dug them out of storage for my review. Through interviews and letters, Charles E. Doll Jr., who succeeded his father as manager of Kresge's Mount Clemens Pottery Company in Michigan, told the story of this important dime store factory. In upstate New York, William Armistead, Frank Fenno, Paul V. Gardner, Lilla Cortright Halchin, John Hoxie, Margaret Lapp, George S. Maltby, Helen Martin, Winifred Maltby Nixon, June Packard, Guy Stong, Lucy E. N. Walbridge, and Jerry E. Wright described their jobs or those of relatives at Corning. Carl U. Fauster and Freda Diamond spoke about Libbey's postwar strategies. The tapes, transcripts, and notes of these oral histories remain in my possession; I will eventually donate them to a research library.

Secondary Sources

In developing my approach to the study of business, design, and consumer society, I drew on the work of scholars in several historical disciplines, from social history to design theory. Although I perceived the need for an analysis of manufacturers, retailers, and consumerism during the 1980s, my ideas have benefited from new work by scholars probing similar issues.

The cultural historian Lawrence W. Levine's exciting essay, "The Folklore of Industrial Society: Popular Culture and Its Audiences," *American Historical Review* (1992), emphasizes the need to consider producer-audience relations as a means for deepening our understanding of cultural production. Writing from sociology, Richard Butsch ("The Commercialization of Leisure: A Case Study of the Relationship between Production and Reproduction in the Model Airplane Hobby," *Critical Communications Review*, vol. 3: *Popular Culture and Media Events,* edited by Vincent Mosco and Janet Wasko [Norward, N.J.: Ablex, 1985]; and "Home Video and Corporate Plans: Capital's Limited Power to Manipulate Leisure," in Butsch's edited volume, *For Fun and Profit: The Transformation of Leisure into Consumption* [Philadelphia: Temple University Press, 1990]) effectively demonstrates consumers' input into product design and their resistance to media manipulation

Joy Parr's research on women and appliances offers similar insights ("What Makes Washday Less Blue? Gender, Nation, and Technology Choice in Postwar Canada," *Technology and Culture* 38 [1997]; and "Shopping for a Good Stove: A Parable about Gender, Design, and the Market," in *His and Hers: Gender, Consumption, and Technology*, edited by Roger Horowitz and Arwen Mohun [Charlottesville: University Press of Virginia, 1998]). In *Hope in a Jar: The Making of America's Beauty Culture* (New York: Metropolitan Books, Henry Holt, 1998), Kathy Peiss describes the not-so-manipulative relationship between cosmetics firms and women customers. Leora Auslander offers a thoughtful analysis of household fashions and national identity in *Taste and Power: Furnishing Modern France* (Berkeley: University of California Press, 1996). Using this scholarship as a springboard, *Imagining Consumers* steps inside the firms that made

purview of scholars concerned with consumer culture. This approach suffers from a checkered history, beginning with Thorstein Veblen's biting critique of the Gilded Age's "conspicuous consumption" in *The Theory of the Leisure Class: An Economic Study of Institutions* (New York: New American Library, 1953; originally published in 1899). Veblen's assessment cast a long shadow over mid-twentieth-century liberals, who continued to eye American business with suspicion and contempt. During the 1950s, writers as different as journalist Vance Packard (*The Hidden Persuaders* [New York: D. McKay, 1957]) and economist John Kenneth Galbraith (*The Affluent Society* [Boston: Houghton Mifflin, 1958]) castigated American corporations for manipulating consumer desire. In the 1970s, the newly translated writings of Italian Marxist Antonio Gramsci added new fuel to this critical tradition. Gramsci's theory of hegemony, which maintains that empowered groups in capitalist societies use cultural symbols as tools of coercion, influenced scholars of American advertising and consumption, starting with Stuart Ewen (*Captains of Consciousness: Advertising and the Social Roots of the Consumer Culture* [New York: McGraw-Hill, 1976]). For decades, the hegemony concept shaped widely read works on consumerism written from the perspectives of intellectual history (Richard Wightman Fox and T. J. Jackson Lears, *The Culture of Consumption: Critical Essays in American History, 1880–1980* [New York: Pantheon, 1983]), material culture (Simon J. Bronner, *Consuming Visions: Accumulation and Display of Goods in America, 1880–1920* [New York: Norton, 1989]), and American studies (William Leach, *Land of Desire: Merchants, Power, and the Rise of a New American Culture* [New York: Pantheon, 1993]). Lears popularized Gramsci's work in "The Concept of Cultural Hegemony: Problems and Possibilities," *American Historical Review* 90 (1985).

Imagining Consumers navigates around the hegemonic school to offer a supply-side perspective. In doing so, it reconnects business history to mainstream historical inquiry. Several scholars—Louis Galambos ("What Makes Us Think We Can Put Business Back into American History?" *Business and Economic History,* 2d ser. 20 [1991]), Kenneth Lipartito ("Culture and the Practice of Business History," *Business and Economic History,* 2d ser. 24 [1995]), and David B. Sicilia ("Cochran's Legacy: A Cultural Path Not Taken," *Business and Economic History,* 2d ser. 24 [1995])—address the need for such connections. Focused on big business, the works of Alfred D. Chandler Jr. (*The Visible Hand: The Managerial Revolution in American Business* [Cambridge: Harvard University Press, 1977]), Susan Strasser (*Satisfaction Guaranteed: The Making of the American*

Mass Market [New York: Pantheon, 1989]), and Richard Tedlow (*New and Improved: The Story of Mass Marketing in America* [New York: Basic Books, 1990]) offer powerful explanations of the rise of American capitalism. Yet, by focusing on firms in the core economy, this work for the most part overlooks the producers and retailers who made and sold the goods that consumers used to construct personal identity.

To explore the absence of pottery, glass, furniture, and other home furnishings firms from the compelling Chandlerian narrative, I turned to historians who, in Philip B. Scranton's phrase, study the "other side of industrialization." In European economic history, I used a rich body of literature on craft and batch production, including Maxine Berg, *The Age of Manufactures: Industry, Innovation, and Work in Britain, 1700–1820* (New York: Oxford University Press, 1986); Charles F. Sabel and Jonathan Zeitlin, "Historical Alternatives to Mass Production: Politics, Markets, and Technology in Nineteenth-Century Industrialization," *Past and Present* 108 (1985); and Sabel and Zeitlin, eds., *Worlds of Possibility: Flexibility and Mass Production in Western Industrialization* (New York: Cambridge University Press, 1997). For the American context, I depended on David A. Hounshell, *From the American System to Mass Production, 1800–1932: The Development of Manufacturing Technology in the United States* (Baltimore: Johns Hopkins University Press, 1984), which includes an enormously insightful chapter on consumer taste as the crucial variable that limited the technical choices of nineteenth-century furniture factories. Scranton, as the leading scholar of American batch production, paved the way for others with his work on the textile, metalworking, and furniture trades: "Diversity in Diversity: Flexible Production and American Industrialization, 1880–1930," *Business History Review* 65 (1991); "Manufacturing Diversity: Product Systems, Markets, and an American Consumer Society, 1870–1930," *Technology and Culture* 35 (1994); *Proprietary Capitalism: The Textile Manufacture at Philadelphia, 1800–1885* (New York: Cambridge University Press, 1983); *Figured Tapestry: Production, Markets, and Power in Philadelphia Textiles, 1885–1941* (New York: Cambridge University Press, 1989); and *Endless Novelty: Specialty Production and American Industrialization, 1865–1925* (Princeton: Princeton University Press, 1997).

For background on the pottery and glass industries, the work of several historians, museum consultants, and curators was indispensable. The leading economic historian of New Jersey's ceramics industry is Marc Jeffrey Stern, whose prize-winning 1986 Stony Brook dissertation and *The Pottery Industry of Tren-*

ton: A Skilled Trade in Transition, 1850–1929 (New Brunswick: Rutgers University Press, 1994) must be read as a multivolume work. Ellen Paul Denker focuses on one Trenton firm in *Lenox China: Celebrating a Century of Quality, 1889–1989* (Trenton, N.J.: Lenox and New Jersey State Museum, 1989). Aaron Hamilton Chute's *Marketing Burned-Clay Products, Including an Analysis of Location, Importance, and Development of the Industry* (Columbus: Ohio State University, 1939), provides the only discussion of distribution based on primary research, including interviews with managers. Andrew McGeorge Lamb's "A History of the American Pottery Industry: Industrial Growth, Technical and Technological Change and Diffusion in the Generalware Branch, 1872–1914" (Ph.D. diss., London School of Economics, 1984), uses public documents to examine technological backwardness. Herman John Stratton's "Factors in the Development of the American Pottery Industry, 1860–1929" (Ph.D. diss., University of Chicago, 1929), surveys tariff issues.

To examine the pottery industry's British origins, I used Stern's dissertation; Regina Lee Blaszczyk, "Ceramics and the Sotweed Factor: The China Market in a Tobacco Economy," *Winterthur Portfolio* 19 (1984); George L. Miller, "Classification and Economic Scaling of Nineteenth Century Ceramics," *Historical Archeology* 14 (1980); McKendrick, "Josiah Wedgwood and the Commercialization of the Potteries," in *The Birth of a Consumer Society;* Frank Thistlethwaite, "The Atlantic Migration of the Pottery Industry," *Economic History Review*, 2d ser. 11 (1958); John Thomas, *The Rise of the Staffordshire Potteries* (New York: A. M. Kelley, 1971); Lorna Weatherill, *The Growth of the Pottery Industry in England, 1660–1815* (New York: Garland, 1986); Richard Whipp, *Patterns of Labour: Work and Social Change in the Pottery Industry* (London: Routledge, 1990); Cheryl Buckley, *Potters and Paintresses: Women Designers in the Pottery Industry, 1870–1955* (London: Women's Press, 1990); and Nancy Koehn, "Josiah Wedgwood and the First Industrial Revolution," in *Creating Modern Capitalism: How Entrepreneurs, Companies, and Countries Triumphed in Three Industrial Revolutions,* edited by Thomas K. McCraw (Cambridge: Harvard University Press, 1997).

The best economic and technological histories of the glass industry are Pearce Davis, *The Development of the American Glass Industry,* Harvard Economic Studies 86 (Cambridge: Harvard University Press, 1949); Warren Candler Scoville, *Revolution in Glassmaking: Entrepreneurship and Technological Change in American Industry, 1880–1920,* Studies in Economic History (Cambridge: Harvard University Press, 1948); Gary Everett Baker, "The Flint Glass

Industry in Wheeling, West Virginia: 1829–1963" (master's thesis, University of Delaware, 1986); and David Jardini, "Separate Paths: Batch and Mass Production in the U.S. Pressed and Blown Glass Industries" (paper presented at the Society for the History of Technology Conference, Rosslyn, Va., 1993).

Many art museum professionals, trained as decorative arts experts, produce well-documented books and articles on high-style decorative arts, leaving the objects of daily life to their cohorts in history museums. For the pottery industry, the research of several public historians stands out. Written by William C. Gates Jr., *The City of Hills and Kilns: Life and Work in East Liverpool, Ohio* (East Liverpool: East Liverpool Historical Society, 1984), is a dense community study on the Crockery City's rise and fall. Compiled by Gates and Dana E. Ormerod, "The East Liverpool, Ohio, Pottery District: Identification of Manufacturers and Marks," *Historical Archeology* 16 (1982), features miniature company histories. Cynthia A. Brandimarte documents gender and china painting in "Darling Dabblers," *American Ceramic Circle Journal* 6 (1988), and in "Somebody's Aunt and Nobody's Mother: The American China Painter and Her Work, 1870–1920," *Winterthur Portfolio* 23 (1988). Susan Myers's early research focused on traditional pottery, but her recent scholarship grapples with design and gender ("'Working at the Decorator's Bench': Woman's Proper Sphere in Baltimore Pottery Manufacture," [paper presented at the American Studies Association, Baltimore, 1991]).

For mass-market glass, I consistently depended on a handful of history-oriented museum curators. Jane Shadel Spillman has devoted her prolific writing career to the creation of top-notch publications. I found several of her books and articles especially informative: "Documented Use of Cup Plates in the Nineteenth Century," *Journal of Glass Studies* 12 (1973); *American and European Pressed Glass in the Corning Museum of Glass* (Corning, N.Y.: Corning Museum of Glass, 1981); with Estelle Sinclaire Farrar, *The Cut and Engraved Glass of Corning, 1858–1940* (Corning, N.Y.: Corning Museum of Glass, 1977); and *The American Cut Glass Industry: T. G. Hawkes and His Competitors* (Woodbridge, Suffolk: Antique Collectors' Club in association with the Corning Museum of Glass, 1996). Kenneth Wilson's two-volume set, *American Glass, 1760–1930: The Toledo Museum of Art* (New York: Hudson Hills Press and Toledo Museum of Art, 1995), verified many of my conclusions about early pressing techniques. For information on mold makers, I relied on Dennis Michael Zembala, "Machines in the Glasshouse: The Transformation of Work in the Glass Industry, 1820–1915 (Ph.D. diss., George Washington University, 1984); Kirk J. Nelson, "Chase,

Trace, and Chisel: The Die-Cutting Mastery of Alvin A. White," *Acorn: Journal of the Sandwich Glass Museum* 2 (1991); Nelson, "Progress under Pressure: The Mechanization of the American Flint Glass Industry, 1820–1840" (master's thesis, University of Delaware, 1988); Gay LeCleire Taylor, "The Husted Mold Drawings," *Glass Club Bulletin* 144 (1984); and Taylor, *Out of the Mold* (Millville, N.J.: Museum of American Glass at Wheaton Village, 1990).

Often, the best research on pottery and glassware is embodied in museum exhibitions, an important but ephemeral communications medium. Sheila Machlis Alexander's American Pressed Glass Tablewares, 1875–1900: Varying Perspectives, an exhibit at the National Museum of American History, was a great favorite of museum visitors in 1992–93. This landmark show put commonplace glass on display, using lively labels and head-turning graphics to explain production, design, marketing, and use. At the Historical Society of Western Pennsylvania, Anne Madarasz's permanent installation, Glass: Shattering Notions, and a companion book tell the story of a leading regional industry, transcending the antiquarian perspective that long shaped the study of Pittsburgh glass.

Scholarship on the home as the consumer dominion is legion, with researchers from many disciplines contributing to the literature. A useful synthesis on domestic space as an expression of personal identity is Witold Rybczynski's *Home: A Short History of an Idea* (New York: Penguin, 1986). Kenneth L. Ames's *Death in the Dining Room and Other Tales of Victorian Culture* (Philadelphia: Temple University Press, 1992), provides an unparalleled art-historical model for interpreting nineteenth-century household furnishings. Published early in her career, Angel Kwolek-Folland's "The Useful What-not and the Ideal of 'Domestic Decoration,'" *Helicon Nine* 8 (1983), and "The Elegant Dugout: Domesticity and Moveable Culture in the United States, 1870–1900," *American Studies* 25 (1984), draw on feminist theory to explain the significance of common household items in an accessible, lively fashion. For the twentieth century, the best monographs, including Ruth Schwartz Cowan, *More Work for Mother: The Ironies of Household Technology, from the Open Hearth to the Microwave* (New York: Basic Books, 1983); Susan Strasser, *Never Done: A History of American Housework* (New York: Pantheon, 1982); and Ellen Lupton, *Mechanical Brides: Women and Machines from Home to Office* (Princeton: Princeton Architectural Press, 1993), hone in on domestic technology. Works that consider the use and meaning of artifacts are few and far between. Those that I consulted include Joan M. Seidl, "Consumers' Choices: A Study of Household Furnishing, 1880–1920," *Minnesota History* 48 (1983); and Annmarie Adams, "The Eichler Home: Intention and Experience in Postwar Suburbia," in *Gender, Class, and Shelter: Perspectives in Vernacular Architecture V*, edited by Elizabeth Collins Cromley and Carter L. Hudgins (Knoxville: University of Tennessee Press, 1995).

Readers interested in the meanings that consumers ascribe to artifacts will find the most compelling insights in disciplines outside of history. The French sociologist Pierre Bourdieu offers the fullest theory of class, consumption, and social control in *Outline of a Theory of Practice* (New York: Cambridge University Press, 1977); *Distinction: A Social Critique of the Judgement of Taste*, translated by Richard Nice (Cambridge: Harvard University Press, 1984); and *The Field of Cultural Production: Essays on Art and Literature,* edited by Randal Johnson (New York: Columbia University Press, 1993). The American sociologist Herbert J. Gans presents case studies of class and consumption in *The Urban Villagers: Group and Class in the Life of Italian-Americans* (New York: Free Press, 1962); and *The Levittowners: Ways of Life and Politics in a New Suburban Community* (New York: Pantheon, 1987). In anthropology, classic works on people-object relations include Mary Douglas and Baron Isherwood, *The World of Goods* (New York: Basic Books, 1981); Mihaly Csikszentmihalyi and Eugene Rochberg-Halton, *The Meaning of Things: Domestic Symbols and the Self* (New York: Cambridge University Press, 1981); Arjun Appadurai, ed., *The Social Life of Things: Commodities in Cultural Perspective* (New York: Cambridge University Press, 1986). More recently, Daniel Miller has carried the anthropological banner with *Material Culture and Mass Consumption* (Cambridge: Blackwell, 1987) and two edited volumes, *Acknowledging Consumption: A Review of New Studies* (London: Routledge, 1995), and *Material Cultures: Why Some Things Matter* (Chicago: University of Chicago Press, 1998). Cultural studies has also produced provocative work, aptly sampled in two anthologies: Lawrence Grossberg, Cary Nelson, and Paula Treichler, eds., *Cultural Studies* (London: Routledge, 1992); and Stevi Jackson and Shaun Moores, eds., *The Politics of Domestic Consumption: Critical Readings* (London: Prentice-Hall, 1995).

Historians of mass retailing focus primarily on the department store as a business innovator and a "palace of consumption." Ralph Hower's comprehensive *History of Macy's of New York, 1858–1919: Chapters in the Evolution of the Department Store* (Cambridge: Harvard University Press, 1943), is an enduring example of business history scholarship. Malcolm P. McNair and Eleanor G. May offer a broader perspective in *The American Department Store, 1920–1960; A Performance Analysis Based on the Harvard Reports* (Boston: Harvard University, Graduate School of Business Administration, Division of Research, 1963).

Scholars who emphasize the department store's social and cultural history include Daniel J. Boorstin, *The Americans: The Democratic Experience* (New York: Random House, 1973); Michael Miller, *The Bon Marché: Bourgeois Culture and the Department Store, 1869–1920* (Princeton: Princeton University Press, 1981); Rosalind Williams, *Dream Worlds: Mass Consumption in Late Nineteenth-Century France* (Berkeley: University of California Press, 1982); Susan Porter Benson, *Counter Cultures: Saleswomen, Managers, and Customers in American Department Stores, 1890–1940* (Urbana: University of Illinois Press, 1986); Elaine S. Abelson, *When Ladies Go A-Thieving: Middle-Class Shoplifters in the Victorian Department Store* (New York: Oxford University Press, 1989); and Leach, *Land of Desire.*

In contrast, the history of five-and-tens and other chain variety stores has received far less scholarly attention. For the basic facts, historians must turn to hagiographies such as John K. Winkler, *Five and Ten: The Fabulous Life of F. W. Woolworth* (New York: Robert M. McBride, 1940); William Thomas Grant, *The Story of W. T. Grant and the Early Days of the Business He Founded* (New York: W. T. Grant Company, 1954); F. W. Woolworth Company, *Woolworth's First 75 Years: The Story of Everybody's Store* (New York: F. W. Woolworth Company, 1954); Sebastian Spering Kresge, *S. S. Kresge Company and Its Builder, Sebastian Spering Kresge* (New York: Newcomen Society in North America, 1957); and William L. Walsh, *The Rise and Decline of the Great Atlantic and Pacific Tea Company* (Secaucus, N.J.: Lyle Stuart, 1986). The archiving of the architectural records from S. H. Kress & Company has spurred some new work: Bernice L. Thomas, *America's 5 & 10 Cent Stores: The Kress Legacy* (New York: Wiley, 1997).

For decades, design history took its cues from Nikolas Pevsner's *Pioneers of the Modern Movement* (London: Faber and Faber, 1936), republished as *Pioneers of Modern Design: From William Morris to Walter Gropius* (New York: Museum of Modern Art, 1949), a whiggish account of the evolution of European highbrow modernism. Curators at the Museum of Modern Art turned Pevsner's arguments into canon, with exhibitions and catalogues that celebrated "good design." For decades, coffee table books, including Stephen Bayley's *In Good Shape: Style in Industrial Products, 1900–1960* (New York: Van Nostrand Reinhold, 1979), and Donald J. Bush's *The Streamlined Decade* (New York: George Brazilier, 1975), waved the MOMA banner. Writing from an American studies perspective, Jeffrey L. Meikle broke away from the celebration of European modernism in *Twentieth-Century Limited: Industrial Design in America, 1925–1939* (Philadelphia: Temple University Press, 1979), zooming in on the consultant design profession in the United States. Subsequently, practitioners such as Arthur J. Pulos (*American Design Ethic: A History of Industrial Design to 1940* [Cambridge: MIT Press, 1983]; *American Design Adventure, 1940–1975* [Cambridge: MIT Press, 1990]), design historians such as Penny Sparke (*An Introduction to Design and Culture in the Twentieth Century* [New York: Harper and Row, 1986]), and museum curators such as Wendy Kaplan (*Designing Modernity: The Arts of Reform and Persuasion, 1885–1945: Selections from the Wolfsonian* [New York: Thames and Hudson, 1995]) honed in on consultants without giving up the notions of "good design" and "good taste."

Besides Bourdieu, several scholars offer insight into the social construction of "good taste." Lawrence W. Levine's *Highbrow/Lowbrow: The Emergence of Cultural Hierarchy in America* (Cambridge: Harvard University Press, 1986), probes the nineteenth century for the origins of snobbery. Herbert Gans extends his subtle discussions of working-class culture to aesthetics in both his *Popular Culture and High Culture: An Analysis and Evaluation of Taste* (New York: Basic Books, 1974), and in his "Design and the Consumer: A View of the Sociology and Culture of 'Good Design,'" in *Design since 1945* (Philadelphia: Philadelphia Museum of Art, 1983). David Gebhard challenges the art-historical belief in modernism as the dominant style of the interwar years in "Traditionalism and Rationalism: Old Models for the New," in *High Styles: Twentieth-Century American Design* (New York: Whitney Museum of American Art in association with Summitt Books, 1985). Gert Selle critiques elite standards in "There Is No Kitsch, There Is Only Design!" in *Design Discourse: History, Theory, Criticism,* edited by Victor Margolin (Chicago: University of Chicago Press, 1989). Jeffrey L. Meikle's *American Plastic: A Cultural History* (New Brunswick, N.J.: Rutgers University Press, 1995), looks at one material and product line considered "tacky" in some circles. Terry Smith's *Making the Modern: Industry, Art, and Design in America* (Chicago: University of Chicago Press, 1993), boldly examines the Museum of Modern Art's role as purveyor of "good design," while Allan Wallach's *Exhibiting Contradiction: Essays on the Art Museum in the United States* (Amherst: University of Massachusetts Press, 1998), exposes the structural and ideological underpinnings that led institutions to buttress the status quo. Most recently, Shelley Nickles's "Object Lessons: Household Appliance Design and the American Middle Class, 1920–1960" (Ph.D. diss., University of Virginia, 1999), indicates that postwar manufacturers, designers, and market researchers struggled to reconcile the gap between their own taste preferences and the working-class demand for traditional styling.

To understand the contradictions at the design nexus, I looked beyond the "good design" paradigm and the consultant design profession. Casting a wide net, I reeled in the concepts of "translation" and "mediation" from the histories of technology, advertising, and design. William Leach discusses the brokering personality in *Land of Desire* and "Brokers and the New Corporate Industrial Order," in *Inventing Times Square: Commerce and Culture at the Crossroads of the World*, edited by William R. Taylor (Baltimore: Johns Hopkins University Press, 1996). Hugh G. J. Aitken and Susan Douglas, respectively, consider how technical translators facilitated innovation in *Syntony and Spark: The Origins of Radio* (New York: Wiley, 1976), and *Inventing American Broadcasting, 1899–1922* (Baltimore: Johns Hopkins University Press, 1987). In *Objects of Desire: Design and Society from Wedgwood to IBM* (New York: Pantheon, 1986), Adrian Forty examines the Wedgwood-Bentley partnership, with special emphasis on the merchant as the reader of demand. Similarly, the cultural historian Roland Marchand analyzes the mediating functions of Madison Avenue executives in *Advertising the American Dream: Making Way for Modernity, 1920–1940* (Berkeley: University of California Press, 1985). Ross Thomson's article, "Learning by Selling and Invention: The Case of the Sewing Machine," *Journal of Economic History* (1987), examines how sales functioned as a form of communication that facilitated invention. In *Making America Corporate, 1870–1920* (Chicago: University of Chicago Press, 1990), Oliver Zunz shows how nineteenth-century agents for International Harvester and Du Pont Company conducted informal market research. Finally, Carolyn Manning Goldstein, in both "Mediating Consumption: Home Economics and American Consumers, 1900–1940" (Ph.D. diss., University of Delaware, 1994), and "From Service to Sales: Home Economics in Light and Power 1920–1940," *Technology and Culture* 38 (1997), considers how domestic scientists built an entire profession around the translating function.

Drawing on these works, I broadened the definition of mediation, considered its relationship to the fashion system, and provided company-specific case studies in Regina Lee Blaszczyk, "Imagining Consumers: Manufacturers and Markets in Ceramics and Glass, 1865–1965" (Ph.D. diss., University of Delaware, 1995); "'Reign of the Robots': The Homer Laughlin China Company and Flexible Mass Production," *Technology and Culture* 36 (1995); "'Where Mrs. Homemaker Is Never Forgotten': Lucy Maltby and Home Economics at Corning Glass Works, 1929–1965," in *Rethinking Home Economics: Women and the History of a Profession,* edited by Sarah Stage and Virginia B. Vincenti (Ithaca, N.Y.: Cornell University Press, 1997); and "Cinderella Stories: The Glass of Fashion and the Gendered Marketplace," in Horowitz and Mohun, eds., *His and Hers.* Recently, business historians have demonstrated a similar interest in mediators. Sally Clarke discusses corporate strategy and intermediaries in her historiographical essay, "Consumer Negotiations," while Jill E. Cooper draws on primary sources from the Edison archives in "Intermediaries and Invention: Business Agents in the Edison Electric Pen and Duplicating Press," both in *Business and Economic History* 26 (1997).

INDEX

Page numbers in italics refer to illustrations.

Ceramic Art Company, 47

ceramic art engineering, 133, 136–37, 145, 155, 158

chain store: age, 120; and mass market, 13, 60, 89, 120; products, 24, 85. *See also* five and tens; tea stores

Chandler, Alfred D., Jr., 272

Chase, Stuart, 159, 194

Cherington, Paul T.: consumer theories of, 1, 90, 229, 231–33; as fashion inter-mediary, 274; at HBS, 231, 240; vs. John B. Watson, 233; and Pyrex Oven-ware, 233–34

Chesapeake Pottery, 71

Childs, George Washington, 63, 81

china cabinets, 2, 28, 50, *54, 83,* 104, *112,* 120, 140; demise of, 143, 146

china decorating, *76;* apprenticeships for, 10, 53, 57–58; and decals, 77–78, 85–86, 88; eclipse of, 90, 107, 109; factory, 75, 85–86, 87, 109–10; and feminiza-tion of consumption, 68, 73; and mer-chants, 37–38, 58–59, 68, 81; and nov-elty, 10–11; and outside contracting, 58, 75, 87, 91; and product design, 10, 26, 37–38, 52–53, 57–58, 90; technical innovation and, 75, 77–78. *See also* Dean, Jesse; Lenox, Walter Scott; Mountford, Arthur

china painting: and china decorators, 52, 68–71; and feedback, 70–71, 73–74, 116; and feminization of consumption, 53, 71–74; supplies, 69–71, 81; women and, 61, 68–74, *70*

china shops, 20, *20,* 34, 47, 60, 74, 258; beckon women, 65, 67–68, 70–71, 73; vs. department stores, 68; vs. five and tens, 115

"chromo-enamels," 78

Churchill, William, 212–16, 219–24, 227–29, 241, 266, 268

Cincinnati Industrial Exposition, 73–74

Cincinnati Pottery Club, 69

Cinderella, 14–16; and gift registry, 258; and glass slippers, 25, *26,* 28, 45, 258; and housework, 191; in real life, 27, 42–43, 50

CIT Financial Corporation, 194

Civil War, 1, 15, 19, 21, 27, 28, 34, 44, 56, 58, 59, 61, 68, 69, 74, 211

Claire de Lune, 150

Clarke, George Washington, 87, 90, 93–96, 101–2, 105, 106, 115

cleanliness, 172, 173, 217, 218; and color white, 186–87, 192, 206

Cliff, Clarice, 146

Coates, George M., 55

Cochran, Drugan & Company, 186

coffee drinking, 4, 16

Cold War, 257, 267, 271

Cole, Arthur, 69

Cole, Glenn W., 259, 260

Collamore & Company, Davis, 45, 58

Collamore & Company, Gilman, 39

collecting: art, 27–28; and china mania, 53, 60–61; and men (*see* consumers and consumption)

Colonial Revival: and Fostoria Glass Company, 148; and mythic past, 31, 36; Spanish, 157, 159; tea stores and, 96, 98; and uplift, 134, 177–78, 180

color: experts, 12, 136, 275 (*see also* Adler, Hazel H.); and faience tiles, 197, 198; and fixtures, 194, 196, 276; fore-casting, 162; home economists and, 201; and identity, 160–61, 206; in the kitchen, 147, 151, 196–97, 237, *plate 4;* and mood, 147, 203; and personality, 148; plastics and, 253; Pyrex Ovenware and, 262; riot of, 201; standards for, 201–2; and tableware, 123, 132, 144–45, *145,* 148–50, 155, 166 (*see also* Fiesta; Harlequin; Yellowstone); theo-ries of, 146–47; white, 186–87, 200, 206; women and, 199

Color Ware. *See* Kohler Color Ware

Colt, Caldwell, 28

Commerce Department, 179, 180, 189, 201

Coney Island, 81, 125

connoisseurs, 12, 73; and "good taste," 273

consultant designers. *See* industrial design

consumers and consumption: blacks as, 42–43, 141; and citizenship, 170; conspicuous, 40, 50; elite, 3–4, 6, 9, 59, 139, 140 (*see also* Briggs, Richard; Wedgwood, Josiah); feminization of, 13, 53, 61, 65, 67, 68, 74, 96, 116, 130–31, 275; home economists define, 217; immigrant, 13, 27, 103–4, 121, 139, 141; "mass" vs. "class," 53, 55, 82, 91, 103, 125, 126, 148, 208, 221, 232–34, 236–37, 241, 243; men as, 8, 16–18, 20, 27–28, 31–32, 36, 38–40, 46–47, 48, 50, 60, 62–63, 73, 81–82, 87, 140, 219, 270, 271, 276; middle class, 31, 43, 91, 111, 117, 121–22, 139, 143–44, 220, 251, 268; resistance by, 13, 98, 106, 112–13; rural, 27, 111–12, 116; sovereignty of, 8, 22, 110, 141, 230–31, 233, 257, 266–67; tableware expenditures of, 130; in training, 21, 217–18; women as, 8, 16, 20–21, 28, 36–39, 60, 73, 74, 83, 116, 130–31, 143–44, 170, 189, 191, 195, 199, 204, 205, 217, 220–21, 227–28, 232, 233–37, 242–45, 246, 247–48, 253, 257–58, 262–63, 264, 268, 270–71, 275 (*see also* Perry, Katherine Wicks; Petrowski, Nellie); working class, 26–27, 60, 82, 91, 107, 110–11, *112*, 121, 139

consumer society: artifacts and, ix-x, 1, 2, 3, 4, 15; British, 1, 3–4; emergence in U.S., 1, 11–13, 53; historiography on, ix, 351–54; and producers as focus of book, xiii, 1–3, 12, 15, 272

Cooper, Susie, 146

Copeland, Melvin T., 240, 241

Corning, N.Y. *See* Corning Glass Works; Hawkes, Thomas Gibbons

Corning Glass Works, xi, 275; consumer products by, (*see* Corning Ware; Flameware; Opal; Pyrex Ovenware); Consumer Products Division at, 259, 260, 262, 264, 270; corporate culture of, 209, 212, 247, 267; early history of, 209–12; and glass cutters, 29, 30, 210; and "high-tech" customers, 29, 44, 224–25, 240, 259, 262, 272; Houghton family at, xi, 211–14, *211*, 220, 224, 237, 246, 247, 259, 260, 263–64, 271; housewares and, 208, 212–14; industrial research at, 208–9, 211–12, 214, 218, 240, 246, 247, 259, 267, 272; licensing at, 225–26, 234; and Mac-Beth-Evans Glass Company, 209–10, 246–47, 260; market research at, 209, 214, 240–41, 261, 264, 268; in postwar era, 259–70, 271; press-ware plant of, 246–47; product design at, 263–64, 269–70; railroads and, 29, 32, 209–14 (*see also* Nonex); reorganizations of, 223–24, 225, 239, 240, 259, 260; sales, 223–24, 224, 237, 240, 262, 263, 265, 270; Steuben Division of, 263, 271; and World War II, 259, 260–61

Corning Ware: advertising, 268; developing and promoting, 267–69, 269; as labor-saver, 270; sales of, 263, 270; and space race, 267–69; success of, 270, 271

corporations, stereotypes of, 2

Cortright, Lilla, 262–63

Cook, Clarence, 64

Covey, Arthur, 178–179, *179*

Coxon, Charles, 56

craftsman, 12

Crane Company, 169, 186, 201, 202, 203, 206

creamware, 5, 6

credit. *See* installment sales

Creel, George, 181
Crockery City, 85, 91, 101
Crooksville Pottery Company, 156
crystal, Scandinavian, 251, 271. *See also*
    cut glass
Crystal City, 29, 32, 37, 210
crystal weddings, 47–50, *48*
Curtis Publishing Company, 138, 241
cut glass, 15; "brilliant," 30–31, 32, 38, 43,
    49; critics of, 50–51; elites and, 15–16,
    27–28, 33, 36–40, 43 (*see also* Briggs,
    Richard); and female consumers, 47,
    49–50; figured blanks for, 43; as gifts,
    32, 43, 47–51, *48;* imitation (*see* pressed
    glass); and male consumers, 27–28, 31–
    32, 46, 49; middle class and, 31–32, 43–
    44, 46; origins of U.S. industry, 28–29;
    producers of, *30,* 43–44, 210 (*see also*
    Hawkes, Thomas Gibbons; Libbey,
    Edward Drummond); retailers of, 47,
    49, 50 (*see also* Briggs, Richard). *See
    also* distinction

Dalzell, William A. B., 129
Dana, John Cotton, 133–34
Dean, Jesse: and china painters, 52, 71;
    English roots of, 52, 55; as fashion
    intermediary, 53, 55, 107, 274; and
    market research, 174; and merchants,
    58–59, 83, 85; and photoceramics, 78–
    79, 87; showroom of, 75; workshop of,
    52, 59, 75, 85, 87, 95, 109, 272
decalcomania, 55, 101, 107; and con-
    sumer expectations, 113; demise of,
    155, 164; experimental, 77–78; in Jazz
    Age, 123–26, 131, 144–46; peak sales
    of, 150; and "poorer classes," 107; in
    postwar era, 254, 255, *256;* triumph of,
    85–88, 107. *See also* Gaertner, Rudolph
Decker, William C., 259, *260*
decorative arts, limitations of, 166, 273–74
Delineator Home Institute, 148, 202
demand: creating, 2, 133, 250; origins of,

231; responding to, 1, 2, 8, 11, 13, 23,
    24, 27, 37–40, 52, 90, 98, 105–7, 130,
    133–34, 136–41, 149–50, 154–61, 163–
    64, 167, 195, 218, 231–32, 240–44, 257,
    266, 273, 274; unpredictability of, 99
DeMille, Cecil B., 171, 195
democratization of consumption, 1, 13,
    27, 90
demonstration: homes, 180–81; product,
    218–19, 227, 261–62, 265, 268, *269*
department stores: as consumption
    palaces, 13, 24, 65–68, 104, 105, 142,
    148, 217; emergence of, 33, 65–67; as
    feminine spaces, 49, 105; vs. five and
    tens, 103; in Jazz Age, 142–45; in post-
    war era, 250, 252, 266; pottery and
    glass in, 24, 85, 96, 100, 129, 132, 138,
    142, 143–44, 148, 149–50, 154, 156,
    157, 158–61, 209, 219, 221, 244, 258
Depression glass, 151, 244
design: history, 12, 166; monotonous, 2;
    reform, 12, 64, 81,141; schools, 65, 69,
    70, 71, 74, 75, 80, 134, 135, 250
desire, 2, 138–39
Diamond, Freda, 250–52, *252,* 270, 271
dime stores. *See* five and tens
dining, 64, 138: accessories for, 21–22, 25,
    37–39, 40, 41, 42, 50, 71, 82, 110–11,
    122, 143, 146, 148, 155, *156,* 160; vs.
    eating, 111; formal, 16, 22, 23, 111, 122,
    126, 146, 155; informal, 122, 126, 146,
    149, 155, 157, 165, 249, 251, 266;
    middlebrow vs. lowbrow, 111, 122; in
    postwar suburbia, 249, 251, 258, 262,
    266; prescription vs. practice, *54*
dirt, 171–72, 174
dish night, 151, *152,* 153, *153,* 160
distinction, 4, 6, 15: artifacts of, 7–8, 27–
    28, 31, 81–82; critics of, 50–51; and pro-
    ducers (*see* Briggs, Richard; Hawkes,
    Thomas Gibbons; Libbey, Edward
    Drummond); wealthy men and, 27–28,
    81–82

Shaw, James C., 93
shawl women, 103–4, 110, 121, 126
Shearer, Mrs., 146. n 34, 147
shoppers, demands of, 1, 5, 10, 16, 33, 53
shopping, districts, 8, 17, 33, 34, 66,
102–3, 124; feminization of, 20–21, 20,
67, 130; malls, 2; and shoppers, 104,
105, 221, 226, 227–28, 244–45
"short sets," 146, 149, 150
showrooms: branch office, 75, 173, 189,
192–93, 197, 198, 199–200, 203; and
consumers, 5, 11, 12; factory, 25, 110,
111, 119–20, 131; Fifth Avenue, 271;
hotel, 145; lack of, 197; London, 5, 8, 9,
11, 67
silk screen, 128, 155, 161–62, 163, 164,
167, 256
Simmel, Georg, 139
Simons, Alice, 71–73, 74, 79
simplified practice, 201–2
Singer Sewing Machine Company, 77, 172
skilled labor: and fashion goods, 10–11,
29–30, 52, 56–58, 225, 272; shortage of,
69, 77, 167
Sloan, Alfred P., Jr., 195, 207
Slobodkin, Simon H., 160
Smith, L. L., 181–82, 191, 193–94
Smith, Walter, 68–69
smoking accessories, men's, 17, 31, 32, 46,
271
snobbery, market value of, 6, 9, 15, 37,
82, 83
social class, and American market, 3–4, 9,
27, 120, 139–41, 232–33, 251, 273. See
also consumers and consumption
Society of Decorative Art, 71
Solon, Léon Victor, 136
souvenirs, 28, 45, 62, 81
space savers, 262
speciality shops, 33, 106. See also china
shops
spin-off products, 4, 6, 11, 41–42, 77–78,
82, 87–88, 140, 155, 164, 246

Staffordshire, England: as pottery center,
4–5, 55; practical men from, 52, 55–56,
75, 87–88, 101, 132, 134, 136, 137, 164;
vs. Trenton, 59, 75; and U.S. market,
82, 91
standardization, 111, 186–87, 188, 195,
201–202, 248
Standard Sanitary Manufacturing Company, 169, 185; advertising by, 193–94,
203; and Cardinal tub, 206; and color,
199, 201; design at, 202; diversification
of, 186; marketing by, 172–73; as price
leader, 188
Stern Brothers, 49, 103, 250
Steuben Crystal, 263–64, 271
Steuben Glass Works, 46, 148, 263–64,
271, 276
Steubenville Pottery Company, 165–66,
165, 249, 253
Stewart, A. T., 20
Stone, Gerald S., 149, 160
Stookey, S. Donald, 267
Stowe, Harriet Beecher, 38, 59–60
Straus, Nathan and Isidor, 66–67, 81
Straus & Sons, L., 66, 96
Strauss, Mildred D., 203
streamlining, 129, 133, 162, 209
styling, 129, 133, 142, 144, 154, 195, 196,
202, 250
subcontracting, 56, 58. See also outside
contract system
Sullivan, Eugene Cornelius, 214–15, 218,
219, 223, 225, 225, 240, 245, 246
Sun Also Rises, The, 160
supermarkets, 254–55
Swanson, Gloria, 171, 195

tariffs, 29, 34, 46, 59, 74, 79, 80, 82, 86,
100, 116, 151, 253
Tarpley, Ford, 144, 145, 149
taste: and corporate strategy, 1, 272;
diversity of American, 2, 3, 11, 12, 13,
52, 53, 59, 75, 90–91, 95, 106–7, 109,